Guide to the
Diplomatic Archives
of Western Europe

Guide to the Diplomatic Archives of Western Europe

Edited by

DANIEL H. THOMAS
University of Rhode Island

and

LYNN M. CASE
University of Pennsylvania

Philadelphia
UNIVERSITY OF PENNSYLVANIA PRESS
[c1959]

From its inception this volume was planned as a volume d'hommage
for

WILLIAM EZRA LINGELBACH

by his friends and former students who have written the several
chapters and served as editors of the volume.

A native of Canada, educated at the universities of Toronto,
Leipzig, Chicago, and Pennsylvania, he served on the faculty or
in the administration of the University of Pennsylvania from
1900 to 1946. Since retiring from duties at that university, he
has had a new career as Librarian and Archivist of the
American Philosophical Society.

He is noted for his knowledge of and publications in modern
European history and Frankliniana, for his success as a teacher,
for his administrative talents, and for his leadership in various
learned societies.

We offer this volume in admiration for his achievements, in
deep appreciation of his unfailing ability to inspire us to research in the archives he knows so well, and in gratitude for
his innumerable personal acts of kindness and consideration.

Preface

THE many scholars who have carried on research in the various diplomatic archives of Europe have long recognized the need of a general guide to these records. The many archivists who have answered the same questions incessantly have agreed that a work of this type would be most helpful both to researchers and to archival staffs. The determination to publish such a guide was reached by the editors after experiencing confusion on many occasions concerning the classification of documents and after obtaining misinformation on at least one occasion even as to the very location of the archives of a foreign ministry.

After seeking the advice of a number of investigators and archivists, we decided that the volume should be a *vade mecum* or a scholar's *Baedeker* for those interested in finding and making the fullest use of the original diplomatic documents of western Europe. It was further agreed that the authors of each chapter should be specialists in the particular archives they discussed. We are happy that so many of the authors are former students, or students of students, or colleagues of William E. Lingelbach, for the volume is a *Festschrift* in his honor.

Although it has not always been possible to be consistent, the chapters usually contain four types of information. The first is the history of the principal depositories. This should serve as a background for a better comprehension of the chronological scope, the arrangement, and the condition of the materials. Secondly, there is a description of the organization, arrangement, and classification of records, the most useful and significant section of each chapter. The extent of the detail varies with the chapters and depends in part upon the existence of inventories and guides that may have been previously published for the individual depositories. This part should save time for the researcher and enable him to proceed with greater confidence and accuracy as well as efficiency. A third type of information includes such varied data as the administration of the depositories and the present officials; the regulations concerning admission and use of materials; the rules of the reading rooms or the way to obtain copies of the rules; the hours, the dates on which the rooms are closed because of holidays, vacations, or annual cleanings; the kind of reference material available in the research rooms; the regulations concerning microfilming and the cost of microfilms; the most useful libraries in the area with their hours, their archival holdings, and their facilities for research; and suggestions for living arrangements in the various cities. Finally, most chapters contain a bibliography of two sections: the principal collections of published documents; and a list of the most useful guides, inventories, and volumes cited or referred to in the chapter.

The first fourteen chapters deal with the depositories of the separate countries of western Europe: Austria, Belgium, Denmark, France, Germany, Great Britain, Italy, the Netherlands, Norway, Portugal, Spain, Sweden, Switzerland, and the Vatican City. In addition, there are four chapters on diplomatic archives of a special or unusual nature. Bavaria was chosen as an example of a former state that has been absorbed in a unification movement and yet whose records have unusual significance. The chapter on public opinion in foreign affairs contains not only descriptions of certain major collections of journals but also suggestions for locating manuscripts that reveal opinion as it existed under dictatorships when the press is controlled as, for example, in France under Napoleon III. Just as the great variety of practices has made it impossible to be consistent in the organization of every chapter, so we have felt justified in departing from the strict western European orientation of our work in order to include two chapters dealing with international materials,

They are "The League of Nations and United Nations" and "UNESCO." The growing significance of international organizations and the activities of western European states in them made it advisable to include these chapters.

The authors of the several chapters in this cooperative work grasped at once the objectives and nature of the volume—no doubt because they had experienced all the difficulties of "unguided" research in foreign archives—and have been exceptionally patient during the delays in editing and publishing. We are deeply grateful for their understanding and appreciative of their many contributions to whatever success the volume may enjoy. We appreciate also the immediate recognition by the Directors and the Editorial Committee of the University of Pennsylvania Press of the potential value of the volume and their decision to publish it. All of us have received a vast amount of help from the archivists in the various foreign depositories, and we gratefully acknowledge their specific contributions in the individual chapters.

D.H.T.

April 18, 1958.   L.M.C.

Contents

xi

GUIDE TO THE DIPLOMATIC ARCHIVES OF WESTERN EUROPE

1 AUSTRIA

Arthur J. May
University of Rochester

HISTORY

A LITTLE more than two hundred years ago—in 1749 to be precise—Empress Maria Theresa issued a *Decretum instructivum* ordering Theodor von Rosenthal to assemble certain documentary materials of the Hapsburg family in a central repository. That decree was a minor item in the sheaf of administrative reforms issued by the "noblest of Hapsburg rulers" and pointed toward a better integration of her disjointed lands and peoples. It is saluted as the foundation stone of the *Haus-, Hof- und Staatsarchiv* of Vienna—which will be designated in this survey as HHSA.

In time this storehouse acquired the official literature and large quantities of unofficial papers relating to *la haute politique* of Austria, to the international pursuits of a dynasty that ruled from the Netherlands to the Near East and affected the whole of Europe in one form or another. Before 1749 papers of state and of the Hapsburg family and court had been accumulated in widely scattered repositories, seldom suitable for the purpose, in constant danger of accidental or deliberate destruction, and accessible only with great difficulty, if indeed they were known at all. Beyond that, in Austria as in other countries the retention of official correspondence by individuals who had served in a public capacity was a common practice. The growth of the Vienna diplomatic archives is nearly as complicated (and as fascinating) as the history of the Hapsburg dominions themselves.

Rosenthal, who was a protégé of Baron John C. Bartenstein, chief minister of the empress, displayed exemplary industry and ingenuity in carrying out his assignment. For thirty years he scoured the realm, gathering up original documents or copies from the principal towns of the Hapsburg hereditary estates and forwarding them to Vienna; and he had the Bohemian crown archives transferred from Prague to Vienna. That operation was never forgotten by Czech patriots; the Treaty of Saint-Germain of 1919 prescribed that Austria should turn over all "documents, historical memoirs, manuscripts, maps, et cetera claimed by the present state of Czechoslovakia, which Thaulow von Rosenthal removed by order of Maria Theresa."

The oldest manuscript in HHSA dates from 816, a letter of Emperor Louis the Pious exempting the Archbishop of Salzburg from imperial taxes.[1] The fundamental nucleus of the great collections is the documents of the Babenberg dynasty, accumulated in 1137 at the monastery of Klosterneuberg on the fringe of Vienna, the records of Ottokar II of Bohemia and of the early Hapsburg family of Austria. Maximilian I considered establishing a common repository for the diplomatic and other documentary materials of the Hapsburg House, but nothing came of the idea. During the reign of Ferdinand I, documents that were stored in Vienna and Innsbruck were sorted and classified but there the archival process was allowed to rest for two centuries; that is, until Maria Theresa responded to pressure for a unified storehouse.

For nearly a hundred and fifty years state and court papers were preserved in a section of the imperial Hofburg. The archives were under the jurisdiction of the Court and State Chancery (*Hof- und Staatskanzlei*), which managed foreign relations and looked after the affairs of the ramified Hapsburg

---

[1]This document together with ninety-nine other resplendent jewels of HHSA has been magnificently reproduced in facsimile in Leo Santifaller, ed., *1100 Jahre österreichische und europäische Geschichte in Urkunden und Dokumenten des Haus-, Hof- und Staatsarchivs* (Vienna, 1949).

cousinage.[2] The diplomatic documents of the chancery were entrusted to HHSA, and late in the eighteenth century it was ordered that all public papers should be concentrated in the Viennese repository.

In the course of the era of Napoleon, HHSA was affected in several ways. It was now, for example, that the name *Haus-, Hof- und Staatsarchiv* came into use. Especially valuable archival materials were evacuated to places of safety whenever French armies approached the venerable capital on the Danube; and in 1809 many papers were carted off to Paris on order of Napoleon, but all were reclaimed under the peace settlement of 1814–15. This epoch also witnessed the transfer to Vienna of most of the documentary records of the Holy Roman Empire of the German Nation upon the dissolution of that moribund institution; included in this accession was an immense mass of data on the diplomatic and political transactions of the Imperial Court Council (*Reichshofrat*) and the Imperial Court Chancery (*Reichshofkanzlei*).

Furthermore, in 1851 the archives of the Archbishop of Mainz in his capacity of Archchancellor of the Holy Roman Empire were acquired by HHSA. These files of correspondence and documents significantly enriched the resources pertaining to diplomatic history. By arrangement with the government of Belgium, Vienna obtained the original records of the principal Hapsburg officials in the Austrian Netherlands from the time of Charles V to the end of the eighteenth century, when Austrian control over the province ceased.

During the revolutionary storms of 1848 the ministry of foreign affairs (*Ministerium des Äussern*) superseded the state chancery in the conduct of diplomacy and it carried that responsibility until the smash-up of the monarchy seventy years later. Large masses of diplomatic documents not required by the Ballplatz in current transactions were deposited, from time to time, in HHSA; and, similarly, the records of Austrian

[2]The change-over from Court to State Chancery occurred in 1742.

embassies, legations, and consulates abroad were concentrated there. Personal letters, moreover, and private correspondence of professional diplomatists, statesmen, and aristocratic families were turned over to HHSA, sometimes with reservations on their use for scholarly purposes.

When Lombardy was lost in 1859 and Venetia seven years later, the archival materials belonging to these provinces were transferred to them and some documents of particular concern to Hungary passed to Budapest upon the making of the *Ausgleich* in 1867.[3] Under the dualistic regime, HHSA became the common property of the two partners in the monarchy, though only one Magyar, Arpád von Károlyi, ever served as director.

The desirability of a specially designed building in which to store the Viennese archival treasures came under discussion as early as the 1850's, but only in 1902 did the idea become a reality when an archives office was completed at the rear of the historic Ballhaus. That structure, a *modèle de luxe*, envied and imitated in other capitals, still houses the diplomatic and related collections. Gustav Winter, who as director had supervised the construction of the archives office, presently set plans in train for a general catalog of the immense resources, a project that was fulfilled in the five stately volumes of the *Gesamtinventar des Wiener Haus-, Hof- und Staatsarchivs*, published in the years 1936–40.

In the meantime, HHSA suffered some subtractions by reason of World War I. It was stipulated in the Treaty of Saint-Germain that the Republic of Austria should negotiate with the heirs or successors of the Danube Monarchy for "an amicable arrangement on all objects which ought to form part of the intellectual patrimony of the ceded districts, . . ." Fortunately, the chief archivists of the succession states greatly

---

[3]For a short account of the archives of Hungary, consult Dionys Janóssy, "Das Archivgesetz in Ungarn," in Leo Santifaller, ed., *Festschrift zur Feier des Zweihundertjährigen Bestandes des Haus-, Hof- und Staatsarchivs*, 2 vols. (Vienna, 1949), I, 13–22. (This work is hereafter cited as *Festschrift*.)

respected the provisional director of HHSA, Professor Oswald Redlich, who had been the teacher of many of them. Records were distributed on a reasonable basis, with all the Austrian diplomatic documents remaining in the Vienna depository. Several leading noble families now entrusted their archives to HHSA. As of 1939, the archives building held more than two hundred collections of papers, about one hundred fifty thousand bundles and cartons of documents, some sixty thousand parchment records, fifty thousand manuscripts, and a considerable body of newspaper materials—upward of sixty million items altogether. The unpublished holdings of this inexhaustible treasure house are inversely proportional to the number of native scholars available to study them.

In the middle of World War II, on orders from Berlin, the riches of HHSA and of other Viennese archives—about three hundred truckloads in all—were moved for purposes of security to the basements of buildings in the capital or to castles and abandoned salt mines in rural Austria and Czechoslovakia. After the war the records were gradually trundled back, the vital diplomatic papers being recovered without loss.[4] At present, HHSA forms the first division of the *Österreichisches Staatsarchiv*, set up July 26, 1945, which has custody of all archival collections in Vienna.

Almost from the beginning, limited access to the jealously guarded documents was granted to disinterested historical investigators.[5] But throughout most of the nineteenth century the cautious, vigilant paternalism that pervaded the Austrian administration generally ruled in HHSA. It was feared by the makers of policy that secret papers might be examined less to achieve impartial and judicial history than to distort or discredit the conduct of Hapsburg diplomacy. Permission to consult the diplomatic archives was extended only to scholars

[4]See R. John Rath, "The war and the Austrian archives," *Journal of central European affairs*, VI (1946–47), 392–396.

[5]See Walter Pillich, "Staatskanzler Kaunitz und die Archivforschung, 1762–1792," in *Festschrift*, I, 95–118.

who were absolutely trustworthy from the standpoint of monarchical interests. That precautionary attitude discouraged, of course, well-informed criticism of foreign policy. Even Leopold von Ranke was denied in 1863 the privilege of studying the correspondence of Prince Kaunitz with his representative in France more than a century earlier.

During the long tenure of Alfred von Arneth as director of HHSA, extending from 1868 to 1897, the overcautious, convention-ridden censorship, which severely hampered authoritative historical study, was substantially eased. Arneth also instituted path-breaking innovations in the organization of archival materials, greater efficiency in the administration of HHSA, and greater vigilance in the preservation of historical records. It was the high responsibility of the archivist, he kept saying, to preserve and prepare original sources for investigation by living and oncoming generations of scholars. Not only qualified citizens of the Hapsburg monarchy, but accredited foreign scholars were welcomed, though diplomatic documents that were requested were still meticulously scrutinized to determine whether it would be discreet to allow them to be consulted for private scientific inquiries. Such restrictions ran parallel, to be sure, with common custom in European diplomatic archives and were not abandoned until the collapse of the monarchy in 1918. Not all the relevant papers were made accessible to the Hungarian historian Eduard von Wertheimer, for instance, when he was writing his massive biography of Count Julius Andrássy, foreign minister from 1871 to 1879.[6] The abolition of the censorship after World War I made possible a more authoritative analysis of the diplomacy of Andrássy and compelled revisions in Wertheimer's emphases and judgments.

Beginning with Rosenthal, a notable line of directors administered HHSA, and they displayed industry and sagacity in the discovery, classification, and description of documentary materials. Top officials were flanked by competent and skillful

[6]Eduard von Wertheimer, *Graf Julius Andrássy*, 3 vols. (Stuttgart, 1910–13).

archivists who, at many points, set professional standards for the rest of the world. Directors with scholarly tastes and their colleagues engaged in productive historical pursuits, for the principle prevailed (and still prevails) that the archival staff resembled a learned academy, in the language of one director, not a set of routineering state servants.

Apart from enlarging the archival collections substantially, Joseph von Hormayr, director from 1808 to 1813, produced historical studies on his native Tyrol that glowed with romantic color and provincial pride. A fiery Austrian patriot, Hormayr exploited his familiarity with the contents of the archives in the cause of political propaganda; for his flair for effective pamphleteering, he was likened to Thomas Paine. After helping to organize the heroic Tyrolese rebellion of 1809, Hormayr fell into disfavor at the Vienna court and eventually drifted into the service of Bavaria.

Alfred von Arneth, both before and during his tenure as keeper of HHSA, prepared elaborate histories—or, more exactly, compilations of source materials—on two outstanding Austrian celebrities of the eighteenth century, Prince Eugene of Savoy and Empress Maria Theresa. Gustav Winter, who succeeded Arneth as head archivist, earned distinction as an authority on the economic and legal history of Austria.

Possibly the most distinguished archivist of his generation, Ludwig Bittner, presided over HHSA from 1925 to 1940 and then took charge of *Reichsarchiv Wien*. Respected throughout the world as an archival administrator and a scholar of front rank, Bittner was elected to membership in ten foreign learned societies and was chosen, in 1933, as chairman of a commission on diplomatic history instituted by the International Congress of Historians. Three major monuments honor his memory and bear witness to his indefatigable energy and his unusual competence as an editor.

In collaboration with other distinguished Austrian scholars, though the main burden fell on his own shoulders, Bittner prepared for publication *Österreich-Ungarns Aussenpolitik von der bosnischen Krise 1908 bis zum Kriegsausbruch 1914*, 9 vols. (Vienna, 1930). Part of his Trojan energies during World War II was devoted to arranging a supplement to this massive collection, necessitated by the discovery of additional documents. With the help of the archival staff, he presented the world of scholarship with the *Gesamtinventar des Wiener Haus-, Hof- und Staatsarchivs*, 5 vols. (Vienna, 1936–40); for this work Bittner wrote a lengthy and brilliant introduction on the history of HHSA. Again in collaboration, he commenced the publication of *Repertorium der diplomatischen Vertreter aller Länder seit dem westfälischen Frieden bis 1930*. The first volume, ranging from 1648 to 1715, appeared in 1936 and the second, from 1716 to 1763, finished in the midst of World War II, appeared in 1950, after the death of Bittner.

An ardent partisan of the union of the Austrian Republic with Germany, Bittner applauded the *Anschluss* in 1938. But as World War II drew to its agonizing conclusion, with Soviet armies storming irresistibly upon Vienna and the house that Hitler built rapidly collapsing, Bittner and his wife committed suicide in April 1945.

ORGANIZATION OF COLLECTIONS

The scholar contemplating study in HHSA will always be grateful for the *Gesamtinventar*. This indispensable work was hailed immediately upon its appearance as an extraordinary masterpiece, a model for other archives to imitate, and it is hard to see how it could be much improved upon. It is regrettable that all five volumes of the *Gesamtinventar* are available at only a few places in the United States; the Library of Congress has a full set as, of course, has the library in the archives building at Vienna.

The *Gesamtinventar* contains a systematic, remarkably thorough, and learned description of the labyrinthine resources of HHSA. Lists of the collections are accompanied by crisp

summaries of their general contents and detailed indexes open
the door to subjects, personalities, and places of interest to the
diplomatic historian. Almost invariably, the *Gesamtinventar*
discloses whether the literature on a given problem or individual is stored in HHSA, though, obviously a complete
catalog of the treasures would run into scores of volumes.[7]

ADMINISTRATION, REGULATIONS, AND FACILITIES

Over-all supervision of the Austrian state archives is the
responsibility of Professor Dr. Leo Santifaller, with Dr.
Gebhard Rath directly in charge of administration at HHSA.
Associated with him in the actual operation of the archives are
Dr. Anna Coreth and five archivists of second rank. As has been
indicated in the historical sketch, the great bulk of the Austrian
diplomatic records is stored in the archives office attached to
the Ballhaus. In some instances the papers of Austrian noble-
men who served in the diplomatic corps still remain in the
possession of their families or have been deposited in the
Landesarchiv in Linz, Graz, or Klagenfurt. Current information
on the location of specific collections not mentioned in the
Gesamtinventar may be procured by addressing Österreichisches
Staatsarchiv, General-Direktion, Wien I, Minoriten Platz I,
Österreich.

As a standard rule, archival materials may be consulted up to
fifty years preceding the present—in other words, in 1955, the
chronological limit was December 31, 1904. (Annually, the
limit advances one year.) Exceptions to this regulation have
been made by the director of HHSA in the case of individual
scholars requiring more recent documents.

Certain collections of papers have been deposited in HHSA

[7]A colossal *Generalkatalog* (1908), filling a hundred handwritten volumes, lists
the resources of HHSA and their location in the archives building. In 1873
Constantin Böhm published in Vienna *Die Handschriften des Haus-, Hof- und
Staatsarchivs* and a supplement appeared in the following year. Unprinted supplements followed, but all are now out of date, owing in part to transfers of manuscripts to other countries. A new printed inventory of the manuscript resources is
promised.

on the understanding that they may be examined only with the consent of the depositor or only after a stated period of time has elapsed. A case in point is the rich and diversified *Nachlass* of Archduke Francis Ferdinand, who perished at Sarajevo in 1914; after World War II access to this collection was granted to a few scholars by the heirs of the archduke.[8] Among the other private collections for which special permission by the owners is required are the files of Josef M. Baernreither, Count Kheven-hüller, Count Heinrich von Lützow (*Erinnerungen*), Baron Karl von Macchio (*Schriftsammlung*), Count Philip Stadion, and the central family archives of the Princes Trauttmannsdorf. For a description of these collections, see *Gesamtinventar*, IV, 409–448. The chronological limit for papers that may be studied only with the consent of the government of Hungary is December 31, 1894.

Except for the restrictions on the use of diplomatic records mentioned above, permission to study in the resources of HHSA is regulated by a *Dienstordnung* of 1925, which is printed in *Gesamtinventar*, I, 77–78. In the same volume (pp. 78–81), the rules governing the use of the facilities of HHSA are listed; every investigator must sign a *Rechtsverbindliche Erklärung*, a facsimile of which is printed there. Regulation 22, obligating an investigator to present a copy of anything he publishes as the outcome of studies in HHSA to the library of the archives building, has been extended to include doctoral dissertations whether printed or not.

It is advisable, though not at all necessary, for the scholar who intends to study at HHSA to communicate his plans to the director well in advance of his arrival in Vienna. As the present writer can testify from experience, the archival staff is extremely helpful in forwarding studies and in ferreting out documentary materials that the investigator may have overlooked or of

---

[8]Robert J. Kann, "Emperor William II and Archduke Francis Ferdinand in their correspondence," *American historical review*, LVII (1951–52), 323–351. See p. 323, n. 1; p. 324, n. 2.

which he may be ignorant. Professor Dr. Hugo Hantsch, professor of modern history in the University of Vienna and author of *Die Geschichte Österreichs*, 2 vols. (1947, 1950), is another wise counselor to historical scholars from the United States.

The archives building is open from 9 A.M. to 6 P.M. on weekdays, save for Saturday when the closing hour is 1 P.M. Except for the period from Christmas to New Year's Day, facilities may be used at any time in the year. The library of HHSA contains nearly sixty thousand volumes. Books may also be borrowed at the *Österreichische Nationalbibliothek* or at the University library, both within easy walking range of the archives building.[9] Parenthetically, library cataloging in Vienna has not attained the level of an exact science as in the United States; the investigator should be prepared for delays (exasperating sometimes) in obtaining the books he desires.

The scholar who finds it impossible to go to Vienna to carry on research himself can employ a competent person there to search out and copy documents. Application for assistance of this kind should be addressed to the director of HHSA. Through the director, too, a typist may be engaged to copy manuscripts that one has uncovered. It is possible to have documentary records in HHSA microfilmed. The official agency for microfilming is the *Fotostelle des Bundeskanzleramtes und des österreichischen Staatsarchivs*, located at Ballplatz 2, Wien I. At present each page copied costs one schilling and thirty groschen.

The American scholar in Vienna is likely to prefer living quarters in or near the Inner City, easy of access to HHSA. Luxury hotels that were pre-empted by the officials of the four governments occupying Vienna and Austria are gradually

---

[9]Data on these libraries are conveniently available in Ernst Trenkler, "The history of the Austrian National-bibliothek," *The library quarterly*, XVII (1947), 224–231; Johann Gans, "Bibliotheca redivivia, the university library of Vienna," *Library journal*, LXXIII (1948), 993–995; Hugo Alker, *Die Universitätsbibliothek Wien* (Vienna, 1953); see also, Josef Stummvoll, "Austrian libraries, past and present," *The library quarterly*, XX (1950), 33–38; Lawrence S. Thompson, "Research libraries in Vienna," *German-American review*, XIV (1947), 24.

being returned to their owners (*Bristol; Sacher*). More modest facilities may be had not far from the archives building (*Kranz; Regina*); still less pretentious establishments that have preserved something of the distinctive charm of an older and more romantic Vienna are *Zum Goldenen Hirschen* (attractive, with pleasant garden) and *Zum Weissen Hahn*. Information concerning pension accommodations may be obtained from the Austrian State Tourist Department, 48 East 48th Street, New York City. This office may also be called upon for advice on any matters of concern to the traveler.

It is scarcely necessary to call attention to the virtues of Baedeker's *Handbook on Austria*. Other works on Austria of varied interest to the wandering scholar are:

Hiscocks, Richard. *The rebirth of Austria*. New York, 1953. A competent, well-written introduction to post-Nazi Austria.

Gedye, G. E. R. *A wayfarer in Austria*. 1929.

Schnitzler, Henry. " 'Gay Vienna'—myth and reality," *Journal of the history of ideas*, XV (1954), 94–118.

Preyer, David C. *The art of the Vienna galleries*. New ed., 1926.

Hanslick, Edward. *Vienna's golden years of music, 1850–1900*. London, 1951.

Sedgwick, Henry D. *Vienna: the biography of a bygone city*. Indianapolis, 1939.

BIBLIOGRAPHY

Printed Collections of Documents

The principal printed collections of Austrian diplomatic papers are:

1. Arneth, Alfred. "Die Relationen der Botschafter Venedigs über Österreich im 18. Jahrhundert," *Fontes rerum Austriacarum*, II/22 (1863).

2. Bittner, Ludwig. *et al.*, eds. *Österreich-Ungarns Aussenpolitik von der bosnischen Krise bis zum Kriegsausbruch 1914*. 9 vols. Vienna, 1930. This monumental series, which runs into 8,144 pages, was prepared in three years and printed in eight months. For an analysis consult O. H. Wedel, "Austro-Hungarian diplomatic documents, 1908–1914," *Journal of modern history*, III (1931), 84–107.

3. Chroust, Anton. "Gesandtschaftsberichte aus München, 1814–1848," *Schriftenreihe zur bayrischen Landesgeschichte*, XXXIII (1939), XXXVI–XXXVIII (1941–43).

4. Demelitsch, F. "Aktenstücke zur Geschichte der Koalition vom Jahre 1814," *Fontes rerum Austriacarum*, II/49/2 (1899).

5. Fiedler, Josef. "Die Relationen der Botschafter Venedigs über Deutschland und Österreich im 17. Jahrhundert," *Fontes rerum Austriacarum*, II/22, 27 (1866–67).

6. "Die Relationen der venetianischen Botschafter über Österreich im 16. Jahrhundert," *Fontes rerum Austriacarum*, 11/30 (1870).

7. "Josef II und Graf Ludwig Cobenzl Briefwechsel (1780–1790)," *Fontes rerum Austriacarum*, II/53, 54 (1901).

8. Gachard, M. *Documents inédits concernant les troubles de la Belgique*. 2 vols. Brussels, 1858.

9. Gooss, Roderich. *Das wiener Kabinett und die Entstehung des Weltkrieges*. Vienna, 1919.

10. *Diplomatische Aktenstücke zur Vorgeschichte des Krieges 1914*. Ergänzungen und Nachträge zum Österreich-Ungarischen Rotbuch. Vienna, 1919.

11. Mendelssohn-Bartholdy, R. *Brief von Friederick von Gentz an Pilat*. Leipzig, 1868.

12. Oechsi, W. *Die Anfänge des Sonderbundes nach österreichischen Gesandtschaftsberichten*. Zürich, 1914.

13. Pribram, Alfred F. "Privatbriefe Kaiser Leopolds an den Grafen F. E. Pötting," *Fontes rerum Austriacarum*, II/56, 57 (1903–4).

14. Prokesch-Osten, *Dépeches inédits du Chevalier de Gentz au hospodar de la Valachie*. 3 vols., 1867.

15. Reinöhl, Fritz von. "Der Fall Jeftanović-Sola-Gavrila, Grossserbische Umtriebe vor und nach dem Ausbruch des 1. Weltkrieges," *Veröffentlichungen des Reichsarchivs Wien*, I (1944).

16. Schlesier, M. *Mémoires et lettres inédits du Chevalier de Gentz*. 1841.

17. Schlitter, Hans. *Napoléon à St. Hélène. Rapports officiels du Baron Stürmer*. Paris, 1886.

18. "Die Berichte des 1. Agenten Österreichs in den Vereinigten Staaten, Baron de Beelen Bertholff . . . 1784–1789," *Fontes rerum Austriacarum*, 45/2 (1891).

19. *Correspondence secrète entre le Comte A. W. Kaunitz, ambassadeur à Paris, et le Baron Ignaz de Koch, secrétaire de l'Impératrice Marie Thérèse, 1750–1752*. Paris, 1899.

20. *Fürst von Kaunitz, Philipp Cobenzl und Spielmann. Ihr Briefwechsel, 1779–1792*. Vienna, 1899.

21.   *Brief und Denkschriften zur Vorgeschichte der belgischen Revolution.* Vienna, 1900.

22.   *Geheimkorrespondenz Josefs II. mit seinem Minister in den österreichischen Niederlanden, Grafen Ferdinand Trauttmannsdorff (1787–1789).* Vienna, 1902.

23.   *Les correspondences des agents diplomatiques étrangers en France avant la révolution.* 1896.

24.   Srbik, Heinrich, and Oskar Schmid, "Quellen zur deutschen Politik Österreichs, 1859–1865," *Deutsche Geschichtsquellen des 19. Jahrhunderts*, XXIX–XXXIII (1934–38).

25.   *Urkunden und Aktenstücke des Reichsarchivs Wien zur reichsrechtlichen Stellung des burgundischen Kreises.* 3 vols. Vienna, 1944–45.

Guides and Reference Works

The best general historical account of the resources in HHSA for the study of diplomacy is Bittner's description in Volume I of the *Gesamtinventar*. Other works with bearing upon the subject are:

26.   Bittner, Ludwig. "Das wiener Haus-, Hof- und Staatsarchiv in der Nachkriegszeit," *Archivalische Zeitschrift*, XXXV (1925), 141–203.

27.   "Die zwischenstaatlichen Verhandlungen über das Schicksal der österreichischen Archive nach dem Zusammenbruch Österreich-Ungarns," *Archiv für Politik und Geschichte*, III (1925), pp. 58–96.

28.   "Zur Neuorganisation des österreichischen Archivwesens," *Festschrift für Waldemar Lippert* (1937), pp. 36–41.

29.   Gross, Lothar. "Das Haus-, Hof- und Staatsarchiv in Wien," *Archivalische Zeitschrift*, XXXV (1925), 134–140.

30.   *Jahrbuch der österreichischen Wissenschaft*, II (1950), 146–148.

31.   Reinöhl, Fritz von. "Zur Geschichte der wiener Zentralarchive," *Archivalische Zeitschrift*, XXXVI (1926), 220–226.

32.   Schlitter, Hans. "Die Rückstellung der von den Franzosen 1809 aus Wien entführten Archive," *Mitteilungen des Instituts für österreichische Geschichtsforschung*, XXII (1901), 108–122.

33.   Seidl, Jakob. 'Österreichische Archive," *Archivi d'Italia*, II (1935) 234–244.

34.   "Das österreichische Staatsarchiv," *Mitteilungen des österreichischen Staatsarchivs*, I (1948), 3–19.

35.   "Das österreichische Staatsarchiv, dessen Abteilungen und führenden Beamten in den letzten fünfzig Jahren," *Festschrift*, I, 127–138.

36.   Winter, Gustav. "Die Gründung des Haus-, Hof- und Staatsarchivs," *Archiv für österreichische Geschichte*, XCII (1903), 1–82.

37.   *Das neue Gebäude des k.u.k. Haus-, Hof- und Staatsarchivs in Wien*, Vienna, 1903.

38. Wolf, Gustav. *Geschichte der k.k. Archive in Wien*. Vienna, 1871.

At this point may be noted the principal documentary collections pertinent to diplomatic history together with references to the *Gesamtinventar* and to scholarly articles in which the records in question are discussed.[10]

Imperial Court Chancery:
39. *Gesamtinventar*, I, 330–353.
40. Gross, Lothar. "Die Geschichte der deutschen Reichshofkanzlei von 1559 bis 1806," *Inventare österreichischer staatlicher Archive*, I. Vienna, 1933.
41. Kaiser, Hans. "Die Archive des alten Reiches bis 1806," *Archivalische Zeitschrift*, XXXV (1925), 204–220.

Archives of the Arch-chancellor of Mainz:
42. *Gesamtinventar*, I, 393.

Secret Austrian State Register:
43. *Gesamtinventar*, I, 397–398.
Gross, Lothar. "Der Kampf zwischen der Reichskanzlei und österreichischer Hofkanzlei um die Führung der auswärtigen Geschäfte," *Historische Vierteljahrschrift*, XXII (1925), 279–312.

State Chancery:
44. *Gesamtinventar*, I, 401–421.
45. Mayr, Josef K. "Geschichte der Staatskanzlei im Zeitalter des Fürsten Metternich," *Inventare österreichischer staatlicher Archive*, II. Vienna, 1935.
46. Postkurse, *Inventare österreichischer staatlicher Archive*, III. Vienna, 1935.
47. Reinöhl, Fritz von. "Die österreichischen Informationsbüros im Vormärz," *Archivalische Zeitschrift*, XXXVI (1926), 261–288.
48. Stix, Franz. "Zur Geschichte und Organisation der Wiener Ziffernkanzlei," *Mitteilungen des österreichischen Instituts für Geschichtsforschung*, LI (1937), 131–160.

Ministry of Foreign Affairs:
49. *Gesamtinventar*, I, 442–466.
50. Wiedermayer, Rudolf. "Geschäftsgang des k.u.k. Ministerium des Äusseren," *Archivalische Zeitschrift*, XL (1931), 131–152.

Archives of Representatives Abroad:
51. *Gesamtinventar*, I, 471–508.

[10]For nearly all the specific, up-to-date information in this section, I am indebted to the general director of the Austrian archives, Professor Doctor Leo Santifaller, and his associate, Dr. Anna Benna.

52.   Gross, Lothar. "Zur Geschichte des Gesandtschaftsarchivs am Regens-
       burger Reichstag," *Archivalische Zeitschrift*, XXXVI (1926), 204–
       220.

Diplomatic Papers by States:
    a. German States
53.   *Gesamtinventar*, I, 511–528.
    b. Non-German States
54.   *Gesamtinventar*, I, 529–584.

Correspondence of Statesmen:
55.   *Gesamtinventar*, I, 587–594.
       (This section contains selections of the papers of Count F. E.
       Pötting, Prince Eugene of Savoy, Count Karl Cobenzl, Prince
       Wenzel A. Kaunitz, Counts Rudolf and Francis Colloredo, and
       others.)

Diplomatic Collection:
56.   *Gesamtinventar*, I, 594–596.
       (This section is made up of copies of documents from European
       archives, for the period 1605–1726, assembled by Baron Johann
       F. Dumont von Karlscroon, publisher of the *Corps universel
       diplomatique*.)

State Charters (Staatsurkunden):
57.   *Gesamtinventar*, III, 97.

State Treaties:
58.   *Gesamtinventar*, III, 127–128.

Belgium:
59.   *Gesamtinventar*, IV, 81–360.
60.   Brandi, Karl. "Die politische Korrespondenz Karls V," *Nachrichten
       Göttingen*, I (1931), 251–258.
61.   "Die Überlieferung der Akten Karls V im Haus-, Hof- und Staat-
       sarchiv Wien," *Berichte und Studien*, V, VI, VII, XI, Vienna, 1931–
       33.
62.   Laenen, I. *Les archives de l'état à Vienne au point de vue de l'histoire de
       Belgique* (Brussels, 1924).

Manuscript Collection:
63.   *Gesamtinventar*, III, 137–291.
64.   Böhm, Constantin. *Die Handschriften des Haus-, Hof- und Staatsarchiv*.
       Vienna, 1873; Supplement, Vienna, 1874.

(This section contains correspondence of diplomatic officials, some originals, some copies.)

Private Papers (*Nachlässe*):

65. *Gesamtinventar*, IV, 375–406.

66. Reinöhl, Fritz von. "Politische Nachlässe des 19. Jahrhunderts in den staatlichen Archiven Österreichs," *Korrespondenzblatt des Gesamtvereins der deutschen Geschichts-und Altertumsvereine* (1925), 209–220. (This section contains papers of both public personalities and private citizens.)

Works containing Austrian treaties and other diplomatic engagements, as well as data on Austrian diplomatic personalities and Red Books are:

67. Bittner, Ludwig. "Chronologische Verzeichnis der österreichischen Staatsverträge," 4 vols., *Veröffentlichungen der Kommission für neuere Geschichte Österreichs*. I (1902), VIII (1909), XIII (1914), XV (1917). (The first volume in this series covers the period 1526–1763; the second, 1764–1847; the third, 1848–1911; the final volume is an index and supplement.)

68. "Bericht über die Ausgabe einer internationalen Bibliographie der Farbbücher und anderen diplomatischen Aktenpublikationen," *Bulletin of the international committee of historical sciences*, XVI (1932), 411 ff.

69. *Repertorium der diplomatischen Vertreter* . . . , I (1936), xi.

70. *Corpus pacificationum. Systematische Zusammenstellung der Friedensverträge, 1792–1913.* Berlin, 1917.

71. *Repertorium der diplomatischen Vertreter aller Länder seit dem westfälischen Frieden.* 2 vols. Vienna, 1936, 1950. (The first volume covers the period 1648–1715; the second, 1716–63.)

72. Bruns, V. In *Fontes iuris gentium* (on Red Books), series B, section I, vol. I, 1932, p. 38 for the period 1856–71; vol. II, 1937, p. 16 for the period 1872–78.

73. Gooss, Roderich. "Österreichische Staatsverträge, Fürstentum Siebenbürgen (1526–1690)," *Veröffentlichungen der Kommission für neuere Geschichte Österreichs*, IX (1911).

74. Kotasek, Edith. "Die Herausgabe der österreichischen Staatsverträge durch die Kommission für neuere Geschichte Österreichs," *Mitteilungen des österreichischen Staatsarchiv*, I (1948), 248–254.

75. Pribram, Alfred F. "Österreichische Staatsverträge, England," 2 vols., *Veröffentlichungen der Kommission für neuere Geschichte Österreichs*, III (1907), XII (1913). (The first volume covers the period 1526–1748; the second, 1749–1813).

76.   *Die politischen Geheimverträge Österreich-Ungarns, 1879–1914.* 2 vols. Vienna, 1920.

77.   *The secret treaties of Austria-Hungary, 1879–1914,* 2 vols. Cambridge, Mass., 1920–21. English edition of the preceding item.

78.   Srbik, Heinrich. "Österreichische Staatsverträge, Niederlande," *Veröffentlichungen der Kommission für neuere Geschichte Österreichs,* X (1912).

79.   Übersberger, Hans. "Österreich und Russland seit dem 15. Jahrhundert," *Veröffentlichungen der Kommission für neuere Geschichte Österreichs,* II (1906).

For guidance on the general content of collections outside the custody of HHSA, the following descriptions will be found helpful:

80.   *Jahrbuch der österreichischen Wissenschaft,* II (1950), 163, 174, 226, 295.

81.   Jaksch, August. "Katalog des Graf Gössischen Familienarchivs," *Veröffentlichungen der Kommission für neuere Geschichte Österreichs,* XXVIII (1932), 3–54.

82.   Küfstein, Karl. *Das Küfsteinische Familienarchiv* (1906).

83.   Martin, Franz. "Das gräflich Kuenburgische Archiv im Langenhof zu Salzburg," *Mitteilungen des k.k. Archivrats,* II (1916), 99–149.

84.   Nösslböck, Ignaz. "Das Archiv des Reichsgaues Steiermark," *Das Johanneum,* VII (1942).

85.   Seidl, Jakob. "Privat- und Adelsarchive in Österreich," *Archivi d'Italia* (1934), 42–49.

86.   "Archivalienschutz in Österreich," *Archivalische Zeitschrift,* XLIV (1936), 149–163.

87.   Zibermayr, Ignaz. *Das oberösterreichische Landesarchiv in Linz im Bilde der Entwicklung des heimatlichen Schriftwesens und der Landesgeschichte.* 3d ed., Linz, 1950, pp. 196 ff., 206, 302 ff., 306 ff.

2 BELGIUM

Daniel H. Thomas
University of Rhode Island

A HISTORY OF THE *SERVICE DES ARCHIVES*

THE Belgian *Service des Archives* is one of the youngest depositories of national diplomatic archives, but it has had a significant and adventurous history. Although a secretary-archivist was one of the first positions created in the new ministry of foreign affairs in 1831, the *Service des Archives* was not established until 1863, a generation after the creation of an independent Belgian state. It was not made adequate in concept and personnel until 1875. As if to make up for the neglect, the government then made it a "division." The first chief of the service and director was Emile Banning, a scholar with experience as a librarian. Except for a few short intervals, it had always been housed with the ministry of foreign affairs until moved to 56 Avenue des Arts in 1953.

The examination of their holdings by the new archivists disclosed what had been feared—that the records were far from complete. Many of the gaps in the instructions to the foreign service officers and in the reports from these representatives were filled by having the consulates and legations forward their files to the home office. Still other documents were retrieved from the residences of former officials.[1]

Political documents on subjects of particular importance were collected into special dossiers, but the bulk of the political records were classified and arranged chronologically. Then the

[1] Pp. 3–6 of reprint of number 18 in bibliography; November 29, 1878 with addenda, January 1880, of number 13 in bibliography.

staff went to extraordinary lengths to prepare the contents of certain categories for rapid and efficient use. Before the manuscripts were bound, able analysts summarized the contents of each document and placed the summaries in each of some nine hundred volumes. This practice, a godsend for the busy researcher, was continued until interrupted by the war of 1914–18. Thereafter, the amount of material was too extensive for the staff to analyze. It was not abandoned, however, until an experiment indicated that an experienced person could summarize an average of only twenty-four documents a day.[2]

Charles Seeger succeeded Banning in 1898, and he constructed a pleasant and fireproof room, the *Salle de Fer*, which served as a reading room surrounded by shelves on which the relatively small number of volumes could be stored. This was the high point in the physical accommodations of the *Service des Archives*, hereafter referred to as the Service. Once it outgrew these facilities, it was never given a building specifically constructed for the preservation and use of the archives. Instead, the staff has been required to utilize as best it might a conventional office building. Alfred De Ridder, who succeeded Seeger as chief of the Service, was the most prolific author among those who served in the division. While second in command, he was chiefly responsible for having the Service made a depository for the *Correspondance politico-commerciale*,[3] an objective that had been in the minds of the archivists from the beginning of the Service. The duties of the staff were increasing rapidly when disaster struck in 1914.

When the German invasion was not repulsed in August of that year and the government fled Brussels, there was time to remove only ten cases of documents. Upon the fall of the capital the Germans soon learned of the numerous diplomatic and other documents that were still in Brussels. Pius Dirr, a Bavarian

---

[2]Based on information furnished in November 1948 and May 1949 in interviews with A. Henri Lambotte, Chief of the Service and Director at that time.

[3]P. 6 of reprint of number 18 in bibliography.

archivist, claimed to be the discoverer of the materials and their potential value to the Central Powers. In a short time the invaders began to make frequent use of the diplomatic and military documents in German propaganda. Indeed, never before in wartime had such extensive use been made of diplomatic records. Starting with publications in the *Norddeutsche Allgemeine Zeitung* on October 13, 1914, the Germans published a stream of Belgian documents that continued until 1919. The imperial propagandists sometimes made extravagant claims in their introductions and comments which were not supported by the Brussels documents. Belgium and Britain were accused, for instance, of plotting aggression against Germany. In the *Norddeutsche Allgemeine Zeitung* of November 25, 1914 Belgium was declared to have "determined from the outset to join Germany's enemies and to make common cause with them."[4] In 1915 an introduction to a volume of Belgian documents concluded with the charge:

A more complete indictment of English statesmanship as the enemy of the peace of the world, a deliberate and persistent conspirator against an unoffending neighbor, could not possibly be framed. The indictment stretches throughout the nine years. There are no palliations, no extenuations. It is a record of a monstrous crime.[5]

The Allied Powers countered by pointing out inconsistencies between such charges and the documents produced as supporting evidence and by publishing some of their own records. Thus began a famous polemic that lasted a quarter of a century.[6] As long as the war lasted, the Belgians were at a disadvantage, since the mass of their archives were in the hands of the invaders. This was a lesson Belgian authorities would never forget.

In 1916 the imperial authorities decided to go about the

[4]Pt. II, p. 847 of number 9 in bibliography.
[5]P. xii of number 10 in bibliography.
[6]The views of a number of the participants in this well-known and lengthy polemic are treated in number 8 in bibliography.

study of the Belgian material in a more thorough and systematic fashion. Consequently, Bernhard Schwertfeger, military historian and officer, was assigned to Brussels and placed in command. He soon notified Berlin that the documents did not justify the charge that there was a "Belgian departure from the precepts of neutrality" and proposed that the propaganda line be revised. He favored an admission that the Belgian diplomats were capable and neutral observers and urged the publication of a still larger selection of their reports in which they described German policy in the most favorable light. The proposals did not meet with full approval of certain superiors. Thereupon, the archival section was dissolved, and Schwertfeger was transferred to Berlin in 1918.[7]

Ironically, many persons still ascribe to Schwertfeger the authorship of the extreme propaganda claims against Belgium. He was permitted eventually to proceed with the publication of numerous Belgian documents, five volumes appearing in Berlin in 1919 under the title *Zur europäischen Politik: 1897–1914*. These publications appear to have been a factor in the postwar decision to publish extensive collections of German documents culminating in the renowned *Die grosse Politik*.[8]

A tremendously discouraging task awaited the personnel of the Service upon the liberation of Brussels in 1918. Returning to the rue de Louvain, the archivists found the offices in great disorder and many of the unbound materials scattered and damaged beyond use. However, only one volume of the bound documents was lost as a result of the German occupation. Numerous documents had accumulated during the four years, and the number to be preserved increased enormously with the peace treaties and such matters as reparations. A few of the other immediate postwar problems were the training of new

[7]Schwertfeger to the author, November 20, 1950 and March 9, 1951 in which he quoted portions of an unpublished report to General Bissing dated May 26, 1916. See also pp. 169–170 of number 12 in bibliography and pp. 44, 94, and *passim* of number 15 in bibliography.

[8]P. 295 of number 16 in bibliography.

staff members, enlarging the staff, and acquiring adequate quarters, all at a time when the financial condition of the state was critical.

Eventually, order replaced chaos and the Service began to function properly once again. The archives were now opened to private scholars for the first time. A significant addition in this period was the acquisition of copies of numerous Austrian documents. H. Schlitter, a former imperial archivist in Vienna, offered to supply copies of Austrian records relating to Belgium. As a result, copies of the instructions to the Austrian envoys in Brussels and of their reports for the years 1833—1902 as well as a number of miscellaneous documents dealing with Belgian affairs are deposited in the Service and are open to investigation on the same conditions as the documents of Belgian origin.

The most radical action of the period was the preparation of the records for rapid evacuation in case there should come another invasion. Instead of placing the volumes of documents on shelves, they were generally stored in wooden cases, which were then stacked one upon another. These cases were about a yard in length and were constructed to fit the size of the various documents. The fronts were hinged so they might be let down when volumes were needed and had clasps by which they could be closed tightly. In the ends of the cases, hand-holds were cut to facilitate handling. When asked about the peculiar arrangement, the personnel freely explained that the purpose was to prevent a second acquisition and use of the Belgian materials. The Belgians were determined to rush their diplomatic records to a place of safety if conquest threatened. Events were to prove these precautions wise and all the expenditure of money and effort worthwhile.

When the war of 1939 began, Belgium was not at first invaded. Nevertheless, many precautions were taken by various ministers. A number of documents—*archives mortes*—were transferred to hiding places in Brussels, and plans were made for a rapid evacuation of others. With these preparations the staff of the Service remained on the alert during the winter and spring. A. Winandy, who had been in charge of the Service, had retired by the latter season; Charles Lecharlier was chief and A. Henri Lambotte was assistant director.

Belgium was invaded on May 10, 1940, and two days later the final evacuation of the other ministry records to Ostend was begun. When the German breakthrough near Sedan was not sealed off by the Allied forces, the danger to the archives in Ostend was recognized. Space on two ships was found and the loading of the cases was begun. In such a crisis the labor necessary to move the cases was a difficult problem; to solve it, the municipal authorities called out some of the men on the social security rolls. It must have been an impressive sight to see men with varying physical disabilities intent on handling the cases in the midst of the wartime confusion in this busy seaport while it was subject to aerial bombardment. The loading was interrupted when dive bombers approached again, and the ships were quickly put to sea without some of the cases. These numbered fifteen hundred, and they were taken overland to Poitiers. None of them contained diplomatic documents, however.

Lambotte followed the one hundred and twenty-five tons, some two thousand cases (four fifths of which were Service records), to England. The British authorities soon offered a relatively safe depository for the duration. This was a portion of the ancient Caernarvon Castle in Wales. Once again the problem of transportation arose. Despite the need for lorries and manpower in the days following Dunkirk, the cases were hauled to the castle on the northwestern coast of Wales. Here, in the Queen's Tower of the famous medieval structure, Lambotte stored his cargo. Where archers once stood guard, he set up a small office. Making a list of the cases and their new locations, and with his firsthand knowledge of the materials in his custody, he was soon prepared to serve the government in exile. Still concerned about the safety of the archives, a concrete roof was placed over the tower to protect them from incendiary bombs;

and when it looked as though England might be invaded and conquered, the removal of the cases to America was envisaged.[9]

A. Henri Lambotte, the ingenious Belgian archivist, and his colleagues took the deepest pride in the successful evacuation of the documents. "This was our first victory," he has claimed. "The British have their Dunkirk, and the Belgian archivists their Ostend!"

All this was as yet unknown to the German authorities who had decided to seize the documents again as in 1914. A special group, or *Sonderkommando*, had been created for the purpose. It was to secure diplomatic and other types of archives of Belgium, Holland, and possibly Luxemburg. The day after the invasions began, the men were alerted, cautioned, and further instructed; they were to occupy certain offices, gain possession of the documents, and if deemed advisable, ship them immediately to Berlin. The officer who seems to have been responsible for the seizure of the Belgian documents was Baron von Künsberg.[10] The group was collected at Düsseldorf on May 15, and since the Dutch armies had surrendered, the men destined for The Netherlands left the following day.

The men assigned to Brussels grew impatient in the late afternoon of May 17 when they learned that the German forces had halted outside the city and would not enter the Belgian capital until the next day. At this moment a propaganda group was found to be equally impatient, for its members had notified Berlin that the Reich could announce the fall of Brussels that evening. The two groups joined forces and dashed into the heart of the city. They put certain offices and buildings under guard until a thorough search could be made. A full day passed before the other troops occupied the Belgian capital.[11] Thus the

[9]Pp. 3–5 of reprint of number 11 in bibliography; information furnished by Lambotte.

[10]Memo., Berlin, May 11, 1940, Ad. Protocol A. 8191 and tel., Kordt to the German foreign office, May 17, A09001, of number 14 in bibliography.

[11]Zeitsschel to the Service of Protocol, German Embassy, Brussels, May 23, 1940, number 16, D. 511204-5-6, of number 14 in bibliography.

Belgian and Dutch archives became one of the first military objectives when the fighting spread to western Europe.

Künsberg was quick to realize that much of what he sought was missing. Nevertheless, the *Sonderkommando* collected all papers thought to be of interest to the Germans, called in the German ambassador to verify this, and shipped the records to Berlin.[12] Actually, there was no material of any value left in the Service. The Nazi searchers traced the missing cases to Ghent, and two *Kommandos* were among the first Germans to enter the city, only to be disappointed again.[13] When Ostend fell, they were disheartened to discover that the cases they had traced to this port were no longer there. Learning that some had been carried into France, the hunt was extended by Künsberg to that haven for Belgian émigrés,[14] and the fifteen hundred cases were discovered and shipped to Berlin. Since these, too, proved to be of little interest or value to the Germans, it was now realized that the ones most sought had been shipped to England.[15] The tenacious Künsberg did not give up easily, for next he sought to compile a list of the personnel of the Service who had gone to England and to secure their addresses in exile, an investigation he continued through January of 1941.[16]

After four and a half years, that is, in November 1944, the collection of documents was returned to the Belgian capital. A

---

[12]Künsberg to the German foreign office, Brussels, May 30 and note, Künsberg to Halem, Berlin, October 8, Rgen 1/4–179, of number 14 in bibliography.

[13]Report of Schmidt, Feldpolizei, May 22, 1940, D51/207 and report Künsberg to German foreign office, Brussels, May 30, of number 14 in bibliography.

[14]Tel., Künsberg to German foreign office, May 29, apparently from Ostend, HNOX 906, of number 14 of the bibliography. On the last day of May a United Press despatch contained a report that the Belgian diplomatic archives had been "almost entirely located and continue to arrive at Poitiers by truck." (*New York Times,* June 1, 1940, p. 2, c. 2.)

[15]Note, Künsberg to Halem, Oct. 8, Rgen 1/4–179 and supplementary report by Berswordt, May 15–June 14, 18. XIII. 40, of number 14 in bibliography.

[16]Note, Künsberg to Lutter, Berlin, Sept. 4; Künsberg to Bargen, Berlin, Nov. 16, Rgen 1/4–248; Bargen to the German foreign office (intended for Künsberg), Brussels, Jan. 13, 1941, Rgen 7/4–248/Ang.II (also marked D.511169); Künsberg to the Special Group in the German foreign office, Berlin, Jan. 31, number D.11168 (also marked K/LG-153/42), all of number 14 in bibliography.

great amount of money, thought, and energy had been ex-
pended and ingenuity exercised before and during the war in
order to protect the diplomatic documents from loss under fire,
from loss while in unfriendly hands, and from use by an enemy.
The effort had succeeded admirably. All the effort, every
expenditure had proved worthwhile. While in exile the Service
had been utilized by the government; when Brussels was
liberated these documents were returned intact. This success of
the Belgian government was in direct contrast to the experience
of several states that had not taken similar precautions. Archivists of The Netherlands burned many of their prewar records
in 1940 as the Nazi forces approached The Hague. Many Quai
d'Orsay records fell into German hands and some were removed
to the Reich, while still others were lost in a fire during the
hostilities in liberating Paris. Oslo documents were seized and
several were used in the "White Book No. 4" in an effort to
bolster the claim that Norway had forsaken neutrality before
the invasion. Some Greek government materials were hauled to
the Fatherland after the fall of Athens and some had not been
returned to Greece by 1952.[17]

When the war was over, roomier quarters were given to the
archives and as quickly as possible the new offices were opened
to scholars. Soon plans were made for constructing new quarters
in a building to house the ministry of foreign affairs. Nevertheless, the war experiences were still fresh in the minds of the
authorities. They had thwarted the invaders in 1939; but would
the same method be successful in case of another invasion? At
the proposal of Lambotte the Service was given funds to start
microfilming the older records and those currently being turned
over to the Service. This is expected to serve a twofold purpose.
Space can be saved by microfilming many of the documents and
destroying some originals and duplicates. Finally, upon another

---

[17]For an interesting review of the treatment and use of archives during wars in
recent centuries see Ernst Posner, "Public records under military occupation,"
American historical review, XLIX (January 1944), 213–227.

outbreak of war in western Europe, it should be much simpler to rush the film to an apparent place of safety and burn the bulky originals.

ORGANIZATION AND CLASSIFICATION

The general collections of documents deposited in the *Service des Archives* are:

1. *Arrêtés royaux et ministériels,* 1830–   . Arranged chronologically in bound volumes.
2. *Correspondance politico-commerciale,* 1830–   . Records of negotiations and information on commerce, finance, emigration, colonization, the Red Cross, health, social problems, arms, etc.
3. *Correspondance politique,* 1830–   .

> *Légations.* Correspondence with diplomats accredited to foreign states; most frequently arranged by the state to which the diplomat is accredited—Allemagne (after 1870), Grande Bretagne, etc.
>
> *Consulats.* Reports from and communications to the consulates on political matters; arranged by cities in which consulates are located until 1903, but after that date placed with the *légations* correspondence.
>
> *Départements ministériels et autorités belges,* 1830–   . In the main, correspondence of ministers of foreign affairs and commerce with other ministers, the king's secretary, and local authorities. Volume 5, for example, contains correspondence on such matters as *Arbitrage du Roi entre les Etats-Unis et le Chili, Troubles dans le Hainaut, Mission de Général Chazal* (1866), and *Mission chinoise en Belgique.*

Except for the *Arrêtés royaux et ministériels,* the classification and arrangement of these documents are not easily explained and they have gone through an extensive evolution. They may be divided into two groups: dossiers that are not numbered but are known by their titles, and those which are numbered with the titles listed in various catalogues.

The unnumbered dossiers. Most of the earlier records—a good majority of those of the nineteenth century and some after that time—are found in this group. They are usually bound in black morocco leather and canvas; hence, they are familiarly known as *les volumes noires* and *les séries noires reliées.* The first pages of these bound volumes contain *Tables chronologiques.* These indicate the number given to the document, the date, the author, the addressee (if a piece of correspondence), and then the summary. The latter is the most remarkable feature, and the investigator who needs material in this period of the Belgian archives is indeed fortunate. The analysis of the documents was done by trained archivists, and the summaries are thorough and dependable. An example in *Correspondance politique, légation, Grande Bretagne,* Vol. 42, 1861–62, is:

No. 129, Van de Weyer à Ministre
Question du TRENT. Les Ministres se sont réunis pour prendre connaissance de l'opinion des avocats de la couronne. On dit que les Etats du Sud avaient preparé la capture de leurs commissaires, pour forcer l'Angleterre à intervenir. La Légation des Etats-Unis recueille des précédents pour constater qu'en maintes circonstances la marine anglaise a arrêté des agents de parties belligérantes voyageant sous pavillon neutre.

When the war of 1914 interrupted the analysis and binding, the archivists had reached the documents of about 1890. The practice was not resumed after the liberation.

The *Correspondance politique—Légations* and *Consulats,* constitutes the principal material found in the unnumbered arrangement of records. As the documents in this category were bound, a number of other records were forwarded to the Service. The first ones to be received were summarized and bound; these bear the name *Compléments reliés,* and contain documents over the period 1830–70. Still later deposits were neither bound nor analyzed and these are known as *Suppléments non-reliés*. As mentioned earlier, the *Correspondance politique – Consulats* was not classified separately after 1903. Instead, it was placed with the unbound legations correspondence from that date to 1934.

Many original documents on subjects of major political significance have not been placed in the general collections but have been gathered into special dossiers. As time passed the tendency has been to put more documents in special dossiers. In these, there are pieces of the *Correspondance politique*, private papers, and memoranda. The titles of these special and unnumbered dossiers include the following:

Conférence de Londres, 1830–39, 18 vols.

Exécution du traité de paix avec les Pays-Bas, 49 vols.

Convention de Zonhoven, 1833, 1 vol.

Convention des forteresses, vol. I, 1831–32, vol. II, 1839–1873.

Missions extraordinaires en Allemagne, 1833–39, 1 vol.

Système défensif de la Belgique, 1835–64, 1 vol.

Rapports politiques—Belgique, Pays-Bas, 1830–52, 8 vols.

Restitution d'archives anciennes, 1835–81, 3 vols.

Missions étrangères, 1830–70, 6 vols. Correspondence with foreign diplomats accredited to Brussels. After 1870 the correspondence is placed in the numbered dossiers.

Indépendance, neutralité et défense militaire de la Belgique— Garantie des puissances, 1831–87, 3 cases.

Guerre de 1870, 14 vols.

Réfugiés politiques en Belgique, 1842–86, 10 vols. A card catalogue lists the name of each refugee and references to the pieces which concern him.

Incidents franco-belges, 1869–70, 3 vols.

Incidents germano-belges, 1871–76, 4 vols.

Papiers Lambermont, 2 series, 11 vols. The first series is arranged by subject. The second, composed of papers collected at a later date, is arranged chronologically.

Arbitrages du Baron Lambermont, 3 vols.

Rapports Dufourny sur les ports français, 1 vol.

Délits de presse, 1851–78, 6 vols.

Papiers Goblet, 1 folder.

Discussions parlementaires: Neutralité et défense militaire de la Belgique, 1851–1904, 6 vols. Printed debates that have been collected, indexed, and bound.

Conférences du Baron Lambermont avec le Prince Albert, 3 vols. Prince Albert was tutored in foreign and colonial affairs by Baron Lambermont. These volumes consist of the notes carefully prepared for that purpose by the distinguished secretary-general of the ministry of foreign affairs.

Notes et mémoires, 4 vols. Comments and opinions of various officials of the ministry on a number of subjects. Of significance generally, they are of particular importance for the World War I period, since some of them were drawn up after the loss of documents during the war.

Conférence de Bruxelles de 1874: Lois et coutumes de la guerre, 5 vols.

Conférence des armes, 1908–9, 4 portfolios.

As could be anticipated, materials relating to Africa constitute an important part of the Belgian archives. There is a special collection known as *Afrique*. Although most of the dossiers in this collection are numbered and hence will be described later, some are unnumbered. The latter are among *les volumes noires*, which have the summaries of each document included in the volume. They are:

Conférence géographique de Bruxelles, 1 vol.

Association internationale africaine, 1876–84, 1 vol.

Association internationale du Congo, 1878–84, 4 vols.

Conférence africaine de Berlin, 1884–96, 6 vols.

Etat Indépendant du Congo, 1884–1901, 14 vols.

Conférence anti-esclavagiste de Bruxelles, 1889–91, 19 vols. and 1 case of supplements.

Exécution de l'Acte général de Bruxelles, 1890–94, and *Acte général de Bruxelles*, 1891–93, 13 vols. and supplements.

Traité des esclaves, 1839–1891, 3 vols.

Researchers should be reminded that when documents have been collected and placed in the special dossiers and the dossiers on Africa, there may be other significant materials in other collections. As an illustration, political records relating to the Congo may be found also in the *Correspondance politique*, both *Légations* and *Consulats*.

Fortunately, there is a guide for these earlier materials that have been summarized or analyzed. Known as the *Tables de rubrique*, it is a large card catalogue that is available to the investigator upon the consent of the director. The subjects are arranged alphabetically with subtitles. An example is:

Neutralité belge
    Conférence de Londres (1831–39)
    Conflit turco-égyptien (1839–40)
    Révolution de 1848

Other subtitles follow, and the latter subtitle has cross references to *Reconnaissance de la République française* and *Reconnaissance du pouvoir central de Francfort*. Under the titles there are references to the location of protocols, instructions, reports, letters, resolutions, notes, memoranda, circulars, interviews, etc. As helpful as they are, the *Tables de rubriques* are of primary value as suggestions only, for the subjects are not exhaustive and the references are far from complete.

Starting in 1919, another guide was begun. It is a card catalogue using the familiar three-by-five cards. Under this arrangement, which was more comprehensive and extensive, the subject of *Neutralité*, for example, starts:

Neutralité
  Neutralité belge
  Neutralité belge (garantie)
  La garantie de l'Angleterre
     I. La question devant le parlement anglais
    II. Renseignements divers—conversations 1860–1912

III.   Idem (1912–13) et après 1914
Neutralité du Congo

The cards contain references to the various types of documents and their location, and there are cross references. The fact that this guide is not open to examination is not as unfortunate as it might seem, for the members of the archives staff will consult it upon request and are most cordial in lending their assistance.

The numbered dossiers. Speaking very generally, most of these materials bear a date after 1900, relatively few are bound, and the majority are arranged by subject. A major exception of the latter characteristic, mentioned earlier, is the *Correspondance politique*, which was not arranged in this manner until 1934.

The two principal series of numbered dossiers are the *Série politique* and the *Archives politico-commerciales*. The political dossiers bear numbers from 1 to 1,999 and above 10,000. The political-commercial are numbered 2,000 to 10,000.

The lower numbers of the political series are on earlier subjects and contain instructions, reports, clippings of articles directly related to the reports, notes, and memoirs. An example is Number 231, *Projet d'occupation de la Bulgarie par les troupes belges*, 1876–77; another contains materials on the Crimean War. Examples of dossiers bearing numbers above 10,000 are the *Pacte de Locarno, Désarmement*, and the *Politique belge d'indépendance et le neutralité de 1936*.

Among these political dossiers there are the *Archives des affaires étrangères, Vienne*, 1832–1902. This multivolume collection of copies of Austrian correspondence came to be located in the *Service des Archives* in the manner described earlier in the chapter. It contains copies of the instructions to Austrian envoys accredited to Brussels, their reports, some dispatches relating to Belgium and sent by other Austrian diplomats, and correspondence between Belgian kings and the Austrian emperors and chancellors. Most of the material is typewritten. The fifty-year rule applies to the consultation of these documents as it does to those of Belgian origin.

The *Archives politico-commerciales* (numbered from 2,000 to 10,000) are arranged by subject and subtopics. *Négociations commerciales*, for example, is divided into dossiers *Belgique-France*, *Belgique-Pays-Bas*, etc. *Questions financières* is divided into states and then into aspects of the questions, such as *Emprunts*, *Budgets*, etc. Other dossiers are devoted to such subjects as *Les chemins de fer européens*, *L'émigration*, and *Les tentatives de colonisation*.

There is a *fichier* for the political and the politico-commercial dossiers. This card catalogue is arranged alphabetically by subject of the dossiers and has cross references.

The numbered dossiers in the *Série politique* and *Archives politico-commerciales* were deposited in the Service at different intervals by various divisions which had collected the documents into the dossiers because of interest in the subject at the time. It follows that there has been a dispersement of related materials. As a consequence, the Service is undertaking a review and regrouping of these documents for the period 1830–1914. The dossiers on related subjects are examined. Those which are no longer of historical or administrative interest are destroyed. The ones of little interest are microfilmed and then destroyed. The ones considered to be of importance are assembled and microfilmed. These are given the title *Classement B 1* if political and *B 2* if political-commercial archives and a number. A new catalogue of these is being prepared, with cards bearing the number of the films and of the paper dossiers.

The first dossiers to be put into *Classement B* are those relating to the Grand Duchy of Luxemburg from 1830 to 1914. The various dossiers have been *fusionnés* and placed together in cases. On several cards of the catalogue, there will be found a list of all the microfilmed and paper dossiers relating to Luxemburg with identifying names and numbers. An inventory of the files of *Classement B* is to be printed. It is possible that the collection on Africa that is described next will undergo such a rearrangement.

Most of the records on the Congo and the continent of Africa are now found in the numbered dossiers. As the area first assumed some significance, however, many materials were arranged in special dossiers and became a portion of the unnumbered *séries noires reliées*. This fact has been mentioned earlier and titles of the earlier dossiers have been listed. As the area became still more significant, it was decided to make a *grande collection* of these documents. Therefore the collection entitled *Afrique* contains both the unnumbered special dossiers and the numbered dossiers. The numbers of the latter bear the prefix "Af." As an illustration, Af 1–1 contains the correspondence of the consulate at Trondheim on the colony of the Congo from 1908 to 1913. Af 1–13 has *Papiers Strauch— Correspondance avec Léopold II au sujet du Congo*. There is a special *fichier* for the African collection.

Among the numbered dossiers there are over a thousand that make up the *Collection presse*. These consist of clippings and copies of articles on a great variety of subjects and are from both Belgian and foreign journals. The materials came from a departmental office that systematically collected the clippings, and from embassies and consulates. However, when reports from the latter dealt specifically with the articles, the clippings were left with the reports. Practically all the items are in the period since the 1860's. Some titles have only a single folder (or *farde*) with a few dozen articles, such as *Anarchisme* (1893– 1914), which has twenty-six items. Other subjects have many volumes of articles, as for example, *Presse étrangère. Analyses. (1914–1922) Violation du droit des gens par les Allemands. (Déportations, etc.) Divers*, which consists of thirty-two volumes and has an estimated thirty-seven hundred items. These articles are primarily press opinions from the daily papers, though there are articles from commercial and even technical journals. Together with the thousands attached to the reports in the *Correspondance politique,* the articles make the Belgian service a good starting point for research on many aspects of press opinion during the period since 1860. The fifty-year rule does not apply to this collection. It, too, has a special *fichier,* a card catalogue listing the titles alphabetically. Each is preceded by "Pr." and the number of the dossier.

Finally, there are numbered *Dossiers du personnel,* which contain the records of personnel engaged in administering foreign affairs. These carry the indication "Pers." and the number and are listed in a separate *fichier.* These are accessible only after the approval by the chief of the Service.

Although the correspondence concerning treaties is deposited in the *Service des Archives,* the treaties themselves are not. They are found in the *Service des Traités* of the ministry of foreign affairs. Special authorization must be secured before they are opened to investigators.[18]

Two exceptionally valuable private papers in the Service are those of the Beyens family (most significant for relations with France) and the Anethan family (for relations with the Vatican); their use is restricted to established scholars who secure the authorization of the family.

ADMINISTRATION, REGULATIONS, AND FACILITIES

Admission to the use of the archives is gained by a written application to the *Ministre des Affaires Etrangères,* 8 rue de la Loi, Brussels. The applicant should give the place and date of birth, his profession or position, his address, the research topic, its

---

[18]Information on the organization and classification of the documents was gained by observation and from Lambotte when he was *Chef du Service,* P.-H. Desneux, now *Chef du Service des Archives,* J. Willequet, *Chef du Service et Archiviste Adjoint* of the *Direction Général de la Politique,* and Georges Colle when he was a member of the staff. The entire staff is exceptionally cordial to those who use the archives. Arnold J. Briddon was also of great aid in helping the writer comprehend the arrangement of materials in which the latter had not done research. The period of research was made possible by a sabbatical leave and the granting of a C.R.B. Fellowship by the Belgian American Educational Foundation.

dates, and the purpose of the study. Belgian nationals should list publications with publishers and dates of publication and give the names and addresses of scholars and others as references. Foreign nationals should inclose a letter of introduction from their embassy. The Service is now located at 56 avenue des Arts.

The section of the ministry of foreign affairs responsible for the archives is the *Secrétariat Général*. The position of the Service is the organization and the current officials and staff members are:

Secrétariat Général
Secrétaire Général : M. Scheyven

Direction Générale de la Politique	*Direction Générale des Services Généraux*
Directeur Général : J. Delvaux de Fenffe	*Directeur Général :* L. Platteau
Service Historique	*Service des Archives*
Chef du Service et Archiviste Adjoint :	*Chef du Service :* P.-H. Desneux
J. Willequet	*Chef de Bureau :* A. Xhrouet
	Rédacteur : R. Fontaine
	Surveillante de Salle : Mme. Nisol

After receiving authorization to use the archives the investigator should present himself to the chief of the Service and explain in more detail the scope and objectives of the study. The researcher will then be given a list of dossiers pertinent to his subject, a list that is retained in a large envelope. To obtain a volume, the name or number should be indicated on the envelope which is signed upon receipt of the volume by the researcher. He in turn requests a signature when it is returned. Notes are kept in the envelope until checked and initialed by the chief of the Service. This *contrôle* is directed toward lacunae in documentation and errors in reading rather than censorship. The chief may, however, confiscate notes of those whose aims are polemical rather than scholarly or who seek to injure public or private interests, and he may withdraw authorization to use the archives.

The materials open to investigation are those antedating fifty years. On January 1 another year is automatically made available.

The reading room has individual research tables, lights, and *casiers* for the volumes being examined. The members of the staff are extraordinarily cordial and know their materials well. The hours of the reading room are 9:15 to 11:45 and 2:15 to 5:45 Monday through Friday and 9:15 to 11:45 on Saturday. There is no period of summer or annual closing, nor are there more than the usual number of national and religious holidays. Those authorized to use the archives may obtain photographic reproductions or microfilms of individual documents. Printed forms to be used in requesting this service are available in the reading room.

A limited number of serious scholars are permitted to use the library of the ministry of foreign affairs. Application is made to E. Duquenne, who has an accommodating staff. The library, strong in reference works and volumes relating to Belgian history, is located at 5 rue de Louvain. The *Bibliothèque Royale*, a much larger library, is located on rue de Musée just off Place Royale; unlike the Service and the library of the ministry, it is open after dinner until 10 P.M. For mature scholars, it maintains a *salle de travail*, a research room where a limited number of scholars may secure study tables. Volumes may be kept on the tables for a reasonable length of time as long as they are in use. This room has a thoroughly trained reference librarian and an attendant who are on duty during the day. Applications for use of both the library and the *salle de travail* should be made to *le conservateur en chef*. The main reading room and the catalogue are on the second floor. Several of the librarians have an excellent background in history. The manuscript division of this library has thousands of private letters and some diaries of

Belgian diplomats among its deposits. These have not been catalogued or indexed, however.

The residence areas of Brussels most convenient to the Service are in the neighborhood of Porte de Namur, which is also within walking distance of the *Bibliothèque Royale*, and Square Marie Louise, which is quiet and attractive. The Service maintains for its users a collection of folders with hotel and other tourist information.[19]

BIBLIOGRAPHY

Printed Collections of Documents

The Belgians have not published any lengthy collections of their diplomatic correspondence. Alfred De Ridder, one-time Director of the Service, quoted documents frequently in his numerous publications. In the following volumes, he was more of an editor than historian:

1. *La Belgique et la Prusse en conflit, 1834–38.* Brussels and Paris, 1919.
2. *La crise de la neutralité belge de 1848, le dossier diplomatique.* 2 vols. Brussels, 1928. After forty pages of comment, each of 477 documents is summarized briefly and quoted almost *in toto.*
3. *Histoire diplomatique du traité de 1839 (19 avril, 1839).* Brussels and Paris, 1920.
4. *Le mariage du Roi Léopold II.* Brussels, 1925. Consists primarily of Belgian documents dealing with Franco-Belgian relations, 1851–56.
5. *Les projets d'union douanière franco-belge et les puissances européennes, (1836–1843).* Brussels, 1933.

When the Germans occupied Brussels in the war of 1914–18, they selected and copied a number of documents. Some were published by them during hostilities, but the greater number appeared afterwards in:

6. *Zur europäischen Politik 1897–1914: unveröffentliche Dokumente in amtlichem Auftrage.* Edited by Bernhard Schwertfeger. 5 vols. Berlin, 1919. A second edition under the title *Amtliche Aktenstücke zur Geschichte der europäischen Politik, 1885–1914* was published in Berlin in 1924. It had 3 supplementary volumes, which contained some additional Belgian materials published during the war.

Conventions and treaties that were negotiated, whether they were ratified

---

[19]Information on the current administration, regulations, and facilities was supplied by Chief of Service Desneux in recent letters to the author.

or not, may be found in:

7. *Recueil des traités et conventions concernant le royaume de Belgique*. Edited by Baron de Garcia de la Véga and continued by Alphonse de Busschere. 21 vols. Brussels, 1850–1914.

Guides and Reference Works

8. De Ridder, Alfred. *La violation de la neutralité belge et ses avocats*. Brussels, 1926.

9. *Diplomatic documents relating to the outbreak of the World War*. Edited by James B. Scott. London, 1916.

10. *European politics during the decade before the war as described by Belgian diplomatists*. Documents issued by the Imperial German Foreign Office, 1915.

11. Lambotte, A. H. "Les archives des affaires étrangères pendant la guerre," *La revue générale belge* (April 1947).

12. Lancken Wakenitz, Oscar Freiherr von der. *Meine dreissig Dienstjahre— 1888–1918. Potsdam—Paris—Brussels*. Berlin, 1931.

13. "Organisation de la direction des archives au Département des Affaires Etrangères." A special dossier in the *Service des Archives, Ministère des Affaires étrangères*, Brussels.

14. Reports and memoranda by members of the German *Sonderkommando*, which was assigned the task of seizing the Belgian documents in 1940. Photostatic copies are on deposit in the Belgian *Service des Archives*. It is difficult to cite these German materials properly and consistently, for they have not been given uniform classification.

15. Schwertfeger, Bernhard. *Der geistige Kampf um die Verletzung der belgischen Neutralität*. Berlin, 1919.

16. Thomas, Daniel H. "History of the diplomatic archives of Belgium," *The American archivist*, XV (1952), 291–302. A more detailed account of the history of the Service written at the same time this chapter was drafted.

17. Willequet, Jacques. "Les archives du Ministère des Affaires Etrangères," *Archives, bibliothèques et musées de Belgique*, XXII (Number 1, 1951).

18. Winandy, A. "Les archives du Département des Affaires Etrangères," *Expansion belge, revue mensuelle illustrée* (October 1913). By a former director of the Service.

3 DENMARK

Waldemar Westergaard
University of California, Los Angeles

HISTORY

THE archives of the medieval Danish rulers were housed in a variety of places—at first in cathedrals such as Roskilde and Lund, then in Vordingborg Castle, and in the days of Queen Margaret and King Erik, in Kalundborg. The early Copenhagen Castle archives were at first purely administrative, but with the moving of the Kalundborg archives to the vaults of Copenhagen Castle, a central archive was established. The beginnings of the *Geheimearkiv* (privy archives) came under Frederick III, after the establishment in 1660 of the absolute monarchy and when Peder Schumacher (Griffenfeld) was named royal librarian and archivist (1663). Some years later the records were moved to Rosenborg Castle, where they remained until their return to a special building near the later Christiansborg Castle in 1720. The so-called joint archives at Gottorp, set up under Frederick I and Christian III, were brought to Copenhagen in 1734, the ducal Gottorp archives in 1736. The royal archives became centers of research under privy archivist Hans Gram, J. Langebek, and G. Schönning (1730–80), and the first collection of competently edited documents, the *Scriptores rerum Danicarum medii aevi* (1772–1834), began its appearance. The rapid accumulation of documents caused such crowding that much material, including some of historical value, was condemned and destroyed. When C. F. Wegener took office as privy archivist in 1848, he arranged to have most of the ministerial archives up to 1750 deposited in the privy archives. As a result of her defeat by the Germans in the 1864 war, Denmark had to surrender a large part of her valuable Schleswig-Holstein archives to Prussia. Not until 1883 were the privy and state archives united under a single head, the *Geheimearkivaren* (privy archivist). Wegener was succeeded in that year by a trained archivist, A. D. Jörgensen, chief of the state archives. The impractical system partly attempted earlier, of listing each separate document on a card, was abandoned, and the practical modern system of organization, based on the principle of provenience—the institutional source of the document—was introduced. In 1889 the *Rigsarkivet* (main archives) were divided into two sections, *Afdeling I*, corresponding to the old privy archives, and providing a reading room for visitors, and *Afdeling II*, the current governmental archives, with a loan office for the government ministries; and under the chief archivist's administration were placed three provincial archives set up in 1890–93 in Copenhagen, Odense, and Viborg. A fourth was established in Aabenraa for the reunited South Jutland districts and formally opened to the public in 1933. It will be noted that the Danish state archives system is more highly centralized than is that of most European countries. This centralization makes it possible to integrate the functions of the provincial archives with those of the Rigsarkiv so as to avoid duplication and possible friction.

ORGANIZATION AND CLASSIFICATION

The *Rigsarkiv* (State Archives and hereafter abbreviated to RA) is the depository for the central administration of the state, its ministries, and its bureaus, and for the private papers of leading figures in the national life of Denmark, such as statesmen and political figures. The *Landsarkiver* (archives of the provinces) house materials originating in the activities of ecclesiastical as well as lay officials of various ranks. Of interest to genealogists and students of Danish emigration are the files of parish registers, going back in some instances to the seventeenth century, and available to about 1892. Probate records from the archives of private estates and local judicial offices have been deposited to about 1870.

The oldest and most precious group of MSS (mostly parchments) in the central archives is the so-called "Oak Cabinet" collection, deposited in the so-called "Oak Cabinet Vault." The main sections in this collection that have greatest general interest, and of which some important parts bear more or less on Denmark's foreign relations and diplomatic history, are: (*a*) older archives of the royal house from Waldemar II to Christian VII (1230–1766); newer archives since the year 1766, from 1839 open only with royal assent; (*b*) charters (1466–1660) and acts of homage (1467–1656), matters concerning the Calmar Union, the council of state (1438–1660), and the estates; (*c*) laws (1521–76), judicial decisions (1418–1662), feudal documents, relations with the church (1419–1536), royal title deeds (1303–1734), mortgages, etc.; (*d*) relations with Schleswig, Holstein, Norway, Iceland, the Faroes, Greenland, and Sweden; (*e*) foreign relations, under the separate states concerned, including more important documents (to about 1700), and treaties (1700–80); (*f*) archives of princes in territories formerly Danish, as the "joint archives" (mainly from the period 1460–1669), the Glücksborg archives (1564–1773), (only parchment MSS, the papers being elsewhere); (*g*) the oldest church archives, including those of bishops, cathedral chapters, monasteries, and parish churches; (*h*) Varberg (Sweden) feudal archives; (*i*) the oldest town archives; (*j*) the oldest manorial records; (*k*) the oldest private archives, and (*l*) fragments of old parchments. (Of the above (*i*), (*j*), and (*k*) stop at about 1600; later materials for the collections (*i*) and (*j*) should be sought in the provincial archives.) For the sections listed above, there is no printed guide except for the collection of the private archives (see later), but a detailed card index and folio registers are available in the RA reading room; also a chronological list of all parchments and the oldest paper letters (especially before 1513) to be found in the "Oak Cabinet" collection.

Among special collections of note may be mentioned the Öresund (Sound) customs archives, 1624–1857, and the Sound Dues accounts, 1497–1856, published in part by Nina E. Bang. The correspondence that accompanied this material, all of it unpublished, is indexed in folio catalogues kept in the reading room. Among commercial archives may be noted those of the East Asiatic and West India and Guinea companies.[1] For Norway, Iceland, and Schleswig and Holstein, formerly under the Danish crown, the RA has retained the so-called *Forestill-ingsprotokoller* containing collegial representations on matters requiring royal signature, and the resulting royal resolution, whereas most of the original accompanying documents have been turned over at different times to Norwegian, Icelandic, and Prussian archives. For the study of the early history of the former Danish provinces of Skaane (Scania), Halland, and Blekinge, much valuable material is to be found in the RA.

Denmark's correspondence with foreign states was carried on by two departments or chanceries up to 1676. The Danish chancery handled the letters to Sweden and to Russia written in Danish. Letters to other European lands, including Poland, composed in German or Latin, were written ordinarily in the German chancery. Copybooks of Latin letters are preserved from the 1560's, and drafts of such letters from about 1650. Copybooks of outgoing letters in German are preserved from the 1540's; similarly, but a bit later, drafts of letters. Copybooks of instructions to envoys, of *pleinpouvoirs* and the like, exist from the 1530's. After 1676 and down to 1770 all foreign correspondence was carried on in the foreign department of the German chancery under two sections, a "general" and a "special." The former includes an *Ausländische Registrant* (foreign register), 1677–1756, and a more important *Geheimeregistratur* (privy

[1] See Kr. Erslev, *Rigsarkivet . . . en Oversigt* (Copenhagen, 1923), pp. 57–66.

register), 1676–1770, with political communications to foreign princes and to Danish envoys abroad. For the period 1736–60 there is a "protocol of confidential foreign reports, the deliberations concerning them and . . . the royal resolutions," with extracts from letters of Danish envoys abroad, the council of state's discussion of them, and the resulting royal resolutions. The "special" section of the German chancery has the correspondence with each country arranged chronologically from the beginning, to include (1) correspondence with the country's ruler, and papers resulting from negotiations with his representative in Denmark; (2) despatches from the Danish envoy in that state, and (3) the archives of the Danish mission in that country, including instructions and letters from Copenhagen, copybooks, incoming letters, drafts of despatches, and related materials.

In 1771 during Struensee's regime, the foreign department of the German chancery was raised to a new position when it became the department for foreign affairs, which designation it bore until 1848 when its name was changed to foreign ministry. In the "general" section for 1770–1847 are protocols of representations made to the king, and for 1785–1847 there are journals of incoming letters and such miscellaneous topics as navigation, customs business, and transit trade. The "special" section, 1771–1848, is arranged under countries, as was done earlier. The reading room has card indexes to the foreign administration archives to 1848.

Military archives before 1660 must be sought in the Danish and German chanceries. The archives for the "colleges" for land and sea forces established thereafter are in the RA but those of individual elements of the armed forces are in the army archives. The archives of the high command, like those of the navy, often have materials of importance for foreign politics. When administrative colleges were replaced by ministries after absolutism came to an end in 1848, an extensive reshuffling of functions took place. Among the new ministries there are the foreign ministry and two special ministries for the duchies, one for Schleswig, 1851–64, and one for Holstein and Lauenburg, 1852–64. A ministry for Iceland followed, 1874–1904; then in 1896 a ministry for agriculture and in 1908 a ministry for trade and navigation. The number of the ministries and their jurisdiction have varied much in this century.

Private papers in the RA for the period before 1660 are made accessible to the student through Erik Kroman's detailed guide, *Privatarkiver för 1660 i Rigsarkivet* (Copenhagen, 1948; 188 pp.), which lists the collections alphabetically from Aagaard to Örtzen, describes their contents, and names senders and recipients of the letters. A full index enhances the usefulness of the guide. Included among these papers are numerous letters on parchment, royal missives, and "open letters" from German, Swedish, and Danish rulers, letters to and from private persons at home and abroad, drafts and transcripts of correspondence, and a variety of miscellaneous documents. A continuation of Kroman's guide by Miss Henny Glarbo, *Privatarkiver 1660–1800*, was published in 1952. For the nineteenth century the guide is: Kr. Erslev, *Privatarkiver, fra det 19 Aarhundrede* (Copenhagen, 1923); for acquisitions of such archives from the nineteenth century received since 1923 and for private archives from this century the RA MSS catalogue must be the guide. Among well-known names of Danish and Norwegian public figures before 1800 or from the first decades of the nineteenth century may be mentioned a few: the Bernstorffs, Bielke, Bille, Brahe, Brochmand, Johan Bülow, Gyldenstierne, Göye (Gjöe), Huitfeldt, Kaas, Krabbe, Krag, Krummedige, Laxmand, Lente, Luxdorph, Milan, Munk, Oxe, Podebusk, Rantzau, Reventlow, Rosenkrants, the Schimmelmanns, Sehested, Thott, Trolle, Ulfeldt, Valkendorff, and Worm. Among the most important private papers concerned with Danish foreign relations in the nineteenth century are those of political and diplomatic figures such as J. G. Adler, C. A. Bluhme, F. C. Dankwart, C. G. Andrae, C. C. Hall, A. F. Krieger, T. A.

Regenburg, A. F. Tscherning, and P. Vedel.[2] The private archives taken over by the RA are those that have belonged to persons whose achievements and interests have been national rather than local. The provincial archives have private papers from local leaders, as well as papers from private estates. However, the papers of a local person whose career is of national interest should be sought in the RA, where the main bulk of private archives is to be found.

A short but useful guide to the materials in the RA is Erslev's *Rigsarkivet og Hjaelpemidlerne til dets Benyttelse: en Oversigt* (1923). In 1886 the first of a series of guides was published: V. A. Secher, *Danske Kancelli*, which some years ago was replaced by B. Kornerup, *Danske Kancelli* (1943; 182 pp.). For diplomatic relations with Sweden and Russia, which were under the Danish chancery (before 1676, see above), the student may refer to the hints in Erslev's *Rigsarkivet* above noted, but must rely mainly on the detailed and comprehensive card indexes in the RA reading room. The internal department of the German chancery has a similar excellent guide, published shortly after Kornerup's in Johanne Skovgaard's *Tyske Kancelli I og de dermed beslaegtede Institutioner* (1946; 179 pp.), based in part on the late F. J. West's long preliminary labors. It is especially useful for the Schleswig area and has some documents on the treaties of Westphalia and Nimwegen, on imperial diets in Regensburg and Frankfort, and on the *Niedersächsicher Kreis*, *Bremen und Verden, Oldenburg und Delmenhorst, Stift Lübeck, Stadt Hamburg*, and more or less related topics. For the South Jutland (North Schleswig) districts, there is F. Gribsvad and J. Hvidtfeldt's *Landsarkivet for de sönderjydske Landsdele: en Oversigt* (1944). It lists the contents of the provincial archives opened at Aaben-

[2]The *Kongelige Bibliotek* (Royal Library) in Copenhagen has a large MS. division with many collections of personal papers of literary notables, as well as political and diplomatic figures with international connections. For acquisitions up to the first decade of this century, the student should consult E. Gigas, *Katalog over det kongelige Biblioteks Haandskrifter vedr. Norden, saerlig Danmark*, 3 vols. (Copenhagen, 1903–15), and C. Behrend: *Katalog over det kgl. Biblioteks Haandskrifter vedrörende Dansk Personalhistorie* (1925).

raa in 1933, a collection that fills about 3,000 meters of shelving, includes MSS from such counties as Haderslev, Aabenraa with Lögumkloster, Flensburg (part), Sönderborg and Nordborg on Als, Tönder, and some records from Ribe diocese. The parish registers, the oldest starting with 1574, are much in demand by genealogists. S. Nygaard's *Danmarks Kirkeböger* (1933) provides a competent evaluation of Denmark's parish registers.[3] The series published by the RA entitled *Vejledende Arkivregistraturer* (to which the volumes above mentioned belong) also has sections prepared by J. Bloch, devoted to divers governmental bodies such as: *Rentekammert* (1660–1848), the exchequer; *Generaltoldkammert* (1760–1848), the national customs administration; *Kommercekollegiet* (1735–1848),[4] the commerce commission or "college"; and *Finanskollegiet*. It may be noted that West India and Guinea affairs came under the customs administration after 1760, but that the colonies in the East Indies, after the crown took them over in 1777, were placed under the college of commerce.

For acquisitions dated later than 1848 there are no printed guides. Such materials are all in Section II (*Anden Afdeling*), where even recent documents are accepted from the ministries and bureaus, though always with the possibility that they may have to go back on loan to their office of origin. They are arranged under journals, according to their appropriate division in the state administration. On the other hand, Section I (*Förste Afdeling*) is practically free from restrictions. But there are as yet no printed catalogues of the diplomatic correspondence in the German chancery (*Tyske Kancellis udenrigske Afdeling*—TKUA) and the (later) department for foreign affairs (*udenrigske Anliggender*). The investigator desiring specific

[3]An extensive collection of microfilms of Danish parish registers has been made by the Mormon church authorities in Utah.
[4]The largest part of the archives of the earliest college of commerce is in the Copenhagen town hall archives, under designations such as *Politiog Kommercekollegiets Resolutionsprotokoller*, 3 vols. (1704–12 and 1722–30), *Missivprotokoller*, 5 vols. (1704–30), and its *Memorialprotokoller*, 8 vols. (1704–27).

material on Danish foreign relations will be given prompt access to a very detailed card index listing materials in his field of interest.

ADMINISTRATION, REGULATIONS, AND FACILITIES

Certain rules are fixed by royal resolution or by agreement with the department or body in which the documents originated. Ministerial records are generally accessible up to 1901. Limitations apply to cases involving persons, to private papers, and to records of the royal house. Census materials are available up to 1901; special permission for access to later censuses may be granted for securing statistical information. Provincial archives are free of access with respect to everything that has been delivered to them, which in most cases means up to *ca.* 1882. The so-called "private archives" in public depositories are subject to varying rules or agreements. The older ones, from before the middle of the nineteenth century, are in the main accessible to all, but the newer ones usually require the permission of the *Rigsarkivar* (State Archivist), or in some cases of descendants of the person in question.

Rigsarkivar Axel Linvald is in general charge of the *Rigsarkiv* staff. Dr. Holger Hjelholt, *Overarkivar* (associate archivist), is head of Section I; Dr. Björn Kornerup, *Overarkivar*, is head of Section II. Address: Rigsarkivet, Rigsdagsgaarden, Copenhagen K. For the provincial archives: (1) *Landsarkivet* for Sjælland, etc. Jagtvej 10, Copenhagen N. (*Landsarkivar* Harald Hatt); (2) *Landsarkivet* for Fyn, Odense (*Landsarkivar* C. Lindberg Nielsen); (3) *Landsarkivet* for Norrejylland, (North Jutland), Viborg (*Landsarkivar* J. Hvidtfeldt); (4) *Landsarkivet* for *de sönderjydske Landsdele* (the South Jutland districts), Aabenraa (*Landsarkivar* Frode Gribsvad).

No introduction of any kind is needed. Readers may receive a leaflet with a few simple rules by applying to the officer in charge at the reading room desk.

The reading room has a small but useful selection of recent

works on Danish history. Adjoining it is a room with a large collection of seals and a room for microfilm readers and typewriter users.

Private persons may in exceptional circumstances be granted permission to use their own microfilming apparatus. The RA is prepared to accept orders for microfilms at a price, as of the present, of 30 öre (approximately 4½ cents) per exposure; for 25 or more, 25 öre each; for 100 or more, 20 öre each. Enlargements can be provided at the following rates: for size 14, 7 × 21 cm., 85 öre; 21 × 29 cm., 1.50 kroner (approximately 21 cents); 29 × 42 cm., 2.50 kroner (approximately 36 cents).

Hotel rooms at present vary from 8 to 60 kroner per night (the kroner is now worth approximately 14 cents). It is advisable to engage rooms in advance. The RA is centrally located with convenient traffic facilities, so location of living quarters is of minor importance. Inquiries should be directed to Turistforeningen (tourist association) for Denmark, located at Hovedbanegaarden (central station), Copenhagen V.

BIBLIOGRAPHY

For the history of the RA in C. F. Wegener's term as chief archivist (1848–82), including reports on acquisitions, problems of reorganization, and publication of selected groups of historical MSS, see his *Aarsberetninger fra det kongelige Geheimearkiv*, 7 vols. (Copenhagen, 1852–83).

In 1884 shortly after taking office as chief archivist, A. D. Jörgensen published a detailed and authoritative account of what came to be known under his administration as the Rigsarkiv, entitled *Udsigt over de danske Rigsarkivers Historie* (329 pp.). His own important contribution to archival reorganization—the initiating of the classification of materials according to provenience, i.e., to the institution in which they originated—is mentioned briefly on page 140; but the real work of applying the principle throughout the archives fell to Dr. V. A. Secher, first Jörgensen's assistant, and later also state archivist. Jörgensen's *Udsigt* notes the main acquisitions through the centuries, and losses such as those to Norway (1820 ff. and 1850 ff.) and to Prussia (1873 ff.). An interesting list of archival officials from 1523 to 1882 occurs on pp. 151–195, and selected documents from the fifteenth century to 1882, illustrating the checkered history of the archives, conclude the volume. Jörgensen inaugurated a series of RA-sponsored publications entitled *Meddelelser fra det kongelige Geheimearkiv og . . . Kongerigets Arkiv* (later changed to *Meddelelser om Rigsarkivet*), a revised and improved version of Wegener's *Aarsberetninger*. In the volume for 1883–85, an able member of his staff, V. A. Secher, provided a hundred-page history of the Danish chancery and a classified *registratur* of its contents to 1848, the first printed guide of its kind. The arrangement reflects Secher's application of the principle of provenience—*Hjemmehörs Principet*.[5] For Danish history since 1848, when absolutism gave way to constitutional government, it is important to have competent descriptions of administrative changes and dispositions. Three books describe periods of the "civil central administration" from 1848 to 1935: G. N. Kringelbach, *Den civile Centraladministration 1848–1893* (1894); L. Laursen, same title, *1894–1913* (1921); and H. Jörgensen, same title, *1914–1935* (1936). Lists of government officials in the state at various periods are available in: *Den danske civile Centraladministrations Embedsetat 1660–1848* (1889), a list of Denmark's civil officials; G. N. Kringelbach's *Civile Direktioner og Kommissioner samt andre overordnede Myndigheder under Enevælden* (1899), a list of directorates, commissions, and higher authorities under the absolute kings. Useful for biographical (genealogical) research is Fabritius and Hatt, *Haandbog i Slægtsforskning* (1943), an introduction to genealogical study. A list of Danish diplomats abroad, prepared by the late E. Marquard, appeared in 1952 under the title, *Danske diplomater i Udlandet*. The terminal date is 1914.

Among more important works listing, calendaring, or reproducing documents in the RA are: Kr. Erslev and W. Christensen, *Repertorium diplomaticum regni Danici mediævalis*, 13 vols. in 2 series (1894–1939); *Diplomatarium Danicum* (1938 ff.), medieval documents from 1250, in facsimiles, printed text, and Danish translation, published by the Danish Society of Language and Literature; *Kancelliets Brevböger* (1885 ff.), outgoing chancery letters and orders concerning internal affairs, 1551–1641, planned to extend to 1660, edited by members of the RA staff; *Kronens Sköder*, 4 vols. (1892, 1908, 1941, 1950), a selection of royal deeds of conveyance in the RA, 1535–1730, edited by L. Laursen, F. J. West, and S. Nygaard, resp.; L. Laursen, ed., *Danmarks-Norges Traktater 1523–1750*, 11 vols. (1907 ff.), completed to 1700 (vols. 10 and 11 edited by C. S. Christiansen); H. Hansen, ed., *Kabinetsstyrelsen i Danmark 1768–1772*, 3 vols. (1916–23), reproducing the "cabinet orders" issued through Struensee and others.

[5]Secher explains this in detail as applied in the RA in an article entitled "Om Proveniens- (Hjemmehörs) Principet," in *Meddelelser fra det danske Rigsarkiv* (1906), 191–240.

A brief but informing account of the history, organization, and activities of Danish archives is *Rigsarkivar* Axel Linvald's *Dansk Arkivvaesen: Historie, Organization og Virksomhed* (1933), originally published in German in the *Archivalische Zeitschrift*, vol. 41. The notes have references to all the more important printed materials on the subject, with citations on foreign archive practices and problems.

The guide to RA's archival materials on Schleswig by F. J. West, "Arkivalier vedr, Hertugdömmet Slesvig eller Sönderjylland," in *Fortid og Nutid*, III, 40–65, has been largely supplanted by H. Hjelholt, "Den dansktyske Arkivudveksling i April–May 1936: Hvad vi fik, og hvad vi afstod," in *ibid.*, XII (1937–38), 1–12, and by A. Linvald, "Dansk-tysk Arkivudveksling," in *Historisk Tidsskrift*, 10 R., vol. 4, pp. 109–120. An indispensable *vade mecum* to the historical literature and sources bearing on Schleswig's history is Troels Fink and J. Hvidtfeldt, *Vejledning i Studiet af Sönderjyllands Historie* (1944).

Publications dealing with other Danish archives and MS. Collections: Oluf Nielsen, "Bidrag til Kobenhavns Raadstuearkivs Historie," in *Danske Samlinger*, IV, 234–249; Axel Linvald, "Meddelelser fra Raadstuearkivet 1923 ff.," in *Historiske Meddelelser . . . om Köbenhavn* (1924 ff.), both on the Copenhagen town hall archives; Knud C. Rockstroh, "Oversigt over de vigtigste Afdelinger af Krigsministeriets Arkiv og Vejledning med Hensyn til Benyttelsen," in *Fortid og Nutid*, II (1920), pp. 170–176; Carl v. Kohl, *Hærens Arkiv* (1946), on the war department archives and their use; Victor Petersen, "Universitetets Arkiv gennem Tiderne," in *Ex Biblioteca universitatis Hafniensis* (1920), pp. 65 ff. (the archives of the university up to *ca.* 1900 have recently been delivered to the RA); Alfred Krarup, *Katalog over Universitetsbibliotekets Haandskrifter*, I-II (1929, 1935) on MS collection in library of university of Copenhagen; Axel Linvald, "Kommissionen til Undersögelse af de i dansk Privateje bevarede Kilder til dansk Historie 1923 ff.," (for the period 1923–31) in *Oversigt over det danske Videnskaberned Selskabs Forhandlinger* (1923 ff.), an account of the work of a committee appointed by the Danish Academy of Science and Letters in listing and evaluating historical MSS in private possession.

To help in identifying authors of unsigned MSS, the RA has, through archivist Dr. W. Christensen, brought together a collection of twelve to fourteen-hundred photostats of specimen hands. Two valuable palaeographic books are: E. Kroman, *Middelalderlig Skrift: Skrift: Skriftpröver og Transkriptioner* (1951), and H. Hjelholt, *Skriftpröver fra Tiden efter Reformationen til Midten af 19. Aarhundrede* (2d ed., 1948).

4 FRANCE

Vincent Confer

Maxwell School of Citizenship and Public Affairs,
Syracuse University

THE habit of identifying the major European foreign ministries simply by their street addresses may be regarded as a recognition of the timeless and institutional quality of these great agencies of the state. Even when one of them has suspended operations, as has the Wilhelmstrasse at this writing, or been abandoned for more than a quarter-century, as has the Pevtchevsky Bridge, the feeling persists that a closing is temporary and a change of address merely the mark of an old outlook preserved under a new name. In modern France the Quai d'Orsay stands as a symbol of the continuity of foreign policy through domestic political vicissitudes unmatched in the annals of any other power. Its archives are the material legacy of the centuries since Richelieu, when French statesmen were never absent from the council tables of Europe and of the world—when indeed they not uncommonly exercised hegemony there.

The building that the French foreign ministry occupies at 37 quai d'Orsay (Paris VII) was not the scene of the diplomatic triumphs of either Louis XIV or Napoleon I. Planned in Renaissance style by Lacornée, it was constructed in the reign of Louis Philippe but not occupied by the ministry until 1853. The archives are installed at the rear on the first floor of the southwest wing, facing upon the rue de l'Université. Extensive alterations in 1936–37 increased the space available to the archives and adjoining offices in this corner of the building. During the liberation of Paris on August 25, 1944 the Germans

55

made a stand in the Quai d'Orsay. A disastrous fire broke out in the southwest wing as a result of the fighting. It destroyed a part of the recent papers and damaged the reading room and offices of the archives so severely that a remodeling and expansion rather than a simple restoration was undertaken in the postwar years. The architect Niermans carried out a modernization of style and facilities within the limits imposed by the need for harmony with the surviving older portion of the wing. This work was completed in 1951.

Students of medieval history will find little of interest in these archives and must turn to the *Bibliothèque Nationale*, the *Archives Nationales*, and other public or private collections. This situation can be attributed to the careless practices of earlier ages when no clear line separated personal and state papers. Retiring ministers of state often took with them whatever they chose among the documents accumulated during their administrations. Since cases of this kind occur from time to time even in the twentieth century, one can understand more readily how most of Richelieu's papers passed into the hands of his niece, the Duchess of Aiguillon, with the remainder in the possession of Bouthillier de Chavigny. Mazarin later turned over his state papers to the personal custody of Colbert. In 1661, accordingly, the French government did not have possession of its own diplomatic correspondence for what amounted to nearly the whole preceding half-century. This situation was clearly intolerable for a nation whose preponderance in Europe was attributable not only to military superiority but to its success in manipulating the complexities of diplomatic intercourse for its own purposes. Consequently, at the death of Hugues de Lionne in 1671, Louis XIV ordered the retention of all papers by the crown. This marked the beginning of regular and careful preservation of the correspondence and papers of the foreign ministry.[1]

---

[1]The best account of the early history of the archives is to be found in number 22 in bibliography. The most detailed study of the whole development down to the beginning of the Third Republic is number 19 in bibliography.

By 1710 the department had accumulated a mass of manuscript material that was no longer considered current or active. Items of that nature were thereupon assigned to a new depository in the Louvre under the care of the Sieur de Saint Prez as the first keeper. Whether because there now existed an administrator with a proprietary interest in the growth of his domain or because of the development of the historical sense in the seventeenth and eighteenth centuries, a major campaign was inaugurated with the full support of the royal power to recover the missing documents of the early seventeenth century. Fortunately for the historian, nearly all the papers of Richelieu (in 1705 and 1733) and Mazarin (in 1732) were added to the growing collection. The diplomatic correspondence was now nearly complete as far back as 1624, and a not inconsiderable number of items from the sixteenth century were also obtained. These acquisitions, amounting to hundreds of manuscript volumes, constitute the heart of the important series, *Mémoires et Documents*.

The archives have been favored by fortune on at least three occasions. At the time of the disturbances in Paris during the Revolution of 1789 they profited from having been moved to Versailles in 1763. Nonetheless, a threat to their safety did arise in 1793, when the Convention sent out several investigating commissions to search the archives for more evidence of secret expenses of the monarchy. Nicholas Geoffroy, a tactful keeper who had accepted the new state of affairs in France, preserved the papers from damage. In 1796 they were brought to Paris by the Directory and were installed successively in the rue du Bac and the rue de Grenelle. They were not placed under the same roof as the foreign ministry until 1822, two years after that institution had moved into a *hôtel* in the rue Neuve des Capucines. This was the establishment outside whose walls occurred the fateful shooting that set off the February revolution of 1848. The government had expected, in fact, to build a large new foreign ministry on the quai Bonaparte. But delays in construction

had led to the substitution of this address on the Right Bank
in 1820. When the building on the quai Bonaparte was
finally completed in 1838, the foreign ministry did not occupy
it. The structure was turned over instead to the *Conseil d'Etat*
and the *Cour des Comptes*. The latter still occupied the premises
when the place was set on fire during the Commune of 1871 and
almost completely destroyed. If the foreign ministry archives
had been located there as originally planned, they might have
been wholly lost.

As it turned out, the war of 1939 inflicted upon the archives
the greatest damage since their formation.[2] The panic of May
1940, following German military successes in the north and the
fear that Paris was about to fall, reached even into the Quai
d'Orsay. Nearly all the diplomatic correspondence for 1935–40,
as well as a large part of that covering 1930–35, was thrown into
the courtyard and burned on May 16. Of course, certain series
of documents had been evacuated to Touraine as early as the
fall of 1939, but even they were not safe. Some of them were
burned by the captain of the steamer upon which they were
being taken from Bordeaux to America, when the vessel was
turned back by German aircraft. The Germans seized the rest
in Touraine and returned them to Paris for preliminary examination. Later they carried away between four and five thousand
volumes of documents: mostly on the Paris Peace Conference of
1919, the French role in the League of Nations, and French
cultural activities abroad. Then the fire of August 25, 1944 (see
above) destroyed many post-1919 items that the Germans were
still inspecting in the offices of the archives.

These stunning losses were, fortunately, not irreparable. The
French recovered about eighteen hundred volumes of their
diplomatic records in Germany after the war. The staff of the
archives saw that most of the remaining correspondence to and
from foreign posts could be reconstituted by bringing back to

[2] The losses and the restoration now in progress are described in number 32 in
bibliography.

Paris the originals or copies of all incoming and outgoing correspondence kept regularly in the files of the French posts abroad during the years that were still missing at the Quai d'Orsay. The identification of what ought to be found at each foreign post has been simplified by the fortunate survival of the Quai d'Orsay's official registers of all documents received or dispatched (with two exceptions: outgoing dispatches for the second quarter of 1935, and both outgoing and incoming dispatches for the second quarter of 1940). Microfilm copies have been made for retention in the archives. While the decision to microfilm grew inevitably out of the prohibitive cost of reproducing so great a mass of material in longhand or typescript, the staff has ordered the enlargement and printing of the most important documents. This is, however, a slow and expensive process. It is to be hoped that the reconstitution of the missing materials will have been completed by the time the official date for the use of the archives has been advanced to 1919. Meanwhile the problem remains purely academic, since the present limit for research stands well before that year.

The archives were opened on a regular basis to qualified scholars in 1880. Before that date admission came only after special, personal consideration of each candidate by the minister of foreign affairs, whose decision was generally final. The doors were usually closed to all save well-connected amateurs or exceptionally well-known scholars. Of course in the seventeenth and eighteenth centuries not many historians asked for admission. Modern history was looked upon as scarcely a proper field for serious scholarship, and these archives afforded few manuscripts earlier than Richelieu's time. In the eighteenth century, the historians who might have wanted admission were often nonprofessionals such as Voltaire. They were suspected of seeking evidence to discredit the existing order of things. And as for Voltaire, his interests lay rather in the direction of social and cultural history.

After 1789 modern history became more respectable. To Burke the present was inextricably linked with the past in the continuous web of society. Romanticism excited new interest in the bygone as well as in the distant and exotic. Admissions to the archives grew more frequent, but still carried the air of being exceptional favors. This no doubt accounted for the peculiarity that they were more often granted to foreigners than to Frenchmen. The foreign ministry seldom hesitated to deny the plea of one of its own citizens, but occasionally opened its record to influential foreigners as a diplomatic gesture toward the governments supporting the applications. During the Peace of Amiens, Napoleon and Talleyrand admitted Charles James Fox with every show of courtesy toward his research on the last two Stuarts. Perhaps the first American to win access to these archives was Jared Sparks in 1828–29. Somewhat later came George Bancroft, when he was minister to Great Britain. He made a trip to Paris in 1847 and was well received by two fellow historians: Guizot, the premier, and Mignet, the keeper of the foreign ministry archives. Even Germans such as Sybel and Theiner were more likely to succeed in their quest than were French historians.

Keepers of the archives at that time seemed to feel that their principal duty was to preserve their manuscripts as much as possible from the touch of outsiders. But all attempts to liberalize policy failed until 1880.[3] An early commission created by Decazes in 1874 had accomplished very little. Six years later, mounting pressure forced the adoption of the modern practice of appointing an official archival commission, composed of experienced diplomats and eminent historians as well as the leading officials of the archives, to handle applications in accordance with a general policy fixed by law or decree. The victory was due in part to a growing interest in modern history in France. Some of that interest can be attributed to the effect

[3]For an urbane account of the campaign to open the archives in the 1870's and 1880's, see the memoirs of Gabriel Hanotaux (number 26 in bibliography).

of the Franco-Prussian War. Wounded national pride sought, perhaps unconsciously, the solace to be found in contemplating the more victorious past. It is not surprising that among the first Frenchmen to take advantage of the new liberality were Albert Sorel, who ultimately published his *L'Europe et la révolution française*, and Gabriel Hanotaux, who was the youthful secretary of the new Commission for the Diplomatic Archives and later the author of the *Histoire du cardinal de Richelieu*. Each devoted his research to an age when French policy had been pre-eminently successful. But even without the impact of 1870, modern history was coming into its own, partly through the German school of historical scholarship and partly through the activities of such French historians as Gabriel Monod, who founded the *Revue historique* in 1876 and complained that ancient and medieval French history crowded out the more recent period in the faculties and in the training of young research men.

Still, these trends seldom affected the Quai d'Orsay directly and more direct stimuli were required to open the archives. One of these was the precedent set by Great Britain, Prussia, Austria, and Russia. By 1875 all of them had announced policies providing for easier access to their foreign ministry archives. This argument was cleverly used by Armand Baschet, whose history published in 1875 was intended as much as a lever to pry open the French archives as a serious account of their development. Even then the reform came only after the triumph of the republicans in 1877–80, when a new keeper was appointed and the Commission for the Diplomatic Archives was created. Under Freycinet in 1880 the open date was set at 1815, and it has subsequently been changed from time to time. Some ten years later, an American influence made itself felt through Benjamin Franklin Stevens, who was the first research worker to persuade the Quai d'Orsay to recognize photography as a method of transcribing manuscripts. He was even granted permission to set up a photographic room in the gardens of the ministry, where he copied many items for his famous twenty-five volumes of facsimiles.[4]

ORGANIZATION AND CLASSIFICATION

In the eighteenth century the foreign ministry adopted a classification that has been applied to all materials accumulated down through 1896. It comprises three basic series: *Correspondance politique*, *Mémoires et Documents*, and *Correspondance consulaire et commerciale*. Each of these is subdivided into *fonds* (record groups). The *fonds* of the *Correspondance politique* bear the names of states, those in *Mémoires et Documents* are called after states or continents, and in the *Correspondance consulaire et commerciale* they are named for diplomatic or consular posts. Then one comes upon the individual documents, most of which are bound into stout volumes numbered chronologically within the *fonds*.

Except for the unwieldy series *Mémoires et Documents*, which grew to more than twenty-five hundred volumes, this system served well enough until the present century brought a vast increase in daily international communication, nearly all of it requiring preservation. The staff of the archives has accordingly undertaken the most important change in classification since the eighteenth century. For the years up to 1897 the *Correspondance politique* will continue to be organized first by country and then by year. But after 1897 it will be arranged first by country and then by subject. This new policy should greatly aid the scholar who pursues a specific subject through long years and thousands of documents. The plan is to make the topical subdivisions for all countries as much alike as possible. Of course some states will require a number of special headings. The foreign ministry will announce the details of this reorganization when a part of the post-1897 papers has been opened to research.

The year 1897 is notable also because it is in effect the

4Number 16 in bibliography.

terminal date for *Mémoires et Documents*. Always a convenient place to catalogue late acquisitions of materials that for one reason or another had escaped the control of the foreign ministry, *Mémoires et Documents* tended to become a closed series as great new purchases or gifts were added more infrequently after the eighteenth century. Consequently, when the post-1897 documents become available, they will be found to have been distributed only to the other basic series: *Correspondance politique* and *Correspondance consulaire et commerciale*.

I. *The* Correspondance politique:

This series consists in major part of drafts and copies of communications sent by the French foreign ministry to its agents abroad and of the reports of those agents in return. It also includes the correspondence between foreign diplomatic representatives in France and the French foreign ministry. In addition, the series contains valuable minutes, notes, memorials, and drafts, originating in the ministry, as well as reports, clippings, and varied enclosures that once accompanied the letters from French diplomats abroad. The research worker might, for example, ask to see: *Correspondance politique. Angleterre.* vol. 774 (janvier-juin, 1877). In that volume he would find not only dispatches that passed between Decazes and d'Harcourt in London, but also letters between Decazes and Lord Lyons, the British ambassador in Paris. The subjects treated range from the imminent Turkish war and Egyptian financial difficulties to the questions of the Newfoundland fisheries and the king of Dahomey.

Only slightly less important are the supplements to the *Correspondance politique*. There are two: *intercalaire* and *général*. The former consists mostly of papers that were once attached to the original dispatches or have been acquired by the ministry at a later date. They are bound into volumes, generally on an annual basis, and these volumes form a regular part of a particular *fonds*, coming in their natural chronological place immediately after the ordinary volume for the year in question. For example: *Correspondance politique. Espagne.* vol. 397 (*janvier-juin 1732*). *Supplément.*

The *Supplément général* contains very much the same kind of material, but usually a longer period is covered by each volume. It is shelved at the end of a particular *fonds* and its volumes are renumbered consecutively in chronological order. For example: *Correspondance politique. Espagne. Supplément.* vol. 14 (1730–52). The existing official catalogues of the *Correspondance politique* cover the supplements as well as the main series. Both supplements will be found to include some duplicates, as well as early drafts, of documents in the regular series since they have been created in part from the obsolete files of French diplomatic posts returned to Paris many decades after the events which they recorded.

While it has been noted that the files of the Quai d'Orsay date in general only from the time of Richelieu, scholars interested in the sixteenth century cannot afford to neglect them. Depending upon the country, a certain number of documents from that period, especially the latter half, can be found in the *Correspondance politique*. For example, the first six volumes in the *Fonds Hollande* cover 1566–1606. The first thirteen volumes for Switzerland deal chiefly with the sixteenth century; and twenty-two volumes are assigned to Rome for the years 1537–1601.

II. The Mémoires et Documents:

This is one of the greatest and certainly the most complex of the series in the French foreign ministry even if, as was pointed out above, it has now become in fact a closed classification. The archivists of the eighteenth century created it primarily to accommodate the great acquisitions of previously dispersed documents when they came in through royal order, by purchase, or by legacy. Some of these, such as the papers of Richelieu, Mazarin, and Saint-Simon (except his memoirs), are still distinctly visible in its structure. For example, volumes 21 to 46 of the *Fonds France* in this series still bear the subheading *Lettres de Mazarin* and cover the years after 1646 (the letters of Mazarin for 1642–46 are held by the *Bibliothèque Mazarine* in Paris). The task of the investigator is complicated, however, by the fact that many letters of the great minister can be found in other volumes of the *Fonds France*, in the *Fonds France. Affaires intérieures et extérieures* (see below), and in the series *Correspondance politique*. The degree of dispersion varies considerably even for personalities whom history has marked as pre-eminent. Most, if not all, of the papers relating to Mirabeau can be found in volumes 1884–90 of the *Fonds France*, but the state papers of Chateaubriand and Lamartine have to be sought throughout the various *fonds* of this great series and of the *Correspondance politique* as well, in the volumes corresponding to the years when they were involved in diplomacy.

Mémoires et Documents also contains reports and memorials drawn up by the staff of the foreign ministry, as well as documents sent to France by its diplomats abroad and not a part of their regular correspondence. It will be noticed that the distinction between this material and some of the contents of the supplements to the *Correspondance politique* is not very sharp. Finally, other volumes deal with what are really internal administrative problems of France. These are found chiefly in the *Fonds: France. Affaires intérieures* and *France. Petits fonds de province*. Each *fonds* in the series is arranged chronologically and the constituent volumes are numbered consecutively, but there is also an over-all, continuous enumeration from *fonds* to *fonds* in the following order of mention.

Perhaps the most important subdivision in the *Mémoires et Documents* is the *Fonds France*. This group of about five hundred volumes of manuscripts includes the papers of Richelieu, some volumes from the original Saint-Simon collection, a part of the Noailles family correspondence in the eighteenth century, and a wealth of other material. Illustrative of this *fonds* is the *testament politique* of Richelieu—one of two copies in existence, the other being in the *Bibliothèque Nationale*. Its designation is: *Mémoires et Documents. Fonds France*, vol. 82.

Associated with the *Fonds France* are four *fonds* of considerable interest. One of these is the *Fonds Bourbon*, sometimes known as the *Fonds des émigrés*. It contains correspondence dealing with royalist intrigues and counterespionage during the French Revolution. The staff will not permit certain volumes to be used because of the fragile condition of some of the manuscripts. An inventory of this *fonds* for use in the reading room has been completed. The *Fonds Saint-Simon* consists of eighty-four carefully inventoried volumes of manuscripts from the collection of the famous duke, whose papers were acquired by the state in 1760. Much of the material in the *Papiers de Bonaparte*, comprising forty-seven volumes, is now available in printed form. The *Cérémonial* concerns itself with precedence and etiquette at the French and foreign courts.

More than a hundred volumes have been assigned the title *France. Affaires intérieures et extérieures*. Among them are additional manuscripts of Richelieu and some of the volumes of Mazarin's correspondence. Here too can be found many of the manuscripts originating with the *"jurisconsultes et publicistes spéciaux"* in the era between the reign of Louis XV and 1930, when the policy of paying certain publicists for services to the state had not yet been officially abandoned. A special inventory of this material, scattered as it is through several *fonds*, will soon be available in the reading room.

About four hundred volumes in the *Fonds France et divers états* constitute a valuable source for drafts of treaties, as well as for reports drawn up by the ministry on various subjects. They are arranged geographically. As an example, one might note: *Mémoires et Documents. Afrique*. vols. 67 and 68 (Madagascar, 1800–85), where the subjects treated include the relations of the Hovas with France and England, Catholic missionary activity, and notes on the island by Thouvenel, the *directeur des affaires politiques*.

The next two *fonds* reveal the impossibility of separating foreign affairs from domestic matters, particularly in the *ancien régime. France. Affaires intérieures* contains more than six hundred volumes. It includes that part of the Mazarin papers which concern internal problems—for example, the Fronde; the correspondence of Fleury; royal ordinances on army, navy, and financial matters; and letters and memorials addressed to the foreign ministry by private French citizens. Some three hundred volumes in *France. Petits fonds de province* are devoted to the pre-revolutionary administration of such provinces as Provence, Dauphiné, Franche-Comté, and Brittany, which retained a right to special treatment as a result of the vagaries of political history.

There are, in addition, a few comparatively new *fonds*, such as *France. Commerce*, which covers the years 1700–1830 (with emphasis on the eighteenth century) in thirty-six volumes of reports, memorials, letters of chambers of commerce, etc., that are useful for economic history and the study of colonial policy. The series *Mémoires et Documents* is concluded with a small *Supplément* composed of manuscripts which, for some reason, were not bound into one of the regular *fonds*.

III. The Correspondance consulaire et commerciale:

Although it is the least known and the least inventoried of the three great series, the *Correspondance consulaire et commerciale* possesses a historical value vouched for by no less an authority than Hanotaux himself.[5] It is also the only series not entirely housed at the Quai d'Orsay. For consular correspondence and papers of an earlier date than 1793 one must go to the *Archives Nationales* because French consulates were controlled by the ministry of marine until that year (except briefly in 1761–66). When the consulates became part of the ministry of foreign affairs in 1793, the two ministries divided the consular records accumulated up to that time. Those retained by the ministry of

[5] II, 67, of number 26 in bibliography.

marine were turned over to the *Archives Nationales* in 1898 and classified as: *Série Ministère de la Marine. Sous-série B⁷*. In 1929 and 1933 the Quai d'Orsay relinquished most, but not all, of its consular holdings earlier than 1793, and these materials are found in: *Série Ministère des Affaires étrangères. Sous-séries Bᴵ et Bᴵᴵᴵ*.

Since the division of the files in 1793 seems to have been carried out on a principle the logic of which is obscure, the research worker nearly always will have to examine at least two of the subseries for a particular period or consular post. It is possible, however, to distinguish three major kinds of material and, in a general way, their location. The instructions and reports drawn up in France prior to January 1, 1756 are to be found in the marine subseries B⁷ (registers 48–202). For 1756–93 they are in the foreign affairs subseries Bᴵ (registers 1–74). The correspondence sent in by consuls abroad was not so neatly divided. It can be noted only that most of the early manuscripts dating from the seventeenth century (and even from the sixteenth in the case of Morocco) can be studied in Bᴵ (registers 75–1188), while B⁷ (registers 204–462) covers mostly the last years of Louis XVI. The former has the larger number of manuscripts. Its bound volumes (*registres*) bear an inclusive enumeration applied by the *Archives Nationales*, but their former designation by post, by old volume number, and by years has been preserved. For example: *Sous-série Bᴵ. Registre 843. Maroc.* vol. 19 (1786–89), in which the French vice-consul on February 2, 1786, acknowledges his instructions to treat the expected American agent to the sultan with a "*conduite amicale et prudente.*" This volume also illustrates the exceptions to the terminal date of 1793 for the consular material in the *Archives Nationales*. When certain volumes taken over from the marine in 1793 were filled out with manuscripts of slightly later date, the ministry of foreign affairs chose to retain them under its own control. They form a part of the series Bᴵᴵ, which still remains at the Quai d'Orsay.

The accession from the foreign ministry in 1929 gave the *Archives Nationales* a third category of consular records: miscellaneous commercial documents that do not fall into either of the first two classifications. While this group might have been very rich for historical research, it has been reduced in value by the withholding of many items and the destruction of many others as useless. As it stands now, foreign affairs subseries B^{III} covers the period 1750–1850 in general, with an important number of earlier items, especially for the Levant, and a few of later date. It is divided into three parts. The largest, called *Levant et Barbarie* (322 volumes), includes a considerable correspondence of the marine ministry with the chamber of commerce and municipal authorities of Marseilles, the *Compagnie d'Afrique*, and other commercial enterprises. A second group of 138 volumes consists of reports and statistical tables that originally accompanied the consular correspondence. Only Spain and Italy are well represented, however, and many of these items pertain to the nineteenth century. A final section of twenty-six volumes, labelled *Correspondance commerciale générale*, incorporates a very incomplete selection of commercial reports from consuls in various countries, chiefly in the eighteenth century and down to 1818.

It should be noted that the *Archives Nationales* hold two other kinds of documents of peripheral interest for this survey. One group consists of the papers for the administration of Champagne, Normandy, and Guienne in the seventeenth and eighteenth centuries, when these provinces were under the secretary of state for foreign affairs. They are, for instance, useful for a study of the Fronde. Furthermore, a student concerned with the internal development of the ministry would want to see the collection of orders of the *Conseil des dépêches* for those which affected this ministry in particular.

All consular documents after 1793 remain at the Quai d'Orsay. They have been neither so well inventoried nor so well arranged and filed as have the other great series. Consequently, the staff may withhold some of them from use for the period after 1870, even though the regular open date is much later. From 1793 down to 1826 all consular manuscripts are arranged chronologically under the post or other consular jurisdiction rather than by country, and are called the *Correspondance consulaire*. For example, Nanking, Naples, and New Orleans might appear in that order. A major change occurred in 1826. Thereafter, the consular material was divided into two parts: the *Correspondance politique des consuls* (not to be confused with the major series, *Correspondance politique*, described above) and the *Correspondance commerciale*, both including much material in addition to correspondence in the strict sense and together known as the *Correspondance consulaire et commerciale*.

The *Correspondance politique des consuls* was intended to distinguish the more political from the more economic matter in a rapidly growing consular network. From 1826 to 1830 it was either incorporated in the volumes of the *Correspondance politique* or filed as *volumes intercalaires* in that major series, but after 1830 it was given the distinct identity contemplated in the reform of 1826. Thenceforth, while it continued to be arranged by states rather than by posts, it was shelved separately from and directly after the corresponding *fonds* in the *Correspondance politique*. And, like that series, it will be reorganized on a subject matter basis for the years since 1897 (see above). There has been some variation in its internal organization after 1830. In the case of certain countries, such as the United States, the correspondence with all consular posts was thrown together chronologically. In other instances, as for Italy both before and after unification, the documents for each post were classified separately and then chronologically. It is interesting to note, too, that political matters involving Morocco were treated entirely within the *Correspondance politique* although much of the material concerning that state originated with French consular officials located there.

The *Correspondance commerciale* with its emphasis upon trade

and industrial opportunities perpetuated, after 1826, the old
arrangement by posts inherited from the *Correspondance consulaire*. Under each post, it was bound chronologically down to
1901. The great increase in papers since that date has led the
staff to plan a post-*cum*-subject arrangement for the more recent
years similar to the one now in progress for the *Correspondance
politique*.

IV.   *Treaty series and other collections:*

The archives of the Quai d'Orsay also hold several special
groups of documents to which access is much more limited than
for those mentioned above. One of these is an unsurpassed
group of treaties and *droits du roi* dating from far back in the
history of the French monarchy. While they are normally to be
seen only on great occasions in the oval "treaty room," their
texts have in most cases been published and can easily be found
by the historian in more accessible and less fragile form. Drafts
of treaties should be sought in the *Fonds France et divers états* in
the series *Mémoires et Documents* (see above).

There is also a small collection known as the *Fonds du cabinet*,
which consists of collections of papers pertaining to the careers
of some prominent officials of the ministry in the past. They
grew out of the confidential dossiers maintained traditionally by
the ministry on each of its staff members, and include routine
administrative papers respecting promotions, pensions, etc., as
well as documents concerning the individual's political or
diplomatic career. In view of the nature of this material, the
staff of the archives usually grants permission for its use only if
the dossier covers a period prior to 1815. It should be added
that these files vary greatly in historical value, have suffered a
good deal of attrition from changes of regime, and number less
than a dozen for the whole period since 1870. The archives also
contain   some private papers, including correspondence,
of certain former members of the foreign ministry or foreign
service. The originals of the letters of Paul Cambon that

were edited and published by Henry Cambon as *Paul Cambon, Correspondance, 1870–1924*, 4 vols. (Paris, 1940–46), were deposited there after publication. But only one of these sets of personal papers is now open for research: the *Papiers de Cercay* consisting of the papers of Thouvenel and Rouher. Lastly, the archives have recently made available for examination the financial records of the ministry itself, including such matters as budgets, current accounts, and pensions, for the years prior to 1840.

V. Availability of guides and inventories:

The scholar who is planning to do research in the above series will find that certain official printed inventories of part of the holdings are obtainable at the Library of Congress and some other American libraries. For the *Correspondance politique* the archives began a calendar that could not be continued on the same scale after World War I because of a reduced budget and staff. Only three volumes were published.[6] As the title implies, these inventories do not pretend to give a thorough listing of the contents of each volume. Unpublished but available at the Quai d'Orsay is the volume that covers the *Fonds Etats-Unis* in this series. To carry the work down to 1871 and to include states not yet in print, the staff published in 1936 an even more summary but still useful volume.[7] It can convey an impression of the extent of the material available on a particular diplomatic mission or personage. For the years after 1871 one has still to rely upon manuscript catalogues in the reading room of the archives.

To aid research in the *Mémoires et Documents* three official inventories have been published.[8] The first two cover holdings down to 1814; the third carries the inventory down to 1830. All are provided with a good subject index. For the period since

6 Number 24 in bibliography.
7 Number 23 in bibliography.
8 Number 25 in bibliography.

1830 the archives have a manuscript volume containing brief notices of a general nature. In view of the size of this series, the calendaring cannot be considered exhaustive in its detailing of the contents. There is some variation among the *fonds* in this respect, with the Saint-Simon papers being treated with especial care.

For the consular documents acquired by the *Archives Nationales* from the ministry of marine (subseries B7) there is a published survey.[9] While the calendaring is brief, there are valuable footnotes for certain volumes. The inventories for the two groups of consular records from the Quai d'Orsay have not been published, but microfilm copies are available in the Library of Congress, which will supply additional prints to other libraries or research centers in the United States.[10]

For the consular papers since 1793, still in the possession of the foreign ministry, published inventories are generally lacking. The only exception is the *Correspondance politique des consuls* for 1826 to 1870.[11] It should be noted, however, that A. P. Nasatir is preparing a guide to the materials in both parts of the *Correspondance consulaire et commerciale* that relate to the United States, as well as a calendar of those that bear upon the history of California.

All the above inventories (except the unpublished items listed as numbers 20 and 21 of the bibliography) can be consulted in the *Bibliothèque Nationale* (*Salle des Manuscrits* or *Salle de Bibliographie*) at hours when the foreign archives are closed. Scholars interested in certain parts of the archival holdings will owe a debt to a few specialized guides.[12]

---

[9]Number 31 in bibliography.

[10]Numbers 20 and 21 in bibliography. Any research worker who expects to use these inventories and the documents in the *Archives Nationales* will profit from some suggestions made by Howard C. Rice, Jr., in Appendix A, 41–47, of number 18 in bibliography.

[11]Included in number 23 in bibliography.

[12]Numbers 18, 27, 30, 33, 34, and 35 in bibliography.

ADMINISTRATION, REGULATIONS, AND FACILITIES

The French foreign ministry plans gradually to advance the present open date of January 1, 1897 until it is established on the fifty-years-ago basis not uncommon in similar European archives.[13] The intervals at which these steps are announced will depend upon the speed with which the staff can carry out the current reorganization of the documents dated since 1897. In view of limited budgets and the enormous increase after that date in the number of items to be preserved, delays should not be unexpected. The archives already hold more documents for the years from 1914 to the present than for the whole period from Richelieu to 1914.

The minister of foreign affairs is authorized by the council of ministers to determine by ordinance, with the advice of the Commission for the Diplomatic Archives, the open date and the regulations governing the use of the documents. This power is derived from the decree of May 11, 1951 (*Journal officiel*, May 14–16, 1951), which established the general rules applied by the staff of the archives. The commission upon whose recommendation he makes his decision is a distinguished group of about thirty-eight statesmen, diplomats, archivists, and historians. The last group comprises nearly one third of the total. All members are appointed by the premier after nomination by the minister of foreign affairs.

The scholar seeking admission to the archives must keep the commission in mind. While he will never see that body in session, it may in fact settle the fate of his request. He should remember that even if his field of interest lies in the years before the official open date at the time of his application, this does not guarantee automatic admission. Not only will each project be considered in itself, but a proper protocol must be followed. Occasionally, disappointments can be traced to ignorance of

[13]The present date was fixed by ministerial order of April 19, 1952 (*Journal officiel* of April 24, 1952).

procedure or to impatience with requirements and delays which, upon reflection, would be recognized as unavoidable in all countries, considering that the *bona fides* of a foreign applicant is naturally not so quickly perceived as it might be at home.

The first obligation of most scholars seeking admission is a formal application made out to the minister of foreign affairs. Careful attention must be given to the content of this document. It should include a clear and specific statement of the subject to be investigated, the purpose for which this research will be used, and the expected duration of the visit to Paris. Above all, the applicant must avoid phrasing his subject in terms that are too general and elusive. The more precise and limited they are, the more likely they are to be accepted. For example, one should ordinarily not ask to look at everything pertaining to the foreign policy of *Louis Philippe*, but instead to see the *Correspondance politique* and the *Correspondance consulaire et commerciale* for certain countries and certain posts in, say, the years 1838 to 1845. Even if it seems possible that the research worker will find one line of investigation leading to another so that he will ultimately want to examine more materials than he requested at first, he should remember that there is no rule against asking for new related material after one has been admitted to the archives and has exhausted the first supply of documents. Nor need any time so be wasted, for the chief of the archives can approve the new petition unless it raises issues that only the commission can determine. Finally, the applicant must include some indication that he has the training or experience to profit from access to the archives. This is usually satisfied by mention of an academic or other institutional connection, or previous publications. If these are lacking, letters of recommendation will ordinarily serve the purpose.

A United States citizen should then go in person to the office of the United States cultural attaché (41 rue du Faubourg Saint-Honoré, Paris VIII), where he will explain his intent, show a valid passport, and indicate the evidences of seriousness of purpose just mentioned. He must ask for a supporting letter from the United States embassy. This official letter, which is required by the French government as an introduction to the foreign ministry, can usually be obtained within a day or two. It refers only in a general way to the objective the research worker has in mind.

Then the applicant may send the two basic documents (his embassy's introduction and his personal, much more detailed, request for entry) by mail to the *Service des Archives, Ministère des Affaires Etrangères,* 37 quai d'Orsay, Paris VII. But the better procedure is to go in person to that address to present the two papers, for this will not only gain several days but also provide the advantage of a preliminary conversation with a staff member who often will make invaluable suggestions for effective approaches to the problem at hand. The chief officials of the archives are: Jean Baillou, *Chef du Service des Archives;* Jérôme de Ribier, *Conservateur des Archives;* Jean de Pins, *Secrétaire de la Commission des Archives Diplomatiques;* and for the *Archives Nationales,* Charles Braibant, *Directeur.*

The minister of foreign affairs has final authority over all applications, but he will normally consult the chief of the archives. If the recommendation is favorable, only a few days will pass before the applicant is notified that entry has been granted. This notification then serves as entry card for all future visits to the archives, which should thereafter be approached through a special entrance at 130 rue de l'Université. On the other hand, if an objection arises in the minds of the French authorities, they may refuse the request or submit it to the Commission for the Diplomatic Archives for a ruling. Since that body meets only irregularly, usually two or three times a year, a delay of many weeks may follow. For the majority of scholars this unfortunate *dénouement* will never materialize, but obviously no one wants to take the risk of wasting a long trip only to be turned down. With their natural courtesy toward foreign visitors, the members of the archival staff are as eager as anyone to avoid disappointments by the wider dissemination of information about their regulations. Under some circumstances, precautionary measures ought to be taken before departure for France. If the applicant is a scholar without academic or institutional ties or established reputation it would be wise to submit his project to the cultural attaché, and then to the archives, in advance by mail. If the applicant wishes to see the *Correspondance consulaire et commerciale* since 1826, he would do well to send a written preliminary inquiry directly to the chief of the archives since parts of that series can be refused to him on the ground of their physical condition.

An investigator interested in the consular records of France prior to 1793 should have little difficulty in gaining entry to the *Archives Nationales* (60 rue des Francs-Bourgeois, Paris III). Again he must go to the office of the cultural attaché, where he will ask for an official letter mentioning briefly his purpose and qualifications. When the letter is presented by the applicant at the office of the director an admission card can usually be obtained without much delay.

Plans for research in Paris must be determined in part by the dates of the annual closings, which are an inevitable feature of all French governmental archives. The archives of the Quai d'Orsay close on July 14 and do not reopen until the first Monday in September. For the *Archives Nationales* the date is July 1 to July 15. Neither institution will be open on Christmas, New Year's Day, Armistice Day, or on such religious holidays as Easter week end and the Mondays after Pentecost, Assumption, and All Saints. In addition, the foreign ministry archives cannot be used in the mornings, the daily hours being 2 P.M. to 7 P.M. The *Archives Nationales* operate on an eight-hour basis, from 10 A.M. to 6 P.M.

The regulations of the reading room in the foreign ministry require that volumes wanted for a certain day be requested in the preceding afternoon. Normally, no more than three volumes can be delivered each day. They can be retained for a week at the reader's place. Ink may be employed for note-taking, but the use of typewriters is not permitted. The auxiliary facilities of the reading room are limited. For biographical and other data the scholar will probably resort in the mornings to the *Bibliothèque Nationale* in the rue de Richelieu. At the *Archives Nationales* no volumes are delivered to readers between 11.30 A.M. and 1.30 P.M., or between 4 P.M. and 6 P.M. While the *Archives Nationales* also have the printed catalogues of the foreign ministry archives and are open in the mornings, they are less conveniently located than the *Bibliothèque Nationale*, except for those visitors who intend to use the consular records prior to 1793.

The foreign ministry archives will permit a person whose application has been approved to designate a second person to do the actual research in his name, but the second individual must also have the approval of the foreign ministry. It is important to remember that the right to take notes does not confer the right to copy a whole series of documents. That can be done only by special permission and only when publication of the material is intended. Notes taken on documents dated before January 1, 1871 can be used at the reader's discretion, but all other notes must be submitted to the staff of the archives before being used in any form. Infractions of this rule will be punished by permanent exclusion from the archives. The decree of May 11, 1951 also requires that two copies of all works based upon material found in the archives, whatever its historical period, must be deposited there.

While authorization is necessary for microfilming, it is ordinarily obtainable when scattered documents or limited series of documents are involved. No one will be allowed to microfilm a long, continuous series of items without the consent of the Commission for the Diplomatic Archives or of a subcommission designated by it. Such requests will normally be granted only to societies or institutions that can provide evidence of intent to publish. This rule is aimed primarily at the person who might like to photograph volume after volume without troubling at the time to separate the valueless items (for his purpose) from the useful ones. His requests for volumes of manuscripts would become a heavy burden upon a limited staff, particularly because no microfilming can be done on the premises of the archives. All volumes must be sent to the *Bibliothèque Nationale* to be microfilmed by its regular service for that purpose (the user of the archives is never given permission to photograph items himself or through some agent of his own choice). The cost for each negative frame amounts (1952) to about four cents, with a minimum of a dollar for each order and a charge of fifteen cents for the first frame of each additional volume. The charge for prints enlarged to about 8 × 11 inches is a little more than twenty cents. Finally, the scholar must keep in mind that the photographic service of the *Bibliothèque Nationale* is closed during the month of August.

If he expects to use materials at both the Quai d'Orsay and the *Archives Nationales* the investigator who is a stranger to Paris will find it most convenient to live in the Louvre section in the first *arrondissement*. But if the Quai d'Orsay is his daily objective there are less commercial and perhaps quieter areas which he might choose. The archives themselves lie on the Left Bank in the agreeable seventh *arrondissement*. The sixth and eighth also merit consideration, for they afford direct bus connections to within a block or two of the archives if one lives near such well-known streets as the boulevard Saint Germain, the avenue Marceau, the boulevard Malesherbes, or the boulevard Raspail. Because French hotels vary so greatly by American standards no specific recommendations are made here. It is suggested that the newcomer may wish to limit his original reservation to a week or two so that he can be free to explore and to move perhaps to more congenial quarters.

BIBLIOGRAPHY

Students of North American history are singularly fortunate in having access on this side of the Atlantic to copies of a large part of the manuscripts of the seventeenth and eighteenth centuries that bear upon the history of the United States and Canada, as well as a considerable number concerning Mexico and the Caribbean. The Archives of Canada in Ottawa hold a large collection of extracts of material relating to that country.[14] Since 1913 the Library of Congress has carried on, with the support of the Carnegie Institution of Washington, a monumental task of copying and photographing that has produced by far the most extensive collection in this country.[15] More recently, the joint program of the American Historical Association and the Library of Congress for microfilming of selected historical documents has added to the holdings of the latter, chiefly through reliance upon Fulbright scholarships awarded to research men for that purpose. Howard C. Rice, Jr., made available the unpublished inventories of the foreign ministry documents in the *Archives Nationales*. A. P. Nasatir prepared copies of the complete French consular correspondence relating to the United States before 1792 (from the *Archives Nationales, série Ministére des Affaires Etrangères, sous-séries* B^I *et* B^{III}).[16] For the latest accessions the Division of Manuscripts should be consulted. The collection in the Library of Congress also contains the Benjamin Franklin Stevens facsimiles, transcripts, and catalogue index of manuscripts relating to American history from 1763 to 1784. Stevens published twenty-five volumes of the facsimiles, many of them from the Quai d'Orsay, in a limited edition of two hundred sets.[17]

The Bancroft Library of the University of California has microfilm copies of all the California material in the *Correspondence politique des consuls* (vols. 1–38), as well as some limited series of microfilms based upon other series in the foreign ministry and related to such subjects as Mexico, New Grenada, Honolulu, and the Sandwich Islands.[18] The *Guide to the Diplomatic*

---

[14] Some of it is listed in number 34 in bibliography; all of it is available as photostats in the Library of Congress, and on microfilm at Stanford University (which also has thirteen reels of microcopies of Library of Congress photostats of selected items in *Mémoires et Documents* dealing with Anglo-French colonial relations, 1632–1766).

[15] A valuable list of the series and volumes acquired by it down to 1942 can be found in Appendix A, 1065–1070, of number 27 in bibliography.

[16] A summary of this work conducted under the auspices of the special committee for France (Richard W. Hale, Jr., chairman) appears in number 18 in bibliography.

[17] Number 16 in bibliography.

[18] 48, of number 18 in bibliography.

History of the United States, 1775–1921 by Samuel F. Bemis and Grace Gardner Griffin (Washington, 1935) gives references to other collections in the United States, as well as to numerous published works based in whole or in part upon the French foreign ministry materials. Important notes on collections of copies or transcripts in this country can be found also in the general preface of the Leland guide to the libraries and archives of Paris; the second volume in this series is the well-known Leland, Meng, and Doysié guide to the American materials in the archives of the Quai d'Orsay.[19]

For the history of areas other than North America, comparatively little in the way of reproduction of the French records is available in the United States. The research worker should, however, consult the list of acquisitions by the Library of Congress printed in Appendix A of the Leland, Meng, and Doysié guide.[20] It comprises a not unimportant number of volumes dealing with European history in both the *Correspondence politique* and the *Mémoires et Documents*. Students of Mazarin's policy will find in the John Frederick Lewis Collection of the Free Library of Philadelphia (with a microfilm copy in the Duquesne University Library) four volumes of manuscript letters of Mazarin, by the hand of a secretary or copyist, which provide some five hundred items not printed by Chéruel and d'Avenel and pertain to the years 1647 to 1651. For certain fields of interest, valuable material may be found in some collections of printed documents of the French foreign ministry. The more important of these are listed below.

Printed Collections of Documents

1. Avenel, Denis, ed. *Lettres, instructions diplomatiques et papiers d'état du cardinal de Richelieu.* 8 vols. Paris, 1853–77.

2. Basdevant, Jules, ed. *Recueil des traités et conventions en vigueur entre la France et les puissances étrangères.* 3 vols. Paris, 1918–20.

3. Bertrand, Pierre, ed. *Lettres inédites de Talleyrand à Napoléon, 1800–1809.* Paris, 1889.

4. Chéruel, P. A., and Georges d'Avenel, eds. *Lettres du Cardinal Mazarin pendant son ministère.* 9 vols. Paris, 1872–1906.

5. Clercq, Alexandre and Jules de, eds. *Recueil des traités de la France depuis 1713 jusqu'à nos jours.* 23 vols. Paris, 1864–1917.

6. Doniol, Henri. *L'Histoire de la participation de la France à l'établissement des Etats-Unis d'Amérique.* 5 vols. Paris, 1886–92.

France. Commission des Archives Diplomatiques. *Inventaire analytique des archives du Ministère des Affaires Etrangères. Correspondance politique :*

---

[19] I, iii–x, of number 27 in bibliography.
[20] Number 27 in bibliography.

7. Kaulek, J., and others, eds. *Correspondance politique de MM. de Castillon et de Marillac, ambassadeurs de France en Angleterre, 1537–1542*, Paris, 1885.

8. Kaulek, J., ed. *Papiers de Barthélemy, ambassadeur de France en Suisse, 1792–1797*. 6 vols. Paris, 1886–1910.

France. Ministère des Affaires Etrangères:

9. *Documents diplomatiques* (Livres jaunes). 229 vols. Paris, 1856–   .

10. *Documents diplomatiques français, 1871–1914*. 36 vols. in 3 series. Paris, 1929–   .

11. *Les origines diplomatiques de la guerre de 1870–1871*. 29 vols. Paris, 1910–32.

12. Meng, John J., ed. *Despatches and instructions of Conrad Gérard, 1778–1780*. Baltimore, 1939.

13. Plantet, Eugene, ed. *Correspondance des beys de Tunis et des consuls de France avec la cour, 1577–1830*. 3 vols. Paris, 1893–99.

14. *Correspondance des deys d'Alger avec la cour de France, 1579–1833*. 2 vols. Paris, 1890.

15. Sorel, Albert, Gabriel Hanotaux, and others, eds. *Recueil des instructions données aux ambassadeurs et ministres de France depuis les traités de Westphalie jusqu'à la révolution française*. 25 vols. Paris, 1884–1929.

16. Stevens, Benjamin Franklin. *Facsimiles of manuscripts in European archives relating to America*. 1773–1783. London, 1889–98.

17. Turner, Frederick J., ed. *Correspondence of the French ministers to the United States, 1791–1797*. In *Annual report of the American Historical Association, 1903*. Vol. 2. Washington, 1904.

18. American Historical Association. Committee on Documentary Reproduction (Edgar L. Erickson, chairman). "Report and appendices A and B," *Annual report of the American Historical Association, 1951*. Washington, 1952, I, 39–49.

Guide and Reference Works

19. Baschet, Armand. *Histoire du dépôt des archives des affaires étrangères*. Paris, 1875.

20. Celier, Léonce. *Archives Nationales. Affaires étrangères. Répertoire numérique de la correspondance consulaire: sous-série B¹* (typescript dated November, 1934).

21. *Répertoire de l'ancien bureau des consulats* (manuscript dated 1935).

22. Delisle, Léopold. "L'origine des archives du Ministère des Affaires Etrangères," *Bibliothèque de l'Ecole de Chartes*, XXXV (1874), 356–372.

France. Ministère des Affaires Etrangères:

23. *Etat numérique des fonds de la Correspondance politique de l'origine à 1871.* Paris, 1936.

24. *Inventaire sommaire des archives du Département des Affaires Etrangères. Correspondance politique:*
Tome I. "Allemagne, Angleterre, Argentine, Autriche." Paris, 1903.
Tome II, partie 1. "Bade, Bâle, Bavière, Brésil, Brunswick-Hanovre, Chili, Cologne, Colombie, Corse, Danemark, Dantzig." Paris, 1908.
Tome II, partie 2. "Espagne." Paris, 1919.

25. *Inventaire sommaire des archives du Département des Affaires Etrangères. Mémoires et Documents:*
Tome I. "France." Paris, 1883.
Tome II. "Fonds divers." Paris, 1892.
Tome III. "Fonds France et Fonds divers. Supplément." Paris, 1896.

26. Hanotaux, Gabriel. *Mon Temps.* 4 vols. Paris, 1933– . Especially vol. I, 321–331; vol. II, 17–19, 23–25, 38–48, 52–58.

27. Leland, Waldo G., ed. *Guide to materials for American history in the libraries and archives of Paris.* 2 vols. Washington, 1932– . Vol. 2: Leland, Waldo G., John J. Meng, and Abel Doysié, eds. *Archives of the Ministry of Foreign Affairs.* Washington, 1943.

28. Lévis-Mirepoix, Emmanuel de. *Le Ministère des Affaires Etrangères.* Angers, 1934.

29. Masson, Frédéric. *Le Département des Affaires Etrangères pendant la révolution, 1784–1804.* Paris, 1877.

30. Nasatir, A. P. *French actitities in California: An archival calendar-guide.* Stanford, 1945.

31. Neuville, D. *Etat sommaire des Archives de la Marine antérieures à la révolution.* Paris, 1898.

32. Outrey, Amédée. "Note sur les pertes subies du fait de la guerre par les archives du Ministère des Affaires Etrangères et sur les mesures qui ont été prises en vue de la reconstitution des documents détruits," *Cahiers d'histoire de la guerre,* numéro 2 (October, 1949), pp. 31–33.

33. Paz, Julian. *Catálogo de documentos españoles existentes en el archivo del Ministerio de Negocios Extranjeros de Paris.* Madrid, 1932.

34. Roy, Edmond. *Rapport sur les archives de France relatives à l'histoire du Canada.* Ottawa, 1911.

35.   Surrey, N. M. Miller. *Calendar of manuscripts in Paris archives and libraries relating to the history of the Mississippi Valley to 1803.* 2 vols. Washington, 1926–28. Copies of a number of these documents are in the United States (Library of Congress and Mississippi Department of Archives and History).

5 GERMANY

Raymond James Sontag
University of California, Berkeley

DURING World War II, Prussian and German archives relating to foreign policy were scattered, disorganized, and in part lost or destroyed. In 1943, when the air attacks on German cities became intense, dispersal of the noncurrent files of the German foreign office began. As the Soviet forces advanced, many of the evacuation centers in eastern Germany were, in their turn, evacuated.

The fate of the documents that remained in East Germany remains obscure. The Nazis destroyed parts of the foreign office archives; other parts were lost during the fighting in Berlin. When Soviet forces occupied Berlin they were, at first, indifferent to the fate of historical records. Even after Americans reached the city, the floors of Hitler's ruined New Chancellery were littered with papers of historical value, and occasionally the Soviet guards allowed Western soldiers to take such papers as souvenirs.

One of the largest documentary collections that remained in East Germany was the Prussian Privy State Archives. In the early postwar years there were many reports, circumstantial but impossible to verify, that this collection suffered irreparable damage from damp, that volumes of documents were burned to heat soldiers' and peasants' quarters, and that parts of the collection were systematically destroyed while other parts were removed to Moscow.

Apparently it will soon be possible to test the accuracy of these reports. The East German government has announced the establishment of archival centers at Potsdam and Merseburg. The Prussian Privy State Archives are among the collections housed at these centers. When scholars are permitted to examine the Prussian archives, and early access has been promised, it should be possible to ascertain what has survived. ·

Press reports state that these centers will also contain materials from the archives of the German foreign office and from German missions abroad. These documents will be of great importance, if all materials in Soviet possession are made available. For instance, the photostatic copies of foreign office documents that the U.S.S.R. has published show that parts of the Reich foreign minister's file were in Soviet possession. That file contained documents, particularly on Nazi-Soviet relations, of which copies were not deposited in other files of the foreign office. The press reports on the East German archival centers mention many other foreign office files that will be made available; the reports do not mention the foreign minister's file. It will be a great loss if access to this file is not granted, and indeed if this file is not made available to scholars, doubt will be cast on the integrity of the East German collection as a whole.

It is possible to speak with much greater precision on the German archives that came into Anglo-United States possession at the end of the war. By the last days of the war the bulk of the archives of the German foreign office were secreted in the Harz Mountains and in Thuringia. Shortly before the end orders were given to destroy the most important files for the years after 1920. Paper is, however, difficult to destroy in quantity, and the Western documents teams moved quickly. As a result, only a fragment of what had been evacuated westward was destroyed although that fragment was of great importance.[1]

[1]The material in this, and in some of the succeeding paragraphs, is based in part on the general introduction to *Documents on German foreign policy, 1918–1945* (Series D, vol. I, *From Neurath to Ribbentrop*, Washington, 1949, pp. vii–xiii), which was written when the author was American editor in chief. This general introduction, and the analysis of the foreign ministry archives (*ibid.*, 1177–185), give many details which it has not seemed necessary to repeat here.

Capture did not end the migration of the foreign office archives. They were first moved west, because the territory in which they were found was to be part of the Soviet zone of occupation. Later they were moved to Berlin. In 1948, during the Soviet blockade of Berlin, they were taken to England. From the day of their capture, the archives have been under the vigilant care of archivists and historians. And so the ironical conclusion emerges that most of the record of German foreign policy from 1867 to 1945 survives for return to the Germans because of the efforts of the Western enemies of Nazi Germany and despite the efforts of the Nazis to destroy large portions of the record.

What has survived? In bulk, an enormous mass of paper. The foreign office materials now in Anglo-United States custody weigh about 400 *tons*. In this mass are materials not properly a part of the foreign office archives. There are the files of the Old and the New Reich Chancellery, running from 1920 to the end of the Nazi period; these contain some materials of interest to students of German foreign policy. There are collections of private papers, such as those of Fritz von Holstein and of Stresemann. There are even manuscripts of books that the rulers of Germany thought too dangerous for publication.

The archives of the foreign office proper fall into three large chronological divisions: 1867–1920; 1920–1936; 1936–1945. While the materials for the first of these periods have not been systematically examined, they seem to be intact. A few tests have been made to determine, on the one hand, whether the documents printed in *Die grosse Politik* have survived, and, on the other hand, whether all important documents were printed in *Die grosse Politik*. For the periods tested, all the documents which were printed survive. On the other hand, while the tests did not reveal essential documents in the main political files that were not printed by the editors of *Die grosse Politik*, they did reveal that the editors, in making their selection, were influenced by a desire not to make the task of the rulers of the

Weimar Republic more difficult, and not to injure the reputation of foreign statesmen who were still active after World War I and who were sympathetic to Germany. The tests clearly demonstrate that *Die grosse Politik* is not the complete story of German diplomacy before World War I.

In 1920 changes were made in the organization of the German foreign office. The old files, which run from 1867 to 1920, were closed. New files, conforming to the changed organization of the office, were begun. This set of files runs to 1936, when there were further changes in the organization of the office. The filing system begun in 1936 continued, with some modifications, to the end of the Nazi period.

The files for the years from 1920 to 1936 are not intact. Some volumes of documents dealing with German rearmament were destroyed by the Nazis. The very important secret files of the political division were damaged by a fire that occurred while the Germans were moving them to the evacuation center. However, it is probable that copies of many of the documents in the volumes that were deliberately or accidentally destroyed are in other parts of the files. The German foreign office—like the agencies of other governments—made many copies of most documents.

From 1936 the problem of reconstructing the story of German diplomacy from the foreign office archives becomes unbelievably complex. In the first place, the archives never contained all the evidence. Policy was determined by Hitler, and he did not always take even the higher officials of the foreign office into his confidence. The execution of policy was often entrusted to party representatives, intelligence officers, or the military; evidence of their activity reached the foreign office archives only by accident. In the second place, we do not know what the archives contained when they were intact, because the foreign office registers for these years are lost. We know what files were destroyed by the Nazis, but we do not know what was in those files.

We can form some idea of what is missing from a source that is probably unique in the history of historical evidence: pieces of microfilm prepared by Ribbentrop's secretariat during the war, on which are photographed some ten thousand pages of documents from his working file. The films were made in 1943 as insurance against the destruction of the records in his file by bombing. Toward the end of the war, when the Nazis realized that the record of their diplomacy would soon fall into Allied hands, the destruction of these films was ordered. Instead, their custodian buried them, and in 1945 Allied officers found them. These officers immediately took the films to the air ministry in London. There the strips were spliced together, to make reels of conventional length, and duplicate films were made, before the deterioration of the original further impaired legibility. The whole operation was performed so hastily that the duplicate films follow no logical order: not only may closely related documents appear on different reels; in some cases parts of a single document are widely separated on the reels. However, what is important is that the filmed portion of the Reich foreign minister's file did survive. There are a few scattered volumes of documents from the Reich foreign minister's file in Anglo-United States possession, and other foreign ministry files contain copies of many documents that appear on the film prepared by Ribbentrop's secretariat. However, some of the most important pages of German history under the Nazis can be documented only from bits of film, which survive because a German official disobeyed orders, and Allied officers were alert.

How much evidence did not survive, we do not know, and may never know. We do not know whether, when Ribbentrop's secretariat selected the material for filming, important material was passed over. We cannot be certain that the film, as we have it, is all that was filmed; the fact that the strips were of varying lengths is puzzling. We do not know what was in the missing portion of other captured files. And, finally, we do not know what was in the files that remained in Berlin or in the evacuation centers in eastern Germany.

A few generalizations are possible. The foreign office archives never contained the complete story of Nazi diplomacy. While parts of the archives are missing for the whole Nazi period, and indeed for the years after 1920, the gaps probably are not of major importance until about 1940. Until 1943, large parts of the story are preserved in the record. From 1943, the record is fragmentary.

Microfilming of documents in the foreign office files began as soon as they were captured. Until the end of 1946, the filming was done by United States and British intelligence officers, who were interested primarily in materials with value for intelligence purposes, or for the Nuremberg trials. In June 1946 the United States department of state and the British foreign office decided to publish a documentary collection that would tell the story of German foreign policy from 1918 to 1945; later, the French government joined the project. At the end of 1946 historical scholars began microfilming materials that might be useful for the project, and in 1949 the first volumes of *Documents on German foreign policy, 1918–1945* were published. By 1956 eight volumes had been published. These volumes cover the years 1937 and 1938, with some material on 1936, 1939, and 1940. Filming has proceeded more rapidly than publication. All significant documents on German foreign policy between 1933 and 1945 have been microfilmed, and microfilming of the documents for the period 1918–33 is approaching completion. One set of the film is in the United States department of state; another is in the British foreign office.

Little of this film has yet been released for use by private scholars. When it is released, scholars are likely to be overwhelmed by the amount of the material and by the faulty organization of the material. Anyone who uses the archives of the German foreign office comes to wonder how the Germans acquired their reputation for efficiency. Undoubtedly, before the archives were dispersed, there were archivists in the Wilhelmstrasse who could, with the aid of the document registry books, find any document in the collection. But the registers have disappeared and the old archivists are gone. By trial and error, the American, British, and French scholars now working through the surviving mountain of paper have learned to find their way in the collection. But anyone who tries to use the miles of microfilm now stored in Washington and London will need guidance.

Such a guide has been prepared for the years from 1933 to 1937 and from 1941 to 1945 in the form of a special film whose immediate purpose is to assist the editors in chief of the tripartite German document project. The editors working in the archives prepare a note card for each document that they consider worthy of consideration by the editors in chief. On the card is noted the location in the files and the film number of all other papers referred to in the document. The card is then attached to the document and both are photographed. Roughly, twice as many documents are photographed on this special film as are thought likely to merit publication.

For most scholars, the documents that are finally selected for publication will suffice. Those who wish more exhaustive documentation will find a wider selection on the special microfilm prepared for the editors in chief, together with the information needed to secure still further documentation. If the heroic researcher is not exhausted by then, the documents identified on the note card will undoubtedly contain references to still other documents, which the scholar may (or may not) be able to track down in the film collection. But anyone trained to the standards of exact research by the individual scholar is bound, in the end, to admit defeat in face of the overwhelming size of modern official archives. Cooperative research has many defects, but no scholar could, by himself, sift the evidence on any major problem in the history of Nazi foreign policy, either from the microfilm or from the documents themselves, as they are now filed.

The more obviously important files for the period of the Weimar Republic have been microfilmed by the editors of the tripartite German document project, but the whole story of German foreign policy cannot be written from these files. Take, for instance, the file that is most obviously important, that of the Reich foreign minister. When negotiations such as those that led to the Rapallo agreement with the U.S.S.R. had advanced to the point where they were likely to lead to agreement, the minister's secretariat would retain a copy of every significant paper for his file. For the early stages of the negotiations, however, it would be necessary to search through the voluminous files of the political and economic divisions. Again, important episodes in the history of Austro-German relations can be documented from the Reich minister's file, but to trace the history of these relations over the years it would be necessary also to read many thousands of pages in the files of the political division. In general, the Reich foreign minister's file is invaluable for the culminating stages and the consequences of an episode; it is inadequate for origins or for long-term developments.

As the tripartite project continues, the significant materials in the lower level files for 1920–33 are being microfilmed, and special films, similar to those for the later years, are being prepared for the editors in chief.

The agreement between the United States, British, and French governments calls for the exploitation of only those parts of the archives dealing with the period after 1918. Because some of the events after 1918 might be understandable only in the light of events during World War I, some papers of the war years were microfilmed. When the captured archives were first examined, it seemed that all documents relating to World War I and the Paris Peace Conference had been kept in a set of special topical files. The most obviously important of these "Weltkrieg" files were filmed. The United States' copy of these films has been deposited in the National Archives and is available for use by scholars. Photographic enlargements from the British copy of the films are available for use in the British Public Record Office. Undoubtedly, most scholars, faced with the problem of selecting what they need from the possibly one hundred and fifty thousand exposures of film of thousands of documents, will envy their British colleagues, who can work as easily from the photostats as from the original documents. As further portions of the filmed documents are made available for study by private scholars, it is the British intention to continue the practice of permitting use of photographic enlargements, rather than the films.

The "Weltkrieg" files filmed by the United States and British governments do not tell the whole story of German diplomacy from 1914 to 1920. If, for instance, one wishes to assemble the evidence on some phase of the diplomatic history of submarine warfare, one document may be found in the file kept by the representative of the foreign office at the headquarters of William II. The sequel may be in the "Weltkrieg" files relating to submarine warfare. The next succeeding document may be in some part of the regular country file on the United States, within the general files for the period 1867–1920! In other words, the voluminous "Weltkrieg" files supplement other regular foreign office files for the period 1867–1920, but much important material is not in these special files.

When it was discovered that the "Weltkrieg" files did not give a complete picture of German diplomacy from 1914 to 1918, St. Antony's College, Oxford, financed the filming of sufficient material from the general files to fill the gaps. A copy of their film is being secured by the United States government for deposit in the National Archives.

The more important files for the 1867–1914 period are now being microfilmed. The most ambitious project is that of the University of California. To date, nearly half a million pages have been photographed for this project. This is only a small fraction of the total collection which runs to millions of sheets of paper. However, filming is continuing, and it must be remembered that in any such collection there is much material which is not worth recording. Various other filming projects have been completed, or are now in progress. The French government has filmed the most important papers on Franco-German relations, and the documents relating to the Moroccan crises of 1905–06 and 1911 have been filmed in some detail. The South African government has filmed materials relating to that area, and particularly to the Jameson Raid and its diplomatic repercussions. The University of Florida is filming materials on the Egyptian question, the Far East, the Congo basin, and German relations with the countries of Central and South America. Undoubtedly all these governments and institutions will permit the purchase of duplicate films. Among the materials filmed by the University of California are the foreign office registers, which have survived for these years. While these give only a general description of the contents of a volume (e.g., Germany Number 143, Secret, "Military conversations between Italy, Austria, and Rumania, 1887–1908," Vol. I, Oct. 3, 1887–Dec. 4, 1887), they do facilitate the search for materials. The University of Michigan has also microfilmed large sections of the diplomatic documents (1867–1930) and has issued a catalogue of these holdings.

Other collections of materials are useful for the study of German foreign policy. The archives of the Old (pre-Hitler) and the New Reich Chancellery are in Anglo-American custody. Some materials have been filmed, notably the minutes of cabinet meetings of the Weimar period, and these are useful. There are also films of part or all of several collections of private papers such as those of Fritz von Holstein and Stresemann. The Stresemann papers have been deposited in the National Archives and may be used by scholars. The department of defense has microfilmed parts of the military archives of Germany; when this film is released, it will shed much light on German foreign policy.

The labors of all these agencies and institutions are being supplemented by the recently formed American Committee for the Study of War Documents, working under the supervision of the American Historical Association and with generous grants from the Ford Foundation and the Old Dominion Foundation. This committee is completing the filming of the foreign office archives, and in addition is filming German military documents made available by the United States department of defense, many of which are important for the study of German foreign policy. The Committee hopes also to prepare a guide to the location of captured German documents filmed or unfilmed.

At the present time it is possible for American scholars to secure almost complete documentation on film for the study of German foreign policy from 1867 to 1920. Very shortly, when the film collection of the department of state is deposited in the National Archives, documentation for the years 1920 to 1933 will be available. As the volumes of *Documents on German foreign policy* are published, the films for the later years covered in the volumes will be deposited in the National Archives, and made available to scholars. For this unique contribution to scholarship, students are indebted to those American, British and French scholars whose patient labor of selection has not only made the materials accessible on film but has greatly facilitated research in these voluminous materials.

BIBLIOGRAPHICAL NOTE

The best brief guide to the use of German foreign office documents is Hermann Meyer's *Das politische Schriftwesen im deutschen auswärtigen Dienst; ein Leitfaden zum Verständnis diplomatischer Dokumente* (Tübingen, 1920). For a description of the organization of the foreign ministry and its files, see the general introduction and the appendices in *Documents on German foreign policy*, Series D, Volume I, described below.

The contents of the Prussian Privy State Archives are described in Archivverwaltung: *Uebersicht über die Bestände des geheimen Staatsarchivs zu Berlin-Dahlem*, 3 vols. (Leipzig, 1934–39). The great collection of documents from German and other archives relating to the years 1858–71 was not completed when publication was halted in 1945 (Reichsarchiv historische Kommission: *Die auswärtige Politik Preussens, 1858–1871*, Oldenburg, 1932–45). The following volumes were published: Vol. I, November 1858–December 1859 (1933); Vol. II, Pt. 1, January–December 1860 (1938); Vol. II, Pt. 2, December 1860–October 1862 (1945); Vol. III, October 1862–September 1863 (1932); Vol. IV, October 1863–April 1864 (1933); Vol. V, April 1864–April 1865 (1935); Vol. VI, April 1865–March 1866 (1939); Vol. VIII, August 1866–May 1867 (1934); Vol. IX, May 1867–April 1868 (1936); Vol. X, April 1868–February 1869 (1939).

The period from 1871 to the outbreak of war in 1914 is covered by *Die grosse Politik der europäischen Kabinette, 1871–1914*, edited by Johannes Lepsius, Albrecht Mendelssohn Bartholdy, and Friedrich Thimme, 40 vols. in 54 (Berlin, 1922–27). Earlier official publications are described in Johann Sass, *Die deutschen Weissbücher zur auswärtigen Politik, 1870–1914. Geschichte und Bibliographie* (Berlin and Leipzig, 1928).

Scholars representing the United States, British, and French governments are now selecting documents for the period 1918–45 for filming. The original plan to publish all significant documents for the years from 1918 to 1945 has been abandoned; only materials relating to the years from 1933 to 1945 will be published. The general title of the publication is *Documents on German foreign policy* (Washington, 1949–   ). The following volumes, all in Series D, have been published (all by the Government Printing Office, Washington, except for Vol. VI): Vol. I, *From Neurath to Ribbentrop, September 1937–September 1938* (1949); Vol. II *Germany and Czechoslovakia, 1937–38* (1949); Vol. III, *Germany and the Spanish Civil War, 1936–39* (1950); Vol. IV, *The aftermath of Munich, 1938–39* (1951); Vol. V, *Poland, the Balkans, Latin America, the smaller powers, 1937–39* (1953); Vol. VI, *The last months of peace, March–August* [8], *1939* (London, Her Majesty's Stationery Office, 1956); Vol. VIII, *The war years, September 4, 1939–March 18, 1940* (1954); Vol. IX, *The war years, March 18–June 22, 1940* (1956). The documents are also being published in German (*Akten zur deutschen auswärtigen Politik*, Baden-Baden, 1950—   ). Selected documents are being published in French (*Les archives secrètes de la Wilhelmstrasse*, Paris, 1950-   ).

Documents bearing on relations between Argentina and Germany, Spain and the Axis, and the Soviet Union and Germany were published by the United States department of state in the following publications: *Consultation among the American republics with respect to the Argentine situation* (Washington, 1946), *The Spanish government and the Axis* (Washington, 1946), and *Nazi-Soviet relations, 1939–1941* (Washington, 1948). The U.S.S.R. has published or sponsored the publication of the following volumes of German documents: *Documents secrets du ministère des affaires étrangères d'Allemagne*, Vol. I, *Turquie, 1941–1943*; Vol. II, *Hongrie, 1937–1943*; Vol. III, *Espagne, 1936–1943* (Paris, 1946); also *Ministry of foreign affairs of the Soviet Union: Documents and materials relating to the eve of the Second World War*, Vol. I, *November 1937–1938*; Vol. II, *The Dirksen Papers* (New York, 1948).

There have, of course, been many other documentary publications, and many studies of German archives and archival practices. These may be found in Dahlmann-Waitz, *Quellenkunde der deutschen Geschichte*, 9th ed., ed. by Hermann Haering (Leipzig, 1931). A systematic survey of German documentary collections in the possession of the United States government, especially of German documentation in custody of the Army, was made by the War Documentation Project under sponsorship of the Human Resources Research Institute of the Air University in Montgomery, Alabama. The inventory of classified materials is accessible only to government agencies, but a *Guide to* (unrestricted) *captured German documents* has been published (December 1952).

For further information on captured German documents see: Richard A. Humphrey, "War-born microfilm holdings of the department of state," in *The journal of modern history*, XX (1948), 133–136; Wolfgang Mommsen, "Deutsche Archivalien im Ausland" in *Der Archivar* (Düsseldorf), Vol. IV, 4 (1951), cols. 1–14: The files of the Auswärtige Amt; and Fritz T. Epstein, "Zur Quellenkunde der neuesten Geschichte; ausländische Materialien in den Archiven und Bibliotheken der Hauptstadt der Vereinigten Staaten," in *Vierteljahrshefte für Zeitgeschichte* (July 1954), pp. 313–325.

6   GREAT BRITAIN

Keith Eubank
North Texas State College

HISTORY

THE chief repository of the diplomatic archives of Great Britain is the Public Record Office, Chancery Lane, London. Officially this repository began with the act of parliament of 1838; however, the history of modern diplomatic archives of Great Britain began with the development of the State Paper Office as an adjunct of the office of the secretary of state.

After the creation of the office of the secretary of state in the reign of Henry VIII came the need to find some site for storing records. This step was necessary because outgoing secretaries of state were prone to take important papers with them. In 1578 the State Paper Office was created to serve as a repository for the papers from the archives of the secretaries of state. The first official State Paper Office was located in rooms near the banqueting hall in Whitehall palace, and Dr. Thomas Wilson was appointed "clerk of the papers." He was succeeded by his nephew, Sir Thomas Wilson, who took over the duties of guarding the papers with the title of "keeper of the paper." Sir Thomas began the first attempt at a systematic arrangement of the papers, dividing them into domestic and foreign classes, but few attempts were made either by Sir Thomas or the later keepers to institute any regular system of calendaring the papers until the Public Record Office Act of 1838.

In spite of the labors of the early keepers, secretaries of state continued to carry documents away with them when they left office. Gradually many of these documents found their way into the great manuscript collections in the British Museum, the university libraries, and many important private libraries. These papers were thus permanently removed from official custody.[1]

During the reign of James I the papers of the State Paper Office were moved to the king's apartments in the tower over the gateway which stood across what is now Whitehall. Little was done to protect these papers and they suffered great damage during the Civil War and the Restoration. In 1705 some of the papers were moved to the lord chamberlain's lodgings at Cockpit, known as the Middle Treasury Gallery.

The papers remaining in the tower over Whitehall were gradually forgotten as the tower fell into disuse; in time it became a pigeon house. About 1763 they were discovered and moved to a house in Scotland Yard. Here the papers lay until it became obvious that the constant overflow of the Thames flooded the lower floors of the house and endangered them. In 1819 they were moved to an old house in Great George Street where they remained until 1833 when, together with the papers in the Middle Treasury Gallery, they were moved to the new State Paper Office in St. James's Park.[2]

Numerous parliamentary reports attested to the deplorable condition of the papers, but nothing definite was done until a select committee of the house of commons brought in a report in 1836. The committee recommended that in view of the way the records were scattered and uncared for, a central record office should be erected on the site known as the Rolls Estate in Chancery Lane. These recommendations were embodied in a bill passed in 1838, which pertained only to the records of royal justice and revenue. The admiralty and the treasury began sending their records to the Public Record Office as early as 1841. Through an order in council of March 5, 1852 all

[1]Number 57 in bibliography, pp. 351–353; number 64 in bibliography, p. 506.
[2]Number 65 in bibliography, pp. 41–42; number 33 in bibliography, pp. 199–203.

departmental records were placed under the charge and super-intendence of the master of the rolls. Under a warrant of August 19, 1854 the master of the rolls empowered the deputy keeper of the papers to take possession of the State Paper Office. By 1861 the foreign office gave permission for the removal of all records through the reign of George III to the new office for the public records. Thus began the periodic transfers of the foreign office records to the Public Record Office, commonly known as the PRO.

The master of the rolls was given the care and preservation of the documents of the foreign office entrusted to his custody. The foreign office, like every department, could retain any papers or documents that were needed for the work of the government. Today the foreign office indicates to what year the papers shall be available for independent research.[3]

When the crisis over Poland developed in August 1939, the planned evacuation of about three hundred tons of documents from the PRO began and continued after the declaration of war until over eighty seven thousand bundles and cartons had been evacuated by 1942. Throughout the war the PRO was open for business, although a bomb destroyed one of the turrets. The evacuated documents were kept in seven repositories outside London for the duration of the war. In September 1945 the reassembling of the documents, which numbered over half a million, was begun. It was completed by June 1946 without a single document being mislaid or lost.[4]

The steady accumulation of records has made space a prime problem for the officials of the PRO. After storing a portion of the overflow in an abandoned air raid shelter, better housing was secured in 1952 at Ashridge Park, Hertfordshire.[5]

[3]Number 34 in bibliography, pp. 2–5, appendix II, 15.
[4]Numbers 28–31 in bibliography.
[5]Number 32 in bibliography.

ORGANIZATION AND CLASSIFICATION

The organization and classification of the materials in the PRO relating to foreign relations have evolved through the years, progressing from simplicity to complexity. The first classification began with the division into foreign and domestic state papers. The State Papers Foreign began in 1547 and continued until 1780. During this period the papers are classified as: general correspondence, foreign entry books, foreign ministers in London, news letters, treaty papers, treaties, archives of legations, ciphers, confidential, and various.

The most important of these is general correspondence, which contains the correspondence with British ambassadors regarding policy. The years 1547–77 are arranged chronologically with no pretense to arrangement by country, but in 1577 the arrangement was changed to chronological within each country. By 1700 the drafts of the letters to the ambassadors were filed separately from the ambassadors' dispatches.

The confidential class is of value since it contains intercepted correspondence from foreign ambassadors in London; some of this is in cipher, but most has been deciphered. The class designated as "foreign ministers in London" contains the official communications from these diplomats to the British government.

For the years 1781–1878 the classification varies somewhat: general correspondence, supplement to general correspondence, Great Britain and general, slave trade, king's letter books, letters to public offices, treaties, miscellaneous, seals, chief clerk's department, embassy and consular archives, archives of commissions, and private collections.

The general correspondence class by this time had begun to take a definite pattern of arrangement. The documents were arranged by country and chronologically within this category. Under each year the drafts of letters to the embassy came first, dispatches from the embassy next, followed by correspondence with British consuls, correspondence with foreign consuls in Britain (listed as consular domestic), correspondence with foreign ambassadors (listed as domestic), and correspondence with other departments of the government and with private individuals in Britain (listed as domestic various). In general, the documents in each of these subdivisions are bound separately.

Further changes in classification and arrangement came with the materials for the years 1879–85. There were now three main classes: general correspondence, treaties, and embassy and consular archives. Much of the arrangement for the period 1885–1902 is similar to this period.

The general correspondence for the years 1879–85 is arranged by country and within each country by the year, beginning with the drafts to the ambassadors. Then come the dispatches from the embassies, drafts of telegrams and the telegrams received from the embassies, recorders of the telegrams,[6] drafts and dispatches of correspondence with the embassies about consular affairs, drafts and dispatches of correspondence with the embassies over commercial subjects, correspondence with the consuls, correspondence with the departments of the British government, commercial negotiations, and then the dossier type files. This is the general arrangement for each year under each country.

The treaties class contains the protocols of the treaties, ratifications of the treaties, miscellaneous matters, and the chief clerk's department. The embassy and consular archives class comprises the correspondence in the files of these offices, letter books, registers, and miscellaneous documents. The correspondence is arranged with the dispatches from the foreign office first, then commercial correspondence, consular correspondence, correspondence with the foreign government to which

[6] A recorder of a telegram was the full message before it had been shortened for telegraphing, and which followed by diplomatic pouch as a check on accuracy. The recorders are often helpful when the sense of the telegram is unclear. The recorder also gives a better idea of the intentions and thinking of the sender.

accredited, and any particular problems that might be in the dossier type files.

There is a slight variation in the arrangement and classification for the years 1885–1902. The separate class for treaties disappears and treaties are placed after telegrams in the general correspondence class.

As British foreign affairs increased in complexity, more and more use was made of the dossier type file in regard to specialized problems, i.e. "Designs of the French on Morocco" or "Newfoundland fisheries, 1885–Jan.–June." Owing to the limitations of space, it is impossible to mention every dossier. The scholar should be aware of this fact because he may not find his subject in the regular files of drafts and dispatches. It may have become so specialized that a separate file has been set up and no notice of this fact will be evident except in the list of the volumes. As a result of this condition, when the work of an ambassador is studied, all the dossiers for this period have to be consulted.

To give some idea of the manner in which the volumes are listed and described in the manuscript lists, an example is given below. It is a condensed and partial listing of the volumes of documents concerning France in 1897.

Vol. No.	Date	Ambassador or Agent	
3312	Jan.–May 1897	Sir E. Monson Mr. Gosselin	Diplo Drafts 1–228
3313	June–Dec. 1897	do.	do. do. 229–432
3314	Jan.–18 Feb. 1897	Sir E. Monson	Diplo Desps 1–120
3315	19 Feb.– March 1897	Sir E. Monson Mr. Gosselin	do. do. 121–242
3324	1897	Sir E. Monson Mr. Gosselin	Consular
3325	1897	do.	Commercial Drafts

Vol. No.	Date	Ambassador or Agent	
3331	1897	Sir E. Monson	Commercial Telegrams, Paraphrases
3332	1897	do.	Treaty Drafts
3335	Jan.–16 Sept. 1897	Sir E. Monson	Africa Drafts 1–271
3339	1897	Various	Diplomatic
3375	1897	Newfoundland Fisheries	
3378	Jan.–March 1897	French proceedings in Madagascar	

The volume described above as "various" contains interdepartmental correspondence related to foreign affairs. These volumes may often prove useful in throwing light on a particular problem if it has been discussed in a department other than the foreign office.

The volumes classed as "domestic" contain the memoranda, letters, etc., between the embassies in London and the foreign office. For the most part, the subject matter is only that of routine affairs, i.e., publication of colored books, claims for nationals, etc.

The researcher may save much time by using the registers of the British embassy accredited to the particular country in which he is interested. These helpful registers list every dispatch sent and received and give a short description of each.

In addition to the regular diplomatic archives of the British foreign service, the PRO has transcripts from foreign archives including Milan, 1428–1786; Rome, fifteenth to eighteenth centuries; Swedish archives, sixteenth to eighteenth centuries; Spanish archives, fifteenth to seventeenth centuries; the Venetian manuscripts, 1485–1787 (valuable for the reports of the Venetian ambassadors in England); and Baschet's transcripts of the dispatches of the French ambassadors to England, 1509–1714.

There is a large collection of semiprivate papers among the foreign office records in the PRO that deal directly with foreign affairs. The Aston papers contain the correspondence of Sir Arthur Aston, minister at Rio de Janeiro, Paris, and Madrid, 1827–43. In the Bloomfield papers there are drafts, dispatches, and the entry books of Sir Benjamin Bloomfield while serving in St. Petersburg and Berlin from 1823 to 1871. The Clarendon papers cover the years 1867–70, and comprise copies of Lord Clarendon's letters and original letters to him when he was foreign secretary.

The Granville papers consist of letters to Lord Granville and the drafts of his letters during the years 1870–74. James Henderson's papers include his correspondence when he was British consul general in Columbia, 1818–31. For Prussia and the United States, 1763–1856, there are the papers of Francis James Jackson and Sir George Jackson. The Simmons papers contain the private letters and reports of Lieutenant General Sir J. L. A. Simmons and deal for the most part with the Russo-Turkish war. There are also the original correspondence and diplomatic papers of Stratford Canning, Lord Stratford de Redcliffe; these cover the years 1808–63. The papers of Sir William White deal mainly with Turkey and the Near East during the years 1857–90. The letters and letter drafts of Lord Tenterden, undersecretary of state for foreign affairs, cover the years 1873–82. The papers of Woodbine Parish include his correspondence and reports while consul general in Buenos Aires, 1813–55.

Among the private papers more recently acquired by the foreign office and now in the PRO are the papers of Lord Cowley for the years 1852–67 when he was ambassador in Paris; Lord Hammond's papers while he was working with Stratford Canning, 1831–34, and later serving as permanent undersecretary in the foreign office, 1854–73; Howard de Walden papers, 1817–34, including his work as undersecretary for foreign affairs and minister to Sweden and Portugal; Sir

Edward Malet's papers while ambassador in Berlin; the papers of Baron Stuart de Rothesay, 1801–14, dealing with the early years of his career in Madrid and Lisbon.

There are other private papers in the same repository classed as "gifts and deposits," and among them can be found the correspondence of Andrew Snape Douglas, secretary of the legation and chargé at Palermo and Naples, 1811–14, 1816–18, 1822. In the Cornwallis papers there is some material relating to Lord Cornwallis' mission to Flanders in 1794 and his mission as plenipotentiary to the congress of Amiens, 1801–2, in addition to the volumes relating to the American Revolution. Among the papers of Sir John Nicholl are drafts and notes on international affairs that were referred to him for opinions when he was king's advocate general, 1798–1808. The Napier papers contain some letters to British ministers and consuls in 1854. In the Stuart papers there is correspondence relative to Turkey, 1864–66, Russia, 1867–68, Argentina, 1868–69, 1871, Uruguay, 1869, Greece, 1871–77, the Netherlands, 1877–88. The Cardwell papers have some correspondence with the foreign secretary when Viscount Cardwell was secretary of state for war, 1868–74. There are also the papers of Lord John Russell, the First and Second Earls of Granville, and the Carnarvon papers, the latter containing correspondence with foreign secretaries for the period, 1874–90. The Satow papers cover the years 1865–1902 and deal with Lord Satow's missions to Japan, Siam, Uruguay, Morocco, China, and the second Hague Peace Conference. The papers of Sir John Ardagh contain his diaries for the years 1867–1900, correspondence relating to the Turkish and Bulgarian frontier commission, 1867–79, the Turkish-Greek frontier commission, 1880–82, his correspondence while serving in Egypt and the Sudan, 1882–87, and in India, 1888–94. The most important items in this collection are Ardagh's memoranda and correspondence while he was director of military intelligence. The diplomatic correspondence of both the Pitts is found in the thirty-eight volumes of the Chatham papers. The Calonne papers cover the years 1787–1802 and contain reports and memoranda relating to European affairs. England's activities with the *emigrés* are in the Bouillon papers which contain secret reports of underground royalist activities in France, intelligence reports, and reports of spies during the years 1794–1802.

ADMINISTRATION, REGULATIONS, AND FACILITIES

In order to use the PRO the researcher must apply there on the appropriate form for a "student's ticket" to the Search Department where he will do his work. Foreign scholars must also request their embassies or legations to ask the foreign office for a letter of introduction on their behalf. This process usually takes about a week but in exceptional circumstances can be shortened. The ticket is valid until further notice. In addition the researcher will sign the register of the PRO every day when arriving to use the records.

After the researcher has obtained his ticket, registered, and found a seat in the Round Room where the Search Department is located (seats are often at a premium in the summer and other rooms must be used), he will find the lists of the documents in the bound volumes, both printed and typscript, around the walls of the Round Room.[7] A ticket must be filled out for each volume that the researcher wishes to consult. Owing to lack of personnel there is some delay in bringing the documents to the reader at the present time. Whenever possible the documents should be requested a day in advance. Most of the documents after 1885 are kept in the repository at Ashridge and should be ordered two days in advance. Each researcher is limited to three volumes that he may use at one time. If the researcher expects to need a number of volumes over a short period of time, he may call for a new volume every time that he finishes one and hands it in. Or he may indicate a need for more than three volumes and request three at a time for his desk.

[7]Numbers 44–50 in bibliography.

All records are produced subject to the closing date set by each department. For the foreign office, the war office, and the admiralty that date is now 1902. Anyone desiring to see documents after that date will first have to obtain the permission of the department concerned, but permission is granted only in very exceptional circumstances. The archives of the board of trade are not open beyond 1885. In order to prepare for a trip most efficiently, the foreign scholar should write beforehand to ascertain the date of closing of the documents since the open date may have been extended.

The PRO is open every day except Sunday and such legal holidays as Good Friday, Saturday before Easter, Easter Monday, Saturday before Whitsunday, Whitmonday, August Bank Holiday, Christmas, and December 26 (Boxing Day). In September the Search Department of the PRO is closed for a short time for the purpose of cleaning. Anyone using the records during September should write ahead to ascertain the exact dates during which the PRO will be closed. Researchers may work in the Search Department daily from 10:00 A.M. to 5:30 P.M., except Saturdays when the hours are 10:00 A.M. to 2:00 P.M.

Among the reference aids available in the Round Room are Guiseppi's *Guide to the public records*, which has been kept up to date with interlinear annotations; the *Dictionary of national biography;* copies of the *Bulletin of the Institute of Historical Research;* Oxford bibliographies of British history; C. M. Andrews' guides to materials for American history in the PRO; and the publications of the Historical Manuscripts Commission. Further information regarding the other books in the Round Room can be found by consulting the "Press list of books in the literary search room." In addition there is the "General catalogue of the lists, indexes, calendars, and other means of references to the records preserved in the Public Record Office." The "Summary of records" includes a list of all the records kept in the PRO; naturally this includes documents that as yet are not open to public inspection.

Through its own facilities and personnel, the PRO will microfilm documents for the researcher. Owing to lack of space, private microfilming is no longer permitted. Applications for microfilming must specify the context in which the reproduction will be used or will appear. The authorities must also approve any caption or description that will be used.[8]

The officers whose duties pertain to the diplomatic archives in the PRO are D. L. Evans, O.B.E., the deputy keeper of the records, H. N. Blakiston, assistant keeper and director of the Search Department, R. E. Latham and E. K. Timings, assistant keepers, in charge of the Round Room.

The PRO is not immediately adjacent to a residential area or to hotels. The nearest area of London where the scholar can find accommodation is Bloomsbury, which includes the University of London and the British Museum. It is better to make reservations well in advance of the trip; the London Hotels' Information Service, 88 Brook Street, London, W.1, will provide information on the hotel accommodations that are available. The Non-Commercial Accommodation Service, 64–65 St. James's Street, London, S.W.1, will supply information regarding accommodations for paying guests in private homes, which will be found to be much cheaper than hotels. The more picturesque sections of London are some distance from the PRO, but the excellent public transportation system offsets this disadvantage.

ADDITIONAL ARCHIVES AND LIBRARIES

There are a number of other archives, libraries, and organizations in Great Britain that can be of value to the scholar

---

[8]The charges for microfilming (1956) are: 3d per exposure, 1–100 exposures; 101 exposures to the end of the reel, 2½d per exposure; minimum charge, 3/6. For work of special difficulty the charges are 5d per exposure up to 100 exposures; 101 exposures to the end of the reel, 4½d per exposure, minimum charge 5/-. If there are long runs of documents that can be easily photographed, special rates can be arranged. A surcharge of 7/6 may be made upon orders from abroad to cover costs of collection.

studying British foreign relations. Prominent among these is the library of the British Museum in London. Many state papers of the fifteenth, sixteenth, seventeenth, and eighteenth centuries that were retained by their owners when they retired from public office are now in this repository. They are found in such famous collections as the Harley MSS., Cotton MSS., Stowe MSS., and Lansdowne MSS. There is also a valuable collection of private papers of British diplomats and statesmen.

For the convenience of the student there is a manuscript class catalogue in the manuscript room of the British Museum. Two groups of materials are of special interest. The first of these is state letters, foreign, consisting of single copies of letters relating to British foreign relations. These were either sent by government officials to private individuals, or they were drafts of private correspondence that were sent to government officials. The items are catalogued chronologically beginning with 1558 and continuing up into the late nineteenth century.

A second collection contains state papers, mainly of the sixteenth, seventeenth, and eighteenth centuries, though some material from the nineteenth century is included. This is miscellaneous foreign correspondence for the most part and there are no large single collections. It is composed of official correspondence of Denmark, France, Germany, Greece, Italy, the Low Countries, Portugal, Poland, Russia, Scotland, Spain and its colonies, Sweden, Switzerland, Turkish Empire, Africa, and the United States. There is much here pertaining to French foreign relations during the sixteenth, seventeenth, and eighteenth centuries, particularly instructions sent to the French ambassadors in the sixteenth century.

The British Museum possesses collections of private papers of officials of the British government that did not reach the PRO. Among the better known are the papers of Canning, Newcastle, Gladstone, the elder Pitt, Liverpool, Bolingbroke, Warren Hastings, Aukland, Wellesley, Peel, Russell, Napier, Wellington, Campbell-Bannerman, the Grenvilles, Cobden, Dilke,

Clive, Townshend, and Charles James Fox. In addition there
are the Aberdeen papers, which include semiofficial correspondence while Lord Aberdeen was foreign secretary and
prime minister; Baron Lexington, 1694–97, envoy to Vienna,
1712–13, ambassador to Spain; Francis Drake, 1790–1813,
while he was accredited to Genoa, Germany, Sardinia, and
Corsica; two hundred volumes of the papers of Prince Chris-
topher Lieven and Princess Dorothea Lieven; some papers
of Frederick II of Prussia; Sir Thomas Chamberlayne, ambassador to Spain, 1559– 69; the letter book of William Blathwayt,
secretary for war and acting secretary of state for William III,
1695–1701; James Vernon, secretary of state, 1697–1702; Sir
Charles Hamilton, representative at Naples, 1761–1803;
Charles John Bentinck, 1730–65; Baron Heytesbury, sixty-five
volumes covering his diplomatic career in Naples, Vienna,
Malta, Barbary States, Spain, Portugal, and Russia for the
years 1801–32; Cardinal Pole while legate to England; Sir
Benjamin Keene, envoy to Madrid, 1727–39, 1749–57, and
Lisbon, 1745–49; and Sir Arthur Layard, archeologist and
undersecretary of state for foreign affairs, 1861–66, minister to
Madrid, 1869, and ambassador in Constantinople, 1877–80.

The General Register House, Edinburgh, Scotland, is the
Scottish equivalent of the PRO and possess many items that
relate to the history of diplomacy of the sixteenth, seventeenth
and eighteenth centuries. As the accumulation of materials is
not as extensive as in the PRO, the procedure for calling for the
documents is simplified. Lists are available for the collections.

One of the largest collections includes the official papers of
the Scottish sovereigns, including treaties between the sovereigns and England, France, Norway, Sweden, Denmark, the
Empire, Burgundy, and the Low Countries. There are also
official state letters, commissions, safe conducts, agreements,
warrants, etc., arranged chronologically.

Among the other collections in the General Register are the
Elphinstone MSS., containing letters of James V and James VI

to cardinals, popes, and kings of France, and the letters of Mary Stuart to sovereigns on the continent. The Tyninghame letter book contains diplomatic correspondence of James V. The papers of Regent Mar, 1571–72, have some correspondence with sovereigns, and the Reay papers contain correspondence of Gustavus Adolphus. A collection known as the Society of Antiquaries has letters of Mary Stuart to ambassadors for the years 1568–70. The papers of John, second Earl of Stair, contain his correspondence while serving in the embassy in Paris, 1715–19. In the Hopestoun MSS. will be found official correspondence for the years 1536–95. Prussian affairs are the main subject of the papers of Alex Gibson, British consul in Danzig, and deal with the period 1807–13. Letters to Charles II of England from sovereigns and agents while he was in exile, 1649–51, are in the Newbattle collection. The General Register House also possesses twenty-three manuscript volumes of synopses of state correspondence with Holland for the years 1674–94. While not in the General Register House, a list is available in this repository of the Buccleuch muniments, which are in the Dalkeith House. These contain the Townshend correspondence pertaining to the years when he was chancellor of the exchequer, and they deal with trade in North Africa, Portugal, America, and the Levant; correspondence with Pitt, Newcastle, Burke, and others is included. These documents can be seen by applying to the Duke of Buccleuch, preferably through the Historical Manuscripts Commission, which is discussed in the last section of this chapter.

There are some papers of interest in the Public Record Office of Northern Ireland, Law Courts Building, Belfast. In the Abercorn papers there are documents relating to the First Duke of Manchester, ambassador to France, 1699–1701; others in the same collection deal with Anglo-French relations in the early eighteenth century. The papers of George Macartney, First Earl Macartney, contain dispatches from British diplomats on the progress of the fighting between Austria and France, 1795–

96, and correspondence of the Count of Provence whom Macartney visited on a secret mission in 1795. This repository also possesses a quantity of important materials relating to Anglo-Irish history.

The John Rylands Library of Manchester, England, possesses a catalogue of the younger Pitt's papers, mostly of the 1780's and the 1790's. There are six volumes with a lengthy description of each letter and occasional extracts; also included are transcripts of correspondence between Pitt and George III relating to foreign affairs. The catalogue was compiled by Edward Tomlinson, Bishop of Winchester and the tutor of Pitt. The unique value of this catalogue lies in the fact that it was compiled before Pitt's papers were scattered and many were lost. This library possesses consular correspondence and papers of Viscount Mount-Stuart, later the first Marquis of Bute, including letters and reports from British agents and consuls in southern Europe for the period 1776-83. In addition there are copies of the reports sent by Mount-Stuart in his dispatches for the years 1780-82. The Stapleton MSS. deal with British affairs in the West Indies for the late seventeenth and eighteenth centuries. There are also the Beke papers relating to the official correspondence of Charles T. Beke while he was in Abyssinia. The Rylands Library contains a great deal of material dealing with the East India Company's activities, and for this subject the Bagshame muniments, the Melville papers, and the Pitt papers are useful. This library has some copies of letters from the correspondence of the ambassadors of Henry VIII, which closely resemble parts of the Harleian MSS. in the British Museum.

The Bodleian Library of Oxford University contains materials of value in the study of seventeenth century foreign affairs. The Rawlinson MSS. have diplomatic documents pertaining to the reigns of Charles II and James II. The Clarendon MSS. and the Carte MSS. would be of use in studying the activities of the royalists during their exile at the time of the Civil War.

For the eighteenth century the Bodleian Library has the correspondence and diplomatic papers of Thomas Villiers, first Earl of Clarendon of the second creation, which cover the years 1738–46. The library also possesses the correspondence of the Fourth Earl of Clarendon while he was foreign secretary. These papers deal with the years 1853–58, 1861–66, and they include the correspondence of members of the cabinet with the fourth earl, as well as his letter books, registers, and the papers printed for the use of the foreign office, 1848–58.

The papers of Asquith are in the Bodleian Library and include cabinet memoranda, papers, and circulations for the prewar and war periods. There are also private letters for the period 1892–1916. These documents can be used with the permission of Sir Maurice Bonham-Carter.

The University Library at Cambridge contains items of value. A printed catalogue gives the acquisitions prior to 1856.[9] For later accessions one must use a manuscript catalogue. The library has a number of state papers of the reign of Henry VIII which have not been printed and which relate to diplomatic affairs. There is also material relating to the diplomatic correspondence of Cardinal Wolsey, Reginald Pole, Queen Elizabeth I, James I, James II, Cardinal Mazarin, the younger Pitt, certain popes, and transcripts of the correspondence of Lord Carteret, 1742–45, and the Duke of Newcastle, 1740–64. There are also some items of diplomatic correspondence of the eighteenth century.

One of the most important institutions for historical research in London is the Institute of Historical Research, part of the University of London. The library of this institution is particularly useful in the study of international affairs, and it contains much of the library of Dr. G. P. Gooch. The lists and indexes of the PRO may be studied in this library. Research fellowships of £275 are available for use by American scholars.[10] Those

---

[9] Number 24 in bibliography.

[10] Applications should be requested from the Director, Institute of Historical Research, Senate House, London, W.C.1.

who have research degrees or who have published their work may use the facilities of the institute upon application and payment of a small fee.

The facilities of the Royal Institute of International affairs in Chatham House, London, are also available. The library of this institute contains a complete set of League of Nations publications, a press cutting service for articles on international affairs, and a collection of books and unpublished documents belonging to John Wheeler Wheeler-Bennett.

The library of the Royal Empire Society, London, will be useful for those studying the diplomacy of the empire and commonwealth.

Each of the departments of the British government that deals with matters in the sphere of foreign relations has a departmental library that may be of use. These libraries are not open to the general public, however, and the request for their use must be made in writing.

The Foreign Office Library, Cornwall House, Waterloo Road, London, possesses a limited amount of manuscript materials. Sometimes special permission to use this material is granted to a qualified scholar who has exhausted every other source and who makes a request for a specific item in writing to the librarian. The private papers of the Fourth Marquis of Lansdowne and of Sir Edward Grey are in this repository, but only a portion of the less important ones are now available for study. The library possesses extremely limited facilities for research and one may be requested to clear through his embassy before being granted permission to use its volumes.

The War Office Library in Whitehall does not contain any manuscripts, for they have been sent to the PRO. It is a good reference library and the scholar can use it after obtaining permission by writing to the director of the library.

The Colonial Office Library, located in the Commonwealth Relations Office in Downing Street, contains no manuscripts prior to 1935, the remainder having been sent to the PRO.

Lastly there is the Admiralty Library in Whitehall in which there are no documents prior to 1902. This is one of the finest naval reference libraries in the world and may be used by the researcher who applies for permission in writing to the director of the library. Certain of Lord John Fisher's papers and the German admiralty papers for the period 1848–1945 are in this library. With special permission these documents may be used by qualified scholars, who must apply in writing, giving the documents they desire to see and the purpose of their study.

PAPERS IN PRIVATE HANDS

A number of other archives, libraries, and organizations in Great Britain can be of value to the scholar studying British foreign relations. The foremost among these is the Historical Manuscripts Commission, which was appointed in 1869 to collect information on manuscript materials which were in private hands and to publish such as seemed worthy of publication. In addition, the commission was to make abstracts and catalogues of documents and to issue reports periodically. Since 1869 the commission has reported on manuscripts of over four hundred private owners and two hundred corporate bodies. These amount to over two hundred volumes, most of which are still in print and can be obtained from H.M. Stationery Office, P.O. box 569, London, S.E.1.[11]

The Historical Manuscripts Commission can be of value for the independent scholar in arranging introductions if he wishes to use private archives. Under no circumstances should one write directly to the family, since in all probability he will be denied use of the papers. Indiscriminate applications from total strangers may prejudice the owners and result in denial of access even to accredited scholars. The researcher should write to the Secretary, Historical Manuscripts Commission, Public Record Office, Chancery Lane, London, W.C.2.

Between 1914 and 1945 the commission's resources, never

[11]Number 42 in bibliography.

very extensive, were mainly concentrated on reporting in increasing detail on the manuscripts of a small number of owners. In 1945, however, it was enabled to make a more comprehensive survey in the form of a National Register of Archives, to comprise eventually a card index of all the archives in private hands and to furnish a vast guide to the manuscript sources extant in private archives in Great Britain.[12] Such a step became imperative as the breakup of the estates continued with the resulting loss of private archives.

The work of the register has proceeded with the creation of voluntary county committees which furnish, with the owner's consent, reports to the registrar on the location and extent of individual archival accumulations. These reports form the basis of the index and to a limited extent may be consulted by the scholar. A bulletin of the register's work has been published periodically with selected summaries of the reports, and the current numbers can be obtained from the National Register of Archives. Present plans call for the annual publication of a special number of the bulletin containing reports from national and local repositories as to the historical manuscripts that have been received during the past year. The first such report appeared in the summer of 1955 and included accessions from eighty-six repositories during 1954. These are condensed reports, but the full reports are available for inspection. The *Bulletin of the Institute of Historical Research*, which formerly contained this information, will no longer do so but will report the migrations of manuscripts sold by booksellers.

From modest beginnings the register's work has expanded to cover far more than was originally intended. In addition to reporting on collections of manuscripts, the work has involved obtaining access to manuscripts for students and arranging for transfer of the archives to more suitable repositories. During the early years of the register's work, the chief emphasis was placed on the examination of family and estate archives and parish

[12]Number 23 in bibliography.

records, but the primary reports showed extensive business, professional, and educational records as yet unexplored. Consequently, the original expectation that the work of the register would be completed in two years and a half is as yet unfilled.[13]

Among the many items that have been examined through the work of the National Register of Archives are the diary, letters, and papers of the First Earl of Kimberley in the possession of the present earl; the correspondence of the First to the Fourth Dukes of Portland; and the correspondence of the Earl of Portland, now on deposit in the Nottingham University Library. The Wentworth Woodhouse papers have been deposited in the Sheffield City Library; they contain much of the correspondence of Edmund Burke and the Second Marquis of Rockingham. Other collections include the official correspondence of the Duke of Wellington, now in the possession of the present duke; diplomatic correspondence of the First and Fourth Earls of Sandwich, now owned by the present earl; Lord Galway's papers, which include secret service reports of Sir John Goodrich from the Low Countries during the Seven Years War and the correspondence of General Monckton, Wolfe's successor, and at present owned by Viscount Galway; diplomatic and political correspondence of Pitt the younger, Peel, Russell, and Gladstone in the possession of the Earl of Harrowby; the political papers of Spencer Perceval, covering the years 1800–18 (these are to be given to the British Museum); diplomatic correspondence of the First Duke of Manchester dealing with his diplomatic career in Venice, Paris, and as secretary of state for the northern department, 1697–1707 (the present owner being the Duke of Manchester); additional Peel, Wellington, and Canning papers in the possession of Major General E. H. Goulburn, Surrey; Canning correspondence in the possession of the Earl of Morley; and the correspondence and papers of William Dacres Adams, private secretary to

[13]Number 23 in bibliography, 1953, 1954, 1955.

William Pitt the younger.[14] Individuals who have possession of these documents and others mentioned in the remainder of the chapter should not be approached except through the Historical Manuscripts Commission; if the documents are definitely known to be in a public repository, application should be made to the custodians.

In Scotland the work of the register has been undertaken by H.M. General Register House, Edinburgh, 2. By 1952 the Secretary of the National Register of Archives (Scotland) had received two hundred and five reports and over ninety repositories had been examined. At the present writing, a card index has not yet been established, and the alphabetical files are serving as an index. Interested scholars can obtain copies of the annual reports made by the register from the Secretary, National Register of Archives (Scotland), General Register House, Edinburgh, 2.

Among the diplomatic materials that have been brought to light through the work of the register in Scotland are the papers of Sir Andrew Mitchell, ambassador to Prussia, 1756–71, now in Craigievar Castle; the correspondence and papers of the Second Duke of Argyll, commander-in-chief in Spain during the War of the Spanish Succession, which are among the Argyll muniments at Invereray; and the Panmure papers, which contain correspondence with Palmerston, Clarendon, Queen Victoria, and the Prince Consort.[15]

Some of the most significant collections of private papers are those of the Third Marquis of Salisbury, Joseph and Neville Chamberlain, Castlereagh, Disraeli, Palmerston, and Curzon. Their custodians may be approached through the Historical Manuscripts Commission. The papers of David Lloyd-George are now in the care of the University of New Brunswick, Fredericton, B.D., Canada.[16]

[14]Number 23 in bibliography.
[15]Number 54 in bibliography.
[16]The writer would like to express his appreciation for the extensive help and information so readily given him by the officials of the Public Record Office and of the National Register of Archives.

BIBLIOGRAPHY

Printed Collections of Documents

1. *British diplomatic instructions*, *1689–1789*, James F. Chance, *Sweden 1689–1727* (London, 1922), *Denmark* (London, 1926), *Sweden 1727–1789* (London, 1928), and L. G. Wickham Legg, *France 1689–1721* (London, 1925), *France, 1721–1727* (London, 1927), *France 1727–1744* (London, 1930), *France, 1745–1789* (London, 1934). These are arranged chronologically according to ambassador; the main sources are the PRO, the British Museum, and a few private papers.

2. *British and foreign state papers* (London, 1841–   ). Begun in the nineteenth century by Sir Lewis Hertslet, librarian of the foreign office; it is a collection of the principal documents relating to international affairs that have been made public since 1814.

3. *British documents on the origins of the war.* Ed. by G. P. Gooch and Harold Temperley. 11 vols. London, 1926–38.

4. *Calendar of state papers, Edward VI and Mary.* Ed. by W. B. Turnbull. 2 vols. London, 1861.

5. *Calendar of state papers foreign, Elizabeth, 1558–1589.* Ed. by Joseph Stevenson, A. J. Crosby, A. J. Butter, S. C. Lomas, and A. B. Hinds. 21 vols. London, 1863–1931.

6. *Calendar of state papers and manuscripts relating to English affairs existing in the archives and collections of Venice and in other libraries of northern Italy. 1603–1643.* Ed. by Rawdon Brown, Cavendish Bentick, Horatio Brown, and A. B. Hinds. 26 vols. London, 1864–1947.

7. *Calendar of state papers, Milan, 1385–1618.* Ed. by A. H. Hinds. London, 1912.

8. *Calendar of state papers, Rome, 1558–1578.* Ed. by J. M. Rigg. 2 vols. London, 1916–26.

9. *Calendar of state papers, Spanish, 1485–1558.* Ed. by G. A. Gergenroth. Pesrual de Gayogas, M. A. S. Hume, and Royall Tyler. 13 vols. London, 1862–1954.

10. *Documents on British foreign policy, 1919–1939.* Ed. by E. L. Woodward and Rohan Butler. 18 vols. London, 1947–   .

11. *Letters and papers, foreign and domestic of the reign of Henry VIII, 1509–1547.* Ed. by J. S. Brewer, James Gairdner, and R. H. Brodie. London, 1862–1932.

12. *Manual of collections of treaties and collections relating to treaties.* Ed. by D. P. Myers. Cambridge, 1922.

13. *Notes on the diplomatic relations of England.* Editor in chief, C. H. Firth.

Lists of ambassadors from England to France and from France to England. Ed. by S. C. Lomas. Oxford, 1906. List of diplomatic representatives and agents, England and north Germany, 1698–1727. Ed. by J. F. Chance. Oxford, 1907. List of diplomatic representatives and agents, England and France, 1689–1763. Ed. by W. G. Wickham Legg. Oxford, 1909. List of English diplomatic representatives and agents in Denmark, Sweden, and Russia, and of those countries in England 1689–1762. Ed. by J. F. Chance. Oxford, 1913.

14. Recueil des instructions données aux ambassadeurs et ministres de France, 1648– 1789; Angleterre, 1648–1690. Ed. by J. J. Jusserand. 4 vols. Paris, 1929.

15. Reports of the Royal Commission on Historical Manuscripts. London, 1870– . At present over two hundred volumes have been published; invaluable for calendars and extracts of documents from private archives examined by the commission. A new revised edition of a guide to the reports is in preparation. The eighteenth report (1917) contains a useful guide to the materials for diplomatic history for the years 1509–1783 that have been calendared in these reports. See also number 66 in the bibliography.

16. Sessional papers. Parliament. London, 1803– . Included in these are accounts of diplomatic correspondence laid before parliament. At the present writing, microprints are available up to 1900. A list of those available can be obtained from the Readex Microprint Co., Chester, Vermont.

Guides and Reference Works

17. Archives. The journal of the British Records Association; published twice yearly.

18. Barwick, G. F. The ASLIB directory, a guide to sources of specialized information in Great Britain and Ireland. London, 1928.

19. Bodleian Library record. Published three times a year; useful for information of the latest acquisitions.

20. British Museum quarterly. Contains articles relating to newly acquired manuscripts.

21. Bulletin of the Institute of Historical Research. Semiannual journal.

22. Bulletin of the John Rylands Library.

23. Bulletin of the National Register of Archives. The latest information on new reports of private papers which have been examined; annual report on new acquisitions in repositories.

24. Catalogue of the manuscripts preserved in the library of the University of Cambridge. 5 vols. Cambridge, 1856.

25. Craster, H. H. E. The Western manuscripts in the Bodleian Library. (Number 43 in Helps for students of history.) London, 1921,

26. Davies, Godfrey. *A student's guide to the manuscripts relating to English history in the seventeenth century in the Bodleian Library.* (Number 47 in *Helps for students of history.*) London, 1922.

27. Dennis, Faustine. "British manuscripts project," *American documentation.* I (1950), 130–132.

28. Deputy Keeper of the Public Records. *The hundred and first report.* London, 1939. Current reports are valuable for recent information of developments at the PRO, and past reports are useful in the study of the history of the Public Record Office.

29. *The hundred and second report.* London, 1940.

30. *The hundred and fourth report.* London, 1942.

31. *The hundred and eighth report.* London, 1946.

32. *The hundred and twelfth report.* London, 1950.

33. Edwards, Edward. *Libraries and founders of libraries.* London, 1864.

34. *First report of the royal commission on public records appointed to inquire into and report on the state of the public records and local records of a public nature of England and Wales.* Cd. 6361. London, 1912.

35. Galbraith, H. V. *An introduction to the use of the public records.* Oxford, 1934. Useful to the scholar beginning his first research in the PRO.

36. "General catalogue of the lists, indexes, calendars, and other means of references to the records preserved in the Public Record Office." 8 vols. In typescript at the PRO; to some extent superseded by a card index.

37. Gilson, Julius P., *A student's guide to the manuscripts of the British Museum.* (Number 31 in *Helps for students of history*). London, 1930. Valuable lists of the ambassadors and envoys whose papers are found in the manuscript collections of the British Museum.

38. *Guide to the public records. Part I. Introductory.* London, 1949. There is no completely up-to-date guide to the PRO, although one is in preparation. This is the introduction to the new guide and it explains much of the work of the PRO. Copies can be purchased from H.M. Stationery Office and the British Information Center, 30 Rockefeller Plaza, New York 20, N.Y.

39. Giuseppi, M. S. *A guide to the manuscripts preserved in the Public Record Office.* 2 vols. London, 1924. The most recent guide to the manuscripts; useful but outdated.

40. Hall, Hubert. *Studies in English official historical documents.* Cambridge, 1908.

41. Harrod, L. M. *The libraries of greater London, a guide.* London, 1951. Includes the procedure for obtaining admission with a brief note on the contents of each library.

42. H.M. Stationery Office. *Sectional list number 17. Reports of the Royal Commission on Historical Manuscripts*. London, 1951. List of reports which have been published through January 31, 1951; those still in print have been so noted.

43. Johnson, Charles. *The Public Record Office*. (Number 4 in *Helps for students of history*). London, 1916.

44. *Lists and indexes number XIV, list of volumes of state papers foreign preserved in the Public Record Office*. London, 1904.

45. *Lists and indexes number XVIII, list of admiralty records preserved in the Public Record office*, London, 1904.

46. *Lists and indexes number XXXVI, list of colonial office records preserved in the Public Record Office*. London, 1911.

47. *Lists and indexes number XLIX, list of diplomatic documents, Scottish documents, and papal bulls preserved in the Public Record Office*. London, 1923.

48. *Lists and indexes number LII, list of foreign office records to 1878 preserved in the Public Record Office*. London, 1929.

49. *Lists and indexes number LIII, an alphabetical guide to certain war office and other military records preserved in the Public Record Office*. London, 1931.

50. "Lists of foreign office records from 1878 to 1902 preserved in the Public Record Office." In typescript in the PRO.

51. *List and index of the publications of the Royal Historical Society, 1871–1924 and of the Camden Society, 1840–1897*. Ed. by Hubert Hall. London, 1925.

52. Martin, Charles T. *The record interpreter: a collection of abbreviations, Latin words and names used in English historical manuscripts and records*. 2d ed. London, 1910.

53. Matheson, Cyril. *A catalogue of the publications of Scottish historical and kindred clubs and societies, 1908–1927*. Aberdeen, 1928.

54. National Register of Archives (Scotland). *Reports of the National Register of Archives (Scotland)*.

55. Roberts, R. A. *The reports of the Historical Manuscripts Commission*. (Number 4 in *Helps for students of history*.) London, 1920.

56. Rye, Reginald A. *The student's guide to the libraries of London with an account of the most important archives and other aids to study*. London, 1927.

57. Scargill-Bird, S. R. *A guide to the various classes of documents preserved in the Public Record Office*. London, 1908. Superseded by Giuseppi (Number 39.)

58. Schmitt, Bernadotte E. "British foreign policy, 1919–1939," *Journal of modern history*, XXI (1949), 320–326.

59. "British foreign policy, 1931–1932," *Journal of modern history*, XXIII (1951), 153–157.

60. "Munich," *Journal of modern history,* XXV (1953), pp. 166–180.

61. *Scottish historical review.* Semiannual journal; October issue contains list of accessions to the Scottish Record Office.

62. Temperley, Harold, and Penson, Lillian. *A century of diplomatic blue books, 1814–1914.* Cambridge, 1938. The best guide to the Sessional papers.

63. Terry, G. Sanford. *An index to the papers relating to Scotland described or calendared in the Historical MSS Commission's reports.* London, 1908.

64. Thomas, F. S. *A history of the State Paper Office with a view of the documents therein deposited.* London, 1849.

65. *Notes of materials for the history of the public departments.* London, 1846.

66. Upton, Eleanor S., and Winship, George P. *Guide to sources of English history from 1603–1660 in reports of the Royal Commission on Historical Manuscripts.* Washington, 1952.

67. *Union list of microfilms.* Ann Arbor, 1951, revised. Lists of documents that have been microfilmed for the British Manuscripts Project; they include documents in the British Museum, Public Record Office, Cambridge University Library, Bodleian Library, Library of Congress, and certain private archives.

7   ITALY[1]

Mary Lucille Shay
University of Illinois

THE number and various locations of Italy's diplomatic archives are explained by its history. With the exception of Rome, they are found in the *Archivio di Stato* in the capital of each state that was independent before 1861. Diplomatic papers after the union are in the *Archivio storico* of the ministry of foreign affairs in Rome.

ARCHIVIO DI STATO IN TURIN[2]

HISTORY

In the eighteenth century the reports of the ambassadors of the House of Savoy won the praise of Lord Chesterfield in a letter to his son and of Marco Foscarini in his report to the Venetian senate. They were also acclaimed by two Frenchmen, Jules Flammermont and Charles Victor Langlois, in the nineteenth century, and in the twentieth by the American historian, Carl Russell Fish. Some of the documents are from the twelfth century, but the greater number pertain to the period after 1553, when the practice of sending ambassadors became regular.

As early as 1351 Amadeus VI forbade entrance to the

---

[1]The writing of this chapter would have been impossible without the assistance of Count Gian Carlo Buraggi, retired director of the archives in Turin; the staffs of the archives in Turin, Florence, Naples, Rome, and Venice; and the staffs of the libraries in Turin, Florence, Rome, and Venice. Their unfailing courtesy and invaluable assistance merit only the highest praise.

[2]The earlier names were *Archivi di Corte*, prior to 1848, and *Archivi del Regno*, 1848–61.

archives without his permission. In 1549 Charles III provided for the inspection of an official's residence, after his death, in order to prevent state papers from remaining in private collections. Both of these regulations were repeated by Victor Amadeus II in 1717 and 1720. His son and successor continued this interest in a striking way. Within six months after his accession, Charles Emmanuel III asked Philip Iuvara to submit plans for an archives building. Three years later, in 1734, it was completed and the documents were moved. It is unique in Italy inasmuch as all the other state archives are housed in buildings that were originally used for other purposes. With the exception of the years 1804-14 and during a portion of the 1940's, the papers that were transferred in 1734 have remained there until today, and also most of the subsequent papers to 1861.

In 1742 Charles Emmanuel III issued regulations regarding diplomatic papers. Ambassadors had to take an oath to give all their papers to the secretary for foreign affairs within a month after their return, that is, all copies of their letters written to the court and the original letters received from the court. Also, within the month returning ambassadors were to submit reports of their missions. This was not an entirely new idea. A number of diplomats from the time of Charles Emmanuel I had prepared reports, but this part of the 1742 regulation was not always followed. After three years all such papers were transferred from the ministry to the archives unless the papers pertained to unfinished business.

To such supervision can be attributed the rarity of gaps in these records. According to Nicomede Bianchi, director of the archives from 1870 to 1886, the regulations were closely followed until 1797, but were not as carefully adhered to after 1815. Both the practice after the latter date and the unification of Italy affected the archives. In 1856 the rule was made that papers pertaining to ordinary matters must be transferred to the archives after five years, and papers pertaining to diplomatic questions after ten years. This regulation meant that with the changing of the seat of government to Florence in 1865 and to Rome in 1871 some of the papers were also moved. Some were returned to Turin after 1871, but not all. There is, therefore, a close relation between the archives in Turin and the archives of the ministry of foreign affairs in Rome for the years 1815–61. It would be advisable to work first in Turin and then in Rome. The inventories that have been published by the ministry of foreign affairs are available in the Turin archives; thus a comparison of papers that duplicate or supplement one another may be easily made (see the section *Archivo Storico*).

CLASSIFICATION AND ARRANGEMENT

The diplomatic papers have been classified as *Materie politiche relative all'Estero*, with four subdivisions. The two most important subdivisions are *Lettere Ministri* (not *Lettere estere* as in Fish) and *Negoziazioni*. The *Lettere Ministri* are the ambassadors' original letters and the originals or copies of the court's replies, which are filed chronologically for each country in packets numbered consecutively. The length of the letters determines the separation into packets. Generally half of a packet consists of the ambassadors' letters for six months or a year, and the second half the court's replies, which include one from the sovereign and one from the secretary for foreign affairs. This subdivision contains very few enclosures sent by the envoys. If there are any missing letters, the copies in letter books, called *registri*, may be consulted. While these copies indicate what was put in cipher in the original, they do not indicate which letters were written by the ambassador and which by his secretary, as the originals do.

A newly appointed ambassador received official instructions, letters to the sovereign and other members of the court to which he was accredited, and other papers. Copies of some were kept in Turin, and all were listed. When Count Francis Joseph de Viry went to Holland in 1750, he took seventeen such items. Upon the return of an ambassador he usually submitted a report or *relazione*. All these instructions, copies of letters, lists, and reports are filed together, according to countries, in the subdivision *Negoziazioni*. If the instructions for only one ambassador are read, too narrow a view may be the result. What was old in the instructions may be found by comparing them with those to his predecessor. What was new may be identified by the report of his predecessor.

Some of the enclosures sent by ambassadors were kept with their letters. Those that concerned the internal affairs of the foreign court were filed in a third subdivision, *Corti straniere* (called *Corti estere* in Nicomede Bianchi's books). For example, ambassadors in London sent pamphlets, parliamentary journals, reports of the national debt, copies of treaties, or correspondence with a third state. Such enclosures are by no means uniform or complete, and they are not always endorsed but they should not be neglected. Another subdivision is that of *Trattati nazionali ed esteri*, which is less important because of the printed edition of treaties.

The majority of the papers are logically filed. There are, however, a few special warnings. Some papers in *Negoziazioni* may be in a packet of miscellaneous items, generally the last one in a series. There may be supplementary papers in *Negoziazioni* and *Corti straniere*, which are called simply addition or first addition, second addition, final addition. Also some packets may have two series of numbers.

There are many handwritten inventories. Those most important for diplomatic affairs are as follows: For the first subdivision, one should consult Number 151, *Indice del Carteggio diplomatico, Lettere Ministri*. This inventory consists of five parts, of which only the first two are valuable. The first lists for each foreign state the ambassadors' dispatches from the early sixteenth century to 1814, the court's replies, and packet numbers. The second part contains similar information for 1814–61.

There are several inventories for the subdivision *Negoziazioni;* for example, Number 94, *Inventario delle Negoziazioni con Inghilterra e Ollanda—Materie politiche.* For England, this inventory lists the items for 1281, 1554, 1603, etc., to 1794, with a brief summary that indicates the contents of each. Another inventory that supplements the preceding group is Number 165, *Carte politiche diverse, 1713–1860.* For the third subdivision there are two parts in Number 100, *Inventario delle Scritture relative alle Corti straniere* and *Inventario d'Addizione delle Scritture relative alle Corti straniere.*

There are other divisions in the archives that do not belong to foreign affairs but should be consulted. For example, the collection *Lettere particolari* contains letters written unofficially. There is a three-volume handwritten index of these letters. If a study of Prospero Balbo's missions is being made, the *Archivio Balbo*, given to the *Archivio di Stato*, should be examined.[3] For a study of any phase of diplomacy during the unification, the *Museo del Risorgimento* in Palazzo Carignano will at least be of interest and perhaps its archives of importance.

The best printed guide is Nicomede Bianchi, *Le Materie politiche relative all' Estero degli Archivi di Stato piemontesi.* Published during his long term from 1870 to 1886 as director of the archives, it was based on the inventories. To simplify, however, Bianchi sometimes used inclusive dates and did not give all the information that the inventories do. For Portugal, he gave the inclusive dates 1825–61, while Inventory Number 151 indicates the breaking off of relations between 1829 and 1842. He also listed ambassadors' letters separately from the court's replies, but they are filed together. There are omissions in his lists, such as the important correspondence of Count Viry from London, 1755–63, and of Count Marmora from Paris, 1765–73. Users must be on guard against his inconsistencies in spelling names, use of incorrect titles, and errors in dates. In several respects it is out of date. In case of gaps in the original correspondence he

[3]Such special collections are listed in number 10 in bibliography.

called attention to the possibility of the use of copies in Italian legations. That was good advice when he was writing. Since then the archives of legations have been sent to Rome and now are in the *Archivio storico* of the ministry of foreign affairs. Since the publication of his guide, some documents have been returned from Rome to Turin. Even with such qualifications the book is of great assistance because it can and should be used in preparation for research in Turin, or it can be consulted in the *Biblioteca Nazionale* after the archives are closed.

ADMINISTRATION, REGULATIONS, AND SUGGESTIONS

Certain general comments might be made about all the state archives except the *Archivio storico* in Rome. In the archives of the old states there are no restrictions regarding the examination of papers after the permission of each director has been granted. Each summer the archives and libraries are closed for two weeks and some libraries for a longer period. For a most profitable period of research, especially if the sojourn must be a short one in the summer, it is advisable to write for information, using air mail and international reply coupons to hasten the correspondence.

There is a library connected with the archives in each city, but the shortness of the hours makes it generally more practical to use books in the *Biblioteca Nazionale* and other libraries. If the sojourn must be a short one, a person would make more profitable use of his time by arranging for demipension, thereby enabling him to use all the five hours in the archives and, after lunch in a restaurant, to spend the remaining afternoon hours in the library.

In each city that was an important capital before 1861 the chief library is classified as the *Biblioteca Nazionale*, and one was established in Rome after 1871. Those of Florence and Rome have the word *centrale* added. According to law these two libraries receive copies of all books published and a third copy is given to the *Biblioteca Nazionale* of the province to which its subject matter applies.[4]

The following holidays are observed by all the archives and libraries of Italy: January 1 and 6, March 19, May 1, June 29, August 15, November 1 and 4, December 8 and 25, as well as the movable feasts of Ascension Thursday and Corpus Domini.

For assistance regarding residence in all parts of the country, the latest edition of *Annuario Alberghi d'Italia* may be purchased. This book lists hotels and pensions with several items of information. It is most advisable to reserve rooms in advance, especially in the summer.

As for Turin, the person in charge of the archives is Dr. Gaetano Garretti di Ferrere, Director, *Archivio di Stato*, Piazza Castello 205.[5] A letter of introduction from the president of one's university to the director is the proper procedure for admission. The director's office and the reading room are on the fifth floor. There are very few regulations. A printed form is presented for a brief description of the research. Packets are stored temporarily overnight in the cupboards in the reading room until a reader has finished them. The hours are from 9 to 2 week days, except on holidays and during the annual closing. Microfilming is permitted, and a professional photographer in the archives will do the filming.

The *Biblioteca Nazionale* is located at Via Po 19, on the top floor. A letter of introduction will admit a reader. The hours are from 9 to 12 and 2 to 5 week days, except Saturday afternoon, holidays, and its annual closing.

There is also an American Library of Information at Piazza San Carlo 197.

Pensions located in Piazza Castello or Via Pietro Micca are most convenient for the archives and libraries. For a winter sojourn in Turin, a room with a southern exposure should be requested. The best time of the year is from April to November.

[4]The *Biblioteca Nazionale* in Turin and the *Biblioteca Palatina* in Parma suffered losses from bombardment in World War II.

[5]The other numbers found in books are out of date.

ARCHIVO STORICO DEL MINISTERO DEGLI AFFARI ESTERI IN ROME[6]

HISTORY

The *Archivio storico* is less than a hundred years old. The Kingdom of Sardinia had served as the nucleus for the unification of Italy and some of its archival practices were adopted. According to the regulation of 1856, diplomatic papers were retained for ten years in the office of the secretary for foreign affairs. It was natural and even necessary that this practice be continued in the new kingdom. With the transferring of the capital to Florence in 1865 and to Rome in 1871, papers that belonged to the ten years preceding 1861 were moved. Some of these were returned to Turin, but not all. Other groups of documents pertaining to the Kingdom of Sardinia are the legation archives that were sent to Rome after 1871.

The plans for the centralization of state papers in a national archives in Rome were not followed by the ministry of foreign affairs; the diplomatic papers have remained as a part of the foreign ministry's separate archives as in France and Belgium.

CLASSIFICATION AND ARRANGEMENT

From the preceding paragraphs, it is evident that the papers belong to two different periods: those before 1861, which supplement the archives in Turin and those after 1861, which are the diplomatic papers of united Italy.

The legation archives of the Kingdom of Sardinia are an important part of the records before 1861. Even during the eighteenth century there developed the practice of keeping some papers in the legations, and after 1815 the practice became

[6]Hereafter referred to simply as *Archivio storico*. It should not be confused with the *Archivio di Stato* in Rome. The latter contains parts of the archives of the Papal State prior to 1870 and other papers that do not pertain to diplomatic affairs, with the exception of some special collections that are listed on p. 378 of number 10 of bibliography.

common. For the years 1815 to 1861 there are not the same kinds of documents in Turin as for the period preceding 1797. Prior to the latter date the originals of both the ambassadors' letters and the court's replies are found in Turin. After 1815 only the originals of the ambassadors' letters are in Turin; the court's replies are the copies that were preserved by the secretary for foreign affairs and later turned over to the archives. Conversely, the papers that were sent from the legation archives and are in the *Archivio storico* are the copies of the ambassadors' letters and the originals of the court's replies.

The papers that pertain to the Kingdom of Sardinia have been classified and the following inventories published since 1947 by the ministry of foreign affairs in the series *Indici dell' Archivio storico*:

Bacino, Francesco (ed.), *La legazione e i consolati del Regno di Sardegna in Russia (1783–1861)*; *Le legazioni sarde a Parigi, Berna, l'Aja, Lisbona e Madrid*.

Moscati, Ruggero (ed.), *Le scritture della Segreteria di Stato degli Affari esteri del Regno di Sardegna*.

Pastore, Mario (ed.), *La legazione sarda in Londra (1730–1860)*.

Piscitelli, Enzo (ed.), *La legazione sarda in Vienna (1707–1859)*.

Each of these inventories has a valuable introduction, and very helpful biographical and bibliographical notes as well as full calendaring of the documents and the numbering of the packets. These inventories are not for sale and were not found in 1951 in the *Biblioteca Nazionale*. Copies were most graciously presented to the writer of this chapter, who has deposited them in the Illinois Historical Survey of the University of Illinois. The general plan of publication also provides for other inventories of legations in foreign and in Italian states.

There are several other inventories available in typewritten copies, such as *L'Archivio della Divisione politica, 1861–1888*; *Serie dei Trattati, 1861–1914*; *Serie dei Telegrammi, 1861–1943*.

By far the most important documents in the *Archivio storico* are the diplomatic papers of united Italy. According to the law of December 1939 only the papers prior to 1870 are open to research. There is under way, however, a great project to publish a number of the diplomatic documents for the period 1861–1943 that will provide numerous sources for research. A ministerial decree of September 20, 1946 established the "Commission for the Publication of Diplomatic Documents." The members were: President, Senator Alessandro Casati; vice-president, Professor Mario Toscano, consulting historian of the ministry; secretary, Professor Ruggero Moscati, consulting archivist of the ministry; Professors Federico Chabod, Walter Maturi, Carlo Morandi, Rodolfo Mosca, Giacomo Perticone, Luigi Salvatorelli, Augusto Torre; The Honorable Maurilio Coppini, Envoy Extraordinary and Minister Plenipotentiary; His Excellency, Augusto Rosso, Ambassador.

There will be about one hundred volumes, which will contain papers from private and the royal archives as well as from the *Archivio storico*. According to the first plan, the papers were to be published in eight series, but that was changed to nine according to the following subdivisions: 1. 1861–70, edited by Walter Maturi; 2. 1870–96, Federico Chabod; 3. 1896–1907, Carlo Morandi and Giacomo Perticone; 4. 1908–14 and 5. 1914–18, Augusto Torre; 6. 1918–22, Rodolfo Mosca; 7. 1922–35, Ruggero Moscati; 8. 1935–39 and 9. 1939–43, Mario Toscano.

Eight volumes of this collection have been published (see bibliography of the documents of Rome).

ADMINISTRATION, REGULATIONS, AND SUGGESTIONS

Permission to work in these archives must be received from Dr. Renato Mori, Director, *Archivio storico del Ministero degli Affari esteri*, Piazza dei Crociferi 54. It is most advisable to request permission well in advance, and applicants from across the seas are advised to apply by air mail several weeks before arrival in Rome. The office of the director is on the second floor. The hours are from 9 to 1 on week days. There is no annual closing, but the usual national and religious holidays are observed.

Within a five-minute walk from the *Archivio storico* is the *Biblioteca Nazionale Centrale Vittorio Emanuele II*, on Via del Collegio Romano, which runs parallel with Via del Corso. The procedures for using the library are involved. The custodian will direct a person to the office on the second floor where the permission is granted. A foreigner must show his passport in order to be granted a reader's card; the latter must be presented each day when the reader signs the register. Call slips for books are obtainable and must be left in the *Sala riservata*, to the left of the custodian's desk, after they have been filled out from the card catalogue to the right of the custodian's desk. The hours are from 9 to 7 on week days except the first fifteen days of August and on the usual holidays. It is also advisable that a reader have a letter of introduction to his cultural attaché in case other collections in Rome must be consulted or any advice is needed. Americans will find the United States Library of Information on Via Vittorio Veneto a most useful place for reading such journals as *The American historical review*.

The most convenient section for residence in relation to the archives and both libraries is that bounded by the lower Via Venti Settembre and Via del Tritone.

These comments are supplemented by the general information given in the section on the Turin archives.

ARCHIVIO DI STATO IN VENICE

HISTORY

Of all the documents regarding Italian diplomacy those in Venice are the most famous. The reason for that is the primacy of the Republic of Venice in establishing diplomatic relations and in maintaining them for the longest period. As early as 1268 the Republic made a law that required each ambassador upon returning from a mission to make a report. Another law in 1296 pertained to this practice. At first the report was not written; then in 1425 a law required that the report be written, and another law in 1533 repeated this stipulation. From these laws of 1425 and 1533 the renowned reports or *relazioni* of Venice have resulted.

An account of these archives may be divided into three periods: before 1797, 1797 to 1815, and after 1815. Despite an effort to maintain secrecy during the first period, copies of a number of the reports were made and may be found in various cities of Europe. There are many variations in some copies. In some Venetian collections there are two drafts; perhaps this may explain how some variations occurred. Rawdon Brown thought such differences might have come from the summaries made by senators after hearing a report. Once a copy was made for a collector, it is self-evident that others might be made from it. Second- and thirdhand copies may account for other variations.

The end of the Republic of Venice in 1797 introduced a transitional period, 1797 to 1815, when parts of the archives— the ambassadors' letters from the middle of the sixteenth century to 1797—were taken to Paris, and the official calendars of these dispatches to Vienna. Some documents were also destroyed by the mobs. It was during this period that some of the nobles sold their libraries. An example was that of the purchase of the great Marco Foscarini collection by the Austrian government in 1799. The documents were removed from the doge's palace and housed in three depositories.

Then in 1815 an imperial decree from Vienna provided for a union of all the documents. After 1822 they were housed in the secularized monastery that adjoins the church of *Santa Maria Gloriosa dei Frari*. A popular name for the archives is the *Frari*. In 1866 many papers were taken by governmental order to Vienna, but all these, as well as those that had been taken earlier (and also those taken to Paris), were returned.

The years between 1822 and about 1870 were busy ones for the archivists—the arrangement of the hundreds of files in the two hundred and ninety-eight rooms and corridors of the *Frari*. There was nothing that resembled a catalogue until 1847. It was not until after 1851 that the minutes of the letters sent from Venice to the ambassadors were found and made available and not until after 1868 that the foreign correspondence of the council of ten was arranged.

Moreover, the veil of secrecy was not lifted immediately and completely. It was from foreign and other Italian states that the fame of the Venetian reports burst forth again as it had in the sixteenth century. Ranke is justly accredited with this rebirth, but it is interesting that simultaneously with his research in Berlin, 1825–27, William Roscoe praised the Venetian reports in the collection of the Earl of Leicester at Holkham Hall. Before Ranke published anything from his research in Italy, 1828–31, Luigi Cibrario published three reports in Turin. As a matter of fact, Ranke's first request to examine the reports in the *Frari* was refused, but he was granted permission in 1829 upon his second request. The 1830's were most important in making reports accessible. Soon after Ranke's publication of *Die römischen Päpste* (1834–36), Niccolò Tommaseo published several reports of the sixteenth century about France, and Eugenio Albèri published his first two volumes of reports.[7] Both Tommaseo and Albèri used copies that were available from other collections and not from the archives in Venice. It is very probable that Albèri would not have been allowed to use the *Frari* manuscripts in the first years of his publishing. With the exception of the collation of one copy with the manuscript in the *Frari* in 1846, Albèri published nothing from the Venetian archives until 1855, using them in the last seven volumes in his series of fifteen. The censor had refused permission to the Venetian scholar, Emmanuele Antonio Cicogna, to publish a report, and in 1852 the censor ordered him to make many

[7]Number 52 and number 68 in bibliography.

changes in another before publication. In 1854 Rawdon Brown alluded to restrictions for some of the papers. The archives of the Venetian Republic have been open for unrestricted research for about a century.

CLASSIFICATION AND ARRANGEMENT

It is almost axiomatic that archives reflect the government of their state. Everyone who has done extensive research in the Venetian archives has stressed the necessity of knowing the relationship between the parts of the government and the subdivisions in the archives. The great council had very little to do with foreign affairs; therefore its papers are unimportant for studies in diplomacy.

The diplomatic papers are found in the archives of the college, the senate, the council of ten, and the inquisitors of state. The college prepared the basic or formal instructions (*Commissioni*) for ambassadors, received letters from sovereigns (*Lettere Principi*), and admitted foreign ambassadors to audiences. After 1541 the records of these audiences were called *Esposizioni Principi* for all states except the papacy, which had its own subdivision, *Esposizioni Roma*. Prior to 1541 such records were filed under different headings, such as ambassadors, orators, France.

The archives of the senate contain its deliberations, the dispatches from ambassadors, and their reports. The deliberations were divided as *Misti*, 1293–1440; *Secreti*, 1401 (*sic*)–1630; and *Corti*, 1630–1797. A student's research is simplified if he is studying the last period, when foreign affairs were separated from domestic under the terms *Corti* and *Rettori* respectively. In the earlier periods, a student must examine all papers to find those that are diplomatic. In the period of the *Misti*, the deliberations have been lost for 1293–1331, but an index of them remains. In these deliberations are found the replies to ambassadors abroad or instructions supplementing the formal instructions. Inasmuch as there are very few dispatches and reports in the archives for the years prior to 1554, the deliberations of the senate may supply the necessary information.

After the invasion of Charles VIII the council of ten became important in foreign affairs, and its papers may also help to fill the gaps between 1494 and 1554 in the dispatches to the senate. After 1579 the inquisitors of state took an active part in foreign affairs. Letters to and from ambassadors abroad are in the separate archives of the council of ten and the inquisitors.

There are handwritten inventories in the archives, such as Number 254/II, *"Dispacci degli Ambasciatori veneti al Senato"*; and Number 174/II, *"Relazioni."*[8] The inventory of the dispatches lists the ambassadors sent to each state from the early sixteenth century to 1797 and has helpful comments. The inventory of the reports is arranged similarly. The comments indicate whether the reports are still unedited or have been published. So recent a note as "destroyed at Naples, 30 September, 1943" reflects an unexpected effect of war (see the history of the state archives in Naples).

None of the inventories has been exactly reproduced in the printed lists or catalogues. The most valuable of these publications is that by Andrea da Mosto, *L'Archivio di Stato di Venezia.* It would have been more useful if it had included the names of ambassadors. It gives, however, the beginning and ending dates or single dates when the latter are necessary, for all the papers named in the preceding paragraphs, and accordingly any gaps are readily seen.

Two other publications contain a quantity of information about these records. Before going to Venice, a beginner should read the book, *Les archives de Venise*, by Armand Baschet, and the preface by Rawdon Brown in the first volume of the *Calendar of state papers and manuscripts, relating to English affairs, existing in the archives and collections of Venice, and in other libraries of northern*

---

[8]The roman numeral II refers to the Republic prior to 1797 and I on other inventories to the governments after 1797.

Italy.[9] If the dispatches, reports, and other papers escaped fires and other mishaps prior to 1822, the research task is comparatively easy. If there are gaps in the material needed, one may benefit from the great amount of work and invaluable advice left by these veteran scholars. For the gaps between 1496 and 1533 the Sanuto diaries are most helpful.[10] Other gaps may be filled by letterbooks of ambassadors and copies of reports in the *Biblioteca Nazionale Marciana* and Correr Museum. Even if the originals are in the *Frari*, sometimes they are illegible because of dampness; then the letterbooks are of great assistance. With the donation of family collections to these two libraries, some private correspondence and enclosures in the letterbooks appeared that are not found in the archives. If relations were broken between Venice and any state, the investigator should search the dispatches from the nearest state, such as those from France about England or from Milan about Turin. One of the comments written in Inventory Number 254 under France

[9]This preface has been translated and published in Venice (see number 74 in bibliography). The prefaces to the other volumes (37 to date) in the *Calendar* are also important. They consist of two parts: information about the papers in the *Frari* that were used for each volume and a summary of the period covered in that volume. Of the two hundred and eleven volumes of transcripts from the Venetian archives in the Public Record Office in London (in 1923), one hundred and twenty-nine were made by Brown. See the Deputy Keeper's 45th Report, *Parliamentary papers* (London: Eyre and Spottiswoode, 1885), XL (1884–85), appendix II, number 2. See also "Venetian manuscripts: Catalogue of, bequeathed to the Public Record Office by the late Rawdon Brown, Esq., of Venice," the Deputy Keeper's 46th Report, *ibid.* (1886), XXXVII, appendix II, number 3. Regarding the purchase of some of these manuscripts, see Edward Cheney, "Despatches of Venetian ambassadors from the court of Louis XIII during the years 1618–38," *Miscellanies of the Philobiblon Society*, XVII (1863–64), number 2. A similar collection made by Ranke is described in *The Leopold von Ranke manuscripts of Syracuse University* (Syracuse: University Press, 1951).

[10]To appreciate that tireless Venetian's records, one look at the fifty-eight (in thirty-five) large printed volumes will be a starting point. Two more impressive facts about him are that he had the permission of the council of ten to use government papers, and upon his death the council took his diaries into its archives. After the end of the Republic, the original manuscript volumes were temporarily in the Marciana Library, where a careful copy of them was made. This copy was bequeathed to the Marciana and was its property from 1817 to 1868. In 1805 the original was taken to Vienna and kept until 1868; then it was exchanged for the copy in the Marciana.

states that packets "114–118 contain letters from England of Lorenzo Paolucci." This example illustrates the advisability of using the dispatches of a nearby state. It pertains to the news letters or *avvisi* that were evaluated by Baschet and Brown. As the former so aptly observed, a dispatch from Paris might be no more interesting about France than one written from another capital but which gave information about France.

In some respects Baschet, Brown, and Albèri are out of date. Their references to Sanuto's diaries are to the manuscript copy or the original inasmuch as the diaries were not published until 1879–1903. Some of their references to the great private collections in the nineteenth century might be misleading. Today those collections are mainly in the Correr Museum and the *Biblioteca Nazionale Marciana*. The nineteenth-century writers did not mention the Querini-Stampalia collection, which is now a third library to be consulted, especially for the papers of some eighteenth-century ambassadors.[11]

[11]Although credit and praise must indeed be given to Albèri for his editing, a wrong impression may come from certain comments about his work. In 1877 Baschet reported that Albèri had published the complete reports of the sixteenth century. As late as 1911 Theodore F. Jones made a similar statement and added that it was no longer necessary to go to Venice to read the reports as Ranke had done. Ranke had shown in his books published between 1824 and 1836, that he did not find all the reports in Venice. The *Archivio di Stato* does not possess originals or complete copies of every report. In that respect one of Ranke's experiences was most interesting. He found in the archives an incomplete copy of Giovanni Gritti's report about Rome. When he found another copy in the Ambrosian Library, he read it eagerly, but to his disappointment this copy contained no more than the other. These two copies were evidently only the first four pages published by Albèri, whose copy from the Manin collection provided twelve more pages. Another example of the gaps at the *Frari* is shown by comparing the sixteen reports there as listed by Andrea da Mosto for Constantinople and the thirty-two (not counting the summaries from Sanuto's diaries) published by Albèri. The incompleteness of Albèri may be seen by using the references in the bibliography under Andreas, Brown, Cérésole, Fulin, Mosto, and Segarizzi. An example of incompleteness, actually known by Albèri, is found in the report of 1590 about the Ottoman Empire. A comparison of the report published by him with a contemporary manuscript copy in the Hiersemann collection at the University of Illinois reveals that Albèri's fifty-five pages contain the same as twenty-six folios of the Hiersemann manuscript. On folio 53 is the note "to here Albèri published." There are eleven additional folios, a sizeable difference. The seventeenth-century reports as published by Barozzi and Berchet have been corrected by Hinds, who was one of Rawdon Brown's successors in editing *Calendar of state papers and manuscripts.*

ADMINISTRATION, REGULATIONS, AND SUGGESTIONS

The person in charge is Dr. Raimondo Morozzo della Rocca, Director-in-Chief, *Archivio di Stato*, 3002 Campo dei Frari. A reader's passport must be shown in order to obtain permission to use the archives. The director's office and reading room are on the second floor. A reader must sign the register each day when he leaves. The hours are from 8:30 to 1:30 week days except on holidays and during the annual closing. The permission of the director must be obtained for microfilming.

The following libraries contain unpublished and published manuscripts that supplement those in the archives: the *Biblioteca Nazionale Marciana* (often called St. Mark's Library by English writers), Piazzetta San Marco 3, with hours varying according to seasons; the Correr Museum, Piazza San Marco 52, open from 9 to 12 and 2 to 5; and the *Biblioteca Querini-Stampalia*, San Zaccaria 4778, with hours from 3 to 11.

The most convenient section of the city in relation to the archives is the right bank of the Grand Canal if one is coming from the railway station, while the three libraries are located beyond the opposite bank. Perhaps in no other city in Italy is it so necessary to reserve a room in advance during the summer season (June through September).

These suggestions supplement those of a general nature given in the discussion of the Turin documents.

ARCHIVIO DI STATO IN FLORENCE

HISTORY

In 1852 Archduke Leopold II appointed a commission to plan the union or centralization of the separate archives. The report of the commission was accepted, and a portion of the Palazzo Uffizi was selected as the depository. Three years later, the archives were opened. After 1859 the papers of the House of Lorraine were added.

CLASSIFICATION AND ARRANGEMENT

The papers have been grouped according to the different governments: under the Medici, 1373–1737, and under the House of Lorraine, 1737–1801, 1814–59. One of the special collections is a part of the ducal archives of Urbino, which contains diplomatic correspondence. Two other great collections are the Strozzi and Torrigiani papers.

The handwritten inventory for the Archivio Mediceo is being replaced by an excellent guide, three volumes of which have been published: *Archivio Mediceo avanti il Principato* and *Archivio Mediceo del Principato*. Only two volumes of the *Archivio Mediceo avanti il Principato* have appeared. (When completed, there will be two other volumes and one of indexes.) Scattered through these papers are letters from and to the ambassadors in other capitals. Diplomatic relations became more regular in the sixteenth century, as is shown in the *Archivio Mediceo del Principato*.[12]

ADMINISTRATION, REGULATIONS, AND SUGGESTIONS

The person in charge is Dr. Sergio Camerani, Director, *Archivio di Stato*. A letter of introduction to the director is the procedure for obtaining permission to use the collection, and foreigners must show their passports. The entrance to the archives is on the Uffizi Lunghi, or Piazzale degli Uffizi, the fourth door from the Arno. The director's office is at the top of the first flight of stairs, and the reading room at the top of the second. The hours are from 8:30 to 1:30 week days except on holidays. There is no annual closing. The permission of the director must be obtained for microfilming. A member of the staff in the reading room will supply the names of photographers who are frequently employed by researchers. According

---

[12]Professor Panella's warning, *Archivio Mediceo del Principato* (Rome: Tipografica fiorentina, 1951), p.31, should be heeded: diplomatic papers will be found in other subdivisions—*Carteggio universale, Carteggio dei segretari, Viaggi* as well as in the obvious sections, *Istruzioni ad ambasciatori, Relazioni con stati italiani ed esteri.*

to regulations, a duplicate set of microfilms must be left at the archives.

The *Biblioteca Nazionale Centrale*, Piazza dei Cavalleggeri 1, is open from 9 to 1 and 2 to 6 on week days and 9 to 1 on Saturday, except on holidays and during the annual closing, which usually is the month of August. A general letter of introduction will admit a reader. The library has two special regulations: everything must be left in the coat room; in the reading room certain tables are reserved for men and others for women.[13]

Another important library is the *Gabinetto G. P. Vieusseux* in Palazzo Strozzi, Via Tornabuoni. Its hours are from 9 to 1 and 3 to 7 in the summer. There is also a United States Library of Information at Via Tornabuoni 2.

The most convenient area in which to live, in relation to the archives and the two Florentine libraries, is that bounded by the Lungarno Acciaioli, Lungarno Generale Diaz, and Via Tornabuoni.

Additional information may be found in the general comments made in the Turin section of this chapter.

ARCHIVIO DI STATO IN NAPLES

HISTORY

Several decrees of Murat provided for a union of all records in Castel Capuano, but it was not large enough to house them all. In 1835 the former abbey of Saints Severino and Sossio was selected as the depository.

An important collection consisted of the Farnesian archives, which had an unusual history. Originally they were in Parma, where Ranuccio I had established the archives in 1592. Between 1621 and 1725, papers were brought to Parma from the Farnese Palace in Rome and from other family possessions. In 1734 Don

---

[13]In books of the early nineteenth century, the references were to the separate libraries, the *Magliabechiana* and the *Palatina*, which today are united in the *Biblioteca Nazionale Centrale*.

Charles ordered that the papers be moved to Naples. Not all, however, were sent. After he had succeeded to the Spanish throne, some of the papers were returned to Parma, but the greater part remained in Naples. When Louis Prosper Gachard, the Belgian archivist, went to Naples in 1868, he had some difficulty in finding this collection. It had lain almost forgotten in the Royal Palace. The collection was moved to the archives building in 1868, where it was arranged and inventoried by the close of the century.

In 1943 the archives were moved for safekeeping to Villa Montesano, near Nola, where, nevertheless, large sections were burned by the Germans on September 30, 1943. Among the papers were documents that had been lent by other archives for an exhibition and upon the outbreak of war had been transferred to the *Archivio di Stato*. This destruction explains the note in Inventory Number 174 in Venice.

CLASSIFICATION AND ARRANGEMENT

Before 1943 the diplomatic papers belonged to two groups: those of the Bourbon kings from 1734 to 1860 and those of the Farnese rulers before 1731. Useful information about the Bourbon records could be gained from such prewar scholars as Fish and Flammermont, or from the report by the director, Francesco Trinchera, *Degli Archivi napolitani*. The destruction in 1943, however, makes it necessary to qualify some of their statements. In 1911 Alfred Cauchie and Léon van der Essen published the excellent *Inventaire des archives farnésiennes de Naples au point de vue de l'histoire des Pays-Bas catholiques*. Parts will be of assistance for those papers that escaped destruction.

ADMINISTRATION, REGULATIONS, AND SUGGESTION

The person in charge is Dr. Iole Mezzoleni, Director, *Archivio di Stato*. A letter of introduction is the procedure for admission. The *Archivio di Stato* is on Via Grande Archivio, which was formerly Vico S. Severino. The office of the inspector and the reading room are on the second floor. The hours are from 8:30 to 1:30 week days except on holidays and during the annual closing. The permission of the inspector must be obtained for microfilming. She or other members of the staff will supply the name of a photographer.

The *Biblioteca Nazionale*, located in the Palazzo Reale, is the chief library.

The residential section most convenient to the archives is that between Via Roma and Corso Garibaldi or on Corso Umberto I.

This information may be supplemented by the general comments given in the discussion of the documents in Turin. Again, researchers are advised to write for precise information on dates of the annual closing, etc.

ARCHIVI DI STATO IN PARMA, GENOA, LUCCA, AND MODENA[14]

Between 1734 and 1943 the Farnese papers were divided between the archives in Naples and Parma, as explained in the preceding section. Today a very small part of the Farnese archives remains in Naples, having escaped destruction in 1943. The archives in Parma contain some of the diplomatic papers for the Farnese period, 1545–1731, the correspondence of ambassadors with secretaries of state and foreign affairs under the Bourbons, 1749–1802, under Marie Louise, 1814–47, and again under the Bourbons, 1847–59.

There are similarities between the diplomatic papers of these less publicized and the more important Italian states. In the archives of Genoa, Lucca, and Modena there are some early documents, but diplomatic relations were more regular during the sixteenth and succeeding centuries and the records have survived better. Dispatches from representatives of Genoa abroad date from 1506 to 1805; of Lucca, 1369 to 1799 and

[14]These archives were not visited by the author.

1815 to 1847; and of Modena, 1265 to 1796 and 1814 to 1859. In the early history of Genoa and Lucca there were officials who looked after the boundaries, and some of their records resemble those of a secretary of foreign affairs. In Modena there is a collection of news letters or *avvisi* from 1393 to the eighteenth century.

For Parma and Lucca there are excellent guides, which are listed in the bibliography.

The persons in charge of these four archives are:

Dr. Ettore Falconi, Director, *Archivio di Stato*, Via Massimo D'Azeglio 45, Parma.

Dr. Giorgio Costamagna, Director, *Archivio di Stato*, Via Tommaso Reggio 14, Genoa.

Dr. Domenico Corsi, Director, *Archivio di Stato*, Palazzo Guidiccioni, Lucca.

Dr. Giovanni Battista Pascussi, Director, *Archivio di Stato*, Corso Cavour 21, Modena.[15]

General information and suggestions are given in the first section of the chapter.

BIBLIOGRAPHY

Certain journals often print documents or are most useful in obtaining information that is not included in inventories. *Archivio storico italiano*, *Miscellanea di storia italiana*, *Rassegna storica del Risorgimento*, and *Rivista storica italiana* are more national in scope than the *Atti* and *Memorie della Reale Accademia delle Scienze di Torino*, *Archivio veneto*, or *Archivio storico per le Province napoletane*. The journals can be more effectively used through the indexes or through bibliographies such as:

1. *Archivio storico italiano, indice 1842–1941*. 3 vols. Florence: L. S. Olschki, 1945—47.
2. *Archivio storico per le Province napoletane, indice generale*. vols. I–XX, Naples: F. Giannini and Figli, 1897; XXI–XXV, Pierro e Veraldi, 1902; XXVI–XXX, L. Pierro and Figlio, 1908.
3. "Indice generale . . . 1871–1930," *Archivio veneto*, Ser. 5, XXV (1939), 3–269; XXVIII (1941), 1–629.

[15]Both the new number 21 and the old 12 appear on the building.

4. "Indice generale delle prime venticinque annate," *Rassegna storica del Risorgimento*, XXVI, 1 (1939), 11–126.

5. *Indice della Rivista storica italiana dal 1884 al 1901.* 2 vols. Turin: The *Rivista*, 1904.

6. *Il primo secolo della Reale Accademia delle Scienze di Torino, notizie storiche e bibliografiche (1783–1883).* Turin: G. B. Paravia, 1883.

7. *Catalogo metodico degli scritti contenuti nelle pubblicazioni periodiche italiane e straniere, Biblioteca della Camera dei Deputati.* Vol. I, Rome: Camera dei Deputati, 1885; supplements 1–2, 1889, 1890; supplements 3–4, 1895, 1902; supplement 5, 1907; new series, vols. I–II, 1914, 1921; III–IV, 1928, 1935.

8. *Pubblicazioni edite dallo Stato o col suo concorso, spoglio dei periodici e delle opere collettivi, 1901–25.* I, Rome: Libreria dello Stato, 1926; II, 1928; *1926–30.* I–II, 1931.

General Guides to Archives and Libraries

9. Apolloni, Ettore, and Arcamone, Guido (ed.). *Le Biblioteche d'Italia fuori di Roma, storia, classificazione, funzionamento, contenuto, cataloghi, bibliografia. (Bibliothèque des "Annales Institutorum,"* vol. III.) 3 parts. Rome: Biblioteca d'Arte, 1934–38.

10. *Gli Archivi di Stato italiani.* ("Ministero dell' Interno, Ufficio centrale degli Archivi di Stato.") Bologna: N. Zanichelli, 1944. For each archives there is a chapter which gives a history, summaries of documents (part of which consists of diplomatic papers), lists of the private papers, and bibliography. It is a revision of *L'Ordinamento delle carte degli Archivi di Stato italiani, Manuale storico archivistico.* Rome: delle Mantellate, 1910.

11. Camerani, Sergio. "Gli archivi italiani e la Guerra in recenti pubblicazioni," *Archivio storico italiano*, (1945–46), 196–200.

12. Fish, Carl Russell. *Guide to the materials for American history in Roman and other Italian archives.* Washington: Carnegie Institution, 1911.

13. Flammermont, Jules. "Rapport à M. le Ministre de l'Instruction publique sur les correspondances des agents diplomatiques étrangers en France avant la Révolution conservées dans les archives de Berlin, Dresde, Genève, Turin, Gênes, Florence, Naples . . . ," *Nouvelles archives des missions scientifiques et littéraires*, VIII (1896), 307–451.

14. *Guide international des archives, Europe. (Bibliothèque des "Annales Institutorum,"* vol. IV.) 3 parts. Paris: Institut international de Coopération intellectuelle; Rome: Biblioteca d'Arte, 1934. An important item of information; lists of the private papers that have been added to the state archives in the different Italian cities.

15. Langlois, Charles Victor, and Stein, H. *Les archives de l'histoire de France.* (*Manuels de bibliographie historique.*) Paris: A. Picard, 1891.

Turin

Documents

16. Alberti, Mario degli (ed.). *La politica estera del Piemonte sotto Carlo Alberto, secondo il carteggio diplomatico del Conte Vittorio Amadeo Balbo Bertone di Sambuy, Ministro di Sardegna a Vienna (1835–1846).* (*Biblioteca di Storia italiana recente*, vols. V–VII.) 3 vols. Turin: Fratelli Bocca, 1913–19.

17. *Carteggio Cavour—Salmour.* ("R. Commissione Editrice de' Carteggi cavouriani.") Bologna: N. Zanichelli, 1936.

18. *Il carteggio Cavour—Nigra dal 1858 al 1861.* (*Ibid.*) 4 vols. Bologna: N. Zanichelli, 1926–29.

19. *Cavour e l'Inghilterra, Carteggio con V. E. d'Azeglio.* (*Ibid.*) 2 vols. Bologna: N. Zanichelli, 1933.

20. Curato, Federico (ed.). *Le relazioni diplomatiche fra il Regno di Sardegna e la Gran Bretagna.* Third series, 1848–60. (*Fonti per la Storia d'Italia*, vols. XXII–XXIII.) 2 vols. (1848–49). Rome: Istituto storico italiano per l'Età moderna e contemporanea, 1955.

21. *La liberazione del Mezzogiorno e la formazione del Regno d'Italia, carteggi di Camillo Cavour con Villamarina, Scialoja, Cordova, Farini, ecc.* ("Commissione per la Pubblicazione dei Carteggi di Camillo Cavour.") 4 vols. Bologna: N. Zanichelli, 1949–54.

22. *La Questione romana negli anni 1860–1861, carteggio del Conte di Cavour con D. Pantaleoni, C. Passaglia, O. Vimercati.* ("R. Commissione Editrice de'Carteggi cavouriani.") 2 vols. Bologna: N. Zanichelli, 1929.

23. Manno, Antonio; Ferrero, Ermanno; and Vayra, Pietro (eds.). *Relazioni diplomatiche della Monarchia di Savoia dalla prima alla seconda Restaurazione (1559–1814).* (*Biblioteca storica italiana*, vol. IV.) France, 1713–19: 3 parts. Turin: Fratelli Bocca, 1886–91.
   "Nota F.—Conservazione e ritiro delle carte di Stato dai privati e dai pubblici ufficiali usciti di vita o di carica," I, 454–463.

24. Morandi, Carlo (ed.). *Relazioni di ambasciatori sabaudi, genovesi e veneti durante il periodo della Grande Alleanza e della Successione di Spagna (1693–1713).* (*Fonti per la Storia d'Italia*, vol. I.) Bologna: N. Zanichelli, 1935.

25. Solar de la Marguerite (Solaro), Clemente (ed.). *Traités publics de la Royale Maison de Savoie avec les puissances étrangères depuis la Paix de Cateau=Cambrésis jusqu'à nos jours.* 8 vols. Turin: Imprimerie royale, 1836–61.

Guides to the Archives

26. Bianchi, Nicomede. *Le carte degli Archivi piemontesi, politici, amministrativi, giudiziari, finanziari, comunali, ecclesiastici e di enti morali.* Turin: Fratelli Bocca, 1881.

27. *Le materie politiche relative all' estero degli Archivi di Stato piemontesi.* Bologna: N. Zanichelli, 1876.

28. Buraggi, Gian Carlo. "Gli Archivi di Corte e la loro storica Sede," *Atti della Reale Accademia delle Scienze di Torino,* LXXII, 2 (1936–37), 89–104.

29. "Archivisti italiani, Nicomede Bianchi," *Notizie degli Archivi di Stato* ("Ministero dell' Interno"), Anno 2, number 4, ottobre-dicembre, 1942.

30. Segre, Arturo. *Il primo anno del Ministero Vallesa (1814–1815), saggio di politica sarda, interna ed estera nel primo anno della Restaurazione. (Biblioteca di storia italiana recente,* vol. X.) Turin: Fratelli Bocca, 1928.

Rome

Documents

31. *I documenti diplomatici italiani.* ("Ministero degli Affari esteri, Commissione per la Pubblicazione dei Documenti diplomatici.")

31. Maturi, Walter (ed.). Ser. 1, I, 8 gennaio–31 dicembre 1861. Rome: Libreria dello Stato, 1952.

32. Morandi, Carlo, and Perticone, Giacomo (eds.). Ser. 3, I, 10 marzo 1896–30 aprile 1897. Rome: Libreria dello Stato, 1953.

33. Moscati, Ruggero (ed.). Ser. 7, I, 31 ottobre 1922–26 aprile 1923. Rome: Libreria dello Stato, 1953.

34. Ser. 7, II. 27 aprile 1923–22 febbraio 1924. Rome: Libreria dello Stato, 1955.

35. Torre, Augusto (ed.). Ser. 5, I, 2 agosto–16 ottobre 1914. Rome: Libreria dello Stato, 1954.

36. Toscano, Mario (ed.). Ser. 8, XII, 23 maggio–11 agosto 1939. Rome: Libreria dello Stato, 1952.

37. Ser. 8, XIII, 12 agosto–3 settembre 1939. Rome: Libreria dello Stato, 1953.

38. Ser. 9, I, 4 settembre–24 ottobre 1939. Rome: Libreria dello Stato, 1954.

In press

39. Chabod, Federico (ed.). Ser. 2, I, 21 settembre–31 dicembre 1870.

40. Maturi, Walter (ed.). Ser. 1, II, 1 gennaio–31 dicembre 1862.

In preparation

41. Mosca, Rodolfo (ed.). Ser. 6, I, 1918–19.

42. Perticone, Giacomo (ed.). Ser. 3, II, 1897–98.
43. Torre, Augusto (ed.). Ser. 4, last volume, 1914.
Other volumes of this monumental project will follow. See the description of it in the discussion of the archives in Rome.

For "Treaties and Conventions between Italy and other States," 1861–; lists of Green Books, 1861–   ; and other documents which have been published, see part II, "Affari esteri," in *Pubblicazioni edite dallo Stato o col suo concorso (1861–1923)*, *Catalogo generale* (Rome: Libreria dello Stato, 1924; supplemento, 1924–30, e aggiunte . . . , 1931).

Guides to Archivio storico *and Libraries*
44. *Annuario diplomatico del Regno d'Italia, 1937.* Rome: R. Ministero degli Affari esteri, 1937. Biographical sketches of ambassadors. Published for other years: 1865, 1886, 1890, 1902, 1909.
45. Bacino, Francesco (ed.). *La legazione e i consolati del Regno di Sardegna in Russia (1783–1861)*. (*Indici dell' Archivio storico*, vol. V.) Rome: Ministero degli Affari esteri, 1952.
46. *Le legazioni sarde a Parigi, Berna, l'Aja, Lisbona e Madrid.* (*Ibid.*, vol. III.) Rome: Ministero degli Affari esteri, 1951.
47. Brusasca, Giuseppe (ed.). *Il Ministero degli Affari esteri al servizio del popolo italiano (1943–1949)*. 2d ed. rev. Rome: Ministero degli Affari esteri, 1949. Information on the history of the Foreign Office, 1861–1943, and lists of ambassadors and ministers, 1861–1948.
48. *Guide-manuel des bibliothèques de Rome.* (*Bibliothèque des "Annales Institutorum,"* vol. I.) Rome: Biblioteca d'Arte, 1932.
49. Moscati, Ruggero (ed.). *Le scritture della Segreteria di Stato degli Affari esteri del Regno di Sardegna.* (*Indici dell' Archivio storico*, vol. I.) Rome: Ministero degli Affari esteri, 1947.
50. Pastore, Mario (ed.). *La legazione sarda in Londra (1730–1860)*. (*Ibid.*, vol. IV.) Rome: Ministero degli Affari esteri, 1952.
51. Piscitelli, Enzo (ed.). *La legazione sarda in Vienna (1707–1859)*. (*Ibid.*, vol. II.) Rome: Ministero degli Affari esteri, 1950.

Venice
Documents
52. Albèri, Eugenio (ed.). *Relazioni degli ambasciatori veneti al senato durante il secolo decimosesto.* 15 vols. Florence: Societa editrice fiorentina, 1839–63.
53. Barozzi, Nicolò, and Berchet, Guglielmo (ed.). *Relazioni degli stati europei letti al senato dagli ambasciatori veneti nel secolo decimosettimo.* 10 vols. Venice: P. Naratovich, 1856–78.

54. Berchet, Guglielmo (ed.). *Relazioni dei consoli veneti nella Siria.* Turin: G. B. Paravia, 1866.

55. Brown, Rawdon (ed.). *Four years at the court of Henry VIII, selection of despatches written by the Venetian ambassador, Sebastian Giustinian, and addressed to the Signory of Venice, January 12th, 1515, to July 26th, 1519.* 2 vols. London: Smith, Elder & Co., 1854.

56. Brown, Rawdon, Brown, Horatio F., and Hinds, Allen B. (ed.). *Calendar of state papers and manuscripts, relating to English affairs, existing in the archives and collections of Venice, and in other libraries of northern Italy.* 38 vols. (to date). London: Longmans, Green (and other companies), 1864–1947.

57. Cessi, Roberto (ed.). *Dispacci degli ambasciatori veneziani alla corte di Roma presso Giulio II (25 giugno 1509–9 gennaio 1510).* (*Monumenti storici,* Ser. 1, Documenti, vol. XVIII.) Venice: R. Deputazione di Storia Patria per le Venezie, 1932.

58. Cibrario, Luigi (ed.). *Relazioni dello Stato di Savoia negli anni 1574, 1670, 1743; scritte dagli ambasciatori veneti, Molino, Bellegno, e Foscarini.* Turin: Alliana, 1830.

59. Cicogna, Emmanuele A. (ed.). "Dispacci al Senato veneto di Francesco Foscari e di altri oratori presso l'Imperatore Massimiliano I nel 1496," *Archivio storico italiano,* Ser. 1, VII–2 (1844), 721–948, 1089–95.

60. Fulin, Rinaldo; Stefani, Federico; Barozzi, Nicolò; Berchet, Guglielmo; and Allegri, Marco (eds.). *I diarii di Marino Sanuto (1496–1533) dall'autografo marciano italiano CL. VII, Codd. CDXIX–CDLXXVII.* 58 vols. in 35. Venice: F. Visentini, 1879–1903.

61. Lazzarini, Vittorio (ed.). *Dispacci di Pietro Cornaro, Ambasciatore a Milano durante la Guerra di Chioggia.* (*Monumenti storici,* Ser. I, Documenti,* vol. XX.) Venice: R. Deputazione di Storia Patria per le Venezie, 1939.

62. Ljubić, Simeon (ed.). *Commissiones et relationes venetae.* (*Monumenta spectantia historiam slavorum meridionalium,* vols. VI, VIII, XI.) 3 vols. Zagreb: Societatis typographicae, 1876–80.

63. Morandi, *see* above under Turin.

64. Moscati, Ruggero (ed.). *Relazioni degli ambasciatori veneti al senato (Secolo XVIII), Francia.* (*Fonti per la Storia d'Italia,* Vol. XI.) [Rome: Istituto storico italiano per l'Età moderna e contemporanea, 1943.] Milan: Instituto per gli Studi di Politica internazionale, 1943.

65. Pasini, Luigi (ed.). *I dispacci di Giovanni Michiel, Ambasciatore veneto in Inghilterra (1554–1557).* Venice: Grimaldo, 1869.

66. Segarizzi, Arnaldo (ed.). *Relazioni degli ambasciatori veneti al senato.*

(*Scrittori d'Italia*, vols. XXXVI, XLIX, LXXIX, LXXX.) 3 vols. in 4. Bari: G. Laterza and Figli, 1912–16.

67. Sneyd, Charlotte Augusta (ed.). *A relation, or rather a true account, of the Island of England, with sundry particulars of these people and of the royal revenues under King Henry the Seventh, about the year 1500.* ("The Camden Society," vol XXXVII.) London: J. B. Nichols and Son, 1847.

68. Tommaseo, Niccolò (ed.). *Relations des ambassadeurs vénitiens sur les affaires de France au XVIᵉ siècle. (Collection de documents inédits sur l'histoire de France,* Ser. 1.) 2 vols. Paris: Imprimerie royale, 1838.

Articles, Guides and other Books

69. Andreas, Willy. *Staatskunst und Diplomatie der Venezianer im Spiegel ihrer Gesandtenberichte.* Leipzig: Koehler and Amelang, 1943.

70. Antonibon, Francesca. *Le relazioni a stampa di ambasciatori veneti.* (*Opera della bibliografia veneziana, Collana di Bibliografie minori,* vol. I.) Padua: Tipografia del Seminario, 1939. This is a very important bibliography with annotations.

71. Baschet, Armand. *Les archives de Venise, histoire de la Chancellerie secrète, le Sénat, le Cabinet des Ministres, le Conseil des Dix et les Inquisiteurs d'Etat dans leurs rapports avec la France* . . . Paris: H. Plon, 1870.

72. *La diplomatie vénitienne, les princes de l'Europe au XVIᵉ Siècle* . . . *d'après les rapports des ambassadeurs vénitiens.* Paris: H. Plon, 1862.

73. "Mémoire sur le recueil original des déspêches des ambassadeurs vénitiens pendant le XVIᵉ, le XVIIᵉ et le XVIIIᵉ siècle et sur la copie qui en a été entreprise pour être déposée au département des manuscrits de la Bibliothèque Nationale," *Archives des missions scientifiques et littéraires* [France], Ser. 3, IV (1877), 495–524.

74. Brown, Rawdon. *L'Archivio di Venezia con riguardo speciale alla storia inglese. (Nuova collezione di opere storiche,* Vol. IV.) Translated by V. Cérésole and R. Fulin with preface by Count Agostino Sagredo. Venice: Antonelli and Basadonna, 1865.

75. Cadorin, G. "Degli Archivi veneti generali," *Venezia e le sue Lagune,* II, 2, Appendix. Venice: Antonelli, 1847. This summary is of historical interest inasmuch as it was the first printed item concerning the contents of the archives. It was followed by others:

76. Bartolomeo Cecchetti and Francesco Gregolin, *Titoli e note cronologiche degli Archivi dell' ex Repubblica veneta e dei governi successivi* (Venice: P. Naratovich, 1866);

77. *Il R. Archivo Generale di Venezia.* (Venice: P. Naratovich, 1873);

78. Teodoro Toderini, and Bartolomeo Cecchetti, *L'Archivio di Stato in Venezia nel decennio 1866–1875.* (Venice: P. Naratovich, 1876).

79. Cantù, Cesare. *Scorsa di un Lombardo negli Archivi di Venezia.* Milan: G. Civelli, 1856.

80. Cérésole, Victor. *La République de Venise et les Suisses, premier relevé des principaux manuscrits inédits des archives de Venise se rapportant à la Suisse.* Venice: Antonelli, 1864.

81. Foscarini, Marco. *Della letteratura veneziana ed altri scritti intorno ad essa.* Venice: T. Gattei, 1854.

82. Fulin, Rinaldo. "E. A. Cicogna . . . ," *Archivio veneto*, III (1872), 211–240.

83. Gar, Tommaso. "I codici storici della Collezione Foscarini conservata nella Imperiale Biblioteca di Vienna," *Archivio storico italiano*, Ser. 1, V (1843), 281–476.

84. Jones, Theodore F. "The archives of the Venetian Republic," *Annual Report of the American Historical Association for the Year 1911*, I, 71–77.

85. Michel, Ersilio. "La Biblioteca marciana di Venezia," *Rassegna storica del Risorgimento*, XIX, 1 (1932), 793–808.

86. "La Biblioteca del Museo Civico Correr di Venezia," *Ibid.*, XVIII, 1 (1931), 164–192.

87. "La Biblioteca della Fondazione Querini-Stampalia a Venezia," *ibid.*, XXII, 1 (1935), 69–84.

88. Mosto, Andrea da. *L'Archivio di Stato di Venezia, Indice generale, storico, descrittivo ed analitico.* (Bibliothèque des "Annales Institutorum," vol. V.) 2 parts. Rome: Biblioteca d'Arte, 1937–40.

89. Ranke, Leopold von. *Die römischen Päpste in den letzten vier Jahrhunderten.* (*Sämmtliche Werke*, vol. XXXIX.) Leipzig: Duncker & Humblot, 1907.

90. English ed., vol. III. London: G. Bell & Sons, 1913. See also *Französische Geschichte* (*Sämmtliche Werke*, vol. V.).

91. Ricci, Seymour de. *A handlist of manuscripts in the library of the Earl of Leicester at Holkham Hall, abstracted from the catalogues of William Roscoe and Frederic Madden.* Oxford: University Press, 1932.

92. Roscoe, William. "Some account of the manuscript library at Holkham, in Norfolk, belonging to T. W. Coke, Esq.," *Transactions of the Royal Society of Literature of the United kingdom*, II (1834), 352–379.

93. *Statistica degli Archivii della Regione veneta.* 3 vols. Venice: P. Naratovich, 1880–81. Inventory of manuscripts in *Biblioteca Nazionale Marciana*, III, 68 *et seq.*, and list of ambassadors' dispatches, 79 *et seq.*, should be supplemented by Apolloni and Arcamone.

Florence

Guides

94. *Archivio Mediceo del Principato, Inventario sommario.* ("Ministero dell'

Interno, Pubblicazioni degli Archivi di Stato," vol. I.) Rome: Tipografica fiorentina, 1951.

95. *Archivio Mediceo avanti il Principato, Inventario* (*ibid.*, vols. II and XVIII.); vol. I. Rome: Tipografica fiorentina, 1951; vol. II. Florence: Empoli Poligrafico toscano, 1955.

96. Renaudet, Augustin. *Les sources de l'histoire de France aux Archives d'Etat de Florence, des Guerres d'Italie à la Révolution* (*1494–1789*). Paris: F. Rieder, 1916.

Naples
Documents

97. Bazzoni, Augusto (ed.). "Carteggio dell'Abate Ferdinando Galiani col Marchese Tanucci (1759–1769)," *Archivio storico italiano*, Ser. 3, IX, 2 (1869), 10–36; X, 1 (1869), 40–57; XX (1874), 345–353; XXI (1875), 516–527; XXII (1875), 37–51, 416–427; XXIII (1876), 242–252; XXIV (1876), 32–46, 242–254; XXV (1877), 195–207; XXVI (1877), 26–42; Ser. 4, I (1878), 14–31, 445–459; II (1878), 23–31, 364–374; III (1879), 171–183; IV (1879), 35–43, 361–375; V (1880), 187–200, 367–375. According to Jules Flammermont, these letters were published from a copy that was incomplete and inaccurate.

98. Carignani, Giuseppe (ed.). "Carteggio diplomatico tra il Marchese Tanucci e il Principe Albertini," *Archivio storico per le Province napoletane*, III (1878), 102–126, 211–232; IV (1879), 365–376, 497–515.

99. Gachard, Louis Prosper (ed.). *Correspondance de Marguerite d'Autriche, Duchesse de Parme, avec Philippe II.* (*Correspondances françaises des Gouverneurs généraux des Pays-Bas.*) Vol. II, Brussels: C. Muquardt, 1870.

Articles and Guides

100. Cauchie, Alfred, and Van Der Essen, Léon. *Inventaire des archives farnésiennes de Naples au point de vue de l'histoire des Pays-Bas catholiques.* (*Académie Royale de Belgique, Commission Royale d'Histoire*, vol. XXX.) Brussels: Kiessling (P. Imbreghts), 1911.

101. Coniglio, Giuseppe. "Carteggi superstiti della Segreteria di Stato borbonica degli affari esteri," *Rassegna storica del Risorgimento*, XXXIX-I (1952), 30–37.

102. Pontieri, Ernesto. "Rovine di guerra in Napoli," *Archivio storico per le Province napoletane*, LXVIII (1943), 269–283.

103. Trinchera, Francesco. *Degli Archivi napolitani, relazione a S. E. il Ministro dell Pubblica Istruzione.* Naples: Fibreno, 1872.

Parma

104. Drei, Giovanni. *L'Archivio di Stato di Parma, Indice generale, storico, descrittivo ed analitico.* (*Bibliothèque des "Annales Institutorum,"* vol. VI.) Rome: Biblioteca d'Arte, 1941.

Genoa

Documents

105. Ciasca, Raffaele (ed.). *Istruzioni e relazioni degli ambasciatori genovesi, Spagna, 1497–1655.* (*Fonti per la storia d'Italia,* vols. XIV, XX, XXI.) 3 vols. Rome: Istituto storico italiano per l'Età moderna e contemporanea, 1951–55.

106. Colucci, Giuseppe (ed.). *I Casi della Guerra, per l'Indipendenza d'America, narrati dall'ambasciatore della Repubblica di Genova presso la Corte d'Inghilterra (Francesco Ageno), nella sua Corrispondenza ufficiale inedita.* 2 vols. Genoa: R. Istituto de' Sordomuti, 1879.

107. Morandi, *see* number 24 above.

108. Vitale, Vito (ed.). *La diplomazia genovese.* (*La diplomazia italiana.*) Milan: Istituto per gli Studi di Politica internazionale [1941].

109. "I dispacci dei diplomatici genovesi a Parigi (1787–1793)," *Miscellanea di storia italiana,* LV (1935), 1–680.

Guide

110. Vitale, Vito. "Diplomatici e Consoli della Repubblica di Genova," *Atti della Società ligure di Storia Patria,* LXIII (1934), 1–341. Sources in archives and bibliography for 1494–1814.

Lucca

Documents

111. Bongi, Salvatore (ed.). *Ambasceria della Repubblica di Lucca a Enrico IV, Re di Francia.* Lucca: Canovetti, 1863.

112. Pellegrini, Amadeo (ed.). *Relazioni inedite di ambasciatori lucchesi alla corte di Vienna (Secoli XVII–XVIII).* Lucca: A. Pellici, 1902.

113. *Relazioni inedite di ambasciatori lucchesi alle corti di Firenze, Genova, Milano, Modena, Parma, Torino* (Secoli XVI–XVIII). Lucca: A. Marchi, 1901.

Guide

114. Bongi, Salvatore (ed.). *Inventario del R. Archivio di Stato in Lucca.* 4 vols. Lucca: Giusti, 1872–88. A supplement or 5th vol.: Lazzareschi, Eugenio (ed.). *Inventario del R. Archivio di Stato di Lucca.* Pescia: Benedetti, 1934.

Modena

115. *Archivio di Stato di Modena, Archivio segreto estense, Inventario.* ("Ministero dell'Interno, Pubblicazioni degli Archivi di Stato," vol. XIII.) Rome: Società tipografica modenese, 1953.

116. Bonaini, Francesco. *Gli Archivi delle Provincie dell'Emilia e le loro condizioni al finire del 1860.* Florence: M. Cellini, 1861. Also, but not quite complete, in *Archivio storico italiano,* new series, App. V (1861), 142–176.

8 THE NETHERLANDS

D. P. M. Graswinckel
Formerly of the State Archives, The Hague

and

Willard Allen Fletcher
University of Colorado

INTRODUCTION

THE Archive Service in the Netherlands was founded in 1802 when Hendrik van Wijn was appointed *archivarius* of the Batavian Republic. Satisfactory quarters for the Central State Archives were obtained in 1854, the year in which the well-known historian, Dr. R. C. Bakhuizen van den Brink, was nominated state archivist. In the course of the second half of the nineteenth century public archival repositories were established in the provincial capitals, under the control of a state archivist. The supervision of these was entrusted to the keeper of the repository at The Hague, on whom the title of General State Archivist was conferred.

Gradually, the larger towns started to give greater care to their archives. Especially at the end of the nineteenth century and the beginning of the twentieth, a great deal of influence was exercised on the development of the Dutch Archives Service by the Netherlands Society of Archivists (*Vereniging van Archivarissen in Nederland*), founded in 1892.

The present organization of the state archives was regulated by the Archives Act of 1918 and by subsequent royal decrees which settled various aspects in detail. In the provincial capitals and larger towns the repositories are under the control of officials who must have passed a professional examination. For the state repositories as well as for the archives of the larger municipalities the law requires that the keeper hold a degree of *doctorandus* in history or law. In the small towns the care of the archives is left in the hands of the local secretary, who is subject to the supervision exercised by the professional archivist of the province.

ORGANIZATION AND CLASSIFICATION

Before discussing the organization of the General State Archives at The Hague certain facts peculiar to Dutch foreign relations should be pointed out. The assembly of the states general (1581–1795) consisted of deputies of the seven independent provinces, in whose councils all foreign affairs were likewise discussed. Thus, in order to obtain a profound knowledge of the foreign relations during that period, it is usually necessary that the researcher consult the archives of the provincial governments of Holland, Zeeland, Utrecht, Gelderland, Overijssel, Friesland, and Groningen, in addition to those of the states general.

In the days of the Republic of the United Provinces the maintenance of foreign relations belonged to the competence of the states general. However, one should not overlook that Holland, and particularly the states of that province along with the grand pensionary (originally called state advocate), exerted a considerable and often determinant influence on foreign policy. The dominant role of the province rests upon historical developments. Holland and Zeeland were delivered from the Spanish rule as early as 1572, whereas the other provinces were liberated some decades later. Thus, the two provinces maintained relations with foreign states well before their sister provinces. Furthermore, commercial interests played a prominent part in Dutch foreign affairs, and commerce was largely concentrated in Holland. Finally, Holland contributed more than half toward the charges of the generalty and therefore was entitled to a great deal of influence in foreign policy. The unusual constitution of the Republic gave no special place to "foreign affairs" and therefore tended to maintain the prominent role of the province of Holland. It was not unusual that foreign affairs were discussed first of all in the states of Holland. Only after that was it ascertained whether the other provinces had objections, whereupon the matter would be taken up by the states general. It is obvious then that the resolutions of the states of Holland are often of prime importance for the study of Dutch foreign affairs prior to 1795.

The archives and collections that make up the General State Archives consist of three major sections. The first of these contains the materials from the department of the generalty: the states general, the council of state, the chamber of accounts of the generalty, and the admiralties. These collections generally extend down to March 1, 1796, when the Batavian Republic and its national assembly replaced the Republic of the United Provinces and the college of its states general. Two other major groups within the first section contain documents pertaining to the colonial administration and to the administration of the demesne lands of the house of Nassau. The second section contains all the archives of the unified state and its departments—the Batavian Republic, the kingdom of Holland, the governor-general of the Dutch departments, the sovereign principality, and the kingdom of the Netherlands—insofar as these archives have been transferred to the States General Archives. The third section is analogous to the state archives of a province—in this case the province of South Holland—although it is to be noted that the archives of the states of Holland and of other bodies that held authority over the whole of Holland, have been stored there.[1]

[1]Pp. 8–9 of number 6 in bibliography.

Archives and Collections of the First Section (United Provinces 1576–1796)[2]

A.   *Archieven der Staten-Generaal* 1576–1796

   1. *Hoofdarchiev:*
Resolutions (ordinary and secret) 1576 (1592)–1796; dispatches (ordinary and secret) and copybooks concerning peace conferences of Münster, Cologne, Nijmegen, Utrecht, Soissons, Aix-la-Chapelle, 1643–1748; concerning Belgium (Austrian Netherlands) 1716–94, Denmark 1679–1796, England 1576–1795, France 1578–1796, German Empire (Austria, Brandenburg-Prussia, and minor clerical and temporal principalities) 1576–1795, Italy 1594–1795, Poland 1579–1772, Portugal 1641–1795, Russia 1589–1794, Spain 1589–1794, Spain (Spanish Netherlands) 1649–1796, Sweden 1591–1796, Switzerland 1582–1796, Turkey and Barbary States 1596–1795, United States of North America 1782–95.

   2. *Vervolg van hiet Archief der Staten-Generaal:*
Ciphers, loose documents, papers from clerk Fagel, papers from clerk Nieuwenhuizen (sixteenth–eighteenth century).

   3. *Loketkas:*
Loose documents and files, classified in the same order as the dispatches 1576–1700.

   4. *Secrete Kas:*
Secret documents, treaties, and ratifications, classified in the same order as the dispatches 1576–1700.

   5. *Tractaten en Ratificatiën sedert* 1700:
Original treaties in chronological order 1700–97; original ratifications classified in order of the countries 1701–97.

[2]Pp. 5–27 of number 12 in bibliography.

6. *Aanhangsel: Legatie- en Consulaatsarchieven:*

    a. *Hoofdbestanddeel*

    Reports (*Verbalen*) of missions to peace conferences; reports of special and ordinary missions to foreign courts, as well as reports intended for the record office of the States-General; documents originating from Dutch embassy archives, formed and maintained abroad; etc.

    b. *Archief van der Nederlandse legatie te Constantinopel,* 1612–1784

    c. *Archief van het Nederlandse consulaat te Smyrna,* 1611–1817

    d. *Archief van het Nederlandse consulaat-generaal te Tanger,* 1685–1835

    e. *Archief van het Nederlandse consulaat te Tunis,* 1736–1813

B. *Archief van de Landraad van deze zijde van de Maas,* later *Raad van State,* 1581–1795.

C. *Stukken behorende tot het Archief van de Stadhouderlijke Secretarie en Kabinet*

See also Royal House Archives. Correspondence with Dutch and foreign diplomats, deciphered secret correspondence of the Prussian ministers in London and at The Hague and of the French ambassadors at The Hague 1751 (1755)–91.

D. *Archieven van de Companiën op Oost-Indië,* 1594–1603

E. *Archieven van de vereenigde Oost-Indische Compagnie,* 1602–1796

F. *Archieven van de Staatscommissie voor de zaken der Oost-Indische Compagnie,* 1790–95 and *van het Comité tot de zaken der Oost-Indische Compagnie,* 1795–96

G. *Stukken, in* 1862–63, *uit Batavia naar Nederland gezonden, voornamelijk betrekking hebende op het bestuur der hoge regering te Batavia over de Buitenkantoren,* 1602–1827

H. *Bescheiden der voormalige Nederlandse Bezittingen in Voor-*

Indië (Residentie Bengalen, Opperhoofdij Coromandel en Madura, Residentie Suratte), 1703–1826

I. *Archief van der Nederlandse factorij te Canton*, 1739–1828
J. *Archief van der Nederlandse factorij in Japan*, 1609–1890
K. *Archieven van de eerste West-Indische Compagnie*, 1621–74
L. *Archieven van de tweede West-Indische Compagnie*, 1674–1795
M. *Archieven van de Direktie ad interim der West-Indische coloniën*, 1791–92, and *van de Raad der Koloniën in West-Indië*, 1792–95
N. *Archief van de Directie van Berbice*, 1720–95
O. *Archief van de Societeit van Suriname*, 1683–1795
P. *Verzameling verspreide West-Indische Stukken*, 1614–1795
Q. *Archieven van der Nederlandse West-Indische Bezittingen en van Suriname*, 1669–1845 (1876)
R. *Stukken behorende tot archieven, die nog in Nederlands West-Indië en Surinam berusten*, 1829–1911
S. *Archieven van de Nederlandse Bezittingen ter Kuste van Guinea*, 1658–1872
T. *Familiearchieven en andere Verzamelingen:*
    Van Aerssen, sixteenth–seventeenth century
      Papers of Cornelis van Aerssen, clerk of the States General; papers of François van Aerssen, ambassador at the courts of France and England
    Van Aitzema, 1625–69
      Papers of Leo van Aitzema, resident of the Hanse towns in The Netherlands Boreel, seventeenth–nineteenth century
      Papers of Willem Boreel concerning various diplomatic missions; papers of Jacob Boreel Jansz., ambassador at the court of England
    Boreel de Mauregnault, 1667–72
      Johan Boreel, ambassador at the court of England
    Brantsen, 1782–1808
      Papers of Gerard Brantsen, ambassador at the court of France

Calkoen, 1745–46

Papers of Cornelis Calkoen, envoy to the king of Poland, to the elector of Saxony

Van der Capellen van de Poll, 1767–84

Papers of J. D. van der Capellen van de Poll, supporter of American independence

Van Citters, 1621(1540)–1694

Papers of Arnout van Citters, ambassador at the court of England

Dumas, 1776 (1700)–95

Papers of C. W. F. Dumas, secret agent of the American Congress during the American Revolution and later chargé d'affaires of the United States

Fagel, 1640–1881

Papers of Gaspar Fagel, clerk of the States General and afterward grand-pensionary of Holland; papers of François Fagel, Sr., clerk of the states general; papers of Hendrik Fagel, Sr., clerk of the states general; papers of François Fagel, Jr., second clerk of the states general; papers of Hendrik Fagel, Jr., second clerk of the states general; papers of Jacob Baron Fagel, envoy at the courts of Denmark and England; papers of Robert Baron Fagel, envoy at the court of France.

De Groot, 1606–67

Papers of Hugo de Groot, ambassador of Sweden in Paris, former legal adviser of the East India Company; papers of Willem de Groot

Van Hill, 1672–75

Papers of Govert van Hill, secretary to various envoys

Ortel, 1581–90

Papers of Joachim Ortel, Dutch agent in England

De Witt, 1670–71

Papers of Johan de Witt Johansz., ambassador to Denmark, Danzig, and Poland

U. *Losse Aanwinsten, 1820–heden:*

Aanw. 1831 A I. Original letters addressed to the Swedish envoys in Paris, 1711–64

Aanw. 1882 A VI. Journal of a member of a Dutch embassy to Dresden and Warsaw, 1744–45

Aanw. 1883 A V. Copy of the correspondence of Mozes de Montaigne, Dutch agent at Frankfurt, 1688–89

Aanw. 1888 26. Report on a mission of Boelensz. co. to the court of Denmark, 1607

Aanw. 1891 nr. 7. Letters from Paris by Abraham de Wicquefort, 1645–47, 1651–53

Aanw. 1899 XXIII 13. Journal of the ambassadors François van Aerssen and Caspar van Vosbergen at the court of France, 1628–29

Aanw. 1902 XIV 8. Report on the embassy of Aerssen and Vosbergen at the court of France, 1628–29

Aanw. 1911 XV 6–9. Notes of Gerard Schaep concerning treaties and foreign relations in the seventeenth century

Aanw. 1915 XV, 1, 2. Journal of Thomas Hees, resident at Algiers, 1675–80

Aanw. 1929 XIII, 2. Documents concerning difficulties with Denmark over the Icelandic fishery, 1740–41

Aanw. 1930 XI 1. Correspondence of Pieter de Groot with Abraham de Wicquefort, 1672–74

Aanw. 1948 First Section III. Correspondence and notes of Professor J. E. Heeres about the sovereignty of Miangas, 1918–19

Archives and Collections of the Second Section[3]

A. *Archieven van 1795/96 tot 1813:*

    I.   *Archieven van de (zo genoemde) Wetgevende Colleges, 1796–1801*

    II. *Archief van het Wetgevend Lichaam, 1801–10*

---

[3]Pp. 31–67 of number 12 in bibliography.

III. *Archief van de Staatsraad*, 1805–10

IV. *Archieven van de met de taak der Rekenkamer belaste instanties*, 1796–1810

V. *Archieven van het Uitvoerend Bewind*, 1798–1801

VI. *Archief van het Staatsbewind*, 1801–5

VII. *Archief van de Raadpensionaries*, 1805–6

VIII. *Archief der staatssecretarie van het Koninkrijk Holland*, 1806–11

IX. *Archief van de Prins-Stedehouder van de Keizer van Frankrijk in te Hollandse Departementen*, 1810–13

X. *Archieven van het Ministerie van Buitenlandse Zaken*, 1795–1810

XI. *Archieven van Nederlandse Gezantschappen en Consulaten*, 1795–1810:

1. Duitse Rijk (Wenen), 1786–1808
2. Keurvorstendommen Keulen, Mainz, en Münster, de Opper- en Nederrijnse Kreits en de Westfaalse Kreits (Mainz), 1778–1800
3. Pruisen (Berlijn), 1795–1810
4. Hanzesteden (Hamburg), 1795–1809
5. Hessen-Kassel (Kassel), 1796–1804
6. Württemberg (Stuttgart), 1797–1809
7. Baden (Mannheim) (Karlsruhe), 1807–9
8. Denemarken (Kopenhagen), 1793–1809
9. Zweden (Stockholm), 1795–1806
10. Rusland (St. Peterburg), 1791–1810
11. Frankrijk (Parijs), 1795–1810
12. Portugal (Lissabon), 1802–4
13. Spanje (Madrid), 1795–99
14. Turkije (Konstantinpel), 1741–1811
15. Noord-Amerika (Philadelphia), 1795–1801
16. Antwerpen (consulaat), 1804–10

B. *Archieven van 1813 tot begin 20e eeuw :*

I. *Archief van de Algemene Staatssecretarie en het Kabinet de Konings*, 1813–97

II. *Archief van de Raad van Ministers*, 1823–1920

III. *Archieven van het Ministerie van Buitenlandse Zaken*, 1813–70

IV. *Archieven van Commissies en andere bijzondere organen, ressorterende onder het Departement van Buitenlandse Zaken :*

1. *Regeling der grensscheiding tussen Nederland en Pruisen en Hannover*, 1815–27

2. *Conferentie te Londen tot regeling der aangelegenheden van Nederland en België*, 1830–39

3. *Liquidatie met Oostenrijk*, 1828

4. *Regeling van de grensscheiding tussen Nederland en Pruisen*, 1816–68

5. *Regeling van de grensscheiding tussen Nederland en Hannover*, 1819–69

6. *Regeling grensscheiding Nederland-België*, 1839–52, 1864–69

7. *Regeling grensscheiding Nederland-Frankrijk*, 1816–26

8. *Commissaries grensregeling Nederland-Frankrijk*, 1816–26

9. *Scheidsgerecht Oostenrijk-Hongarije*, 1922–23

V. *Archieven van Nederlandse Gezantschappen :*

1. Groot-Brittanië en Ierland, 1814–1914

2. Frankrijk, 1814–84

3. Duitse Bond en Frankfort, Hessen, en Keur-Hessen, 1816–67

4. Oostenrijk, 1814–42

5. Pruisen, 1814–1900

6. Beieren, Wurttemberg, en Baden, 1814–67

7. Saksen, 1828–56

8. Hanzesteden (Hamburg, Bremen, en Lübeck), 1815–41
9. Hannover, 1838–66
10. Denemarken, 1815–62
11. Zweden en Noorwegen, 1814–62
12. Zweden, Noorwegen, en Denemarken, 1863–1910
13. Rusland, 1814–90
14. Turkije en de Levant, 1814–57
15. Kerkelijke Staat, 1826–30 (the archives for the period 1842–70 are in the Vittorio Emmanuele Library in Rome)
16. Toscane, 1826–28
17. Sardinië, 1818–55
18. Zwitserland, 1817–1915
19. Spanje, 1814–1913
20. Portugal en Brazilië, 1815–21
21. Portugal, 1823–98
22. Brazilië, 1826–33
23. België, 1839–90
24. Italië, 1875–1910
25. Noord-Amerika (Verenigde Staten), 1814–1909
26. Argentinië (tevens consulaararchief), 1880–1919
27. Japan, 1870–90
28. Perzië, 1890–1906
29. Roemenië, 1889–1910
30. Servië, 1903–11

VI. *Archieven van Nederlandse Consulaten en Vice-Consulaten:*

1. Alexandria (Ver. Staten), 1815–25
2. Athene (Nauplia), 1840–43
3. Berlijn, 1867–77

4. Bern, consulaat-generaal (tot in 1867 ook van Luxemburg), 1832–1915
5. Bern, consulaat-generaal van Luxemburg, 1880–90
6. Bern, vice-consulaat, 1865–89
7. Bordeaux, 1873
8. Buenos Aires (cf. legatie Argentinië)
9. Caracas, 1859–77
10. Coruna, 1831–86
11. Cyprus, 1829–31
12. Elmina, 1827–80
13. Genève, 1850–1915
14. Guatamala, 1853–59
15. Kanea, 1828–33
16. Lausanne, 1892–94
17. Lissabon, 1814–61
18. Londen, 1814–99
19. Mogador, 1845–97
20. Mozambique, 1874–76
21. Nagasaki (Desima), 1860–1908
22. New York, 1855–1911
23. Ningpoo, 1868–1908
24. Penang, 1872–1908
25. Philadelphia, 1869–1903
26. Rio de Janeiro, 1826–31 (cf. legatie Brazilië)
27. Singapore, 1863–1905
28. Stockholm, 1821–1920
29. Tanger, 1830–1907
30. Truxillo, 1826–34
31. Tunis, 1814–64
32. Yokohama, 1860–70
33. Zürich, 1850–74

VII. *Archieven der Nederlandse Overzee Trust Maatschappij*, 1914–19

VIII. *Archief van het Koninklijk Nationaal Steuncomité,* 1914–26

IX. *Archief van het Centraal Vluchtelingen-Comité,* 1914–19

X. *Archief van de Dienst der Geinterneerde Krijgsgevangenen,* 1917–19

XI. *Archieven of Verzamelingen van bijzondere Personen:*

1. C. J. Asselbergs, 1869–1949
   Military attaché accredited to the Boer forces during the South African War

2. Mr. G. Beelaerts van Blokland, 1772–1844
   Attorney-General at the Cape of Good Hope, 1802–17

3. Bartinck - Varel - Kniphausense lening, 1809–54

4. F. G. Baron van Dedem van de Gelder, 1743–1815
   Resident at Pera and in Constantinople, 1785–1808

5. P. A. Dumont Pigalle
   Political refugee in Paris, 1788–1801

6. A. R. Falck, 1777–1843
   Ambassador in London, 1823–32, and Resident in Brussels, 1839–43

7. Baron van der Goes, squire of Dirxland, 1751–1826
   Resident in Denmark, 1785–93, Hamburg, 1793–96, Spain, 1796–97, Negotiator at the peace conference of Lille, Minister for foreign affairs 1798—1808

8. J. Goldberg, 1763–1828
   Resident in Berlin, 1807–9

9. J. G. H. Hahn, 1761–1822
   Member of the Committee of foreign affairs, 1796–98

10. C. Hiddingh, 1809–71
    Resident of the Orange Free State
11. D. van Hogendorp, 1761–1822
    Resident in Vienna, 1807–9
12. Jhr. J. W. Janssens, 1762–1838
    Governor-General of the Cape of Good
    Hope, 1802–6
13. Dr. W. J. Leyds, 1859–1940
    Resident of the Boer Republic in Europe,
    1898–1902
14. Jhr. P. Th. van der Maesen de Sombreff,
    1827–1902.
    Minister for foreign affairs, 1862–64
15. A. W. C. Baron van Nagell tot Ampsen,
    1756–1851
    Minister for foreign affairs, 1814–24
16. Dr. F. E. Posthuma, 1874–1943
    Papers dealing with commercial treaties
    and international agriculture, 1918–40
17. Jhr. W. F. Roell, 1767–1835
    Minister for foreign affairs, 1809–10
18. Jhr. D. A. W. van Tets van Goudriaan,
    1844–1930
    Minister for foreign affairs, 1905–8
19. C. H. Verhuell, 1794–1845
    Resident in St. Petersburg, 1807–8; in
    Paris, 1808–10
20. J. G. Verstolk van Soelen, 1776–1845
    Resident in Russia, 1816–23, Arbitrator of
    Anglo-American dispute 1824, Minister
    for foreign affairs, 1825–41
21. Hugo Baron van Zuylen van Nyevelt,
    1781–1853
    Envoy to Brussels, 1814, to Stockholm,
    1814, to Madrid, 1816–22, to Smyrna,

1825, to Constantinople, 1825–29, to London, 1831–33, ambassador in Brussels and Paris, 1840, minister for foreign affairs, ad. i. 1833–41

22. J. P. J. A. Baron van Zuylen van Nyevelt, 1818–94
Minister for foreign affairs, 1860–61, 1866–68

Archives and Collections of the Third Section[4]

A. *Archieven van de Staten van Holland en Gecommitteerde Raden in het Zuiderkwartier*, 1572–1795:

Nrs. 11–280	printed resolutions 1575–1795
Nrs. 281–298	printed index on the printed resolutions 1572–1790
Nrs. 299–315	printed secret resolutions 1653–1795
Nrs. 316–317	index on the foregoing
Nrs. 325–1208	minute resolutions 1575–1795
Nrs. 1226–1250	minute secret resolutions 1651–1705
Nrs. 1384–1481	registered outgoing letters 1621–1795
Nrs. 1871–2029	original letters and other documents submitted to the assembly of the states 1691–1763
Nrs. 2244–2577	copies of documents concerning foreign affairs, classified in order of the various countries in which the Republic had representatives 1653–1702

B. *Archieven van de Raadpensionarissen*, 1572–1795:

In respect to foreign affairs the grand pensionary of the province of Holland occupied a most important position. He was in charge of the formulation of proposals, the leading of discussions, and the drafting of resolutions of the states of Holland, thus being in effect the president of

[4]Pp. 71–103 of number 12 in bibliography.

the states assembly. In his capacity as the only permanent member he was the leader and spokesman of the states of Holland in the assembly of the states general. He also took part in the sessions of the Secret Council, in which foreign affairs were discussed, as well as in meetings of other committees of the generalty. Although the Dutch representatives abroad were obliged to report to the states general and to the clerk of that college (in which case secrecy was not always maintained), they adopted the custom of addressing important and confidential dispatches to the grand pensionary in person. These facts account for the importance of the archives of the grand pensionaries in matters of foreign relations, especially those of Oldenbarnevelt, Johan de Witt, Gaspar Fagel, Anthonie Heinsius, Simon van Slingelandt, and Laurens Pieter van de Spiegel. The archives of the grand pensionaries are kept partly as a subdivision of the archives of the states of Holland, partly as separate collections.

1. Paulus Buys, 1572–86
2. Johan van Oldenbarnevelt, 1586–1619
3. Jacob Cats, 1629–31, 1636–51
4. Johan de Witt, 1653–72
5. Caspar Fagel, 1672–88
6. Anthonie Heinsius, 1688–1720
7. Isaac van Hoornbeek, 1720–27
8. Anthony van der Heim, 1737–46
9. Peter van Bleiswijk, 1772–87
10. Laurens Pieter van de Spiegel, 1787–95

Provincial Archives of The Netherlands

In addition to the General State Archives the researcher should also be aware of archival collections in the provincial repositories that might be of value for certain topics in the field of Dutch foreign relations.

1. Province of Gelderland:
   The archives are located at 1, Marktstraat, Arnhem. Of interest are the papers of the counts of Culemborg, concerning diplomatic relations with various countries, as well as the archives of the manor houses of Waardenburg, Keppel, and Enghuizen, relating to embassies and diplomatic missions entrusted to functionaries from Gelderland.

2. Province of Zeeland:
   The archives, located at 3, Abdij, Middelburg, house the papers of Van den Warck, a Dutch envoy to Denmark and England, as well as the Verheye-Van Citters collection, which concerns peace negotiations with France 1709-13.

3. Province of Utrecht:
   This repository, at 27, Drift, Utrecht, contains the following collections: the papers of G. Hamel, counsel of the states; the family archives of De Geer van Jutphaas on diplomatic and commercial relations with Sweden, seventeenth–nineteenth centuries; the family archives of Huydecoper, on relations of members of the family with foreign countries, seventeenth–eighteenth centuries; the family archives of De Pesters, on diplomatic missions of members of the family, seventeenth–eighteenth centuries; miscellaneous papers on foreign engagements, 1618–69, and concerning the Barrier Treaty, 1753–54.

4. Province of Friesland:
   These archives, at B 13, Turfmarkt, Leeuwarden, house various resolutions on foreign affairs, concerning the United States, 1782, Cologne, 1673; Denmark, 1720; England, 1672, 1704; France, 1584, 1660, 1672; Lübeck, 1653; Münster, 1643–62; Poland, 1669; Portugal, 1644; Prussia, 1720, 1727; Spain, 1660, 1672; Sweden, 1644, 1719; and the Gabbema collection, a group of papers on foreign relations, including the peace negotiations with Cologne, 1579–83.

5. Province of Overijssel:
   This collection, at Sassenpoort, Zwolle, contains the archives of the nobility and towns in Overijssel, as well as missives of the deputies to the army, 1706–8, 1711, 1712.

6. Province of Groningen:
   Papers of interest, at 2, St. Jansstraat, Groningen, are those concerning independent actions of the province regarding East Friesland and Germany.

7. Province of Drente:
   The archives are at 4, Brink, Assen, and include papers concerning boundary disputes between the county of Bentheim and the bishopric of Münster.

8. City of Amsterdam:
   During the Middle Ages the city of Amsterdam pursued a more or less independent policy in respect to the Hanseatic League. Particulars concerning these relations might be found in the following: the charter collection of the Iron Chapel, the grand-memorandum registers since 1474, and the resolutions of the city council since 1536. During the period 1578–1795 Amsterdam exerted a great deal of influence on foreign policy and at times maintained foreign relations of its own. For details one may consult the resolutions of the municipality as well as the correspondence of its college. Moreover, there are embassy reports, copies of treaties with foreign powers, and missives of Dutch envoys.

ADMINISTRATION, REGULATIONS, AND FACILITIES

The General State Archives are located at 7, Bleijenburg, The Hague. Admission to the archives is readily granted and the researcher, native or foreign, need not present any papers of identification or letters of introduction. Upon entering the reading room the investigator is given access to the index files and can place his request for documents with the attendant. Documents are released to the user upon the presentation of a requisition bulletin and the delay necessary for bringing documents from the stacks to the reading room is very brief. The researcher is not permitted to use ink in the reading room for the purpose of transcribing documents. A speaking knowledge of the Dutch language is not essential since most, if not all, of the archivists and attendants speak English. Consultation with members of the staff on matters of research is possible but should of course be limited to essentials. All archives dating from before 1813 are open to research without any restriction whatever; most of the records are open to about 1900, and some may be consulted down to the year 1920.

A well-equipped reproduction department is attached to the General State Archives, where documents from the public archives may be photostated or microfilmed for the use of researchers. It may be noted that transcriptions by a researcher for the use of another party are only permitted in exceptional cases. The schedule of the archives is that of government offices, thus permitting adequate periods of uninterrupted consultation.

BIBLIOGRAPHY

Guide and Reference Works

In respect to the contents of the General State Archives it may be noted that typed inventories of virtually all the materials listed above are available to the researcher at the repository at The Hague. There has also been a consistent effort to print the inventories of the archives. In 1854 R. C. Bakhuizen van den Brink, Keeper of the State Archives at The Hague, published a survey entitled *Overzicht van het Nederlandsche Rijksarchief, eerste stuk*. It was his intention to follow this initial survey with a second part and then to continue with annual reports. However, this plan did not materialize and it was only in 1866 that his successor, L. Ph. C. van den Bergh, issued an annual report for the minister of the interior, which was published in the *Staatsblad*, as were the reports of the years following. Beginning in 1878, the annual reports from the Keeper of the State Archives and the keepers of other state repositories were published as *Verslagen omtrent 's Rijks oude archieven*, consisting of a first series from 1878 to 1927 and a second series beginning in 1928. In the first series inventories were published as appendixes to the reports; since 1914 they are divided into two volumes, of which the first is solely consecrated to the General State Archives.

The annual report of 1928 was the first to appear without the appended inventories, and the latter were printed thenceforth as a separate publication of the Dutch government, entitled *Inventarissen van Rijks—en andere archieven*. The gap between 1854 and 1878 was filled by the publication of a survey of the administration of Bakhuizen van den Brink, published by R. Fruin in 1926 under the title *De Gestie van Dr. R. C. Bakhuizen van den Brink als archivaris des Rijks, 1854–1865*, and by the publication, in 1914, of the annual reports from 1865 to 1877.

In *Verslagen* . . . , 1926, I, 87 ff., can be found a survey of the contents of the General State Archives; the researcher's attention is also directed to the inventory of the foreign office archives in *Verslagen* . . . , XLI, pt. 1 (1918), 291–469; XLIV, pt. 1 (1921 [1923]), 111–240; XLVI, pt. 1 (1923 [1924]), 174–207.[5]

Other guide and reference works are:

1. Bakhuizen van den Brink, R. C., L. Ph. C. van den Bergh, and J. de Jonge. *Nederlandsch Rijksarchief, verzameling van onuitgegevene oorkonden voor de geschiedenis des vaderlandes.* Amsterdam, 1855–57.

2. Bakhuizen van den Brink, R. C. *Overzicht van het Nederlandsche Rijksarchief.* The Hague, 1854.

3. Bijlsma, R. *De regeeringsarchieven der Geunieerde en Nader Geunieerde Nederlandsche Provincien.* The Hague, 1926.

4. Bosmans, Cornelis J. E., and M. Visser. *Répertoire des traités et engagements internationaux concernant les Pays-Bas, 1845–1900.* The Hague, 1928.

5. Formsma, W. J., and B. van 't Hoff. *Repertorium van inventarissen van Nederlandse archieven.* Groningen, 1947.

6. Fruin, R. *The General State Archives and their contents.* The Hague, 1932.

7. Heeres, Jan E., and F. W. Stapel. *Corpus diplomaticum Neerlando-Indicum. Verzameling van politieke contracten en verdere verdragen door de Nederlanders in het Oosten gesloten, van privilegebrieven aan hen verleend, enz.* 4 vols. The Hague, 1907–38.

8. Heeringa, Klaas. *Bronnen tot de geschiedenis van den levantschen handel.* 2 vols. The Hague, 1910–17.

9. Van 't Hoff, B., and M. W. Juriaanse. *Het archief van Anthonie Heinsius.* The Hague, 1950.

10. Japiske, N., and H. H. P. Rijperman. *Resolutien der Staten-Generaal van 1576 tot 1609.* 12 vols. The Hague, 1915–50.

[5]P. 7 of number 6 in bibliography.

11. Muller, S., J. A. Feith, and R. Fruin. *Manual for the arrangement and description of archives; drawn up by the direction of the Netherlands Association of Archivists.* 2nd ed. Trans. by A. H. Leavitt. New York, 1940.

12. Nederland, Ministerie van Onderwijs, Kunsten, en Wetenschappen. *De Rijksarchieven in Nederland.* The Hague, 1953.

13. Riemsdijk, Theodorus H. F. *De griffie van Hare Hoop Mogenden; bijdrage tot de kennis van het archief van de Staten-Generaal der Vereenigde Nederlanden.* The Hague, 1885.

14. Scheltema, P. "Het historisch-diplomatisch archief van Amsterdam," *Amstel's oudheid, of gedenkwaardigheden van Amsterdam.* Vol. III. Amsterdam, 1859.

15. *Inventaris van het Amsterdamsche archief.* 3 vols. Amsterdam, 1866–74.

16. Schilfgaarde, Antonie P. *Het archief der heeren en graven van Culemborg.* The Hague, 1949.

17. Wabeke, Bertus H. *A guide to Dutch bibliographies.* Washington, D.C., 1951.

9 NORWAY[1]

Florence Janson Sherriff
Wesleyan College, Macon, Georgia

HISTORY

NORWAY has been an independent state three times in its long existence since Viking days. The earliest period of sovereignty began with its emergence as a nation in Viking times about A.D. 900. Independence was lost when Norway was merged with Denmark in 1387, and in the Union of Kalmar in 1396 Denmark, Norway, and Sweden were united. During the early part of this union Norway had a personal relationship with the Danish crown, but after 1572 Danish stadholders governed Norway as an integral part of Denmark. Foreign relations were carried on by the Danish chancellor for both countries.

During the Napoleonic wars when Denmark became an ally of France in 1807, Norway was the subject of much diplomatic correspondence between the nations united against Napoleon. After the Battle of Leipzig in 1813, Bernadotte, now crown prince of Sweden and allied with Napoleon's foes, invaded Denmark and in December forced it to sign the Treaty of Kiel, granting Norway to Sweden. Norway has always refused to accept this treaty. A national convention was elected in Norway to meet at Eidsvoll, and independence was proclaimed on May 17, 1814. A constitution was drafted providing for the government of the country by the Storthing as parliament. The

[1]The author wishes to acknowledge indebtedness to the archivists of *Riksarkivet* for information and guidance in obtaining many facts for this chapter. Others who have been of assistance through correspondence are Hedvig Schanning, Head Librarian of *Utenriksdepartementets Bibliotecket*, Odd Hjorth-Sorensen, Press Attaché, and Tordis Dreyer, Assistant in Archives, Norwegian Embassy in Washington.

crown of Norway was offered to the Danish regent, Prince Christian Frederick, but Bernadotte returned to Sweden and threatened to enforce the Treaty of Kiel by the invasion of Norway. At the Convention at Moss an agreement was reached that Christian Frederick was to refuse the crown and in November 1814 the Norwegian Storthing voted a union with Sweden. In this personal union Norway lost her independence a second time.

The union of Norway and Sweden lasted until 1905. During this period foreign affairs for both countries remained at first under the Swedish chancellor; after 1840 with the reorganization of the Swedish administration, foreign affairs were under the Swedish minister of foreign affairs. The Joint Council for Sweden and Norway, which always met in Stockholm, had Norwegian representatives but never achieved any control over foreign affairs. As time went on, the growing Norwegian merchant marine found it humiliating and difficult to deal with Swedish consuls in foreign ports, and although some Norwegian consuls were appointed, this controversy finally led to the separation of the two countries in 1905. The cabinet of the Norwegian government includes a minister of foreign affairs. Diplomatic correspondence that has accumulated since 1905 may be found in the archives of the *Utenriksdepartementet* (department of foreign affairs) at Solplass 1.

The first written documents in Norway's history appeared in the twelfth century, and its first commercial treaty was negotiated between Henry III of England and Haakon IV of Norway in 1217. During King Haakon's reign Norway corresponded with the Emperor of the Holy Roman Empire, with France, England, the Christian states of Spain, and with the Sultan of Tunis. The capital of Norway had been moved from Nidaros, old Trondhjem, to the southern commercial town of Bergen, where the Hanseatic League in the next century established the fish market of Europe. The Archbishop of Nidaros remained the political influence in the North and carried on a correspondence with the pope and various members of the clergy in Europe and England until the time of the Reformation.

The third and permanent capital of Norway was established in Oslo by King Haakon V at the end of the thirteenth century. Akershus, the imposing fort that overshadows the city, was built as a castle for the residence of the king and as a fortification for the defense of the city. It is first mentioned as Akersnaes in a letter written by King Haakon Magnusson dated June 22, 1300, granting gifts and privileges to *Mariekirken* (St. Mary's) in Oslo. A copy was found in the archives at Akershus. Queen Margaret, the regent of Denmark who promoted the Union of Kalmar in 1396, advised the heir apparent, King Erik, to investigate his title to the throne of Norway in the letters patent at Akershus during his tour of Norway in 1405. Registered at Akershus is a donation of money from him to the Archbishopric of Nidaros. From 1572 to 1809 the Danish stadholder for Norway was resident at Akershus and the archives were continued here. A change of government for Norway took place in 1809 when a commission was appointed instead of the stadholder with a Danish prince as regent. Under the Norwegian union with Denmark from 1387 to 1814 the foreign affairs of the two countries were conducted by the Danish chancellor in Copenhagen. In the sixteenth century Danish "agents" were sent to foreign countries, and in the seventeenth century resident ministers were exchanged with other powers. Their diplomatic correspondence was deposited in the *Kongelige Geheimearchivet*, (Danish Royal Archives) which was established from the accumulated archives of the chancellor by Frederick III and is now located in Christiansborg Palace in Copenhagen. Very few of these archives have been sent to Norway, but the *Riksarkivet* (National Archives) has copies of some made by its own officials. The documents concerning the period of independence in 1814 are in the Norwegian National Archives in Oslo. The diplomatic correspondence for the period of the union between

Norway and Sweden, 1814–1905, can be found in the Swedish National Archives in Stockholm. The archives of the Norwegian department of foreign affairs contain all the diplomatic correspondence of Norway since 1905.

The origin of the National Archives of Norway was the archives of government documents at Akershus. In 1494 a register of the government papers at Akershus was made by Ion Paalsson, Provost of *Mariekirken* and Chancellor of Norway; Odd Alfsson, Governor at Akershus; and Hallstein Jonsson, the king's chaplain and designated *Registrum om de Breve, som ligge oppaa Akershus (og) Kronen ere anrörende.* From that time it was customary to make a register each time the official at Akershus was changed, and Akershus remained the chief depository for government documents until 1866. From time to time there were also other depositories such as the one at the Cathedral of Nidaros. Archbishop Olaf Engelbrektsson's papers were among those recovered from Munich with the archives of King Christian II.[2] For a short time, dating from 1483, King Hans made Bergen a depository. The documents that had accumulated at *Mariekirken* in Oslo with the church jewels, etc., were deposited for safekeeping at Akershus at the time of King Christian II's flight to Holland in 1523. An inventory was made upon order from Christian IV, who rebuilt Oslo after the fire and renamed it Christiania in 1622.[3] In the eighteenth century various attempts were made to catalogue the materials at Akershus and to appoint an archivist, but the compensation offered was too small to attract such an official. In 1800 Carl Deichman Moller accepted the position; he did arrange all the original kings' letters from 1572 to 1751 and gathered into seventeen folio volumes the registers and catalogues of a part of the archives.[4] General Gustav Grüner arranged the military archives in 1760, and these were deposited at Akershus in 1822.

[2] See numbers 18 and 27 in bibliography.
[3] See number 24 in bibliography.
[4] See number 17 in bibliography.

Norway received many archives from Denmark during the first half of the nineteenth century as provided in the Protocol of 1819, an addition to the treaty that made provisions for the separation of Norway and Denmark. Some eleven hundred sacks and various cases of government documents were sent to Norway in 1820–22. This archival exchange continued until 1851, but very little diplomatic correspondence was included.[5] The famous *Arnamagnaeanske Samlingen* (Arne Magnusson Collection) at the University of Copenhagen library contains some valuable documents on Norway's medieval history, which the University has refused to give to Norway. Professor Magnusson, a medievalist of the eighteenth century, had borrowed these manuscripts from the Danish Royal Archives and had neglected to leave any records of the loans. Upon his death in 1730 all his library and papers were donated to the University of Copenhagen library, and they were so intermingled with his private collection that it has been impossible to separate the papers from the archives. Another exchange of archives was that with Munich and involved Christian II's papers and documents. This also comprised documents that were claimed by Sweden and Denmark. In 1829 Professor G. F. Lundh of the University of Christiania was sent to the Bavarian Archives in Munich to select the archives that Christian II in his flight in 1523 had taken from Stockholm and Copenhagen to Holland. Strangely, these archives had appeared in Munich in the early nineteenth century.[6]

The Norwegian National Archives were officially established by the Storthing in 1836. The archives at Akershus had been placed under the finance department of the government in 1817, but no efforts had been made to appoint an archivist and the documents were in a state of chaos. In the Law of 1836 the Archives at Akershus were transferred to the *Kirkedepartement* (Department of the State Church). The first official archivist

[5]See number 19 in bibliography.
[6]See number 18 in bibliography.

to be appointed was the poet, Henrick Wergeland, in 1840.[7] The organization and cataloguing of the archives was the work of two historians, J. C. Berg and G. F. Lundh of the University of Christiania. It was in 1866 that the archives were moved from Akershus to a wing in the newly constructed Storthing building. At the present time the archives are housed in a separate building at Bankplass 3. Since 1875 there has been a *Förstearkivaren* (Head Archivist) of the *Riksarkivet*. It is now under the Department of Church and Education.

ORGANIZATION AND CLASSIFICATION

The *Riksarkivet* is the central depository for government documents and other archives. It includes collections of private papers of diplomats, statesmen, and foreign ministers. The method of classification used in the archives may be obtained from a published guide, *Kort oversigt de i det norske Rigsarkiv samt Stiftsarkiverne i Trondhjem og Bergen beroende arkivsager* [A short summary of the archives of the National Archives of Norway and those of the diocesan archives of Trondhjem and Bergen]. The following excerpts have been chosen because of their value in a study of international relations and because of their pertinence in a study of the relations between Norway and Denmark.

I. *Rigsarkivet* (1200–1900)

    B. *Diplomsamlingar*—A list of original manuscripts with a summary of their contents, including correspondence since 1196.

    D. *Historisk-kronologisk Samling*—Foreign correspondence and other documents relating to Norway's independence movement in 1814.

    F. *Kongebrev o. Lign*—Royal correspondence of the Danish kings.

        1. a. *Originale Kongebrev fra Arkivet paa Akershus, 1572–*

[7]See number 17 in bibliography.

1700—Original letters from the kings in the archives at Akershus.

b. *Kongebrev fra andre Arkiver, 1664–1813*—Royal correspondence from other archives.

2. *Afskrifter fra Danske Rigsarkivet*—Copies from the Danish Royal Archives.

   a. *Norske registre og tegnelser, 1523–1719*—Copies of Norwegian registers or copybooks.

   b. *Kongebrev fra Danske Arkivafdelninger, 1560–1660*—Copies of royal correspondence from the Danish Archives.

   c. *Afskrifter*—Copies from

      1. *Kancelliets Arkiv*—Chancery archives.

      2. *Krigskollegiets Arkiv, 1660–1663*—Ministry of war archives.

K. *Personalia*—Collections of correspondence and papers of government officials.

   1. Documents arranged according to family name.

   3. Manuscript collection.

Q. *Privates Samling*—Private collections and correspondence.

II. *Statsarkiver fr 1814 afleverade fra Danmark*—State archives prior to 1814 received from Denmark.

A. *Kancelliets Arkiv*—Chancery archives.

   1. a. *Forestillinger, 1681–1700*—Memorials

      b. *Aabne Breve og Missive, 1559–1588, 1623–1799*—Correspondence.

   2. *Aabne Breve og Missive, 1800–1813.*

M. *Udenrigsdepartementets Arkiv*—Archives from the Danish department of foreign affairs concerning boundary agreements between Norway and Sweden, 1690, 1725–1808, and between Russia and Norway, 1727–1810,

III. *Norske Centralmyndigheter for 1814*—The central administration of Norway before 1814.

    A.   1. *Statholderskabets Arkiv til 1704*—Archives of the
stadholder to 1704.

          2. *Vicestatholderskabets Arkiv, 1722–1814*—Archives of
the vice stadholder.

    C. *Regjeringskommissionens Arkiv, 1807–1814*—The Gov-
ernment Commission's archives.

IV. *Regjeringsarkiver efter 1814 til 1850*—Archives of the Norwegian government after 1814 to 1850.

    A. *Statsekreteriats Arkiv, 1810–1850*—Archives of the
Secretariat.

    B. *Statsraadafdelningen i Stockholm, dens Arkiv, 1814–1905*
—The archives of the national council in Stockholm,
which included Norwegian councilors.

The diplomatic correspondence of Norway since 1905 is
located in the *Utenriksdepartementets Arkivet* (Archives of the Department of Foreign Affairs) at Solplass 1. No law has been
passed for its final deposit nor is there any law restricting its use.
This is left to the discretion of the archivist, and the earlier parts
are open for research. The diplomatic archives are divided into
five classifications: I. General and Political, II. Commerce, III.
Inheritance and Legal Affairs, IV. United Nations, V. The
North Atlantic Pact. All diplomatic correspondence is recorded
in copy books designated as *Journaler* or *Protocol*. The classification of I. General and Political is divided into head titles
numbered from 1 to 99. Head Title 1 deals with "State Organization and State Administration." Subdivision 2 under this,
designated as "International Co-operation," includes conferences, meetings and expositions, etc. The title of Subdivision
3 is "Nordic Co-operation," co-operation with the Scandinavian countries. This includes the making of conventions and
treaties, and even of bilateral treaties. Diplomatic correspond-

ence may be found under Subdivision 4, "Norway's Intercourse with Foreign Powers," negotiation and the making of bilateral treaties. Subdivision 4 is divided into geographical areas according to the Norwegian alphabet. The United States is Number 47 (*Forenede Stater, Tallet* 47), while Sweden (*Sverige*) is Number 106.

ADMINISTRATION, REGULATIONS, AND FACILITIES

The National Archives on Bankplass 3 are open to the public with the exception of a few archives that have been closed by the government or in the case of private collections by the families. Under certain circumstances even these may be consulted upon the discretion of the archivist. The reading room is open from 9 A.M. to 3 P.M. and from 5 to 8 P.M. on week days. In the reading room are guides, bibliographies, published source materials, the journals of the *Riksarkivet, Meddelelser fra Riksarkivet*, and of the Norwegian Historical Society, *Historisk Tidskrift*. A card catalogue lists the contents of the archives. Assistants at the desk are most helpful in aiding the researcher. It is possible to arrange for microfilming and photostating.

The Archives of the Department of Foreign Affairs is located at Solplass 1. The diplomatic correspondence of Norway since 1905 is found here. There is no published catalogue of these archives, but a card catalogue arranged alphabetically may be consulted in the reading room. It is open to the public from 9 A.M. to 3:30 P.M. during the week days, closing at 2 P.M. on Saturdays and 3 P.M. in the summer. The administration of these archives is under the *Förstearkivaren* (First Archivist). His staff includes an archivist, a secretary of archives, and several attendants. A research student should present a letter of introduction to the archivist, either from his research professor or from a historical association of which he is a member. He must also present in writing a petition to use the archives, stating his field of research. At the present time there is a microfilming service available. Archives may be photostated with special permission of the archivist for each document so reproduced.

The library of the department of foreign affairs is also at Solplass 1. It contains 104,000 volumes and a good collection of maps. It is open to scholars and a card catalogue is available in the reading room.

The University of Oslo library located at Drammenveien and Observatoriegaten was founded in 1815. It has occupied its present building since 1882. All books published in Norway are deposited here, and its annual publication serves as a bibliography. There is a Dewey catalogue for the 1,100,000 books in this library, which possesses some 26,000 volumes of newspaper files. The library is open to the public at the usual hours. The city library of Oslo (*Deichmanske Bibliotheket*) is a circulating library of 350,000 volumes, and in its reading room bibliographies, published source materials, and journals may be found. This library dates back to 1790 when Carl Deichman, a merchant of Oslo, gave his private library to the city.

The Norwegian parliament and the supreme court (*Hoeiestrett*) have their own archives in the *Storthingbäude* (Storthing building). *Statsarkivet* or the District of Oslo archives are also in this building. These archives include those of the southeastern Norway and the ecclesiastical archives of the Bishop of Oslo. The city archives of Oslo are at *Grev Wedels Plass* 2. The *Statsarkivet* for Trondhjem and northern Norway include the archives of the Archbishopric of Nidaros and may be found on Hoiskolveien in Trondhjem. The old Hanseatic city of Bergen also has a *Statsarkiv* located on Aarstaveien in that city, which serves as a depository for southwestern Norway. Two of Norway's statesmen, W. K. Christie, the president of the first Storthing in 1814, and Christen Michaelson, the first premier of free Norway in 1905, were natives of Bergen. There is also the Nobel Institute of Oslo, located at Drammenveien and Parkveien, with a reading room open to the public and a library of books on international affairs and peace.

Housing in Oslo should not be a difficult matter. A number

of small hotels may be found in the vicinity of the National
Archives, and pensions are numerous in the university library
locale. There is a student hotel near the university. A service
for housing at various prices is maintained by the Norwegian
Railways at the terminal station in Oslo at a nominal cost.
Travel bureaus such as Bennett's and the American Express will
find hotel and pension accommodations. It is recommended
that the researcher be fortified with a letter of introduction for
the National Archives, the libraries, and university circles. A
general letter may fit more occasions, and should be obtained
from the university with which he is associated or from a
historical association. Registration with the consulate or the
cultural attaché will be of help if the researcher expects to
remain for some months in the city.

BIBLIOGRAPHY

Published Collections of Source Materials

1. Allen, C. F. *Aarsberetningar fra det Konglige Geheimearchiv: Breve og
    Aktstykker till Oplysning af Christiern den Andens og Frederick den Forstes
    Historie.* Copenhagen, 1854. Letters and documents of the reigns of
    Christian II and Frederick I from the Foreign Affairs Archives.

2. Bricka, C. F. and L. Laursen. *Kancelliets Brevboger vedrorende Danmarks
    indre Forhold, 1551–1615.* 13 vols. Copenhagen. Copybooks of the
    chancery concerning the internal affairs of Denmark.

3. Erslev, K., and W. Mollerup. *Kong Frederick den Forstes danske Regis-
    tranter.* Copenhagen, 1878–79. The registers of Frederick I (1524–
    1533).

4. *Danske Kancelliregistranter, 1553–1550.* Copenhagen, 1881–82.
    Registers of letters of the Danish chancery.

5. Kongelige norske Videnskabersselskab (Royal Norwegian Learned
    Society), *Skrifter* and *Forhandlinger.* Serial publications that contain
    historical sources, although the Society is primarily for science.
    Following are some of the publications of diplomatic correspondence.
    Nielsen, Y. "Aktmaesigge Bidrag til de nordiske Rigers politiske
    Historia i 1813 og 1814," *Forhandlinger i Vedenskabsselskabet i
    Christiania.* Christiania, 1877, Nr. 2. A discussion with excerpts of
    the diplomatic correspondence between Sweden and Vienna
    about Norway in 1813–14.

"Aktstykker vedkommende stormagternes Mission till Kjöbenhavn i Aaret 1814," Videnskabsselskabet i Christiania, *Skrifter*. Christiania, 1897, Hist.-fil. Klasse, Nr. 3. Source material from the diplomatic archives of Denmark, England, Prussia, Austria, and Russia concerning Norway in 1814.

6. Laursen, L. *Danmark-Norges Traktater, 1523–1750, med derti horende Aktstykker*. Copenhagen. Danish-Norwegian Treaties and Documents.

7. Norske Generalstaben (Norwegian General Staff). "Akstykker vedrörende Fredsunderhandlingerne med de mod Frankrig forbundne Magter," *Meddelelser fra Krigsarkivene*. vol. IX. Christiania, 1902. The diplomatic correspondence between the powers allied against Napoleon.

8. Norske historiske Forening (Norwegian Historical Society). *Historisk Tidskrift*. Historical journal which contains articles, with source material, diaries, etc.

Christie, W. F. K. "Dagbog mai-oktober 1814," *Historisk Tidskrift* (1901), R.4, I, 28–213. A diary of the first President of the Storthing.

Manthey, A. C., "Aug. Chri. Mantheys Dagboger for Arene, 1856–1874," *Historisk Tidskrift* (1909–1919), Supplement (Bilaga). Manthey was active in the Scandinavian movement of 1864.

9. Norske historiske Kildeskriftskommission (Norwegian Commission for the Publication of historical sources). *Historiske Samlinger*. Collections of historical sources. Some examples of this publication are given as follows:

"Diplomatisk Brevveksling om Norge mellen Wien og London (1814) og mellen Berlin og London (1813–14)," *Historiske Samlinger* (1902–07), II. Diplomatic correspondence.

"Diplomatiske Aktstykker fra 1814," *Historiske Samlinger* (1908–14), III, 179–244. Austrian and Prussian dispatches to London and the correspondence between Bernadotte and Alexander I of Russia.

Nielsen, Y., "Aktstykken om Bödosagen," *Historiske Samlinger* (1900), I, 113–464. Diplomatic correspondence between London and Norway over British smuggling at Bödo in northern Norway.

10. *Regesta diplomatica historiae Danicae*. Copenhagen, 1847–1907. Source materials to 1660, including some Norwegian.

11. Riksarkivet, *Meddelelser fra Riksarkivet*. Journal of the National Archives, which publishes source materials from time to time.

12. *Norske Rigs-registranter*. Christiania, 1861–91. Norwegian national registers.

13. Udenrigsministeriets Foranstallning. *Danske Traktater, 1751–1800.* Copenhagen, 1882. Danish treaties.

14. Utenriksdepartementet, *Norges Traktater, Recueil des traités de la Norvège.* Christiania, 1907–1926. Norwegian treaties from 1905 to 1926, published by the Norwegian Department of Foreign Affairs.

15. Utrikesdepartementet (Svenska). *Sveriges och Norges traktater med främmande magter 1814–1905.* Stockholm, 1906. The treaties of Sweden and Norway published by t˙e Swedish Department of Foreign Affairs.

16. Wegener, C. F., and A. D. Jörgensen. *Aarsberetninger fra det Kongelige Geheimearchiv indeholdene Bidrag til dansk Historie af utrykte Kilder.* 7 vols. Copenhagen, 1852–83. Annual reports from the foreign affairs archives of Denmark with supplements of the publication of source materials of Danish history, some pertaining to Norway.

Guides and Reference Works

17. Birkeland, M. *Om arkivvaesenets Ordning. Erklaering fra Rigsarkivaren til Kirkedepartementet.* Christiania, 1877. Reprinted in *Historiske Skrifter* (Christiania, 1922). A report of the history and the condition of the archives by the archivist to the ecclesiastic department of the Norwegian government in 1876.

18. Bowallius, R. M. "Bidrag till historien om K. Christiern II :s arkiv och dess delning mellen Sverige, Norge och Danmark," *Meddelanden från (svenska) Riksarkivet* (1875–79), III, 21–46. A good discussion of the archives obtained from Munich and their distribution.

19. Brinckmann, Christian. *Norges Arkivsaker i Danmark.* Oslo, 1927. Discusses the exchange of archives between Denmark and Norway from 1820 to 1851, the archives remaining in Denmark, which includes diplomatic correspondence, and the Arne Magnusson collection (Arnamagnaenska Samlingen) at the University of Copenhagen library.

20. Bring, Samuel E. *Bibliografisk handbok till Sveriges historia.* Stockholm, 1934. This excellent bibliography contains many references to the diplomatic correspondence of Norway and other source materials for Norwegian history.

21. Erichsen, B., and A. Krarup. *Dansk historisk Bibliografi.* 3 vols. Copenhagen, 1918–27. A Danish historical bibliography, valuable for Norwegian international affairs.

22. Erslev, Kristian. *Rigsarkivet.* Copenhagen, 1923. A discussion of the organization of the Danish Royal Archives.

23. International Institute of Intellectual Co-operation of the League of Nations. *Guide international des archives - Europe,* "Norvège," p. 224.

24. Koht, Halvden. *Det gamle norske Riksarkive og restane fraa det.* Oslo, 1927.

25. Kolsrud. "Arkivregistrering paa Akershus i 1622," *Meddelelser fra det norske Riksarkiv.* (Oslo, 1921–28), pp. 257–286. A discussion of the archives lost since 1622.

26. *Kort oversigt de i det norske Rigsarkiv samt Stiftsarkiverne i Trondhjem og Bergen beroende Arkivsager.* Christiania, 1907. The classification of the National Archives of Norway and the diocesan archives of Trondhjem and Bergen.

27. Secher, V. A. "Das Archivwesen im skandinavischen Norden," *Archival Zeitschrift* (Munich), V, 249–259.

28. "Opdagelsen og Erhvervelsen af Kong Kristiern II: s Archiv fra hans Ophold i Nederlandene 1523–31," *Meddelelser fra det danske Rigsarchiv* (1906–18), I, 335–383. A discussion of the Munich archives obtained by the Scandinavian countries.

29. Thomle, E. A. "Rigsarkivets Organisation, almindelige Forhold vedkommende Arkivvaesenet," *Meddelelser fra norske Riksarkivet* (1896–1902), pp. 403 ff. A good account of the history of the Norwegian National Archives.

30. Universitätsbibliotheket. *Norske Aviser, 1763–1929.* Christiania, 1929. A bibliography of Norwegian newspapers.

31. Utenriksdepartementet. *Bibliografiske Opplysninger om Norsk Utenrikspolitikk etter 1905.* Oslo, 1951. A bibliography on Norwegian foreign affairs since 1905 containing publications by the Norwegian department of foreign affairs and the Storthing; also magazine articles.

10 PORTUGAL[1]

Manoel Cardozo
The Catholic University of America

THE PRINCIPAL DEPOSITORIES

THE archives and libraries of Portugal, both public and private, are surpassingly rich in unpublished materials for the study of diplomatic history. These materials are especially valuable for the study of the relations of Portugal with the other European powers (notably England, Castile, France, Holland, the Holy See, and Austria) and with the Order of Malta, but they are also important, as one would expect in a country with old and widespread imperial connections, for the diplomatic history of nations and territories outside Europe.

Despite this abundance of sources, foreign scholars, and in particular the American scholars who concern themselves with the diplomatic history of Europe, have not been fully aware of the opportunities for research afforded them in Portugal. The eight centuries of Portuguese history (since the political organization of the nation) have profound diplomatic implications, and the existing Portuguese materials, ancient as they are and covering as they do even the remote areas beyond the seas, have a real significance for the historian today.

[1]This survey was largely made possible by a grant from the American Philosophical Society of Philadelphia. In Portugal Dr. Manuel Santos Estevens, Director of the National Library of Lisbon; Dr. Virginia Rau, Professor of History in the Faculty of Letters of the University of Lisbon; and Dr. António Cruz, Director of the Municipal Public Library of Oporto, were especially kind. It was not possible to visit the District Archives of Evora or get through correspondence the information needed. For these reasons these very rich archives are not listed. However, the title of the printed catalogue is included in the bibliography. Most of the manuscripts are extremely well described by the compiler of the work.

Arquivo Nacional da Torre do Tombo, Palácio de São Bento (also known as Palácio da Assembleia), Lisbon. Founded during the second half of the fourteenth century. Open daily, except Sundays and holidays, 11 A.M. to 4 P.M. Dr. João Martins da Silva Marques, Director. Reading is by natural light only.

The *Arquivo Nacional da Torre do Tombo* (generally referred to as *Torre do Tombo*), the oldest secular public archives of Europe, are the largest, richest, and most distinguished archives of Portugal. Most of the papers are housed in a wing of the Palácio de São Bento, the national legislative palace, where the offices of administration and the principal reading room are located. The vast collections of the National Archives and its dependencies run into the millions of pieces. These have not been fully inventoried, but some catalogues are available. For special help in locating materials, the reader is directed to Dr. Emília da Piedade de Carvalho Félix, an official of the Archives.

For the study of diplomatic history, the largest and most important single source is the Historical Archives of the Portuguese Foreign Office, which were transferred to the *Torre do Tombo* in 1950. These papers—717 boxes and numerous bundles—include (1) the correspondence of Portuguese and foreign diplomatic missions and consulates (known as *Correspondência das Caixas*); (2) internal records of the foreign office; (3) letters of cardinals; (4) letters of princes; (5) records of the Mixed Commission on the Suppression of the Slave Trade; (6) the Congress of Vienna; (7) reports of the Desembargo do Paço (or Court Royal); (8) correspondence with France; (9) the commerce commission (Junta do Comércio); (10) reports (*ofícios*) of the governors of Portugal; (11) the Order of Malta; (12) documents on slavery; (13) miscellaneous protests (*reclamações*); (14) miscellaneous petitions; and (15) international treaties, acts, and conventions.

The foreign office records that are in this depository date for the most part from about the middle of the eighteenth century and end in 1851. Papers of this collection are not numerous for the period before 1756. There is nothing, for example, on the period from the Restoration of 1640 to the peace with Spain of 1668, and only miscellaneous documents from 1668 to 1736, when the Archives of the Foreign Office were officially created. The collection is more or less complete beginning with 1756. Its lacunae may be attributed to three reasons: (1) the Lisbon earthquake of 1755, which destroyed the Archives of the Foreign Office; (2) the custom followed by the Marquess of Pombal (who was in office from 1750 to 1777) of removing state papers from the Archives of the Foreign Office, many of which were never returned (they are now for the most part in the Pombaline Collection of the National Library of Lisbon); and (3) the considerable bodies of materials transferred to the *Torre do Tombo* during the nineteenth century.

For the period before 1756 (and in some instances after that date), there are other collections of manuscripts in the *Torre do Tombo*, notably the Collection of Bulls (beginning with 1099), the Papers of the Portuguese Factory at Antwerp (1411–1796), the Royal Chancelleries (beginning with the thirteenth century), the *Corpo Cronológico* (1123–1699), Diplomatic Correspondence and Instructions (1641–1785), papers filed by drawers or *gavetas* (from the twelfth century to the present), papers of the *Mesa da Consciência e Ordens* (beginning with the sixteenth century), papers of the Military Order of Christ, papers of the Holy Office, the São Vicente Collection (sixteenth and seventeenth centuries), and Miscellaneous Treaties (eighteenth and nineteenth centuries).

Except for the personal papers of Conselheiro José Luciano de Castro and the papers of the extinct religious communities, which may be consulted only with the permission of the director, all the manuscripts of the *Torre do Tombo* are at the disposal of any scholar in accordance with the Archives' rules and regulations.

Arquivo e Biblioteca do Ministério dos Negócios Estrangeiros, Largo do Rilvas, Lisbon. Founded in 1736. Open daily, except

Sundays and holidays, 9 A.M. to 12 noon, 2 to 5 P.M. Dr. Alberto L. M. Martins, Director. Open only to scholars who secure the permission of the secretary-general of the foreign office.

The records of the foreign office for the period since 1851 are in the foreign office's own archives. This material is distributed in numerous codices and 1,157 boxes, classified chronologically by origin. It comprises the following sections: (1) Correspondence of the Portuguese and Foreign Diplomatic Missions, of the Portuguese Consulates—for consular information before the nineteenth century, see the collection of papers of the Junta do Comércio in the *Torre do Tombo*—and of the Ministries; (2) Correspondence on the Lourenço Marques Railway; (3) Boundaries; (4) Correspondence of the Civil Governors and of the Governors of the Overseas Provinces; (5) the Church of St. Anthony of the Portuguese in Rome; (6) Concordats and Negotiations with the Holy See; (7) Letters of Cardinals; (8) the Question of Bolama, Portuguese Guinea; (9) Portuguese Sovereignty in Zambezia; (10) Wills; (11) the Boer War; (12) Miscellaneous Manuscripts; (13) Miscellaneous Subjects; and (14) Miscellaneous Protests.

Biblioteca Nacional, Largo da Biblioteca Nacional, Lisbon. Founded in 1796. The main reading room is open daily, except Sundays and holidays, 11 A.M. to 5 P.M., 8 P.M. to 11 P.M. The library is closed evenings during August and September. The reading room of the Rare Book and Manuscript Division is open daily, except Sundays and holidays, 11 A.M. to 5 P.M. Dr. Manuel Santos Estevens is the Director, and Dr. Carlota Gil Pereira is Chief of the Rare Book and Manuscript Division.

The Pombaline Collection, acquired from the heirs of the Marquess of Pombal (1699–1782), is made up largely of papers of the first part of the eighteenth century. These may be consulted freely. There is a printed catalogue of the collection. The National Library also has diplomatic correspondence of the Marquess of Niza, António da Silva e Sousa, Francisco de Sousa Coutinho, Father António Vieira, Count of Ericeira,

Alexandre de Gusmão, Count of Tarouca, Dom Luis da Cunha, Caetano Lima, Duke of Palmela, Duke of Saldanha, Anselmo José Braamcamp, José Estêvão, Count of Lavradio, Count of Bonfim, Bishop of Viseu, Duke of Ávila, António Ribeiro Saraiva, etc. It has papers that deal with the diplomatic relations of Portugal with Spain, France, England, the Low Countries, Russia, Morocco, Tripoli, Algiers, Rome, Mazagan, Persia, China, etc. The manuscript division of the National Library is made up of 12,681 codices, 2,284 bundles of manuscripts, and 234 boxes of manuscripts.

Arquivo Histórico Militar, Museu Militar, Largo dos Caminhos de Ferro, Lisbon. Founded by decree of May 25, 1911. Open daily, except Sundays and holidays, 1 to 6 P.M. Captain Jorge da Costa Pereira, Director. Foreigners may not work in these archives without the written authorization of the office of the minister of war, duly countersigned. The foreign scholar should first approach the director of the archives. However formidable the law may be, the fact remains that working conditions for the scholar in the War Archives are excellent.

The *Arquivo Histórico Militar* is one of the largest archives of Portugal. The papers of the council of war (1640–1834) are now in the *Torre do Tombo*, but arrangements have been made to transfer them to the War Archives. These will eventually form the oldest group of records in the archives.

The holdings of the archives are divided into three sections. The first concerns military campaigns in Europe and in Portugal. The oldest existing documents of the archives, before 1640, are to be found here. The second deals with overseas expeditions and campaigns. Brazil is included in this section. The third comprises a collection of papers on general military matters, such as the defense of Portugal, uniforms, iconography, etc. Within the three sections are the papers of the secretariat of state for foreign affairs and war, papers on the wars of the period of Liberalism (the so-called Archives of Terceira), the papers of the now extinct Infantry and Cavalry Offices

(*Inspecções Gerais de Infantaria e Cavalaria*), etc. The archives are organized chronologically by subject, and the materials are easily located. The subjects are in many cases the wars in which Portugal has taken part, the War of the Restoration, the War of the Spanish Succession, the Seven Years' War, the wars with Spain in South America, the Napoleonic wars, the independence of Brazil, the civil wars during the liberal period, the colonial wars, and the First World War.

Arquivo Histórico do Ministério das Finanças, Rua de Santa Marta, 61–E., Lisbon. Founded in 1938. Open daily, except Sundays and holidays, 9 A.M. to 12 noon, 2 to 5 P.M. José Augusto Mendes da Cunha Saraiva, Director. Although not generally open to the public, permission to work here is granted by the *Director-Geral da Fazenda Pública* and is not difficult to obtain. The director of the archives will make the necessary arrangements.

Most of the material in these archives concern domestic affairs, but certain collections are of special interest for the history of diplomacy. Among these are the archives of the royal house which contain, *inter alia*, the reports and correspondence of Alexandre de Gusmão, the private secretary of King John VI and the person most directly involved in the negotiations for the boundary treaty of 1750 (dealing primarily with South America). The papers of the Order of Malta, some of which are here, and those of the council of finance will also be of use to the historian of diplomacy.

The papers of the archives are not catalogued, but there are a number of printed guides and studies the scholar will find useful. Arrangements must be made with the director to consult papers housed in the annexes of the archives in Santa Joana, Santa Luzia, Trinas, and Calçada da Ajuda, all in Lisbon.

Arquivo Histórico Municipal, Paço do Conselho, Lisbon. Founded in 1940. Open daily, except Sundays and holidays, 9 A.M. to 12 noon, 3 to 5 P.M. The archives may be used only with the permission of the Director of the Central and Cultural

Services of the Lisbon City Council. The archivists immediately in charge are Dr. Lia Ferreira do Amaral and Dr. Idalina Mota Grilo Ribeiro Rodrigues.

The papers of these archives, collected in about 6,000 codices and numerous bundles and boxes, are of considerable interest for the history of diplomacy. The current records of the city government of Lisbon are kept in the *Arquivo Geral da Câmara Municipal de Lisboa*. Any document over fifty years old is automatically transferred from the *Arquivo Geral* to the *Arquivo Histórico Municipal*.

The collection known as the *Chancelaria Régia* (Royal Chancellery) begins with the first king of Portugal and extends to the overthrow of the monarchy in 1910, a record of about 800 years. The collection known as the *Chancelaria da Cidade* (Chancellery of the City) is divided into three parts: (1) *Livros de Chancelaria* (1627–1824), (2) *Livros de Vereação* (1515–1900), and (3) *Editais e Posturas* (1419–1753). There is a miscellaneous *Colecção da Coroa* (Crown Collection) that has nothing to do with the administration of the City of Lisbon.

There are general guides to the collections. The cataloguing of the codices began only in 1945. A card index is now being prepared.

Biblioteca e Arquivo da Assembleia Nacional, Palácio de São Bento, Lisbon. Founded in 1836. Not open to the public. Permission to use the archives or the library must be secured from Idalino Ferreira da Costa Brochado, Secretary of the National Assembly. The archivist-librarian immediately in charge is Dr. Joaquim Rosado Carmelo Rosa.

The archives contain the papers of the royal parliamentary regime in Portugal, beginning with the Liberal Côrtes of 1821 and extending to the overthrow of the monarchy in 1910. The papers of the congresses of the republic (1911–26) are also here, as are those of the national assembly and the corporative chamber, both created since 1926. There is no adequate index of the archives' holdings except for the 1821–23 period.

Arquivo Histórico Ultramarino, Palácio da Ega, Calçada da Boa Hora, 30, Lisbon. Founded in 1931. Open daily, except Sundays and holidays, 2 to 7 P.M. Dr. Joaquim Alberto Iria Júnior, Director.

These archives (formerly known as the *Arquivo Histórico Colonial*) are part of the ministry for overseas territories. They are especially well known to historians for the papers of the overseas council (1643–1833), in its time the most important administrative agency for the Portuguese empire, but the archives also contain the papers of the colonial offices that have since superseded the council.

The *Arquivo Histórico Ultramarino* are the largest and most important archives of Portugal for the study of the history of the former and present overseas possessions of Portugal, including Brazil. There are about 4,380 codices, 2,284 bundles of manuscripts, and 810 boxes of manuscripts. There is also an uninventoried collection of miscellaneous papers. These archives, like nearly all the other archives of Portugal, do not have a special section devoted to diplomatic affairs, but many of the documents have a direct bearing on diplomatic history. For the boundary settlements in South America (as they involved Brazil), as well as those in the Portuguese areas of Africa and elsewhere, the records of the *Arquivo Histórico Ultramarino* are indispensable. Actually, the history of the imperial aspects of Portuguese diplomacy cannot be adequately treated without consulting the papers of these archives.

Biblioteca da Ajuda, Palácio Nacional da Ajuda, Lisbon. Founded in 1756. Open daily, except Sundays and holidays, 10:30 A.M. to 4 P.M. Dr. Frederico Guilherme Gavazzo Perrÿ Vidal, Director.

The Ajuda Palace Library was founded in 1756 as a royal library by order of King Joseph I after the old royal library was destroyed in the earthquake of 1755. The rare book and manuscript section of the library comprises a total of 5,526 bound volumes. Many of the manuscripts are of prime value for the

diplomatic history of Portugal, notably the (1) papers on the
Jesuits in Asia (beginning in 1541); (2) records on the government of Portugal and Spain (beginning with the sixteenth
century); (3) correspondence of the governors of India, Africa,
and Brazil (beginning with the sixteenth century); (4) papers
on the Council of India (seventeenth century); (5) records of
the council of the exchequer (beginning with the seventeenth
century); (6) records of the Desembargo do Paço or Court
Royal (1587–89); (7) diplomatic papers that deal with Rome,
Spain, Germany, England, France, etc. (from the sixteenth to
the eighteenth centuries); (8) correspondence of important
personages of the period of the Restoration; (9) correspondence
of Sebastião José de Carvalho e Melo (the future Marquess of
Pombal) during his diplomatic mission in Vienna (eighteenth
century); and (10) *Symmicta Lusitana* or *Rerum Lusitanicarum*,
eighteenth-century transcripts of manuscripts from the Roman
archives. There are adequate guides and catalogues.

Biblioteca da Academia das Ciências, Rua da Academia das
Ciências, 19, 1º, Lisbon. Founded in 1779. Dr. António Eduardo
Simões Baião is Inspector of the Library and the librarian
immediately in charge is Virgílio Leão Nunes.

There are 1,936 codices bound in blue, and 950 bound in red.
The former are properly those of the Academy of Sciences,
collected by the academy since its foundation in 1779. The
latter belonged to the Franciscan Friars of the Convento de
Jesus (in a part of whose convent the Academy is now housed)
and extend to 1825. Papers of diplomatic interest are scattered
through the collections.

Biblioteca Geral da Universidade de Coimbra, Coimbra. Reorganized in 1722. Open daily, except Sundays and holidays,
9:30 A.M. to 12:30 P.M., 2 to 6:30 P.M., 8:30 to 11 P.M. Dr. Manuel
Lopes d'Almeida, Director.

The manuscript section of this library contains about 6,000
codices and boxes and a considerable quantity of miscellaneous
papers. Its materials are especially valuable for the diplomacy

of the seventeenth century, notably of the Restoration. Here are papers that deal with the missions that were sent to the various European courts in connection with the recognition of John IV, first of the Bragança line, as king of Portugal.

The university library is the only library of Portugal (except for the National Library of Lisbon) that is officially classed as a national library. It contains about a million volumes.

Arquivo e Museu de Arte da Universidade de Coimbra, Coimbra. In existence since the sixteenth century but opened to the public only in 1903. Open daily, except Sundays and holidays, 9:30 A.M. to 12:30 P.M., 2 to 5 P.M. Dr. Mário Mendes dos Remédios de Sousa Brandão, Director.

These extremely important archives, housed in a superb modern building and provided with every convenience, are under the immediate control of the Faculty of Letters of the University of Coimbra. Among its extensive holdings of interest are papers on Dom Luis da Cunha (the Portuguese delegate to the Congress of Utrecht), the Napoleonic invasions, the relations of the university with the Holy See, Society of Jesus, and Nova Colónia do Sacramento. The catalogues are incomplete.

Biblioteca Pública Municipal, Oporto. Founded in 1833. Open daily, except Sundays and holidays, 10 A.M. to 10 P.M. Dr. António Augusto Ferreira da Cruz, Director.

This is the principal library of northern Portugal and indeed one of the largest and best in the country. Its collection of manuscripts comprises about 2,500 codices and 1,500 bundles of papers. This collection is of considerable interest for the study of nearly all periods of the diplomatic history of Portugal, but particularly since the seventeenth century. A catalogue is available.

Biblioteca Pública e Arquivo Distrital, Braga. Founded by decree of August 11, 1917. Open daily, except Sundays and holidays, 9 A.M. to 12 noon, 2 to 5 P.M., 8 to 10 P.M. Closed evenings during the months of August and September. Dr. António Gomes da Rocha Madahil, Director.

The archives' collection of about 10,000 medieval documents, from the ninth to the thirteenth centuries, is rich in papal bulls. The manuscripts of the Count of Barca Collection in 18 boxes are of some interest for the study of diplomacy, particularly as it involves Brazil. Other Barca papers are in the National Library of Rio de Janeiro. There is a catalogue.

Arquivo Distrital, Palácio Bettencourt, Angra do Heroísmo, Azores. Founded by decree of April 20, 1948. Open daily, except Sundays and holidays, 9:30 A.M. to 12:30 P.M., 2 to 5 P.M., and on Monday, Tuesday, and Wednesday evenings (except during the months of July, August, and September) from 8 to 10. Dr. Manuel Coelho Baptista de Lima, Director.

This youngest of the important archives of Portugal has some material for the diplomatic history of the period of Liberalism.

Private Family Archives. It is difficult to know what precisely is contained in the numerous private family archives of Portugal, but the materials in them are abundant and some of them, at any rate, are bound to be important for the study of diplomatic history. These archives are not open to the public, but qualified scholars are at times allowed in them. Scholars interested in visiting them must first get in touch with the owners concerned, preferably in writing or through mutual friends.

The owners of the principal family archives of Portugal, together with their places of residence (all in Lisbon unless otherwise indicated) are as follows:

Duke of Palmela, Rua da Escola Politécnica, 140.

Duke of Lafões, Calçada do Duque de Lafões, 1.

Marchioness of Cadaval, Quinta da Piedade, Sintra.

Marquess of Fronteira, Palácio do Marquês de Fronteira.

Marquess of Abrantes, Travessa do Patrocínio, 15.

Marquess of Ponte de Lima, Largo da Rosa, 4.

Marquess of Rio Maior, Rua Eugénio dos Santos, 124.

Marchioness of Alegrete, Largo das Amoreiras, 24.

Count of Castelo Melhor, Avenida Joaquim António de Aguiar, 9, 2°.

Count of Val de Reis, Largo de Santo Estêvão, 6.

Countess of Sabugosa and of Murça, Rua 1° de Maio, 120.

Ecclesiastical Archives. Many of the archives of the religious orders and of other Catholic organizations have been taken over by the state and are now in public archives, notably in the *Torre do Tombo* and the District Archives. Many other archives, however, have remained in the possession of the Church. Permission to use these records should first be sought in the chancery offices (*cúrias*). It is difficult to know how important these archives are for the history of diplomacy—these are on the whole the least accessible of all the archives of Portugal—but certainly they must be consulted to document fully the history of the diplomatic relations between Portugal and the Holy See. It is also in some of these archives that new material will be found on the history of Portuguese patronage.

ADMINISTRATION, REGULATIONS, AND FACILITIES

It is well for the foreigner who expects to carry out his research in Portugal to write in advance of his arrival to the directors of the archives and libraries he plans to visit. He should also write in this connection to The Secretary, *Instituto de Alta Cultura*, Praça do Príncipe Real, Lisbon. The *Instituto* is a special agency of the ministry of national education charged specifically with intellectual and cultural affairs, and its influence over the public archives and libraries of the country (since many of them are under the same ministry) is very great.

Upon arrival in Lisbon, the foreigner should apply at his embassy or legation for letters of introduction to the directors of the archives and libraries he wishes to see. By decree of June 27, 1931, a foreigner may not work in any archives or library without first presenting his passport and such a letter of introduction to the director in charge. The National Library of Lisbon further requires the reader to provide himself with a card of admission, for which two passport photographs are also needed. Such a card is issued only by the Director of the

Library, upon application. The directors of archives and libraries in the provinces are much more prone to overlook the inflexibility of the law, but even in the provinces it is indispensable for the scholar from abroad to identify himself properly. In Lisbon many of the directors of archives and libraries rigidly follow the law, and in some institutions no foreigner is allowed to see a book or a manuscript without the required credentials from one's diplomatic mission. These credentials may also be secured from the *Instituto de Alta Cultura*, the *Secretariado de Informação, Cultura Popular e Turismo*, or, in the provinces, from one's consular representative or from any competent official Portuguese agency. The law seems to look upon every foreigner as a potential thief, but the intransigence of the law is fortunately tempered very often by the good humor of the Portuguese and their thoughtfulness.

The reader should understand fully the regulations under which he is permitted to make use of the facilities of each archive and library. This will avoid unnecessary friction. In some institutions pens may be used; in others, only pencils. Typewriters are never furnished, but the reader will often be allowed to use his own.

Directors and other officials are accustomed to receive more consideration from the readers than their colleagues ordinarily receive in the United States. A foreign scholar in particular should make a point of greeting the director or, in the case of larger archives and libraries, the presiding official of the reading room when he arrives and of saying goodby when he leaves. Bowing will not be enough, even for women, for the Portuguese custom is to shake hands.

All public archives and libraries in Portugal have persons on their staffs who are glad to help the reader with occasional problems of paleography. No gratuities are commended for service, but a gift to a member of the staff who has been consistently kind will help to smooth the path of the next scholar. Needless to say, such a gift must be presented discreetly, preferably upon one's departure. (The director, if he has been unusually friendly, may be entertained at dinner.)

In some of the Lisbon archives the reader is supposed to handle no more than five or six pages of manuscripts at one time. If one is anxious to go over very quickly a substantial number of documents, even the most particular archivists will make it possible for one to do so. There have been a number of unfortunate cases of theft, a notable one on the part of a foreigner, and many of the regulations are designed to prevent a recurrence.

Some researchers may want to take their own microfilming equipment to Portugal. In general the Portuguese customs are lenient about passing duty free unused film for scholarly purposes. If a great amount of such film is to be taken into the country, American scholars should ask the Portuguese Embassy or a Portuguese consulate for a letter of introduction to the customs officials of Lisbon. Portuguese archives and libraries are equally lenient in permitting properly qualified foreigners to photograph their materials. This is rather true everywhere except at the National Library and at the *Arquivo Histórico Ultramarino*, both of Lisbon. These two institutions have their own photographic laboratories and insist that all work be done by them. The quality of such work is high, but their prices may make the cost of an extensive project of microfilming quite prohibitive. Some difficulties may be encountered at the *Arquivo Nacional da Torre do Tombo*, which is not wired for electricity. As a special favor, an extension is provided from one of the outlets in another part of the Legislative Palace. In every instance, of course, special permission must be obtained before any type of photography is allowed.

Since most of the great archives of Portugal are in Lisbon, it is likely that scholars will make their headquarters in the capital city. Scholars may, if they like, stay in one of the several residential hotels of Lisbon, such as the Aviz, which is the most expensive of all, but they should not overlook the substantial savings and comforts offered by the *pensões*. In the smaller cities of Portugal it would be well to stay in a hotel, or in a boarding house recommended by a friend. The nineteenth edition of the *Indicador dos Hotéis e Pensões de Portugal*, giving the official ratings of the establishments listed and the tariffs in each case for room and board, was published in Lisbon in 1953. Portuguese hotels and *pensões* are generally conducted on the American Plan. Arrangements may be made in most cases with the management if only room is desired.

Since steam heat is not widespread in Portugal, winters will often be uncomfortably cold. Scholars planning to work in Portugal in the wintertime should provide themselves with woollen underwear and a heavy coat. Summers are infinitely more pleasant than they are on the east coast of the United States. The light cotton suits worn by men in Washington and New York will not prove practical in Portugal. In all libraries and archives the scholar will be required to wear a necktie and work with his coat on.

BIBLIOGRAPHY

Guides and References

1. Almada, José de. *Tratados Aplicaveis ao Ultramar, Apendices e Indices.* Lisbon, 1942.

2. Almeida, Eduardo de Castro e. *Bibliotheca Nacional de Lisboa. Archivo de Marinha e Ultramar, Inventario. Madeira.* Coimbra, 1903.

3. *Bibliotheca Nacional de Lisboa. Archivo de Marinha e Ultramar. Inventario. Madeira e Porto Seguro, 1613–1833.* 2 vols. Coimbra, 1907–9.

4. *Catalogo de mappas, plantas, desenhos, gravuras e aguarellas. Bibliotheca Nacional de Lisboa. Archivo de Marinha e Ultramar.* Coimbra, 1908.

5. *Inventario dos documentos relativos ao Brasil existentes no Archivo de Marinha e Ultramar.* Vols. 31 (Bahía, 1613–1762), 32 (Bahía, 1763–86), 34 (Bahía, 1786–98), 36 (Bahía, 1798–1800), 37 (Bahía, 1801–7), 39 (Rio de Janeiro, 1616–1729), 46 (Rio de Janeiro, 1729–47), and 50 (Rio de Janeiro, 1747–55) of *Annaes da Biblioteca Nacional do Rio de Janeiro.* Rio de Janeiro, 1913–36.

6. Almeida, José Gaspar de. *Inventário do Cartório do Cabido da Sé do Pôrto e dos cartórios anexos.* Publicações do Arquivo Distrital do Pôrto, 1, Oporto, 1935.

7. Almeida, Manuel Lopes d', and César Pegado. *Livro 2° do Registo das Cartas dos Governadores das Armas (1653–1657).* Biblioteca da Universidade. Coimbra, 1940.

8. Alves, Francisco Manuel. *Catálogo dos manuscritos de Simancas respeitantes á história portuguesa.* Coimbra, 1933.

9. Andrada, Ernesto de Campos de. "O Palacio dos Marquezes da Fronteira e os seus manuscritos," *Revista de Historia* (Lisbon), XII, Nos. 47–48 (July–December 1923), 241–268.

10. Anselmo, António. *Os códices alcobacenses da Biblioteca Nacional.* Lisbon, 1926.

11. Arquivo Nacional da Torre do Tombo. *Indice geral dos documentos registados nos livros da chancellarias existentes no Real Archivo da Torre do Tombo mandado fazer pelas Cortes Na Lei do Orçamento de 7 de Abril de 1838.* Lisbon, 1841.

12. *Inventario dos livros das portarias do Reino.* Lisbon, 1909.

13. Ataíde, A. P. de Bettencourt. "Bibliografia portuguesa de Biblioteconomia e Arquivologia Subsídio para o estudo do nosso problema bibliotecário e arquivístico," *Revista de Historia* (Lisbon), VIII, No. 30 (April–June 1919), 87–106.

14. Azevedo, Pedro A. d', and António Baião. *O Archivo da Torre do Tombo, Sua historia, corpos que o compóem e organisação.* Lisbon, 1905.

15. Baião, António. *O Arquivo Nacional da Torre do Tombo.* Lisbon, 1929.

16. Barreto-Feio, Florêncio Mago. *Memoria historica e descriptiva, á cêrca da biblioteca da Universidade de Coimbra e mais estabelecimentos anexos; contendo varios esclarecimentos officiaes, e reflexões bibligraphicas.* Coimbra, 1857.

17. Basset, René. *Notice sommaire des manuscrits orientaux de deux bibliothèques de Lisbonne, mémoire destiné à la 10ème session du Congrès International des Orientalistes.* Lisbon, 1894.

18. Bethencourt, Cardozo de. *A bibliotheca da Academia Real das Ciências de Lisboa noticia summaria.* Lisbon, 1909.

19. Biblioteca Geral da Universidade. *Catálogo de manuscriptos.* Vol. 1 (Códices 1 a 250)—Coimbra, 1940– .

20. Biblioteca Pública Municipal do Porto. *Documentos para a sua historia.* Oporto, 1933.

21. Biblioteca Nacional de Lisboa. *Inventário dos Códices Alcobacenses.* 5 vols. Lisbon, 1930–32.

22. *Inventario Secção XIII—manuscriptos collecção pombalina.* Lisbon, 1889.

23. *Inventario Secção XIII—manuscriptos.* Lisbon, 1896.

24. *Boletim do Arquivo Histórico Colonial* (Lisbon), I (1950).

25. Cardozo, Manoel S. "A guide to the manuscripts in the Lima Library,

The Catholic University of America, Washington, D.C.," *Handbook of Latin American studies*, VI (1941), 471–504.

26. Carvalho, José Branquinho de. *Roteiro do Arquivo Municipal de Coimbra.* Coimbra, 1947.

27. Castro, Luis de. "O Arquivo Municipal," *Revista municipal* (Lisbon), Numbers 18–19 (1944), pp. 29–34.

28. *Catálogo dos Manuscritos Ultramarinos da Biblioteca Pública Municipal do Porto.* I Congresso da História da Expansão Portuguesa no Mundo, 5.ª secção. Lisbon, 1938.

29. *Catalogue de la bibliothèque de M. Fernando Palha.* 4 vols. Lisbon, 1896.

30. Centro de Documentação Científica. *Instituições científicas, literárias e artísticas portuguesas.* Lisbon, 1953.

31. Costa, Santos. "O Arquivo do Hospital de S. José," *Anais das Bibliotecas e Arquivos* (Lisbon, 1920), 1–7.

32. Cruz, António. *Catálogo dos manuscritos (codices n. os 1225 a 1364).* Biblioteca Pública Municipal do Porto. Oporto, 1952.

33. Danvers, F. C. *Report to the secretary of state for India on the Portuguese records relating to the East Indies contained in the Archivo da Torre do Tombo and the public libraries at Lisbon and Evora.* London, 1892.

34. Diffie, Bailey W. "Bibliography of the principal published guides to Portuguese archives and libraries," *Proceedings of the International Colloquium on Luso-Brazilian Studies, Washington, October 15–20, 1950, under the auspices of The Library of Congress and Vanderbilt University* (Nashville, Tenn., 1953), pp. 181–188.

35. Estevens, Manuel Santos. *Arquivo Geral e Biblioteca Central da Marinha.* Lisbon, 1945.

36. *Sinopse Cronologica da Legislação Portuguesa sobre Bibliotecas e Arquivos (1796–1948).* Coimbra, 1949.

37. Ferrão, António. *Os arquivos e as Bibliotecas em Portugal,* Ciências auxiliares da historia bibliografia e bibliotecografia. Coimbra, 1920.

38. Ferreira, Carlos Alberto. *Inventário dos Manuscritos da Biblioteca da Ajuda Referentes á América do Sul,* Faculdade de Letras da Universidade de Coimbra, Instituto de Estudos Brasileiros. Coimbra, 1946.

39. Figanière, Frederico Francisco de la. *Catalogo dos manuscriptos portuguezes existentes no Museu Britannico. Em que tambem se dá noticia dos manuscriptos estrangeiros relativos á historia civil, politica e litteraria de Portugal e seus dominios, e se transcrevem na integra alguns documentos importantes e curiosos.* Lisbon, 1853.

40. Figueiredo, A. Mesquita de. *Arquivo Nacional da Tôrre do Tombo roteiro prático.* Lisbon, 1922.

41. Fitzler, M. A. Hedwig. *Os tombos de Ceilão da secção ultramarina da*

Biblioteca Nacional, Publicações da Biblioteca Nacional. Lisbon, 1927.

42. Fitzler, M. A. Hedwig, and Ernesto Ennes. *A Secção Ultramarina da' Biblioteca Nacional. Inventários. I-Códices do Extincto Conselho Ultramarino. Estudos e Notas por M. A. Hedwig Fitzler. II-Códices vindos de Moçambique por iniciativa de António Ennes. III-Códices do Arquivo da Marinha publicados, anotados e prefaciados por Ernesto Ennes.* Lisbon, 1928.

43. Fonseca, Francisco Belard da. *O Arquivo Geral da Alfândega de Lisboa,* Publicações da Inspecçao Superior das Bibliotecas e Arquivos, Vol. 3. Lisbon, 1950.

44. Fonseca, Martinho da. *Catalogo resumido da Preciosa collecção de manuscriptos da Casa Cadaval.* Lisbon, 1915.

45. Guimarães, J. G. de Oliveira. *Catalogo dos pergaminhos existentes no archivo da insigne a real collegiada de Guimarães.* Lisbon, 1909.

46. *Index Codicum Bibliotheca Alcobatiae.* Lisbon, 1775.

47. *Indices e summarios dos livros e documentos mais antigos e importantes do archivo da Camara Municipal de Coimbra. Segunda parte do inventario do mesmo archivo.* Coimbra, 1867. Fasc. 2 and 3 of the second part, Coimbra, 1869 and 1872.

48. *Indice chronologico dos pergaminhos e foraes existentes no archivo da Camara Municipal de Coimbra. Primeira parte do inventario do mesmo archivo.* Coimbra, 1863. 2d ed., Coimbra, 1875.

49. Lavadinho, Domingos. *Manuscritos e outros documentos da Biblioteca Municipal de Elvas.* Elvas, 1945.

50. Lima, Henrique de Campos Ferreira. *Documentos manuscritos e cartográficos relativos ao Brasil que existem no Arquivo Histórico Militar.* Lisbon, 1942.

51. Lima, Manoel de Oliveira. *Relação dos Manuscriptos portuguezes e estrangeiros, de interesse para o Brazil, existentes no Museu Britannico de Londres.* Rio de Janeiro, 1903.

52. Marques, João Martins da Silva. *Arquivo Nacional da Tôrre do Tombo (ensaio de um manual de heurística e arquivologia).* Vol. 1 (Index Indicum). Lisbon, 1935.

53. Mellander, Karl, and Edgar Prestage. *The diplomatic and commercial relations of Sweden and Portugal from 1641 to 1670.* Watford, England, 1930.

54. Melo, Arnaldo Faria de Ataíde e. "Arquivo historico Municipal," *Revista Municipal* (Lisbon), Numbers 30–31 (1947), pp. 21–25.

55. Morel-Fatio, Alfred. *Catalogue des manuscrits espagnols et des manuscrits portugais, Bibliothèque Nationale, Département des Manuscrits.* Paris, 1892.

56. Norton, Luiz. *Notícia sobre o "Arquivo Militar de Lisboa" encontrado no Ministério das Relações Exteriores do Brasil.* Rio de Janeiro, 1938.

57. Pereira, Gabriel. *Catalogo dos pergaminhos do cartorio da Universidade de Coimbra.* Coimbra, 1880.

58. *Bibliotecas e arquivos nacionais.* Lisbon, 1903.

59. *Biblioteca Nacional de Lisboa.* Lisbon, 1898.

60. *O archivo ultramarino, Bibliotheca Nacional de Lisboa.* Lisbon, 1902.

61. Prestage, Edgar. *Chapters in Anglo-Portuguese relations.* Watford, England, 1935.

62. *The diplomatic relations of Portugal with France, England, and Holland from 1640 to 1668.* Watford, England, 1925.

63. Proença, Raúl de. "A Bibliotheca Nacional Breves noções históricas e descritivas," *Publicaçoes da Biblioteca Nacional* (Lisbon), I (1918), 7–57.

64. Rau, Virginia. "Arquivos de Portugal: Lisboa," *Proceedings of the International Colloquium on Luso-Brazilian Studies, Washington, October 15–20, 1950, under the auspices of The Library of Congress and Vanderbilt University* (Nashville, Tenn., 1953), pp. 189–213.

65. Rebello, José Pedro de Miranda. *Extracto do Real Archivo da Torre do Tombo offerecido á augustissima rainha, e senhora D. Maria I.* Lisbon, 1904.

66. Ribeiro, João Pedro. *Memorias authenticas para a historia do Real Archivo.* Lisbon, 1819.

67. Rivara, Joaquim Heliodoro da Cunha. *Catalogo dos manuscriptos da Biblioteca Publica Eborense.* 4 vols. Lisbon, 1850–71.

68. Sampaio, Luiz Texieira de. *O Arquivo Histórico do Ministério dos Negócios Estrangeiros (subsídio para o estudo da história da diplomacia portuguesa).* Coimbra, 1926.

69. Santarém, Visconde de. *Noticia dos manuscriptos pertencentes ao direito publico externo diplomatico de Portugal, e á historia, e litteratura do mesmo paiz, que existem na bibliotheca R. de Paris, e outras, da mesma capital, e nos archivos de França.* Lisbon, 1827.

70. Silveira, Luís. *Portugal nos arquivos do estrangeiro. I Manuscritos portugueses da Biblioteca Estadual de Hamburgo.* Lisbon, 1946.

71. Tarouca, Carlos da Silva. *Inventário das cartas e dos códices manuscritos do Arquivo do Cabido da Sé de Evora.* Evora, 1946.

72. Tovar, Conde de. *Catálogo dos manuscritos portugueses ou relativos a Portugal existentes no Museu Britânico.* Lisbon, 1932.

73. Velloso, J. M. de Queiroz. *O Arquivo Geral de Simancas suas importancia capital para história portuguesa.* Coimbra, 1923.

Printed Collections

74. Biker, Julio Firmino Judice. *Supplemento á collecção dos tratados, conven-*

ções, contratos e actos publicos celebrados entre a corôa de Portugal e as mais potencias desde 1640 compilados, coordenados e annotados pelo Visconde de Borges de Castro. Vols. 9–30. Lisbon, 1872–79.

75. Castro, José Ferreira Borges de. *Colecção dos tratados, convenções, contratos e actos publicos celebrados entre a coroa de Portugal e as mais potencias desde 1640 até ao presente.* Vols. 1–8. Lisbon, 1856–58.

76. Cruz, António. *Subsídios para a história das relações diplomáticas de Portugal com a Holanda (1640–1668).* Oporto, 1948.

77. Santarém, Visconde de. *Corpo diplomatico portuguez, contendo todos os tratados de paz, de alliança, de neutralidade, de tregua, de commercio, de limites, de ajustes de casamentos de cessóes de territorio e outras transacçóes entre a corôa de Portugal e as diversas potencias do mundo, desde o principio da monarchia até aos nossos dias.* Vol. 1 (Portugal e Espanha). Paris, 1846.

78. Santarém, Visconde de, and Luiz Augusto Rebello da Silva. *Quadro elementar das relações politicas e diplomaticas de Portugal com as diversas potencias do mundo, desde o principio da monarchia portugueza até aos nossos dias.* 16 vols. Paris and Lisbon, 1842–60.

79. Silva, Luiz Augusto Rebello da, and Jayme Constantino de Freitas Moniz. *Corpo diplomatico portuguez contendo os actos e relaçoes politicas e diplomaticas de Portugal com as diversas potencias do mundo desde o seculo XVI até os nossos dias.* 10 vols. Lisbon, 1862–91.

11   SPAIN

Lino G. Canedo

Academy of American Franciscan History

(*Translation by* Rhea Marsh Smith, *Rollins College*)

THE role of Spain in European international politics began to be preponderant as soon as the union of the kingdoms of Castile and Aragon was realized as a consequence of the marriage of Ferdinand and Isabel. Only then, in reality, could Spain be considered as a political unity, although this was not to be completed until the conquest and incorporation of Navarre in 1512. During the sixteenth century Spain dominated the European scene under its two monarchs, Charles I and Philip II. It continued to be one of the great powers until the Peace of Westphalia (1648) and exercised considerable influence in the affairs of Europe until the French Revolution. The power of Spain began its final decline in the latter part of the eighteenth century under the inertia of Charles IV. The struggles of the war of independence against Napoleon so shattered the machinery of state and so divided the Spaniards politically that the catastrophe was consummated in the reign of Ferdinand VII with the loss of nearly all the overseas territories and the beginning of internal conflicts which fill the Spanish history of the nineteenth century. Until this time Spain had been one of the leading imperial powers.

This synthesis indicates the fundamental importance of Spanish archives for diplomatic history, especially of Europe in the sixteenth, seventeenth, and eighteenth centuries. But it must not be concluded that only at the end of the fifteenth century did Spain begin to participate in European politics. As the reconquest advanced and the Arab domination in the peninsula ceased to be an absorbing preoccupation, the old Spanish kingdoms intervened more and more in European affairs. The Kingdom of Aragon (Aragon, Catalonia, the Balearic Islands, and Valencia) was the principal Mediterranean power in the fourteenth and fifteenth centuries, while Navarre was in close contact with France. Castile, more absorbed in its struggle with the Arabs, who continued to occupy a good part of its territory, and politically less developed, could not give as much attention to external enterprises; but it never lacked European interests. An example of this was the candidacy of Alfonso X, the Wise, for the imperial crown, which was granted to him in effect, although he never succeeded in enjoying it. This Castilian participation in European politics became more intense as a result of the so-called Schism of the West and after its liquidation at the beginning of the fifteenth century.[1] The documentation on this theme in the Spanish national archives of today (Simancas), however, is very scanty, perhaps because it was neither very extensive nor conserved with due care, or for both reasons. The itinerant condition of the Castilian court during this time did not facilitate the services of the chancellery and archives. It was just the contrary in the Kingdom of Aragon and Navarre, which have left us magnificent diplomatic archives, especially the former. The *Archivo de la Corona de Aragón* in Barcelona, the most important in the Aragonese kingdom, contains not only sources of a medieval character, but also others that are of interest to the history of the modern diplomacy of Spain.

All these historical circumstances make a satisfactory classification of the Spanish diplomatic archives difficult. For the practical aims of this study, it has appeared preferable to consider them as independent entities, while noting the relations that exist between some, like those of Simancas, *Histórico*

[1] Some references to Spaniards who, for example, took a decisive part in the direction of papal diplomacy during the fifteenth century, may be found in Lino Gómez Canedo, *Don Juan de Carvajal. Un español al servicio de la Santa Sede* (Madrid, Consejo Superior de Investigaciones Cientificas, 1947), pp. 8–30.

Nacional and *Ministerio de Asuntos Exteriores*. Therefore, they are considered in the following order:

1. *Archivo General de Simancas* (General Archives of Simancas)
2. *Archivo Histórico Nacional* (National Historical Archives, Madrid)
3. *Archivo General de Indias* (General Archives of the Indies, Seville)
4. *Archivo del Ministerio de Asuntos Exteriores* (Archives of the Ministry of Foreign Affairs)
5. *Archivo General de la Corona de Aragón* (General Archives of the Crown of Aragon, Barcelona)
6. Special Archives and Collections

The objective is to present within the short space assigned the greatest amount of information useful for the investigator. The limitations of a work of this type, especially for its extreme conciseness and the consequent difficulty of giving complete data, are very great. These deficiencies may, nevertheless, be overcome in part through the consultation of the works cited in the general bibliography. In addition to those which are indicated under numbers 1–8, that of Carini (number 43 in the bibliography) is especially recommended. In regard to the collections of treaties, one should refer to the *Repertorio* of López Oliván (number 40 in the bibliography), where the principal series are given.

ARCHIVO GENERAL DE SIMANCAS (GENERAL ARCHIVES OF SIMANCAS)

HISTORY[2]

These archives are assembled in the Castle of Simancas, a short distance from Valladolid, in the dry plain of Castile. The

[2]The history of the Archives of Simancas is narrated in detail in the *Guía histórica y descriptiva* (number 1 in bibliography). See especially pp. 140–158, 343–357.

old castle was designated about 1539 for the conservation and custody of the papers belonging to the royal crown. Already in 1509 the creation of two central archives had been arranged: one in the Chancellery of Valladolid for the original documents and another in the Chancellery of Granada, where authorized copies of such documents would be kept. It is not known to what extent this project was realized, especially for the Archives of Granada.[3] There is evidence that many documents perished during the War of the Comuneros (1521), and it was this, perhaps, which inspired the selection of a place as secure as the fortress of Simancas.

To it were carried not only the documents collected in the Chancellery of Valladolid after 1509 but also other documents relating to the Crown of Castile, which after the reigns of John II and Henry IV had been ordered secured in the Castillo de la Mota (Medina del Campo) and the Alcázar of Segovia. Successively, there were added other groups of documents proceeding from different offices and depositories. In 1542 these papers were placed in the care of *licenciado*, Catalán, but the first archivist in the true sense of the word was Don Diego de Ayala, appointed in 1561. Only then did the archives begin to be really organized, with the completion of the necessary facilities in the castle. Ayala was able to accomplish a great deal not only because of his intelligence and effort, but also because he enjoyed the confidence of Philip II, who gave the archives their basic regulations by the royal decree of August 24, 1588 at the Escorial. Philip IV promulgated another important regulation in 1633 as a consequence of the inspection made by Antonio de Hoyos.

The *Archivo General de Simancas* suffered a real disaster during the French invasion, at the beginning of the nineteenth century, when it had to contribute enormous quantities of papers to the

[3]It is nevertheless certain that the licentiate Salmerón had been named "Keeper of the Writings concerning the Royal Crown" in 1509. The licentiate Galindo (1519) and the licentiate Acuña (1526) succeeded him. See *Guía histórica y descriptiva*, pp. 148 ff. (number 1 in bibliography).

fantastic Napoleonic caprice of creating the Archives of the Empire in Paris. It is estimated that between 1810 and 1811 some five hundred carts[4] of documents left Simancas for Paris. In being selected for shipment the series was disorganized; and the disaster was later increased with the entrance of parties of irregular troops into Simancas. With the fall of Napoleon in 1814 all this material should have been restored to Simancas, but the French contrived to hide the most important documents on Hispanic-French diplomatic relations, which were left in Paris. The famous canon, Don Tomás González, named in 1815 by a royal commission for the reorganization of the archives, immediately discovered this deceitful maneuver, and Spain initiated a series of official protests, unheeded by France until 1941. Not until after this date did they return the sequestered documents (it is not known whether all were returned) to their place of origin and to the possession of their legitimate owner. Nevertheless, since 1914 there has been a catalogue of these papers, prepared and published by Don Julián Paz (number IV of the series of catalogues of Simancas).

Until the foundation of the *Archivo General de Alcalá de Henares* and the *Archivo Histórico Nacional* (Madrid) in the second half of the nineteenth century, Simancas constituted the only general archives of Spain for official documents, with the exception of those of America, kept in the *Archivo General de Indias* (Seville). For this reason, several shipments of documents were sent to Simancas after its reorganization by Don Tomás González.

ORGANIZATION AND CLASSIFICATION

This description of the *Archivo General de Simancas* is limited to the indications of the sources of a diplomatic character. The documents are divided into sections, according to their content.

---

[4]The estimate of 500 carts is that of Paz in the introduction to the printed catalogue of these documents (number 11 in bibliography). In the *Guía histórica y descriptiva* (number 1 in bibliography) it is stated that 60 carts were taken in 1810 and 172 boxes in 1811, without affirming that these were the only ones sent.

Each section is subdivided into series and, within each series, the distribution by bundles is usually chronological.

The documents of interest for diplomatic history are conserved principally in the section called *Estado* (State), consisting of the papers of the Secretariat of State. In 1570 it was divided into two subdivisions, the North and Italy; it was reunited into one division in 1626 and again in 1630 separated into three: Spain and the Indies, Flanders, and Italy. Finally it was reorganized again into Italy and the North, assigning to the latter the affairs of Spain and Portugal. The bulk of the State documents in Simancas belong to the sixteenth and seventeenth centuries, but there are also many of the eighteenth century, and some of the fifteenth century. In general the remaining State papers for the seventeenth and eighteenth centuries are found in the *Archivo Histórico Nacional* (Madrid) and are continued in the ministry of foreign affairs (formerly called State), which possesses its own historical archives.

The records of *Estado* in Simancas retain their old classification by "negotiations," one for each country. The most important "negotiations" for European diplomatic history are the following:

1. Negotiations with Germany, Saxony, Prussia, and Poland, 1510–1796.
This section consists of
   a. General part: *legajos* 635–712 for the years 1510-1619; *legajos* 2323–2401 for the years 1600–78. (*Legajos* are bundles of papers loosely tied together.)
   b. Minutes of the Consultations *de oficio* for Germany (1620–60), *legajos* 2402–2448.
   c. Minutes of Dispatches for Germany, 1586–1678: *legajos* 2449–2491; 1654–1699: *legajos* 3948–3954.
   d. Letters from Germany, 1604–29: *legajos* 2492–2510; 1620–1683: *legajos* 3918–3947.
   e. Correspondence from Germany, 1699–1733: *legajos* 6392–6542.

f. Saxony, 1738–88: *legajos* 6543–6579.
g. Poland, 1746–91: *legajos* 6580–6597.
h. Prussia, 1744–88: *legajos* 6598–6608.
i. Hamburg, 1725–59: *legajos* 7453–7478.

These sources are inventoried in summary fashion in Catalogue II, prepared by Julián Paz (number 9 of the bibliography). Paz also included in his catalogue (pp. 241–299) the bundles relating to Germany, which are found in the series of "Notable Affairs" of the same section of State. They contain documents from 1511 to 1744. Paz also indicates five bundles of the section, "Royal Patronage," with documents of the years 1493–1661 relating to "Capitulations and Treaties with the House of Austria."

2. Negotiations with Flanders, Holland, and Brussels, 1506–1795.

Its sources and materials are divided into the following groups:

a. Negotiations with Flanders, 1506–1620: *legajos* 496–634.
b. Minutes and Affairs *de partes*, 1600–24: *legajos* 1743–1854.
c. Flanders and Holland, 1600–78: *legajos* 2023–2287; 1632–1699: *legajos* 3860–4019.

In *Negocios Notables* there exists also, as in the case of Germany, a number of bundles with important documents relative to the negotiations with Flanders from 1549 until 1754.

These sources are inventoried in Catalogue III, also by Julián Paz. (Number 10 of the bibliography.)

3. Negotiations with France. It is one of the most important archival collections for the history of European diplomacy. Many of the most important of these papers remained in Paris until after 1941, as has been indicated; but already in 1914 they had been inventoried by Julián Paz in Catalogue IV of Simancas (number 11 in the bibliography). Nearly all these

documents belong to the sixteenth and seventeenth centuries. They include dispatches and minutes of dispatches from the Spanish ambassadors in Paris, consultations of the Council on such dispatches, capitulations and treaties, etc. In the cited catalogue of Paz the bundles marked with the letter "K" are of special value.

4. Negotiations with England. These papers are inventoried in Catalogue XVII of the Archives of Simancas (number 14 in the bibliography). In spite of the dates that appear in this catalogue (1480–1824) the documents begin to be abundant only after 1550. Only *legajo* 806, the first of the series, refers to the years 1480–1549.

The classification of content corresponds to that of the remaining negotiations: letters and dispatches of the Spanish ambassadors in England, the corresponding consultations of the Council, replies to the ambassadors, etc. The most modern papers, "English Embassy," added to the archives in 1841, contain the documents of the Spanish Embassy in London from 1764 to 1824.

5. Negotiations with Portugal, 1478–1784. No catalogue of this series has been published, but brief summaries can be found in the *Guía histórica* (pp. 216–222) and in the *Guía del Investigador* by Alcócer (numbers 1 and 5 in the bibliography, respectively; cf. also number 60 in the bibliography.)

The type of document is similar to those in the other negotiations. There is much material on the boundaries in South America. A group of papers refers to the combination of the Spanish and Portuguese squadrons (1560–64) to eliminate the corsairs from the Straits of Gibraltar.

6. Negotiations with Rome. Under Number XIV of the series of catalogues of the archives was printed (Valladolid, 1936) an old inventory of this section. There is much diplomatic material, but many documents of these negotiations have a merely ecclesiastical character. A very important complement of these negotiations is found in the archives of the Spanish

Embassy to the Holy See, which are in the ministry of external affairs in Madrid. These have a printed catalogue of several volumes.[5] Documents before the sixteenth century are very scarce.

7. Negotiations with Naples. These records are inventoried in Catalogue XVI of the archives (number 13 in the bibliography). Many of the documents of this section refer to the internal government of the Kingdom of Naples as a Spanish possession, but diplomatic references, explicit or implicit, abound.

8. Sicily. Spanish Viceroyalty and Negotiations with Malta. This series has its inventory in Catalogue XIX of the archives (number 15 in the bibliography). That which was said in respect to the "Negotiations with Naples" must be borne in mind, but special attention should be given to the role played by the Order of Malta in all the political affairs of the eastern Mediterranean.

9. Kingdom of the Two Sicilies. Eighteenth Century. Spanish Embassy. The catalogue of this source has been published by Ricardo Magdaleno, present director of the archives (number 15 in the bibliography). Since the Kingdom of the Two Sicilies included Naples and Sicily, this series continues the two preceding ones, with a more strictly diplomatic character. There are negotiations for Denmark, Holland, Russia, Sweden, Switzerland, the small states of Italy, etc.

The diplomatic historian must give equal attention to certain general and miscellaneous series of the State section. Some of these, for example, are the *Registros de decretos de oficio* (Registers of Official Decrees). Under numbers 399–417 are conserved

[5] *Archivo de la Embajada de Espagna cerca de la Santa Sede* (Rome, 1915–1935). The first volume (sixteenth century) was prepared by Father Luciano Serrano, O.S.A.; the four following by Father José Maria Pou y Martí, O.F.M. Another group of documents concerning the relations between Spain and the Holy See, from the source *Nunziatura di Spagna*, in the Archives of the Vatican, has been partially inventoried by José Olarra Garmendia in his *Indice de la correspondencia entre la Nunciatura de España y la Santa Sede, en tiempo de Felipe II* (Madrid, Academia de la Historia, 1940–49).

many documents from 1703 to 1730. In *Libros* (Books) 68–79 there is abundant diplomatic material, especially concerning affairs in Italy in the sixteenth century. Book 583 of *Inconexos* (Miscellaneous—Unconnected) has copies of correspondence (1746–50) of Don José de Aldecoa, minister of Spain in Sweden. Book 584 contains his dispatches from 1746 to 1749, and Book 585 has other copies by the same diplomatic representative, which cover the years 1750–52. In *Sueltos de Estado* (Loose State Papers) there are also diplomatic documents.

Besides the State section, various other sections of the Archives of Simancas contain documents of interest to diplomatic history. Thus, in *Patronato* there is the series of "royal capitulations" or accords between the kings of Spain and other European sovereigns. Their interest frequently transcends the personal sphere by dealing with true treaties between nation and nation. Aside from the treaties with the Moslem states of the peninsula and those with Aragon and Navarre, there are the "Capitulations with England" (1294–1604), "Capitulations with the House of Austria" (1493–1608), "Treaties with Portugal" (1369–1593), "Capitulations with the Popes" (1452–1570), "Naples and Sicily" (1250–1599), "Milan" (1495–1579), and "Diverse Affairs of Italy" (1251–1668). The capitulations with England and the House of Austria are inventoried in the respective catalogues of the section of *Estado*, but there is a more perfect inventory of all these diplomatic sources on the section of Patronage (number 16 in the bibliography). The "Capitulations with France," inventoried in Catalogue IV (number 11 in the bibliography), do not form part of the Patronage section.

In the *Gracia y Justicia* (Justice) section there are papers relating to the relations of Spain with the Holy See, with the Pontifical Nunciature in Spain, and to the Tribunal de la Rota Española. Two series of this section refer to the government of the intruder king, Joseph I, brother of Napoleon (1809–13): "Intruder Government" and "Various Books" (1808–11).

In *Guerra y Marina* (War and Navy) and *Guerra Antigua* (Old

War) (1386–1701) there is much diplomatic material, especially concerning the reigns of Ferdinand and Isabel and Charles I. The material relative to the latter has been inventoried in Catalogue XVIII (number 18 in the bibliography). Documents of diplomatic interest are found in the section *Secretaría de Guerra* (Secretariat of War) (1700–1830). There are the series "Expedition to Algers" (1775–76); "War with Portugal" (1761–63); "War of Catalonia" (1719–21); "Expedition to Sicily" (1718–22); "War with England" (1727–63); "War with France" (1793–99); "Secretaries of State," that is, correspondence with ambassadors and ministers (1724–88). In this section there is also a series of *Inconexos* papers, among which it is possible to find documents of interest to diplomatic history, as for example, the important correspondence of the Marquis of Valladarias on the war in Germany. Documents of similar character appear in the section *Secretaría de Marina* (Secretariat of the Navy). The series "Expeditions of Europe" (1720–83) contains papers relative to Gibraltar and Minorca, two burning preoccupations of Spanish diplomacy.

Of course, these sources usually have only an indirect interest for diplomatic history, but this interest is not on that account any less real. The same must be said in regard to the section *Hacienda* (Finance), where it is possible to find very valuable information on the international enterprises of Spain. It is sufficient to cite such volumes and subjects as: "Sums paid to the galleys of Genoa" (1612–1746); *Armada de la Liga* (Fleet of the League); correspondence with ambassadors on matters of finance (1734–75); presents to foreign courts (1785–99); war with Portugal and England (1796–99); war with France (1791–99); wars in Italy (1727–83); and sieges of Gibraltar (1776–98).

The section called *Secretarías Provinciales* (Provincial Secretariats) contains especially documents relating to the interior government of certain European possessions in Spain, such as the Low Countries, Naples, Milan, etc. Nevertheless, it also contains documents of importance for diplomatic history. The same may also be said for the section *Visitas de Italia*.

ADMINISTRATION, REGULATIONS, AND FACILITIES

The Archives of Simancas are attended by officials of the Corps of the Archives, subject to the General Directorship of Archives and Libraries, of the Ministry of National Education.

Present Director: Ricardo Magdaleno Redondo.

The archives are well arranged in the Castle of Simancas, some seven miles from Valladolid, on a good road. Communications are easy, since the archives possess their own bus which daily carries the researchers and archivists.

They remain open all working days, from 9:00 to 1:30. In the months from April to October inclusive they are also open from 4:00 until 7:00.

To consult the sources it is only required that the investigator identify himself. All the documents may be consulted. There is a reference library connected with the archives, and it may be utilized by the investigators.

The archives also have a microfilm office. In order to make microfilms with one's own apparatus, it is necessary to have special permission.

Valladolid is a large city, with good hotels, including one luxury hotel: *Conde Ansúrez*. The hotels are situated in the center of the city, in a good location for taking the archives bus. Apartments have also been completed for researchers in Simancas near the castle. The researcher who works during the months from November to March (usually intensely cold but dry) can use his afternoons to advantage in the library of the *Instituto de Historia Moderna*, a center of studies installed in the principal building of the university, where nearly all the officials of the Archives of Simancas work. Besides, Valladolid has other attractions that can occupy the time of the studious: a good museum of polychrome sculpture, important architectural monuments, and the possibility of excursions to neighboring

historic places with magnificent monuments, such as Tordesil-
las, Medina del Campo, Medina de Rioseco, Peñafiel, etc.

From the end of June until the end of August the climate is
warm but dry. It is nearly always much cooler in the evenings,
which are agreeable. In short, it is a good and healthful climate.

BIBLIOGRAPHY

Guide and Reference Works: Those cited in numbers 1, 5, 6, 44,
47, 48, and 60 of the general bibliography. Simancas possesses
a good series of printed catalogues, which have already been
indicated in the appropriate places and are again listed in
numbers 9–19 of the general bibliography. There are also other
manuscript catalogues and files that are at the disposal of the
researcher.

Printed Collections of Documents: Among many others, numbers
21–23, 45, and 50 in the general bibliography.

ARCHIVO HISTÓRICO NACIONAL
(NATIONAL HISTORICAL ARCHIVES)

HISTORY

Don Lorenzo de Arrazola, minister of justice, had intended
in 1847 to put into effect the old project of a central archives in
Madrid, where there would be assembled, as the first objective,
the papers from suppressed offices, such as the Council and
Presidency of Castile, the Council of the Orders, the *Contencioso
de Indias* (Court of the Indies), etc. To this vast quantity of
documents, which filled the administrative offices, there would
be added the archives of the religious corporations and orders
suppressed in 1835. These last sources had been concentrated
in the *Dirección de Propiedades* (Administration of Properties,
Ministry of Finance), but in 1850 were turned over to the
custody of the Royal Academy of History. Eight years later
there was created the Central General Archives, located in the
palace that the archbishops of Toledo had in Alcalá de Henares.

But these archives were principally administrative in character, in accord with the ideas that Riol had already expounded in 1726.[6] There still remained the need for historical archives that should preserve the documents of important organizations.

With this objective, the *Archivo Histórico Nacional* (National Historical Archives) were established in 1866, on the basis of the monastic papers collected in the Academy of History and the archives of suppressed organizations, according to the plan of Arrazola. The new archives were placed in the building of the Academy until 1896, when they were transferred to the Palace of Libraries and Museums, located in the Paseo de Recoletos. At present there is a new building for the National Historical Archives to which the transfer of the records has already begun. Since their installation in the Palace of Libraries and Museums they have received many materials, which have notably increased their quantity. From the General Archives of Alcalá there came, for example, the papers of State, Chamber of Castile, and others. In 1897 the papers belonging to the Council of Castile, Royal Patronage of Castile and Aragon, and others were added. Other documents proceeding from governmental offices have continued to be added since that time.

ORGANIZATION AND CLASSIFICATION

For the objectives of this guide, the section of *Estado* (State) is especially interesting. Its sources proceed from the Secretariat of the Office of State, which after 1714 came to be called the First Secretariat of State and in 1833 became the Ministry of State (today of Foreign Affairs). Consequently, the central archives for the international politics of Spain are found chronologically at Simancas, the National Historical Archives, and the Archives of the Ministry of Foreign Affairs. As has already been

---

[6] The memorial of Riol (number 2 in bibliography) is important not only as testimony of the state in which the archives of the Spanish public administration were then found, but also of the program of organization. This work of Riol has been edited by Valladares, in Vol. III, pp. 73–324, of his *Semanario Erudito*, but merits a new edition and new study.

indicated, many of the papers of the section of *Estado* of the National Historical Archives came in 1897 from the General Archives of Alcalá de Henares, where they had been taken after having remained some time in the National Library. In 1921 the section contained 8,602 bundles, distributed in the following series:

1. Council of State:
   a. Secretariat of the North, Royal Dispatches, 1587–1687;
   b. Consultations relative to the negotiations with Germany (1684-1702), Argel (1696), Sardinia (1647–1709), Flanders (1700–12), France (1700–17), Hamburg (1700–3, 1714–16, 1722), England (1700–18), Milan (1700-7), Naples (1700-7), Oran (1667-69), Low Countries (1651-1717), Portugal (1681–1717), Porto Longone (1708-16), Savoy (1698-1702), Holy See (1679-1717), Sicily (1700-17), Switzerland (1707–17), Venice (1700-13).

2. Government of Joseph Bonaparte (Joseph I). Correspondence and Files (*Expedientes*), 1808–13.

3. Supreme Governmental Committee of the Kingdom (*Junta Central Suprema Gubernativa del Reino*), 1808–14, consisting of 84 bundles. There is a printed index (number 20 in the bibliography). The documents refer, in general, to the conduct of the war against Napoleon, but there are specifically diplomatic bundles. Thus, in *legajo* 22 is preserved the declaration of war on Denmark, on account of its attitude toward the troops of the Marquis de la Romana; the alliance with England etc.; *legajo* 56 contains documents on the intrigues of the Princess Carlotta in the Río de la Plata; *legajo* 69 refers to the armed aid of England and the conflict of the *Junta* of the Kingdom of Galicia with the English representative; while *legajos* 71 and 77 contain communications between the *Junta* of Galicia, cited above, and its representative in London, Don Pedro Sangro.

4. Council of Regency (successor of the committee), 1810–14.

5. Constitutional Epochs: first, 1812–14; second, 1820–23. It is concerned with consultations, orders, decrees, etc.

6. Acts of the Consultative Committee of Government (*Junta Consultiva de Gobierno*), which functioned in 1825, from September 13 to December 29.

7. Council of Government, 1833–36. Contains the acts, correspondence with the different ministries, orders and circulars.

8. Embassies and Legations: Correspondence and files of the following: Germany (1611–61, 1780–1805), Algiers (1787–1800), Austria (1804–72), Bavaria (1804–26), Belgium (1835–49), Brazil (1809–36), Sardinia (1741–1836, 1848–60), China (1843–49), Denmark (1787–1833), Etruria (1801–7), Florence (1789–1800), France (1663–66, 1730–1849), Genoa (1793–99), Greece (1834–49), Hamburg (1779–99), England (1720–23, 1725–28, 1747–98, 1802–43), Luca (1800–48), Malta (1717–98), Mexico (1837–48), Morocco (1766–1850), Naples and the Two Sicilies (1760–1836, 1847–65), Netherlands (1789–1849), Parma (1789–1801), Poland (1760–64, 1790–94), Portugal (1765–1825), Prussia (1789–1833), Cisalpine Republic (1797–1813), Russia (1761–1838), Holy See (1632–43, 1798–1800), Saxony (1739–1832), Sweden (1789–1833), Switzerland (1703–1828), Tuscany (1801–7), Tripoli (1785–99), Tunis (1784–99), Turkey (1778–1833), United States (1785–1833), Venice (1645–65, 1789–99).

9. Consulates. Correspondence and accounts, 1800–50.

10. Treaties, 1701–1869.

11. Board of Commerce and Foreign Dependencies: consultations (1700–1807); files (1815–19).

12. War of Succession: correspondence with the First Secretariat of State (1701–14).

13. Governors of Fortifications and Ports: Correspondence with the First Secretariat of State (1750–1800).

14. Maritime captures and reprisals (eighteenth and nineteenth centuries): France, Prussia, Sweden, Portugal, England, United States.

Documents of a diplomatic character may also be found in other sections. For example, in *Consejos suprimidos* (Suppressed Councils), series "Old Archives of the Council," there is some material relative to foreign policy; in "Extraordinary Council" three bundles are preserved that are related to the Franco-Spanish War of 1793, although nearly all the material concerns French émigrés, especially ecclesiastics; in "Council of Italy," there is a group of papers relating to the State of Piombino (seventeenth century).

Among the documents coming from the *Junta Central Suprema Gubernativa del Reino* there are a certain number of interest to the history of emancipation movements in Spanish America. There is a catalogue of these documents in *Papeles de la Junta Central Suprema Gubernativa del Reino* (Madrid, *Archivo Histórico Nacional*, 1904).

ADMINISTRATION, REGULATIONS, AND FACILITIES

The National Historical Archives are under the care of the Corps of Archives, subject to the Directory General of Archives and Libraries.

Present Director: Dr. Luis Sánchez Belda.

All the documents preserved in the National Historical Archives can be consulted by investigators. These need only to provide themselves in advance with the *tarjeta de lector* (reader's card), which is obtained from the Secretariat of the Archives. In order to obtain the card it is sufficient to identify one's self as a scholar or be presented by a scholar or an official of some cultural body of recognized standing. The criteria of admission are very broad. The regulations that must be respected by all researchers and readers are those current in all the official Spanish archives and are simple and easy.

There are facilities for obtaining photostats.

The archives remain open daily from 9:30 to 1:30 and from 4:00 to 7:00. During the first two weeks of July and the second two weeks of September, they remain open only from 4:00 to

7:00 in the afternoon. From July 15 to September 15, they are open only from 9:30 to 1:30. They are also closed to the public from December 20 to January 6.

BIBLIOGRAPHY

Guide and Reference Books: See numbers 1, 3, 4, and 53 of the general bibliography. The National Historical Archives has published catalogues of several of its sections, but very few of the papers of *Estado* because, perhaps, only from a relatively modern date did the researchers begin to use these sources. The catalogue of documents relating to the United States by Campillo (bibliography, number 53), deserves special mention.

Printed Collections of Documents: There is no important collection that may be considered as being formed principally from the documents of these archives. Yet daily the materials of the section *Estado* are being used in monographic studies.

ARCHIVO GENERAL DE INDIAS

(GENERAL ARCHIVES OF THE INDIES, SEVILLE)

HISTORY

In the last third of the eighteenth century the General Archives of the Indies were established with a view of concentrating in a single place all the papers relating to the conquest, colonization, and government of the Spanish possessions overseas. The idea was promoted by the famous annalist of the Indies, Don Juan Bautista Muñoz, and the strong will of the powerful minister of the Indies, Don José de Galvez, played a preponderant part in its rapid realization.

Basically, the new archives were formed from the American sources already existing in the General Archives of Simancas and from the accumulated papers of the various branches of the government of the Indies (Council of the Indies, House of

Trade, etc.). These governing branches, enlarged in time, increased the sources of the archives with the influx of documents. Among the latest acquisitions of papers were those of section nine, *Estado*, which were transferred in 1871 from the ministry of foreign affairs of Madrid; *Ultramar*, consisting of documents taken in 1887 from the ministry of the same name; and of the "Papers of Cuba," transferred from Havana in 1888–89.

The bulk of State Papers remained at Simancas. Toward the middle of the nineteenth century the National Historical Archives were created in Madrid, where from that time on the papers of the modern diplomacy of Spain have been kept. Consequently, the General Archives of the Indies at Seville can be considered only secondarily as diplomatic archives. Nevertheless, these sources are very important. The classification of papers could hardly be perfect in so extensive and complicated an administration as that of the Spanish possessions in America; and, on the other hand, those possessions were the object of conflicts, negotiations, and agreements with other countries which could not fail to leave many significant documents in these archives.

ORGANIZATION AND CLASSIFICATION

The General Archives of the Indies consist of more than thirty-four thousand large *legajos* divided into fourteen sections and numbered progressively within each section. These sections are the following: (1) *Patronato* (Patronage); (2) *Contraduría* (Accounting); (3) *Contratación* (Trade); (4) *Papeles de Justicia* (Papers of Justice); (5) *Audiencias e Indiferente* (Courts and Miscellaneous); (6) *Escribanía de Cámara* (Notarial Office); (7) *Secretaría del Juzgado de Arribadas, de Cádiz* (Tribunal of the Court of Arrivals, of Cadiz); (8) *Papeles de Correos* (Records of Mail); (9) *Papeles de Estado* (Papers of State); (10) *Papeles del Ministerio de Ultramar* (Papers of the Overseas Ministry); (11) *Papeles de Cuba* (Papers of Cuba); (12) *Papeles de Cádiz* (Papers of Cadiz); (13) *Títulos de Castilla* (Titles of Castile); (14) *Papeles de España* (Papers of Spain). There are handwritten inventories of all these sections at the disposal of the researcher in the archives. These inventories are made *legajo* by *legajo*, are relatively detailed in respect to the first six sections, and very summary for the rest. Some of the latter, for example *Estado*, do have, however, a complete file on their material.

Documentation of a diplomatic character is found scattered in almost all these sections of the archives. Consequently, it is very difficult to give useful information in a brief treatment. The section of greatest diplomatic value, or at least where that documentation predominates, is the ninth: *Papeles de Estado*. The name does not imply, however, that this section contains only documents relating to diplomatic relations. Perhaps it would be more exact to say that it continues the fifth section, consisting of papers of both a political and an administrative character. Yet the references of a diplomatic character are very great in the ninth section for an obvious reason. The dominant problem in the Spanish possessions in America during the period to which the papers of this section refer (the last third of the eighteenth century and the first third of the nineteenth) is brought about by the movements for independence. Various foreign nations, such as England, France, and the United States, intervened in these movements and the questions raised over the struggle for liberation assume thereby an international character.

The sources of the ninth section are subdivided by *Audiencias* like section five. The papers of a general nature form a group apart. In all, there are 108 *legajos*, arranged in the following series:

1. Santo Domingo (Cuba, Puerto Rico, Louisiana, and Florida), 1729–1860: *legajos* 1–19.
2. Mexico, 1707–1853: *legajos* 20–42.
3. Guadalajara, 1686–1818: *legajo* 43.
4. Philippines, 1762–1824: *legajos* 44–47.

5. Guatemala, 1787–1820: *legajos* 48–50.
6. Panama, 1794–98: *legajo* 51.
7. Santa Fe, 1789–1820: *legajos* 52–57.
8. Caracas, 1783–1826: *legajos* 58–71.
9. Quito, 1792–1817: *legajo* 72.
10. Lima, 1700–1824: *legajos* 73–75.
11. Charcas, 1715–1823: *legajos* 76–77.
12. Buenos Aires, 1794–1827: *legajos* 78–84.
13. Chile, 1792–1816: *legajo* 85.
14. America in General, 1768–1836: *legajos* 86–105.

Recently, the publication of the complete file of this section (number 55 in the general bibliography) was undertaken. Its sources had already been inventoried in large part by Torres Lanzas, as seen in his work on the independence of Hispanic America (number 56 in the general bibliography).

Other sections of the General Archives of the Indies contain, as noted previously, materials of a diplomatic character. They are found principally in section 5, in the respective *audiencias* as well as in the mass of material known by the name of *Indiferente*. The conflicts with the Portuguese in Paraguay and Rio de la Plata; the wars with England in the Antilles, Central America, and Florida; the boundary questions with Portugal, the United States, and France; the frictions arising from explorations along the coast of California, all left their trace in the immense source material of this section.

The documents of section 11 (*Papeles de Cuba*), inventoried in detail by Roscoe R. Hill (number 57 in the general bibliography), have great importance for the history of Spanish relations with the United States concerning Florida and Louisiana. In the *Papeles de Ultramar* (section 10) there are eight *legajos* relating to Louisiana and Florida (1717–1822). Material relating to Hispanic-North American relations can be found in the 404 *legajos* of the same section that refers to Cuba (1740–1864).

Even in sections that do not seem to have the slightest bearing on diplomatic material, as in the seventh section (*Secretaría del Juzgado de Arribadas*), there are found some aspects of the wars against England in America, the expedition of Ceballos to Rio de la Plata, etc.

ADMINISTRATION, REGULATIONS, AND FACILITIES

The General Archives of the Indies have been located, from their inception, in the old Casa Lonja of Seville, which is perfectly conserved. It possesses a reading room, a heating system, service for the making of copies and photostats. Except in rare cases no investigator is permitted to make photostats of documents himself, but is obliged to avail himself of the services of authorized photographers.

The archives remain open from 9:00 A.M. to 1:30 P.M. and from 3.30 P.M. to 6.00 P.M. During the latter hours there is no service for getting at the *legajos* or books so they must be requested during the former hours. On Saturday afternoons, Sundays, and holidays of a religious or national character the archives are not open. During the summer months, a reading room is provided in the building below where the investigator can seek respite from the intense heat during the months of July and August.

To be admitted to the archives one must produce the usual evidence of qualifications as a research scholar.

Director: José de la Peña y Cámara.

BIBLIOGRAPHY

Guide and Reference Books: For a general view of the source material of these archives see general bibliography, numbers 58–59. For a more detailed view of the source material one should refer to Canedo's *Los archivos de la historia de America*, now being printed.

Printed Collections of Documents: There has been no publication of any collection of documents that includes as its predominant objective the diplomatic materials of the General Archives of the Indies, but there are many monographic studies, especially recent ones, that have used the same sources.

ARCHIVO DEL MINISTERIO DE ASUNTOS EXTERIORES (ARCHIVES OF THE MINISTRY OF FOREIGN AFFAIRS, MADRID)

HISTORY

These archives were in the Royal Palace until transferred in 1900 to the present building of the ministry. Most of the older papers, those up to the death of Ferdinand VII, had been transferred to the Archives of Simancas, the General Archives of Alcalá de Henares, and the National Historical Archives. The bulk of the documents in the Archives of the Ministry of Foreign Affairs today begin, therefore, about the second third of the nineteenth century. There are, nevertheless, small groups of documents of an earlier date.

ORGANIZATION AND CLASSIFICATION

The sources are arranged according to the different sections of the ministry. The most important sections for this study are the second, *Política* (Policy); the tenth, *Correspondencia* (Correspondence); and the fifteenth, which contains the so-called *Libros Rojos* (Red Books), relating to treaties and annexed documents (1855–1921).

In *Política* there are found documents concerning the following countries: Albania (1780–1829), Germany (1849–1931), Algeria (1786–1931), Argentina (1851–1929), Austria-Hungary (1817–1919), Austria (1919–31), Belgium (1831–1931), Bolivia (1836–1931), Brazil (1851–1931), Bulgaria (1909–31), Colombia (1838–1931), Costa Rica (1857–1931), Cuba (1850–1931), Czechoslovakia (1920–31), Chile (1836–1931), Denmark (1700 –1931), Dominican Republic (1796–1931), Ecuador (1841– 1931), Egypt (1852–1931), Esthonia (1929–31), Finland (1917–

1931), Great Britain (1789–1931), Greece (1807–1931), Guatemala (1849–1931), Haiti (1822–1931), Honduras (1863–1931), Hungary (1919–31), Italy (1781–1931), Latvia (1920–31), Lithuania (1917–31), Luxemburg (1918–20), Mexico (1836–1931), Nicaragua (1850–1931), Norway (1878–1929), Netherlands (1804–1931), Panama (1880–1931), Paraguay (1864–1931), Peru (1842–1931), Poland (1795–1931), Portugal (1820–1931), Puerto Rico (1899–1931), Rumania (1878–1931), Russia (1854–1918), Holy See (1762–1931), Salvador (1858–1931), Serbia (1914–18), Sweden (1845–1931), Switzerland (1848–1931), Turkey (1846–1931), Ukrainia (1919–21), United States of America (1801–1931), Venezuela (1818–1923), Yugoslavia (1918–23). There is also a series of 194 bundles relating to the First World War, 1914–18. This section is composed mostly of files of outgoing dispatches (*expedientes*).

The section of General Correspondence contains the dispatches from Spanish representatives abroad, arranged by order of nations and chronologically. The oldest series, the Holy See, begins in 1789, France in 1831, England in 1837, and Russia in 1834. Some countries that received representatives are not in the section *Política*, as for example, Morocco (1861–1931). The Correspondence of Consulates, the oldest document of which is of 1834, may be considered complementary to this section.

The section of Red Books mentioned above contains the uninterrupted series of treaties from 1869 to 1927. The preceding treaties from 1801 to 1869 are deposited in the National Historical Archives.

In the portion of *Política* concerned with internal policy, there are also important documents for diplomatic history. Thus, in Civil War (*Guerra Civil*) there are papers relative to the British Legion, supplies of Great Britain, the Portuguese Legion, and the French Legion; in Candidates to the Throne (*Candidatos al Trono*), there are some concerning Ferdinand of Coburg, the Duke of Genoa, and the Prince of Hohenzollern,

In Spanish Royal House (*Casa Real Española*) are found documents on the election of Amadeo I to the Spanish throne, as well as credentials to ambassadors and notifications during the presidency of the Duke of la Torre.

The library of the ministry of foreign affairs also possesses some manuscripts of great diplomatic value. Among them are the transcripts of the diplomatic correspondence of Don Cristóbal de Moura (four large volumes) already utilized by Danvila in his well-known work on this influential representative of Philip II (number 69 in the general bibliography); a volume with documents on the marriage of the Infanta Doña Maria, daughter of Philip III, with the Prince of Wales; the original correspondence of Don Melchor de Macanaz, Spanish plenipotentiary at the Congress of Breda (1747-48); memorials of the Marquis of Santa Cruz of Marcenado, ambassador extraordinary of Spain to the Congress of Soissons; diaries of the three divisions of demarcation of the boundaries between Spain and Portugal in South America; the original of the memoirs of León y Pizarro, the text of which notably differs from that published. See the note by Jerónimo Becker in BAH, LXXV (1919), 481-483 (number 75 in the general bibliography).

In line with a general plan that the ministry has been following, the archives of the embassy of Spain to the Holy See have recently been transferred to Madrid and deposited in these archives. This is a collection of great importance for European diplomatic history in spite of the losses suffered from frequent fires. These fires damaged especially the documents of the sixteenth and early seventeenth centuries, although many notable survivals of this period remain. There is a detailed *Indice analítico* (Rome-Madrid, 1915-35) in four volumes, dealing, respectively, with the sixteenth, seventeenth, eighteenth, and first half of the nineteenth centuries. The first volume was prepared by Luciano Serrano, O.S.B.; the following three by José M. Pou y Martí, O.F.M. The latter also published the *Indice analítico de los códices de la Biblioteca contigua al*

Archivo (Rome, 1925). This section likewise contains much diplomatic material.

On the importance of these archives of the Spanish embassy at the Holy See for European diplomatic history, specifically for the nineteenth century, one may refer to the article by Alberto M. Ghisalberti, "L'Archivio dell'Ambasciata di Spagna presso la Santa Sede," *Rassegna storica del Risorgimiento*, XL (1935), 232–237. For more general information, see José M. Pou y Martí, "Los archivos de la Embajada de España cerca de la Santa Sede," *Miscellanea archivistica Angelo Mercati* (Vatican City, 1952), pp. 297–311.

ADMINISTRATION, REGULATIONS, AND FACILITIES

The archives and the library are in the care of officials of the Corps of Archives but under the complete jurisdiction of the minister of foreign affairs.

Present Director: L. García Ribes.

The consultation of documents less than a century old is not permitted. Those of greater antiquity may be consulted, but the authorization of the subsecretary of the ministry must be procured. The personal files of Spanish diplomatic representatives cannot be consulted except in very exceptional cases.

The archives may be used, within the conditions indicated, during the hours of work of the ministry, which are usually 9:30 to 1:30 and 4:30 to 7:30.

BIBLIOGRAPHY

Guide and Reference Works: See number 7, pp. 94–108, in the general bibliography.

Printed Collections of Documents: There are no important ones. The ministry has published, from time to time, partial collections of treaties. They are cited in López Oliván (number 40 in the general bibliography). See also numbers 77–78.

ARCHIVO DE LA CORONA DE ARAGON
(ARCHIVES OF THE CROWN OF ARAGON, BARCELONA)

HISTORY[7]

The Catalan-Aragonese monarchy was the peninsular state that took the most active part in European politics during the Middle Ages and at the dawn of the modern period, before the achievement of Spanish unity through the marriage of Ferdinand of Aragon and Isabel of Castile. In the fourteenth and fifteenth centuries Aragon was a power of the first order in the Mediterranean.

Its magnificent archives correspond to this political importance. They are the best medieval sources that Spain possesses. The origin of these archives dates back to the epoch of the counts of Barcelona (ninth to tenth centuries). They possess manuscripts prior to the invasion of Almansor (986). Alfonso the Chaste (died 1196) took measures for the reorganization of the royal archives, and with James the Conqueror the *Registros* (Registers) were begun, after the practice of the Vatican. James II (1291-1327) and Pedro the Ceremonious (1336-87) especially interested themselves in the archives. To the latter is due the nomination (July 6, 1346) of the first archivist, Pedro Paseya, who died in 1348, after having left an inventory of the papers that the archives then had. Pedro the Ceremonious also ordered the assembly of all the sections of the royal archives in a single place.

The present name, "Archives of the Crown of Aragon," was given during the reign of Charles III. After 1782 this legend appeared on the official seal. It seems that the archives had not been well cared for in the seventeenth century, but in the

[7]This information has been supplied by the present Director of the Archives of the Crown of Aragon, Don Jesus E. Martínez Ferrando, to whom due appreciation is here expressed.

eighteenth century they benefited from the new interest in historical studies. The Mercedarian, Father Manuel Mariano Ribera, accomplished a great work of arrangement during the occupation of Barcelona by the archduke in the War of Succession (1706–13). Later, the great archivist, Francisco Jávier de Garma y Durán (1740–83), attempted without success the unification in Barcelona of the four royal archives of the Crown of Aragon: Zaragoza, Barcelona, Valencia, and Mallorca. In any event, those of Barcelona, which were the most important, were installed in new and better quarters (1770–71). The great archivist of the nineteenth century was Don Prospero de Bofarull, named in 1814, who was succeeded in the office by his son and grandson successively.

ORGANIZATION AND CLASSIFICATION

The Archives of the Crown of Aragon are divided into thirteen sections, of which the ones pertinent to this study are: the first (Chancellery), the third (Supreme Council of Aragon), the fifth (*Generalidad* or Corporation of Catalonia), the ninth (War of Independence), and the eleventh (Miscellaneous) which ends with the archives of the "Old Legation of Spain in Genoa," 1552–1804 (362 bundles).

The principal section for diplomatic history is the first: *Cancillería Real* (Royal Chancellery). To this section belongs the famous series of "Registers,"within which the subseries *Curiae, Curiae Sigilli Secreti, Legationum, Sigillum Secretum, Secretorum,* and *Itinerum* contain diplomatic documents. These must be consulted for each reign. There is also material of interest for diplomatic history in the series *Cartas Reales* (Royal Letters), formed by fifty thousand documents. Likewise within this first section must be considered the series of parchments, in which are included many documents of a diplomatic character. Such is the case for James II, whose parchments include a great quantity of royal correspondence, especially with France and Italy.

In the third section, *Consejo Supremo de Aragón* (Supreme Council of Aragon), the correspondence of the secretariats of Catalonia (French frontier) and Sardinia (Mediterranean frontier) is of diplomatic interest. Yet, as the Supreme Council of Aragon was active in the sixteenth and seventeenth centuries, it must be remembered that foreign policy was then conducted basically from the capital of the united crowns.

There are also diplomatic documents in the fifth section, *Generalidad de Cataluña* (Corporation of Catalonia), especially on the occasions (fifteenth and seventeenth centuries) when this organization was opposed to the crown and sought aid for its aspirations abroad.

The ninth section, *Guerra de Independencia* (War of Independence), contains documents on the interference of the French in Catalonia and the reaction of the Spaniards before the open intervention of Napoleon. Both concepts are involved in the relations sustained from within Spain with the important European governments of the epoch. The two series of which the section is constituted, *Junta Superior de Cataluña* (Superior Committee of Catalonia) and *Papeles de la dominación napoleónica en el Principado* (Papers of the Napoleonic Domination in the Principate) are interesting in this respect.

ADMINISTRATION, REGULATIONS, AND FACILITIES

The Archives of the Crown of Aragon are in the care of the officials of the Corps of Archives.

Present Director: J. E. Martínez Ferrando.

Address: Condes de Barcelona 2, Barcelona, Spain.

In order to be admitted to consult the sources, the identification of the reader, through a letter of introduction or a card from a similar or teaching center is required.

The archives are open all working days from 9:00 to 1:00 and from 4:00 to 7:00. During the summer months the public service is reduced to a single period, from 10:00 to 1:00.

The archives have a library specializing in the history of the Crown of Aragon and related subjects.

They also possess a microfilm service with a projection machine and a laboratory. In spite of the excellence of this service, in special cases the researcher is authorized to photograph documents for himself.

The investigator has at his disposal several manuscript inventories for each one of the sections mentioned. The sources of the "Old Legation of Spain in Genoa" are being inventoried at present in great detail. There are several manuscript catalogues, but none embodies specifically a diplomatic category.

BIBLIOGRAPHY

Guide and Reference Works: See numbers 1, 8, and 80 of the general bibliography. The work of Desdevises du Dezert, "La Junta Supérieure de Catalogne," published in the *Revue Hispanique* (1910), is preceded by an inventory of the respective sources.

Printed Collections of Documents: See numbers 24–30 of the general bibliography.

ARCHIVES AND SPECIAL COLLECTIONS

In this section brief references will be made to certain archives that are either small or not primarily related to diplomacy, but that do have some documents of interest for diplomatic history. It is concerned with public and private archives. Some sources of importance found in the manuscript collections of Spanish libraries will also be indicated.

ARCHIVO GENERAL DE NAVARRA
(GENERAL ARCHIVES OF NAVARRE)

They are located in Pamplona and are under the custody of the Foral Commission of Navarre. Their principal content is the archives of the ancient *Cámara de Comptos* (Chamber of Accounts) of Navarre, the oldest documents of which date back to the end of the twelfth century, although the series does not become continuous until the end of the fourteenth century. Other sections are formed by the remains of the ancient royal archives and by the modern archives of the *Cortes*.

The Chamber of Accounts was an organization of financial control, but among its documents are also found materials of interest to the diplomatic history of Navarre, especially in the series of "Registries" (*Cartularios*).

No special prerequisite is required for the consultation of the archives. They do not have a microfilm service, but the researcher may photograph documents for himself.

Present Director: José Ramón Castro.

BIBLIOGRAPHY: SEE NUMBERS 36-37

BIBLIOTECA NACIONAL
(NATIONAL LIBRARY, MADRID)

Among the varied manuscript sources of the National Library in Madrid, materials of interest for the history of the diplomatic relations of Spain abound. There are, for example:

1. Papers referring to the preliminary negotiations of the Peace of the Pyrenees, conducted by the Count of Peñaranda, ambassador-extraordinary of Spain (May–August, 1658). MS. 5542 (P. sup. 127).

2. Book of registry of the correspondence of the Marquis of Alomodóvar, ambassador of Spain in St. Petersburg (January 8–December 27, 1762). MS. 3526 (L. 243).

3. Book of letters that Don Juan Carlos Bazán wrote on diverse diplomatic matters from some cities in Italy to various princes and lords ("Señores"), as ambassador of His Majesty (January 1, 1689–October 8, 1701); copy of the eighteenth century. MS. 3527 (1.260).

4. Registry Book of the correspondence of the minister of

state of Denmark with the consuls of his nation in Spain, during the years 1781–82. MS. 3833 (M. 485).

5. "Letters of Antonio Rebelo da Fonseca, who accompanied Count Fernão Telles to the Vienna Embassy, for the Count of Assumar," 1705 and 1708; originals, 38 pages in folio and in quarto. MS. 7544.

6. Letters of Antonio Galvão de Castellobranco, envoy of Portugal in London, for the Count d'Assumar (April 1, 1721–February 6, 1727); originals. MS. 7547.

7. Letters and dispatches of the embassy of the Marquis of La Hinojosa, from his departure in May 1623 until his return in July 1624; copies of the beginning of the eighteenth century. MS. 10467 (Jj. 58).

8. Correspondence and documents referring to the diplomatic negotiations of Don Manuel Francisco de Lira at the Hague and Brussels (1671–79); 16 vols., copies of the eighteenth century. MS. 13372(Oo.157).

9. Letters of Don Luis Méndez de Haro to King Philip IV and the replies of this monarch relating to the so-called Peace of the Pyrenees (1659). MS. 4090 (Jj.15).

10. Letters of the Count of Ribeira, ambassador in Paris, for the Count of Assumar (Paris, January 4, 1717 to November 28, 1718); originals. MS. 7545.

11. Journal (*Ephimeri*) of different treaties of peace between Spain and other powers (1508–1713). MS. 12948.

12. Correspondence of Cardinal Granvela (1538–75). *Gayangos 236* (number 32 in the bibliography).

13. Letters from Rome by Don Juan de Zúñiga and others (1579–83). *Gayangos 241.*

14. Venetian Reports from Spain, Portugal, France, etc. (1574–1649). *Gayangos 244.*

15. Diplomatic correspondence of the Count of Fuentes (1593 and 1620). *Gayangos 253.*

16. Sixteen letters of the Infanta Isabel Clara Eugenia, Governor of Flanders, to the Duke of Lerma (1601–6). *Gayangos 256.*

17. "Sir Charles Cornwallis; his Negociation as Liedger Ambassador for Spayne AD 1605"; 752 pages. *Gayangos 259.*

18. Several volumes to and on the Count of Gondomar, Spanish ambassador to England (1605–24). *Gayangos 260.*

19. Letters to Father Nithard by the Duke of Villaumbrosa and others (1676–80). *Gayangos 302.*

20. Correspondence of Don Baltasar Patiño, Spanish ambassador to France, with his brother, Don José (1730–32). *Gayangos 323.*

21. Miscellaneous papers relating to the history of France (1589–1616). *Gayangos 530.*

22. Collection of documents about Louisiana (1767–92); 3 vols. MSS. 19246–19248.

23. Collection of documents on the history of Florida (1709–1817); 2 vols. MSS. 19508–19509.

24. "Memorandum expositivo de las gravísimas consideraciones en que se funda el interés que las grandes potencias y en particular España, tienen en . . . poner un correctivo a la absorción . . . que de todos los Estados independientes, formados a consecuencia de la emancipación de las colonias españolas, aspiran a consumar los Estados Unidos de América, presentado a D. Xavier de Istúriz, Presidente del Consejo de Ministros, por D. Andrés Borrego" ("Expositive memorandum of the very grave considerations on which is founded the interest which the great powers and Spain in particular have in blocking the absorption . . . of all the independent states, formed as a result of the emancipation of the Spanish colonies, which the United States of America aspire to consummate, presented to Don Xavier de Istúriz, President of the Council of Ministers, by Don Andrés Borrego") Madrid, June 24, 1858; 227 pages. MS. 20228.

There are many other documents of diplomatic interest scattered through all the section, principally on the conflicts in America with the Portuguese and the wars with England. See number 62 in the general bibliography.

The Section of Manuscripts of the National Library is open to the public every working day from 9:30 to 1:30 and from 4:00 to 8:00 in the evening.

The researcher needs to provide himself with a *tarjeta de lector* (reader's card), which is valid for one year. It is obtained in the Secretariat of the Library, after the identification of the person and the presentation of some document that proves his aptitude, if this should not be obvious from the offices, profession, or publications of the solicitor. Two photographs are required.

The library possesses a good microphotographic service.

Bibliography: See numbers 32, 62 and 70 in the general bibliography. Some diplomatic material is also listed in the *Catálogo de Tomos de Varios,* published by Julián Paz (Madrid, Biblioteca Nacional, Departamento de Manuscritos, 1938).

In *Codoin* (number 21 in the general bibliography) some diplomatic documents of this section have been published. For example, Manuscripts 1026 and 2795, which contain papers on the negotiations of the Count of Peñaranda with the French plenipotentiaries for the Peace of Münster (1647) were edited in vols. 82–83 of the said collection.

BIBLIOTECA Y ARCHIVO DEL PALACIO REAL
(LIBRARY AND ARCHIVES OF THE ROYAL PALACE)

The manuscript materials of a diplomatic character in this library are abundant, especially collections of correspondence of ambassadors and diplomats. Since the manuscripts are dispersed rather than collected in a series, it is impossible to make a résumé, considering the brief space to be devoted to it in this study. It is sufficient to cite, as an example, the hundred volumes of correspondence of the famous Count of Gondomar,[8] ambassador of Spain in London, 1613–22, 1624–26. Part of

[8]The correspondence of Gondomar is not, for the most part, directly diplomatic in character, although it possesses extraordinary value for a knowledge of the life of this important personage. On the other hand, the correspondence of the son of Gondomar, Don Antonio Sarmiento de Acuña (1635–40), is extremely valuable in regard to the European politics of Spain for these years.

this correspondence has been published in the first four volumes of the new series of *Documentos inéditos para la historia de España* (1936–).

Another notable lot of diplomatic letters conserved in the Library of the Royal Palace is that of Don Diego Hurtado de Mendoza, one of the great craftsmen of the Italian policy of Emperor Charles V. Some of these letters have been published by Alberto Vázquez (number 50 in the general bibliography). There are also numerous letters of Granvela, Lope de Acuña, Antonio Sarmiento, etc., and much material regarding the period of Charles V, Philip II, Philip III, and Philip IV. For the records regarding America, see number 63 in the general bibliography.

There is also material of interest in the General Archives of the Palace, the organization of which dates from Ferdinand VII (1814). In general, it may be said that its documents are concerned principally with the House of Bourbon, although there are papers concerning the House of Austria. In addition to information scattered in other sections, the so-called "Historical Section" is important. It consists, among other series, of the "Confidential Archives of Ferdinand VII," sixty-six volumes. Other sections that should be consulted are *Condecoraciones* (Decorations) (1593–1931); "Matrimonial Contracts" (1570–1701); "Embassies" (seven boxes); "Succession to the Crown" (1700–1904); "Historico-Political Events" (1614–1868); "Treaties of Peace" (1598–1783), one box.

In bundle 4 of this *Archivo reservado de Fernando VII* (Confidential archive of Ferdinand VII) is found the dispatch sent by the Spanish ambassador in Mexico, Bermúdez de Castro, on the plan to convert that republic into a monarchy with a Spanish prince as ruler (1846). In the same bundle is a "confidential dispatch" from the Spanish ambassador in Paris to the minister of state on complaints against Mexico (1861). On this collection see José Moreno Villa in the *Revista de Historia de América* (1938), pp. 57–58.

The section formed by the archives of the Great Steward and Private Secretary of His Majesty may also offer something of interest. It possesses, for example, 24 bundles of "Correspondence with the diplomatic and consular corps" (1874–1936); 4 bundles with the title of "Diplomatic Corps" (1840–1930); "Diary of His Majesty and Audiences" (1902–29), 4 bundles; "International Military Nominations" (1904–27), 2 boxes.

Both the archives and the library of the palace are in the charge of officials of the Corps of Archives, but under the jurisdiction of the Council of Administration of the National Patrimony. To consult the sources, it is necessary to have the authorization of the Manager Delegate Councilor of the Patrimony, which must be requested in writing. Both the library and the archives are located in the building of the Royal Palace. The archives remain open to researchers every working day, from 10:00 to 1:30; the Library from 10:30 to 1:30 and from 3:30 to 6:30 in the afternoon. Both close for eight days in August.

Bibliography: In regard to the archives, see number 7 in the general bibliography, pp. 19–73. For the library, see number 70 in the general bibliography, pp. 165–181.

BIBLIOTECA DE LA REAL ACADEMIA DE LA HISTORIA
(LIBRARY OF THE ROYAL ACADEMY OF HISTORY)

Among the extremely rich manuscript sources in this academy in Madrid there is much that is of interest in respect to diplomacy. Of primary value, in this regard, is the *Colección Salazar* (Salazar Collection), consisting of more than a thousand volumes. These documents are of particular importance for the period covering the reigns of the House of Austria (*Casa de Austria*) and of Philip V. Among the notable portions of them may be cited the correspondence of Charles V and of the famous Spanish ambassador in London, Count Diego Sarmiento de Acuña (1613–18, 1619–22), as well as that of Lope de Acuña y

Avellaneda, the lieutenant-general of the cavalry in Flanders (1557–73) and of Don Luis Méndez de Haro (1639–61).

The papers of Lope de Soria, representative of Charles V in Genoa and commissary of the army of Italy (1526–27), that are in the Salazar Collection are complemented by the *Archivo de Lope de Soria* (Archives of Lope de Soria). This collection of 264 original documents, which illustrate magnificently the policy of Spain in Italy during this period, is also found in the academy.

The collection known as the Lopez Ballesteros Collection, given to the Academy in 1857, consists of some 2,226 copies of documents relating to Don Juan of Austria (1569–78). These documents are copied from the General Archives of Simancas.

Of importance for the relations of Spain in the nineteenth century are the private Archives of Don Francisco Xavier de Istúriz (1785–1871), who was president of the Council of Ministers, was twice ambassador to London (1847–48, 1850–54), and discharged other weighty assignments of a diplomatic and political nature. These papers were given to the Academy in 1919 and are classified in BAH. LXXV, 1919, pp. 101–125 (number 75 in the general bibliography). In the Academy are also, as a gift of their owner and editor, the Duke of Maura, the documents to which number 35 of the general bibliography refers.

Documents of a diplomatic character can also be found in the Lorenzo Folch de Cardona Collection (Colección Lorenzo Folch de Cardona). He was a judge of the Chancellery of Valladolid in the seventeenth century. The collection was given to the Academy in 1857 by Don Antonio López de Córdoba, and summarily inventoried by Don Pedro Sabau in *Noticia de las actas de la Real Academia de la Historia* (Madrid, 1857).

In the *Colección Muñoz* (Muñoz Collection), which is specially important for the colonial history of Spanish America, volume number 56 contains 118 originals, minutes of letters of Emperor Charles V to his ambassador to Rome, the Duke of Sessa, and to others (1522–28). See number 81 in general bibliography.

For the bibliography and reference books, see numbers 38, 39, and 70 in the general bibliography. There is also a general manuscript catalogue, prepared by Don Antonio Rodriguez Villa, which is very useful. The card catalogue is antiquated and imperfect. Many of the documents kept in this library have been published or used. See numbers 21, 64, 65, 66, and 67 in the general bibliography.

The library is located in the building of the Academy (Calle de León, Madrid), and application for its use must be recommended by some academician.

It is open every working day, except Saturday, from 3:30 to 7:30 in the afternoon. It remains closed in the months of July, August, and September and from December 24 until January 6.

MILITARY CENTERS

It is interesting for the investigator of Spanish diplomatic history to be aware of the existence of two centers of military studies in Madrid: the *Servicio Histórico Militar* (Military Historical Service) and the *Museo Naval* (Naval Museum).

In the first, the collection of "Transcribed Documents" (some 6,281), formed between 1844 and 1856 from the Archives of the Indies, Simancas, and the Crown of Aragon, is important. It includes the most significant documents concerning the Spanish campaigns abroad, especially those of Flanders, Germany, France, and Portugal. In addition to this collection of copies, the Military Historical Service also has some 7,264 original documents on the same theme. The most notable groups, both of manuscripts and maps and plans, refer to Africa and overseas. Nevertheless, there is much material of European interest.

A catalogue of all these sources has been published recently in the *Boletín de la Biblioteca Central Militar* (Bulletin of the Central Military Library). The cartographic materials are being edited under the general title *Cartografía y relaciones históricas de Indias*. The second volume refers to the United States and Canada.

The Military Historical Service is located in the old building of the Museum and Library of the Corps of Engineers of the Army (Mártires de Alcalá 9, Madrid), from which it inherited many sources and the activities which it has, in part, continued.

To consult the sources, the permission of the Director-Colonel of the Service is required. It is obtained without any special formality.

The Naval Museum, situated in the building of the Ministry of the Navy (Montalbán 2, Madrid), also has an important section of manuscripts proceeding principally from the defunct *Depósito Hidrográfico* (Hydrographic Depository), founded in 1789. The section of interest to diplomatic history is that constituted by the "Sans Barutell Collection," called thus because it was assembled after 1789 by the naval lieutenant, Don Juan Sans de Barutell. It is concerned with the history of the navy of Castile and Aragon and contains many documents on the naval campaigns in the Mediterranean. In general, the originals of these documents are still preserved, usually in the archives of Simancas and the Crown of Aragon, but this does not annul the value of the work performed by Sans de Barutell.

The general naval archives of Spain are being transferred to the new *Archivo Museo D. Alvaro de Bazán*, at Viso del Marqués, in the old palace of the Marquis of Santa Cruz. They have too some important materials for the history of Spain's external relations. (See numbers 79 and 82 in the general bibliography.)

The *Archivo General Militar* (General Military Archives), founded in 1898 and located in the Alcazar of Segovia are predominantly administrative in character. Their materials belong usually to the eighteenth and nineteenth centuries, as a continuation of the military sources of the General Archives of Simancas. Nevertheless, their indirect value for diplomatic history should not be overlooked. The copious first section, "Personnel," which continues the very interesting series of "Certificates of Military Service," conserved in Simancas, offers unexpected biographical information. The ninth section contains some documents concerning the wars in Portugal and Catalonia. Finally, the tenth section, "Historical," includes a select group of papers that have been judged as particularly important.

To consult these archives special permission of the military authorities is necessary. It must be presented in a request addressed to the Subsecretary of the Army, Ministry of the Army, Madrid.

The trip from Madrid to Segovia, a city of great interest to tourists, is easily made by train (two hours), by bus, or by car.

SOME PRIVATE ARCHIVES

1. Archives of the House of Alba. In spite of the losses suffered in repeated fires and other accidents, these are one of the most important private archives in Spain, perhaps the most important. Their value is due in part to the primary role played in Spanish political affairs by the house of Alba and in part to the fact that through family relationships the archives contain the papers of the houses of Lemos y Monterrey, Modica, Admirals of Castile, Montijo, Count-Duke of Olivares, etc. The Count-Duke retained in his possession, by special authorization of the king, many papers of state from the times of Charles V, Philip II, Philip III, and Philip IV. The justification given for asking this abusive privilege was the bad state of the official archives (certainly a singular motive in the case of the omnipotent favorite who should have remedied the evil); but in fact the Count-Duke carefully bound these papers. Nearly all of them were destroyed, nevertheless, in various fires in the Palace of Alba from 1695 to 1936. Some 120 volumes of correspondence of Don Luis de Haro (1643–61) alone perished in the fire of September 13, 1795.

However, the remaining material is still very important, especially for the history of Spanish relations with Rome, Portugal, and England. At the end of the nineteenth century,

they contained some eight thousand original letters of outstanding historical value, including forty of Don Juan of Austria
and more than twelve hundred of Philip II, many of them
unedited. They contain also many of the famous Count-Duke,
a favorite of Philip IV.

In addition to the selection of documents published previously (numbers 33 and 54 in the general bibliography), the
Duchess of Alba published a very useful *Catálogo de las colec-
ciónes expuestas en las vitrinas del Palacio de Liria* (Madrid, 1898).
Documents of the Archives of the House of Alba have been
published in various historical works, several of which were due
to the inspiration of the late Duke of Alba. Some of them are
listed in Sánchez Alonso (numbers 41, 54, and 61 in the general
bibliography).

2. Archives of the House of Medinaceli. These are located
in the palace of the present Duke of Medinaceli (Génova 28,
Madrid). For reasons similar to those mentioned in regard to
the House of Alba, the private archives of the dukes of Medinaceli are definitely valuable for the diplomatic history of Spain.
Don Antonio de Paz y Melia published the principal sources of
these archives more than half a century ago. (Number 34 in
the general bibliography.)

3. Archives of Altamira. The archives of the House of
Altamira (Counts) are today dispersed in various places: the
British Museum, University of Geneva, archives of the Counts
of Heredia Spinola, and the Institute of Valencia of Don Juan
(Madrid). The portion that belongs to the British Museum is
reviewed in the well-known *Catalogue of the manuscripts in the
Spanish language in the British Museum* (London, 1875–93). The
Geneva documents were listed by Leopold Micheli in his
*Inventaire de la Collection Edouard Favre (Archives de la maison d'
Altamira)*, (Paris, 1914. *Bulletin hispanique*). The documents in
the archives of Heredia Spinola, formerly belonging to Don
Francisco de Zabálburu, are very important. Some documents
have been edited in *Codoin* (number 21 in the general

bibliography) and Serrano (number 64). See also March (number 51 in the general bibliography).

Of the documents preserved by the Institute of Valencia of Don Juan, a very brief summary of titles appears in the recent *Guía de los archivos de Madrid*, pp. 386–392 (number 7 in the general bibliography). From this summary it is obvious that there are documents concerning Spanish foreign policy there, number 8 (Secretariat of Philip II, Correspondence) and number 23, which contains an interesting and copious collection of papers belonging to Mateo Vázquez, secretary to Philip II, are notable. The correspondence of Vázquez with his lord, preserved in these archives, has been studied by Carlos Riva and is being published by the Superior Council of Scientific Investigations. The Institute has also acquired the archives of the Marquisate of Velada, related to the House of Altamira.

4. Archives of the House of Frías. These rich materials are presently being catalogued. Among other collections, one of forty-three bound volumes relating to the activities of the Spanish ambassador to the Congress of Münster, the Count of Peñaranda (1645–50), is preserved there (number 72 in the general bibliography). In the archives of the House of the Marquis del Castelar (Madrid) is preserved a group of papers of Don Gonzalo Fernández de Córdoba and Don Alvaro de Losada, during the campaign of 1621–22 in the Thirty Years War (number 73 in the general bibliography).

Many other private archives undoubtedly contain documents of interest for the history of the diplomatic relations of Spain; but, aside from lacking specific and recent data on such archives, there would not be space to describe them. This refers not to the archives of the nobility alone. An identical supposition might be made in regard to those of politicians and diplomats who notably influenced the destinies of Spain. For example, the archives of Don Antonio Cánovas del Castillo are conserved in the *Museo Fundación Lázaro* (Serrano 122, Madrid) and they consist of some 359 portfolios that were lately being arranged and catalogued. (Number 7 in the general bibliography).

The archives of Zúñiga-Requeséns, of such a preponderant influence in the reigns of Charles I (V) and Philip II, passed recently into the possession of the Society of Jesus and have been used, though in a reduced proportion, by José March, S.J., for the books and articles listed in the general bibliography (numbers 49, 51, and 52). They are in the so-called *Archivo del Palan* in Barcelona.

Other family archives of considerable diplomatic importance are those of the house of the dukes of Alburquerque, in Madrid, in which are collected the archives of the marquises of Alcañices and of Balbases, among others. It is worthwhile to cite five volumes of the correspondence of Don Luis Méndez de Haro (1655–56) and much material relating to the famous ambassador of Charles V to Rome, Juan de Vega, in which are found letters from the emperor, partly in cipher. It should be remembered that the Marquis of Saltillo in his work *Juan de Vega, embajador de Carlos V en Roma* (Madrid, Instituto de Estudios Políticos, 1946) used principally the correspondence of Vega, which was in Manuscript 18.417 in the *Biblioteca Nacional* in Madrid, without having used the archives of the House of Alburquerque.

Furthermore, one should also take into account the already mentioned archives of the marquises of Heredia Spinola, the Count of Guaqui, the Duke of the Infantado, and others in Madrid. The archives of the marquises of Camarasa, united now with those of the dukes of Alcalá, have been recently transferred from Madrid to Seville.

The *Biblioteca Pública de Toledo* (Toledo Public Library) has the registers of the diplomatic correspondence of the embassy of the Duke of Liri to Moscow, 1727–30 (5 vols.). See Francisco Estebe Barba, *Biblioteca Pública de Toledo, Catálogo de la colección de manuscritos Borbón-Lorenzana* (Madrid, 1942), p. 297. Estebe

Barba believes (p. 4) that these registers could have come to the Public Library through Juan Cascos y Vilademoros, who was the duke's secretary during his embassy. Cascos wrote a *Formulario* or *Libro de Gobierne*, which contains all the events concerning ceremonies and other things after the arrival of the duke in St. Petersburg, in November 1727. Estebe Barba describes this manuscript under number 402 of his catalogue.

The same library has the registers of correspondence of the Marquis of San Felipe, as envoy extraordinary to Genoa, 1715–25. There are thirty-five volumes of letters and communications sent to various persons. Many are autographs and others are copybooks (*en borrador*) (catalogue, numbers 404–436).

At least indirect materials for the history of Spanish diplomacy may be found in many other Spanish collections. The simple intent of enumerating the principal ones would expand intolerably the limits of this study. Nevertheless, to avoid a possible erroneous conclusion, it should be added that among the rich manuscript sources of the Escorial relatively few are of interest in not too indirect a manner to diplomatic history. See Julian Zarco Cuevas, O.S.A., *Catálogo da los manuscritos castellanos de la Real Biblioteca de El Escorial.* 3 vols. Madrid, 1924–29.

The examination of the particular bibliography of the diplomatic history of Spain found in Sánchez Alonso and in the *Manuel de l'hispanisant* (numbers 41–42 in the general bibliography) will provide the researcher with indications of other archives.

GENERAL BIBLIOGRAPHY

1. *Guía histórica y descriptiva de los archivos, bibliotecas y museos de España.* Madrid, 1921.
2. *Representación hecha por el secretario D. Santiago Agustín Riol del, origen y estado de los Consejos, tribunales, archivos reales de la Corte y Chancillerías, el de Roma y Simancas, al Rey nuestro señor* (1726). The Academy of

American Franciscan History possesses one copy of this manuscript made in the eighteenth century. This information was widely utilized in the works cited in the two numbers which follow.

3. Vignau, Vicente. *El Archivo histórico nacional.* Madrid, 1898. Reception speech in the Royal Academy of History.

4. Desdevises du Dézert, M. G. *Les Archives historiques nationales de Madrid.* Madrid, 1900. Extract from the *Bulletin historique et philologique.*

5. Alcócer, Mariano. *Archivo General de Simancas. Guía del Investigador.* Valladolid, 1923.

6. Archivo General de Simancas. *Catálogo XV: Papeles sobre la introducción y distribución de la quina en España.* Valladolid, 1937. Gerardo Masa describes the group "Finance" in the introduction, modifying that which was written by Alcocer in his *Guía* (Number 5 in the bibliography).

7. *Guía de los archivos de Madrid.* Madrid, Ministerio de Educación Nacional, 1952.

8. González Hurtebise, Eduardo. *Guía histórica-descriptiva del Archivo de la Corona de Aragón en Barcelona.* Madrid, 1920.

9. Archivo General de Simancas. *Catálogo II, Secretaría de Estado. Capitulaciones con la Casa de Austria y Papeles de las Negociaciones de Alemania, Sajonia, Polonia, Prusia, y Hamburgo (1493–1726).* Ed. by Julián Paz. 2d ed. Madrid, Consejo Superior de Investigaciones Científicas, 1942.

10. Archivo General de Simancas. *Catálogo III, Secretaría de Estado. Documentos de las negociaciones de Flandes, Holanda y Bruselas . . . , 1506–1795,* 2d ed. Madrid, Consejo Superior de Investigaciones Científicas, 1946.

11. Archivo General de Simancas. *Catálogo IV, Secretaría de Estado. Capitulaciones con Francia y negociaciones diplomáticas de los Embajadores de España en aquella corte (1265–1714).* Ed. by Julián Paz. Madrid, 1914.

12. Archivo General de Simancas. *Catálogo XIV. Papeles de Estado de la Negociación de Roma, 1381–1700.* Valladolid, 1926.

13. Archivo General de Simancas. *Catálogo XVI. Papeles de Estado de la Correspondencia y Negociación de Nápoles. Virreinato.* Ed. by Ricardo Magdaleno. Edición del Consejo Superior de Investigaciones Científicas y Universidad de Valladolid. Valladolid, 1942.

14. Archivo General de Simancas. *Catálogo XVII. Secretaría de Estado. Documentos relativo a Inglaterra (1254–1834).* Ed. by Julián Paz and Ricardo Magdaleno. Edition and prologue of the Duke of Alba. Madrid, 1947.

15. Archivo General de Simancas. *Catálogo XIX. Papeles de Estado. Sicilia.*

Vireinato Español y Negociación de Malta. Ed. by Ricardo Magdaleno. Madrid, 1951. The catalogue *Papeles de Estado. Reino de las Dos Sicilias. Siglo XVIII. Embajada Española* (Ed. by Ricardo Magdaleno) has also just appeared.

16. Archivo General de Simancas. *Catálogo V. Patronato Real (834–1851).* Complete edition. Revision and final indexes by Amalia Prieto Cantero. 2 vols. Valladolid, 1949.

17. Archivo General de Simancas. *Catálogo VII. Guerra Moderna. Guerra de Marruecos. Años 1774–1776.* Sources for its study by Mariano Alcócer. Valladolid, 1926.

18. Archivo General de Simancas. *Catálogo XVIII. Guerra y Marina. I: Epoca de Carlos I de España y V de Alemania.* Ed. by Concepción Alvarez Yerán. Valladolid, 1949.

19. Archivo General de Simancas. *Catálogo VI. Secretarías Provinciales. Títulos nobiliarios concedidos por nuestros Reyes en Flandes, Italia y Portugal* (Sixteenth and seventeenth centuries). Ed. by Angel de la Plaza. Valladolid, 1923.

20. Archivo Historico Nacional. *Indice de los Papeles de la Junta Central Suprema Gubernativa del Reino y Consejo de Regencia.* Madrid, 1904.

21. *Colección de documentos inéditos para la historia de España.* 113 vols. Madrid, 1842–95. It was begun by Martín Fernández Navarrete, Miguel Salvá, and Pedro Sainz de Baranda. It is of great importance for the history of the European policy of Spain. There is a good catalogue in two volumes by Julián Paz, Madrid, 1930–31, cited as *Codoin.*

22. Archivo Histórico Español. *Colección de documentos inéditos para la historia de España y de sus Indias.* Valladolid, 1928– . It is patronized by the Academy of Social and Historical Studies of Valladolid, under the direction of the Count of Gamazo, the Duke of Maura, Augustin G. de Amezua, Mariano Alcócer, and others. Vol. I contains documents concerning the Council of Trent; Vol. II (1929) the Invincible Armada; and Vol. III the consultations of the Council of State. Cited *AHE.*

23. *Calendar of letters, despatches, and state papers relating to the negotiations between England and Spain, preserved in the Archives at Simancas and elsewhere* . . . . Ed. by G. A. Bergenroth [and others, among them Pascual de Gayangos]. London, 1862– . Vol. XI, which ends in 1553, appeared in 1916.

24. *Collección de documentos inéditos del Archivo de la Corona de Aragón.* Barcelona, 1864–. This collection was begun by Dr. Próspero Bofarull and continued by his son and grandson respectively, D. Manuel de Bofarull and D. Francisco de Asis Bofarull, who were successively

directors of the Archives of the Crown of Aragon. In a great part, it contains documents that are of interest to the history of the international policy of the Aragonese monarchy.

25. Rubió y Lluch, Antonio. *Diplomatari de l'Orient Català*. Barcelona, 1947.
26. Fincke, H. *Acta Aragonensia. Quellen zur deutschen, italienischen, französischen, spanischen, zur Kirchen und Kulturgeschichte aus der diplomatischen Korrespondenz Jaymes II (1291–1327)*. 3 vols. Berlin, 1908–22.
27. Alarcón, Maximiliano, and Ramon García Linares. *Los documentos árabes diplomáticos del Archivo de la Corona de Aragón*. Madrid, 1940.
28. Baer, Fritz. *Die Juden in dem christlichen Spanien. Aragonien. Navarra.* 2 vols. Berlin, 1929.
29. Torre, Antonio de la. *Documentos sobre las relaciones diplomáticas de los Reyes Católicos*. Barcelona, 1949– .
30. Vincke, Johannes. *Documenta selecta mutuas Civitatis Arago-Cathaloniae et Ecclesiae relationes illustrantia*. Barcelona, 1936.
31. *Documentos inéditos para la historia de España.* Published by the Duke of Alba, Duke of Maura, Count of Gamazo. Madrid, 1936. Vol. I–IV contain letters and dispatches of the Count of Gondomar, ambassador of Spain in London.
32. Biblioteca Nacional. *Catálogo de los documentos que pertenecieron a D. Pascual Gayangos, existentes hoy en la Biblioteca Nacional.* Ed. by D. Pedro Roca. Madrid, 1904.
33. *Documentos escogidos del Archivo de la Casa de Alba.* Madrid, 1891. The Duchess of Berwick y Alba published them.
34. Paz y Melia, Antonio. *Series de los más importantes documentos del archivo y biblioteca del . . . Duque de Medinaceli . . . I: Serie historica, años 860–1814.* Madrid, 1915. Vol. II, a bibliographical series, was published in 1922.
35. Maura, Duque de. *Correspondencia entre los embajadores Don Pedro Ronquillo y el Marqués de Cogolludo, 1689–1691.* Transcription, introduction, and notes by the Duke of Maura. Madrid, 1951–52.
36. Diputación Federal de Navarra. *Catálogo del Archivo General. Sección de Comptos y documentos.* Ed. by José Ramón Castro, Chief of the Archives of Navarre. Vol. I, 842–1331; Vol. II, 1332–1357. Pamplona, 1952.
37. Brutails, Jean Auguste. *Documents des Archives de la Chambre des Comptes de Navarre.* Paris, 1890. It is Fac. 84 of the Bibliothèque de l'Ecole des Hautes Etudes.
38. Real Academia de la Historia. *Indice de la Colección de Don Luis de Salazar y Castro.* Ed. by the Marquis of Siete Iglesias and D. Baltasar Cuartero y Huerta. 8 vols. Madrid, 1949– .

39. *Catálogo de los documentos del Archivo de Lope de Soria, embajador del emperador Carlos V.* Ed. by E. Ibarra Rodríguez and G. Arsenio de Izaga, in *Boletín de la Academia de la Historia* (Madrid), XCVIII (1931), 363–416.

40. López Oliván, Julio. *Repertorio diplomático español.* Index of the treaties concluded by Spain (1125–1935) and of other international documents. Madrid, 1944. In the bibliography (pp. 651–669) are indicated the principal collections of treaties, supported by documents of the Spanish diplomatic archives.

41. Sánchez Alonso, Benito. *Fuentes de la historia española e hispanoamericana.* Third edition corrected and brought up to date. Madrid, 1952.

42. Foulché-Delbosc, R. and L. Barrau-Dihigo. *Manuel de l'Hispanisant.* 2 vols. New York, 1920–25.

43. Carini, Isidoro. *Gli archivi e le biblioteche di Spagna in rapporto alla storia d'Italia in generale e di Sicilia in particolare.* 2 vols. Palermo, 1884.

44. Gachard, Louis Prosper. *Les bibliothèques de Madrid et de l'Escurial.* Brussels, 1875. Information and extracts from the manuscripts which concern the history of Belgium.

45. Gachard, Louis Prosper. *Correspondence de Philippe II sur les affaires des Pays – Bas, 1558–1577, publié d'après les originaux dans les archives royales de Simancas.* 5 vols. Brussels, 1848–79.

46. Gachard, Louis Prosper. *Retraite et mort de Charles-Quint au monastère de Yuste. Lettres inédites publiées d'après les originaux conservés dans les archives royales de Simancas.* 3 vols. Brussels, 1854–56.

47. Lonchay, H. *Les archives de Simancas au point de vue de l'histoire des Pays-Bas au XVII siècle, en compte-rendu des séances de la Commission Royale d'Histoire ou recueil de ses bulletins,* 1907, LXXXVI, annexes XIII–LV.

48. Kybal, Vlastimil. *Über die Bedeutung des General-Archivs zu Simancas für die neuere Geschichte Österreichs.* Vienna, 1910.

49. March, José María, S. J. "Don Luis de Requeséns, Lugarteniente general del mar, y la batalla de Lepanto a la luz de nuevos documentos," *Razón y Fe.* Madrid, CXXVI (1942), 200–225. Re-edited and expanded, Madrid, 1944.

50. Vásquez, Alberto, and S. Selden Rose. *Algunas cartas de Don Diego Huartado de Mendoza.* New Haven, 1935. It contains 125 letters of Hurtado de Mendoza, who was ambassador in Venice, Rome, and Siena (1538–1552). The originals are in Simancas and in the Library of the Royal Palace.

51. March, José María, S. J. *El comendador mayor de Castilla, Don Luis de Requeséns, en el gobierno de Milán.* Madrid, Ministerio de Asuntos Exteriores, Relaciones Culturales, 1943.

52. March, José María, S. J. *Niñez y juventud de Felipe II.* 2 vols. Madrid, Ministerio de Asuntos Exteriores, Relaciones Culturales, 1941–1942.

53. Gómez del Campillo, Miguel, *Relaciones diplomáticas entre España y los Estados Unidos, según los documentos del Archivo Histórico Nacional.* 2 vols. Madrid, 1944, 1946.

54. Berwick y de Alba, Duque de. *Correspondencia de Gutierre Gómez de Fuensalida, embajador de Alemania, Flandes e Inglaterra (1496–1509).* Madrid, 1907.

55. Archivo General de Indias. *Catálogo de documentos de la Sección Novena* . . . Vol. I: *Santo Domingo, Cuba, Puerto Rico, Lusiana, Florida y México.* Seville, 1949.

56. Torres Lanzas, Pedro. *Independencia de América, fuentes para su estudio. Catálogo de documentos conservados en el Archivo General de Indias de Sevilla.* First series, 5 vols. Madrid, 1912. Second series, 2 vols. Seville, 1924–25.

57. Hill, Roscoe R. *Descriptive catalogue of the documents relating to the history of the United States in the "Papeles procedentes de Cuba" deposited in the Archivo General de Indias at Seville.* Washington, 1916.

58. Torre Revello, José. *El Archivo General de Indias.* Buenos Aires, 1929.

59. Torres Lanzas, Pedro and German Latorre. *Catálogo-Cuadro general de la documentación del Archivo General de Indias.* Seville, 1918.

60. Alves, F. M. *No Arquivo de Simancas.* Oporto, 1932.

61. Alba, Duque de. *Epistolario del III Duque de Alba, D. Fernando Alvarez de Toledo, Años 1536–1581.* 3 vols. Madrid, 1952.

62. Paz, Julián. *Catálogo de manuscritos de América existentes en la Biblioteca Nacional.* Madrid, 1933.

63. Bordona, Jesús Domínguez. *Catálogo de la Biblioteca de Palacio.* Vol. IX. *Manuscritos de América.* Madrid, 1935.

64. Serrano, Luciano, O.S.B. *Correspondencia diplomática entre España y la Santa Sede durante el pontificado de San Pío V.* 4 vols. Madrid, 1914.

65. Pacheco y de Leyva, Enrique. *La política española en Italia. Correspondencia de D. Fernando Marín, abad de Nájera, con Carlos I.* Madrid, 1919.

66. Rodríguez Villa, Antonio. *Italia desde la batalla de Pavía hasta el Saco de Roma, Reseña histórica escrita en su mayor parte con documentos originales, cifrados.* Madrid, 1885.

67. Rodríguez Villa, Antonio. *Memorias para la historia del asalto y saqueo de Roma, en 1527, por el ejército imperial, formado con documentos originales, cifrados e inéditos en su mayoría.* Madrid, n.d.

68. Ayerbe, Marqués de, Conde de San Clemente. *Correspondencia inédita de Don Guillén de San Clemente, embajador en Alemania de* . . . *Felipe II y*

Felipe III sobre la intervención de España en los sucesos de Polonia y Hungría, 1581–1608. Zaragoza, 1892.

69. Danvila y Burguero, Alfonso. *Diplomáticos españoles: Don Cristóbal de Moura, primer marqués de Castel Rodrigo (1538–1613).* Madrid, 1900.

70. *Guía de las bibliotecas de Madrid.* Madrid, Ministerio de Educación Nacional, 1953.

71. Alba, Duque de. "Achivos de España. El de la Casa de Alba," *Hidalguía,* I (1953), 145–156.

72. Frías, Duque de. "Breve síntesis del contenido del Archivo de la Casa de Frías y sus agregadas," *Hidalguía,* I (1953), 645–652.

73. Castelar, Marqués del. "Archivo de la Casa del Marqués del Castelar," *Hidalguía,* I (1953), 337–340.

74. Aguarelles, Eugenio Sarrablo. "Archivo de Su Alteza Real Don Carlos de Habsburgo-Lorena y Borbón Duque de Madrid," *Hidalguía,* I (1953), 653–660.

75. *Boletín de la Real Academia de la Historia* (BAH).

76. *Hidalguía. La revista de Genealogía, Nobleza y Armas.* Madrid, 1953– .

77. *Colección de tratados de España con otras naciones a partir de 1939.* Ed. by Justo Gómez Ocerín. Madrid, Ministerio de Asuntos Exteriores, 1954.

78. Cagigas, Isidro de las. *Tratados y convenios referentes a Marruecos.* Madrid, 1952.

79. Guillén, Julio F. *Archivo General de Marina. Independencia de América. Indice de los Papeles de Expediciones de Indias.* 3 vols. Madrid, 1953.

80. *Archivos de Barcelona.* Barcelona, 1952.

81. *Catálogo de la Colección de Don Juan Bautista Muñoz.* 2 vols. Madrid, 1954–55.

82. Giullén, Julio F. *Archivo General de Marina. Indice de los Papeles de la Sección de corso y Presus, 1784–1837.* 2 vols. Madrid, 1953.

12   SWEDEN[1]

Florence Janson Sherriff

Wesleyan College, Macon, Georgia

HISTORY

THE modern state of Sweden was established in 1523 under King Gustavus I Vasa. Sweden had been independent in early Viking days, but was joined with Denmark and Norway in the Union of Kalmar in 1397. During the period of the Union the Danish governor was driven from Sweden by Engelbrecht Engelbrechtsson, who was elected king by the first *Riksdag* (Swedish Parliament) in 1434. Independence lasted only two years, but the *Riksdag* has continued to the present time. The Danish crown was forced to appoint as stadholder such Swedish national leaders as Karl Knutsson Bonde, Sten Sture, and Sten Sture the Younger. The defeat of the latter by the Danish King Christian II led to a nationalist revolt under Gustavus Vasa in 1521 and to his election as King of Sweden by the *Riksdag* at Strängnäs two years later. With the flight of the Danish King Christian II from Sweden in 1523 the independence of Sweden was established.

Written documents began in Sweden in the eleventh century and the first treaty dates from A.D. 822. However, most of the archives prior to 1300 have been lost. When King Birger Magnusson of Sweden fled to the Danish court in 1319, he is supposed to have taken many of the state papers with him. Two

[1]The author wishes to acknowledge with gratitude the assistance of Olaf Jägerskiold of *Riksarkivet* and Harald Bohrn of *Kunglige Bibliotheket* in Stockholm. Various officials at *Riksarkivet*, at *Kunglige Bibliotheket*, and in the libraries of Uppsala and Lund in Gothenburg, and at the *Statsarkiv* in Gothenburg, Visby, and Lund were very helpful and their courtesy was much appreciated.

hundred years later the Danish King Christian II also took the archives of Sweden with him when he fled from the country in 1523. In his continued flight from Denmark to Holland the same year he transported Danish and Norwegian government documents as well as the Swedish and, strangely, some of these documents appeared in the archives of Munich in the early part of the nineteenth century. In an archival arrangement with Bavaria in 1829 the documents were sent to Oslo, and Sweden recovered some of its earliest national registers (*registrum regni*) kept by its chancellor, Archbishop Gustaf Trolle.[2] In another exchange of archives with Denmark in 1929 Sweden received the Sture papers of her famous stadholders.[3] The Bishop of Strängnäs served as chancellor of Sweden during the period of the Union and had the custody of the archives. During the reign of Gustavus Vasa the government documents were removed from Strängnäs to the new chancery in Stockholm. The *Riksarkivet* (National Archives) date from the time of Chancellor Axel Oxenstierna in the reign of Gustavus Adolphus when by orders of council they were established in 1618.

All important foreign correspondence, royal decrees, decisions of the Royal Council, treaties, international agreements, etc., were customarily recorded in a copybook designated the *registrum regni* and later in Swedish *riksens register* (national register). They date from the reign of King Magnus Eriksson (1319–74). At the time of Gustavus Vasa one of the secretaries of the *Rikskanslit* (chancery), Rasmus Ludvigsson, classified and organized the archives that had come from Strängnäs. They were known as the *riksens gamla archivium* ("old archives"). By the end of the sixteenth century the state papers were again neglected and in disorder. The National Archives established by Chancellor Oxenstierna in 1618 were given a permanent location in a wing of the palace. The first official secretary of archives to be appointed was Peder Månsson Utter, whose

[2]See number 31 in bibliography.
[3]See number 22 in bibliography.

system of cataloguing state papers was followed for two hundred years. Under Chancellor Oxenstierna a special register for foreign affairs (*utrikes register*, sometimes designated as *register i utrikes ärenden*) was developed.

Fire in the old palace of Tre Kronor (Three Crowns) in 1697 destroyed two thirds of the archives, including the registers of 1522 to 1648. Other valuable documents lost at the time included much of the medieval correspondence, papers concerning Sweden's foreign relations, royal correspondence prior to 1645, and the records of the chancery prior to 1650. Following the fire the archives were kept in much confusion in two old residences in the "Old City." To add to this calamity, the scare of threatened Russian invasion of Sweden after the defeat of Charles XII at Poltava in 1709 sent the secretary of archives, Elias Palmskiöld, in flight with the state papers by sea to Örebro. He was caught by storm at sea, the ship almost sank, and the archives were soaked with seawater. Charles XII, upon his return to Sweden in 1716, had the government documents returned to Stockholm.

A new royal palace was completed in 1756 and the archives were installed in a special apartment. They remained, however, in a chaotic condition until they were recatalogued in the nineteenth century by the Archivist, Hans Järta. In 1846 a new depository for government documents was established in the old Stenbock Palace on Riddarholmen. The palace was enlarged in 1891 and bears the address of Arkivgatan 3. The bulk of the archives has so increased that it is necessary to provide separate housing for a part. Section IV, dealing with home affairs, the navy, etc., has been moved to the reconstructed prison building at Östermalmagatan 26.

The foreign affairs of Sweden were conducted by the chancellor until 1720. During the Period of Freedom a chancery council presided over by a president took over this function. In 1772 the chancellor was reinstated and remained in charge of foreign affairs until 1840 when the *Utrikesdepartementet* (department of foreign affairs) was established. An official named the *custos archivi* became responsible for the archives at the time of Gustavus Vasa in the sixteenth century. He was directly under the chancellor. The cataloguing and care of the government documents were given to one of the secretaries in the chancery who was designated the secretary of archives. The *custos archivi* was replaced by an *hovkansliren* (court chancellor) in the period following 1720, and he was a member of the chancery council. The directives of the chancery council were called *kansliproto-koll* (chancery protocol). The *rådsprotokoll* (orders in council) were passed by the all-powerful *Riksrådet* (national council), which actually governed Sweden between 1720 and 1772, for the king had become a figurehead.

Within the chancery there was a special secretary for foreign correspondence. He was responsible for the maintenance of the *register i utrikes ärenden* (register of foreign affairs). Soon there were several secretaries for foreign correspondence who formed a council or cabinet of foreign affairs within the chancery. Their archives are now in the National Archives, classified under the names of the secretaries who were responsible for the correspondence. The papers of the presidents of the chancery council are also filed under their respective names. Special dossiers on international problems of the day are filed according to subject matter in a special section of the archives of the chancery council. Registers for foreign affairs from 1645 to 1809 are also in the National Archives. Many secret agreements were negotiated by the *Riksdag* during the Period of Freedom and these still remain in the archives of the *Riksdag* in the parliament building.

In the conduct of foreign affairs the custom of exchanging resident ministers and ambassadors became prevalent in Europe in the seventeenth century; and Sweden was included, for it was the period of her greatness as a power. Hugo Grotius, the father of international law, though an exile from Holland, served as Sweden's ambassador to France from 1634 to 1645.

In his correspondence he used Latin. In the next century German and French were used in foreign correspondence.

With the ascension to the Swedish throne of the enlightened despot, Gustavus III, nephew of Frederick the Great of Prussia, the *Riksdag* lost its power and the office of chancellor was restored. Then in the 1840's many of the functions of the chancery were given to various departments of the new cabinet. What was left in the chancery became the department of foreign affairs. The National Archives remained in this department until later transferred to the Department of Church and Education (*Ecklesiastikdepartementet*). The title of *Riksarkivarie* (national archivist) was first used in 1835. The office of *hovkansliren*, which had had the responsibility of the archives since 1720, was discontinued in 1840. With the administration of Hans Järta as *Chef* (head archivist) from 1837 to 1844 came a complete reorganization of the archives. The National Archives now became not only the depository for government documents, but also a central institution for historical research. In 1859 it began the publication of historical papers and in 1876 its journal, *Meddelanden från Riksarkivet*. The archives are now classified under the principle of provenience or origin, according to the function of an official or an administrative department.[4]

ORGANIZATION AND CLASSIFICATION

For the study of the diplomatic correspondence and the foreign affairs of Sweden the researcher will find the above-mentioned registers of foreign affairs of great value for the period from 1648 to 1809. The registers consist of a chronological record and a copy of all correspondence expedited by the secretaries of foreign affairs in the chancery. Another source is the correspondence itself, which is called *koncepten*. These may be checked with the registers. The registers are usually referred

[4]See number 26 in bibliography.

to in historical works as RR. Some registers prior to 1523 may also be found in the archives. Correspondence of political significance was not entered in the registers after 1720, but can be found in the files of correspondence. So-called *diarierna* (diaries) consist of chronologically arranged summaries of incoming and outgoing correspondence. Before 1720 the complete letter was sometimes included in these documents.[5] Orders in council are important for those periods when the Swedish kings were away in wars and the country was ruled by the Council and later during the Period of Freedom in the eighteenth century when the *Riksdag* ruled. They are designated as *rådsprotokoll*. The papers and correspondence of the kings and queens of Sweden, of chancellors, diplomats, and statesmen may be found in the National Archives. Treaties have been published since 1877 by the department of foreign affairs.[6]

The diplomatic archives in the National Archives are designated the *diplomatica samlingen*. Today diplomatic correspondence is carried on in French and is retained in the department of foreign affairs for fifty years before it is turned over to the National Archives. Such deposit has been made up to 1900. The correspondence in the archives of the department of foreign affairs is not open to research. Before 1813 instructions to Swedish diplomats were filed under the name of the secretary of foreign affairs in the chancery who issued the directives, but since that date they have been filed under the countries to which the diplomats were assigned. Correspondence from foreign countries may be found in the same way. The older diplomatic correspondence is organized under the Latin designation of countries as used in Europe at the time. A series of printed indexes of some of the states have appeared in various numbers of *Meddelanden från Riksarkivet*.[7] Some of the countries covered in these publications include Americana, Anglica

---

[5]See number 27 in bibliography.
[6]See numbers 27 and 34 in bibliography.
[7]See number 35 in bibliography.

(England), Brandenburgico-Borussia (Prussia), Danica (Denmark), Gallica (France), Germanica, Helvetica (Switzerland), Hispanica (Spain), Italica, Muscovitica (Russia), Turcica (Turkey), etc. Reprints of these may be procured in the office of the National Archives. Others may be found in the card catalogue in the reading room. In this card catalogue are listed the names of the secretaries of foreign affairs of the chancery for the period before 1813 arranged alphabetically, and filed by countries since that time.

The department of foreign affairs is organized into five divisions, of which Division V consists of the archives and the library of the department. This is not open to the public. The archives, as has been mentioned, are turned over to the National Archives after fifty years, the last deposit having been made up to 1900. One other division is concerned with diplomatic correspondence. Division I has three bureaus dealing with diplomatic and consular intercourse. The first bureau is concerned with Denmark, Iceland, Finland, the Netherlands, Norway, Switzerland, Germany, Austria, and the colonies of these countries. Included under Bureau II are Great Britain, the United States, Japan, China, and other Asiatic and African states and colonies. The remaining states and colonies are under Bureau III and include the Balkan states, Belgium, France, Italy, Poland, Portugal, Russia and the Slav states, Spain, Hungary, Mexico, other Central American and South American states, and the West Indian republics. Public information and the Swedish and foreign press come under Bureau IV.

Collections of the private papers of the royal family, of statesmen and of diplomats have been deposited in the National Archives, the *Kungliga Bibliotheket* (Royal Library), in various university libraries, and in regional archives. Some of these valuable papers are still on the estates of prominent Swedish statesmen and diplomats. The following list includes a few of these collections:[8]

[8] See number 19 in bibliography.

In the National Archives

Adler-Salvius papers. Johan Adler-Salvius was a diplomat during the Thirty Years' War. Among others he corresponded with Hugo Grotius.

Dahlberg archives. Governor-General Erik Dahlberg administered Finland in the last half of the seventeenth century.

De la Gardie collection. Papers confiscated from Magnus De la Gardie, a confidant of Queen Christina, at the time of her abdication. Other archives of the family are deposited in Esthonia and at the University of Lund. There is an unpublished catalogue of this collection at the National Archives.

Löwenhjelm papers. Baron Gustaf Löwenhjelm was the Swedish ambassador to France from the time of Napoleon to 1828. These archives cover the years 1812–16.

Oxenstierna collection. Chancellor Axel Oxenstierna was the Chancellor of King Gustavus II Adolphus and the regent for Queen Christina during the Thirty Years' War. The nucleus of this collection came from the estate of Vidö in Västmanland in 1848. The correspondence of interrelated historical families include that of Bielke, Bååt, De la Gardie, de Mornay, Grip, and Horn.

Reuterholm collection. Gustaf Adolf Reuterholm was the leader of the regency for Gustavus IV Adolphus (1792–96).

The Skokloster collection. The archives of the Brahe family, friends of King Sigismund of Poland in the sixteenth century and of Per Brahe, Governor of Finland at the time of Gustavus II Adolphus. The collection came from the estates of Skokloster and Rydboholm. The old Salsta archives include medieval manuscripts and correspondence from 1372 to 1681.

Stegeborg collection. The correspondence of John Casmir, Baron of Westphalia, who was elected King of Poland in 1648, that of Duke Adolph Johan, and that of the Crown Prince Charles Gustavus who succeeded Queen Christina to the Swedish throne as Charles X.

Säfstaholm collection. The archives of the Bonde family of which Karl Knutsson Bonde was stadholder of Sweden in 1436. It came from the estates of Säfstaholm and Hörningsholm.

Vellingk collection. These papers of Mauritz Vellingk, Governor-General of Finland, cover the years 1710–21.

In the Royal Library in Stockholm

Engeström collection. Lars von Engeström was the Swedish ambassador to Warsaw from 1787 to 1792, and later ambassador to England and Berlin. He was Sweden's foreign minister from 1809 to 1824. Included are the papers of Jacob Engeström, who was implicated in the assassination of King Gustavus III in 1792.

In the Library of the University of Uppsala

Gustavus II Adolphus collection. Papers and documents relating to the king and also papers of Oxenstierna and Stjernald.

Gustavus III papers. All the papers and correspondence were willed to the library by King Gustavus III and were not to be opened for fifty years.

Literary Booty of the Thirty Years' War. The Swedish armies purposely looted libraries in Germany and many of these books are deposited at Uppsala.

In the Library of the University of Lund

De la Gardie archives. These papers include those of Pontus de la Gardie, French soldier of fortune in the sixteenth century and a Swedish envoy, those of Jacob, Stadholder of Livland in the seventeenth century, those of Magnus Gabriel, favorite of Queen Christina, and those of Jacob Gustaf, diplomat from 1795–1815.

In Private Collections

Björnstjerna papers. General M. F. F. Björnstjerna was the Swedish ambassador to England during the reign of Gustavus III (1772–92); O. M. Björnsterna was foreign minister. The papers are located on the Almare-Stäket estate in Uppland.

Ericksberg collection. This collection on the Ericksberg estate in Södermanland contains the papers of the Bonde family, the old Stenbock archives from the estate of Torsjö in Skåne with the correspondence of Gustaf Otto and Magnus Stenbock and of Bengt Oxenstierna of the period of the Thirty Years' War. There is also correspondence from the time of Gustavus III and the diaries of Queen Hedvig Elisabeth Carolina from 1775 to 1817.

Löwenhjelm correspondence. The archives of C. A. and G. Löwenhjelm, the latter diplomat and a friend of Bernadotte. These are located at Okna in Södermanland.

Queen Louisa Ulrika correspondence. The sister of Frederick the Great of Prussia and the mother of Gustavus III. Her papers are at Stavsund on the Mälaren. The correspondence of Fersen, Swedish ambassador to France and friend of Marie Antoinette, are also here.

ADMINISTRATION, REGULATIONS, AND FACILITIES

The National Archives of Sweden is a subdivision of the *Ecklesiastikdepartementet* (department of church and education). The *riksarkivets chef* (chief archivist) has charge of the administration of the archives. A foreign scholar should have a letter of introduction to him either from his research professor or from a historical society to which he belongs. The reading rooms of the National Archives are open from 10 A.M. to 5 P.M. on week days. From June 1 to August 31 the hours are changed to 9 A.M. to 4 P.M. All materials wanted for research must be procured before 3 P.M. during the winter months, and between 10 and 2:30 P.M. in the summer months. When a researcher enters the reading room he is asked to register and he signs the same registration book when he leaves. There are some published catalogues of special collections, most of them in issues of the journal, *Meddelanden från Riksarkivet*, and most of which are rather outdated. A card catalogue in the reading room covers the archives. It is possible to obtain microfilming and photostating service, the prices ranging from 70 öre to 1 krona for photostating at the National Archives to a slightly higher price in other institutions. The Swedish krona is worth at the present (1953) 19.35 cents in the currency of the United States.

The *Kunglige Bibliotheket* (Royal Library) is located in a park called Humlegården off one of Stockholm's main thorough-fares, Birgerjarlsgatan. It is a depository for many important papers and collections. Since 1661 a copy of every book published in Sweden has been deposited in this library. Here may be found bibliographies, guides, published source materials, and the journals of the National Archives and the Swedish Historical Society (*Meddelanden från Riksarkivet* and *Historisk tidskrift*). The library was started as a palace library by Queen Christina; however, she took the best part of it with her to Rome when she abdicated. The second attempt to establish a library in the royal palace was destroyed by the fire of 1697. A third attempt was made in the new palace; it remained there until 1877, when the library was removed to its present site in Humlegården. It now contains some 750,000 volumes and a valuable collection of 13,000 parchment manuscripts. The library is open to the public during the winter months from 9:30 A.M. to 9 P.M. and in the summer from 9:30 A.M. to 6 P.M. from Monday through Friday. On Saturday the library closes at 6 P.M. in winter and at 4 P.M. in summer. All books that are to be used in the library must be drawn out from 10 A.M. to 4 P.M. Registration of name and address is required of all readers upon entering and leaving the library. There are three catalogues arranged according to title, author, and topic. The library provides a photostating and microfilming service.

In the city of Stockholm there are several depositories of archives, which have not been mentioned. The *Riksdag* archives are located in the Parliament building near the palace and are especially valuable for the secret documents of the Period of Freedom. The city of Stockholm has archives dating from 1474, consisting of ordinances of the Mayor and of the City Council, including dealings with the Hanseatic League. These materials are housed at the city hall, while other archives are located at Birgerjarlstorg 12 in the City Archives and Library. The *Flottans arkiv* (records of the navy) are at Skeppsholmen; those of the *Krigsarkivet* (war department archives) at Östermalmsgatan 87. The family papers of the royal family, the Bernadottes, may be found at *Slottsarkivet* in the palace but can only be consulted upon the special permission of the king.

Landsarkiv (local depositories) have been established in various districts of Sweden since 1897. The one at Vadstena in central Sweden is near the ruins of the famous shrine of St. Bridget, which attracted many pilgrims in medieval times; another is located in the interesting old castle in Uppsala. Visby on the island of Gottland, once a factory of the Hanseatic League, has local archives and an interesting museum. The old warehouse of the Swedish East India Company in Göteborg has been converted into a museum and in the city is another *landsarkiv*. The records of the Archbishopric of Lund, the oldest in the north, have been placed in the local depository in that university town.

Housing in Stockholm may be found in numerous pensions, some located near the Royal Library, which is in Humlegården. Bus and streetcar transportation conveniently connect this region with the National Archives. The Swedish Railways maintain a housing service in the main terminal station which is very reasonable and reliable. Such travel agencies as the Nordiske Resebureau and the American Express will give aid in finding hotel and pension accommodations. Meals are often served in the pensions and Stockholm is famous for its restaurants. The Students' Union of the University of Stockholm (*Stockholms högskolas studenters kårhus*) is located at Holländersgatan 95. The University of Liberal Arts may be found at Norrtullsgatan 2. It is wise for the researcher to possess letters of recommendation to the university. If he is to remain in

Stockholm for some time, he should register at his conlsulate or with his cultural attaché.

BIBLIOGRAPHY

Published Collections of Source Material

1. Fryxell, A. *Handlingar rörande Sveriges historia ur utrikes arkiver.* 1859–84. Extracts from foreign archives concerning Sweden's history.
2. Hallendorff, C. *Tal och skrifter av konung Gustav II Adolf.* 1915. The speeches and documents of King Gustavus Adolphus.
3. Klemming, G. E. *Kongl. Bibliothekets samling af samtida berättelser om Sveriges krig.* 1888–91. Contemporary accounts of Sweden's wars in the Royal Library.
4. *Samtida skrifter rörande Sveriges förhållanden till fremmande magter.* 1881–83. Contemporary accounts of Sweden's relations with foreign powers.
   The two publications mentioned above have been continued by C. Snoilsky in 1892, by J. A. Almquist in 1901–2, and by A. Jorgensen, the latter in Helsingfors in 1918.
5. Kungliga samfundet för utgifvande af handskrifter rörande Skandinaviens historia. *Handlingar rörande Skandinaviens historia.* (HSH). 40 vols. 1816–60. Royal Society for the Publication of Source Materials in Scandinavian History. Series entitled: Documents concerning Scandinavian History.
6. *Historiska handlingar.* (HH). 29 vols. 1861– . A continuation of the above.
7. *Stockholms stadsböcker från äldre tid.* 4 series. 1876– . The archives of Stockholm from 1420 to 1544.
8. Riksarkivet. *Arkiv till upplysning om svenska krigens och krigrättningarnes historia.* 3 vols. 1854–61. Archives of the Thirty Years' War.
9. *Handlingar rörande Sveriges historia.* 1859– . Historical sources including:
   Series I. "Konung Gustaf: s registratur." 29 vols. Covers the dates 1521–60. (1861–1916).
   Series III. "Svenska riksrådets protokoll." 17 vols. 1878–1929. Orders in Council from 1621 to 1657.
10. *Svenska riksdagsakter jämte andra handlingar, som höra till statsförfattningens historia.* 2 series, 1521–1718 and 1718–1800. 1887– . Acts of the Riksdag and other documents concerning constitutional development.

11. Styffe, C. G. *Konung Gustaf II Adolfs skrifter.* 1861. Writings of King Gustavus Adolphus.

12. Utrikesdepartementet, *Sveriges traktater med främmande magter jämte andra dit hörande handlingar.* 1877– . Foreign treaties and other documents concerning foreign relations. 15 parts covering 862 to 1905. Part 8 includes border maps (*Gränskarter*) for the years 1752 to 1766 and 1810.

13. *Sveriges och Norges traktater med främmande magter.* Separate edition of Parts 10–15 of the above.

14. *Recueil des traités, conventions et autres actes diplomatiques de la Suède entièrement ou partiellement en vigueur le 1er janvier 1910.* 1910. Another edition of 1910–11. 1911.

15. *Sveriges overenskommelser med främmande makter.* 1912– . Annual publication since 1912 of Sweden's foreign agreements.

16. Vitterhets-historie-och antikvitetsakademien, *Rikskanslere Axel Oxenstiernas skrifter och brefvexling.* 2 series. 1888– . The Royal Academy of Literature, History, and Antiquity's publication of the works and correspondence of Chancellor Axel Oxenstierna.

Guides and Reference Works

17. Bergh, S. *Svenska riksarkivet.* 2 vols. 1916, 1927. The history of the National Archives of Sweden from 1618 to 1846.

18. Bowallius, R. M. "Bidrag till historien om K. Christiern II: s arkiv och dess delning mellen Sverige, Norge och Danmark," *Meddelanden från Riksarkivet,* I:3 (1879), 21–66. A discussion of the division of the archives taken from Sweden and Denmark by Christian II in his flight to Holland.

19. Bring, Samuel E. *Bibliografisk handbok till Sveriges historia.* 1934. This excellent historical bibliography contains a good account of the history and contents of the National Archives and other depositories, a bibliography of published diplomatic correspondence generally and in historical periods, and lists of guides to archival material. It is indispensable to a researcher in Swedish diplomatic history. The author of this chapter has drawn much of the material from this source.

20. Brulin, H. "Das schwedische Archivwesen," *Archivalische Zeitschrift,* 38 (1927).

21. "Utbyte av arkivalier mellen Sverige och Danmark," *Historisk tidskrift,* 1929, 82–84. The archival exchange between Sweden and Denmark, in which Sweden received the documents of the stadholders Svante Nilsson and Sten Sture the Elder, the so-called Sture papers.

22. Bååth, L. M. "Anteckningar om det s.k. Sturearkivet," *Meddelanden från Riksarkivet*, 1929, 165–170. The same as above.

23. Carlander, C. M., *Svenska bibliotek och ex libris*. 6 vols. 1904. An excellent account of collections of private correspondence in libraries and in private collections in Sweden.

24. International Institute of Intellectual Cooperation of the League of Nations, *Guide international des archives-Europe*, "Suède."

25. Posse, A. "Anteckningar om RA bestammelse och arkivhandlingarnas fördelning," *Meddelanden från Riksarkivet*, I : 1 (1877), 30–45.

26. Weibull, C. G. "Arkivordningsprinciper. Historisk återblick och nyorientering," *Scandia*, 1930, 52–77. Since 1902 the principle of provenience has been used in the Swedish archives.

Guides to Special Archive Collections

27. Bergh, S. "Kungliga kansliets i Riksarkivet förvarade diarier," *Meddelanden från Riksarkivet*, N.F. series I, II (1910), 467. A discussion of the "diaries" kept in the chancery in the seventeenth and eighteenth centuries.

28. Brulin, H. "Gadebuchska samlingen i Riksarkivet," *Nordiska tidskrift för bok- och bibliotheksväsen*, 1916, 40–51. A collection of materials on the history of Swedish Pomerania by Professor Gadebusch.

29. Carlsson, A. B. "Jonas Hallenbergs anteckningar och samling till Gustaf II Adolfs historia," *Uppsala universitatsbibliotheks minneskrift*, *1921*. A discussion of Hallenberg's collection of materials on the history of Gustavus II Adolphus in the library of the University of Uppsala.

30. "Forteckning öfver samlingen af riksregistratur i Kongl. Riks-Archivet," *Meddelanden från Riksarkivet, I* : 1 (1877), 61–72. A discussion of the collection of national registers or copybooks of correspondence of the chancery in the National Archives.

31. Hildebrand, E. "Anteckningar om Registrum Regni eller Sveriges äldsta Riksregistratur," *ibid.*, I : 2 (1878), 45–54. The archives recovered from Munich containing the older papers.

32. Sondén, P. "Forteckning ofver bref till konung Gustaf II Adolf i Riksarkivet," *ibid.*, IV (1897), 21–77. Discussion of the correspondence of King Gustavus Adolphus in the National Archives.

33. "Forteckning ofver bref till konung Karl X Gustaf i Riksarkivet," *ibid.*, V (1901), 104–184. Discussion of the correspondence of King Karl X Gustaf in the National Archives.

34. Taube, B., and S. Bergh. "Forteckning öfver samlingen af originaltraktater i Svenska Riksarkivet," *ibid.* (1897), 99–154. Discussion about the copies of original treaties in the National Archives.

G.D.A.–K

35. Taube, B., and T. Westrin. "Förteckningar over ministeriella handlingar," "Danica," *ibid.*, I : 2 (1878), 85–95; new index in 1901, V. Concerning the diplomatic correspondence with Denmark.

"Muscovitica," *ibid.*, I: 3 (1789), 68–80, with a supplement on Cosaccia, III (1891), 422. Russia and the Cossacks.

"Polonica," *ibid.*, II : 6 (1882), 187–196. Poland.

"Germanica," *ibid.*, II : 8 (1884), 135–218. Germany with a topographical register.

"Brandenburgico-Borussia," *ibid.*, II (1883), 93–102. Brandenburg and Prussia.

"Gallica," *ibid.*, III (1891), 125–144. France.

"Hispanica," *ibid.*, 245–250. Spain.

"Italica," *ibid.*, 237–242. Italy.

"Maroccania," *ibid.*, 421. Morocco.

"Portugallica," *ibid.*, 251–254. Portugal.

"Turcica," *ibid.*, 411–420. Turkey, with supplements on "Transylvania, Moldavo-Valachia, Tatarica, Tripolitana, Tunisica and Algerica."

"Hollandica," *ibid.*, IV (1897), 371–394. Holland.

"Allmänna fredskongreser," *ibid.*, V (1901), 321–324. International conferences.

"Americana," *ibid.*, 318.

"Anglica," *ibid.*, 289–314. England.

"Helvetica," *ibid.* (1901), 316–317. Switzerland.

"Persica," *ibid.*, 319–320. Iran.

"Scotica," *ibid.*, p. 315. Scotland.

"Livonica," *ibid.*, N.F. Ser., I : 1–2 (1902), supplement. Livonia was a part of Sweden in the seventeenth century before annexation to Russia. Most of these are by Taube and Westrin.

13 SWITZERLAND

Lynn M. Case
University of Pennsylvania

HISTORY OF THE ARCHIVES

THERE was no national repository in Switzerland for government records and documents until 1798. Consequently, for
documentary materials on Swiss foreign affairs before 1798 one
must rely on the collections of uneven value scattered in the
various cantonal archives.[1] The cantonal archives of Berne,
Lucerne, and Zurich are the most important for the earlier
materials on foreign relations. However, of considerable value
are also the cantonal archives of Appenzel (Ausser Rhoden),
Appenzell (Inner Rhoden), Basel, Frauenfeld, Fribourg, Glaris,
Nidwald, Obwald, Schaffhausen, Soleure, and Zug. There are
materials of lesser importance to be found in the cantonal
archives of Geneva, Grisons (at Coire), Neuchatel, Schwyz,
and Valais (at Sion). The archives of Uri were burned by the
French in 1799.[2]

The first central repository for confederation documents
came at the time of the establishment of the Helvetic Republic
in 1798 when provision was made for national archives on
December 18 of the same year. In spite of changing regimes the
archives were continued in 1803 and 1848. In 1804 they were
given their permanent location in Berne, where all of the
records on Swiss foreign relations since 1798 have been kept.
After 1803 the archives were designated as the Schweizerische

---

[1] I, 385 of number 30 in bibliography.
[2] Based on information furnished by the Archives Fédérales Suisses, April 7,
1953.

eidgenössische Bundesarchiv.[3] With the founding of the Swiss federal government in 1848 the archives were put under the direction of the federal chancellery, but in 1861 they were reorganized on their present basis and placed under the department of interior. For many years the *Bundesarchiv* occupied part of the basement of the Federal Palace in central Berne, but in 1899 it was moved to the south wing of the new Archives and Library Building in Kirchenfeld (South Berne). In 1931 the library (*Landesbibliothek*) moved to its new, modern building, and the *Bundesarchiv* then took over the rest of the space in the old building left vacant by the library.[4]

ORGANIZATION AND CLASSIFICATION

Although its name, organization, and location may have changed since its founding, the *Bundesarchiv* contains the confederation's documentary materials since 1798. Thus there are three general chronological groupings of the official documents: (1) the archives of the government of the Helvetic Republic (1798–1803), (2) the archives of the Diet (1803–48), (3) the archives of the central federal administration since 1848.

The archival materials of the period of the Helvetic Republic (1798–1803), consisting of 3,775 volumes, are classified under the headings of ten authorities: (1) legislative, (2) executive, (3) finance, (6) war, (7) foreign affairs, (8) judicial, (9) treasury and office of the seals, and (10) pay commissioner (*commissaire ordonnateur*). All these sections have documentary materials relating to foreign affairs, but of course the one containing the materials of the ministry of foreign affairs is the most important. This section of material (7) is subdivided into two subheadings: (*a*) minutes of proceedings (*procès-verbaux*), brief descriptions of the deliberations in the Executive Directory concerning foreign affairs; (*b*) decisions, messages, correspondence, and instructions.

[3]The French and Italian designations for the archives are: Archives Fédérales Suisses and Archivio Federale Svizzero.

[4]I, 496 of number 32 in bibliography; I, 385–386 of number 30 in bibliography.

The archives of the Diet (1803–48) are subdivided into two periods: Period of the Mediation (1803–13) and Period of the Restoration and Regeneration (1813–48). The foreign ministry materials of the Period of the Mediation, consisting of 672 volumes, are further subdivided under the following sub-headings:

1. Political reports from the Swiss diplomatic agents in Paris, Vienna, and Milan.

2. Papers concerning special (extraordinaires) diplomatic missions to foreign countries.

3. Swiss consular papers from France and the Italian states.

4. Papers (diplomatic and consular) originating with the Swiss federal authorities concerning Swiss negotiations and correspondence with foreign countries. These are still further subdivided under the headings of German states, France, Great Britain, Italy, Netherlands, Austria, Prussia, Rome, Russia, Sweden, Austria, Sicily, Spain, Valais, Neuchatel (except for the last subheading, these are arranged alphabetically under the German form of the name).

The foreign ministry materials of the Period of Restoration and Regeneration (1813–48), consisting of 2,230 volumes, are arranged under the following headings and subheadings:

1. Correspondence of the federal authorities with the Swiss diplomatic representatives in Paris, Vienna, and Milan.

2. Special (extraordinaires) diplomatic missions to foreign countries.

3. Correspondence with the Swiss consulates in Marseilles, Lyons, Bordeaux, le Havre, Bastia, Nantes, Algiers, Lisbon, Barcelona, Genoa, Naples, Rome, Milan, Leghorn, Trieste, Turin, London, Liverpool, Leipzig, Hamburg, Amsterdam, Rotterdam, Antwerp, Brussels, St. Petersburg, Odessa, Moscow, Christiania, New York, New Orleans, Philadelphia, Madison, Galveston, Louisville, Alexandria, Mexico City, Rio de Janeiro, Pernambuco, Bahia, and Para.

4. Correspondence, negotiations, and treaties with the

German states, Belgium, Brazil, Denmark, France, Greece, Great Britain, the Italian states outside Sardinia and the Two Sicilies, Liechtenstein, Mexico, the Netherlands, the United States, Austria, Portugal, Prussia, Russia, Sardinia, Sweden, Two Sicilies, and Spain.

The foreign ministry archives of the central federal administration since 1848 have no specially prepared inventory but are classified by files according to the headings given by the registry of the political department. The main collection of diplomatic correspondence is, however, arranged under the heading of *"Rapports politiques"* and then subdivided into the various foreign countries. There is no catalogue for this material. But the following card catalogues in the research room serve as guides to other materials since 1848 and indicate their nature:

1. Catalogue of general bilateral treaties to which Switzerland is a party, listed by number, date, diplomatic personnel, and country.

2. Catalogue of boundary treaties, listed by number, date, country, and place of signature.

3. Catalogue of international (multilateral) treaties, listed by number, date, subject, country, and place of signature.

4. Catalogue of tariff treaties (*Zollauslösungsverträge*).

5. Catalogue of federal and cantonal constitutions.

Other collections in the period since 1848 of interest to foreign relations are:

1. Copies of documents relating to Swiss history obtained since 1876 from the archives of Paris, Italy, London, Madrid, Simancas, Vienna, the Hague, and Stockholm.

2. The original minutes (*procès-verbaux*) of the Swiss Federal Council, the Swiss Council of States (*Ständerat*) and the Swiss National Council (*Nationalrat*). (These contain discussions on foreign affairs and ratifications of treaties.)[5]

[5]Information on the organization and classification of the documents on foreign affairs was obtained from number 32 in bibliography; pp. 338–344 of number 29 in bibliography; and Réponses (by Dr. Leonard Haas) à un questionnaire de M. Case concernant les Archives Fédérales, August 1948.

ADMINISTRATION, REGULATIONS, AND FACILITIES

The *Bundesarchiv* is located at 24 Archivstrasse in Berne, on the south side of the city. Its phone number is 617600. Dr. Leonard Haas is the Federal Archivist.

The research room will be found in the central front area of the second floor, just in front of the staircase. One must ring to obtain entrance at the iron grill at the top of the stairs. The administrative offices are located on the same floor near the research room. The *Bundesarchiv* is open from Monday through Friday, from 8 to 12 A.M. and from 2 to 6 P.M., Saturdays 8 to 12 A.M. only. (Actually the hours are fifteen minutes earlier than those indicated.) It is closed for two days in the spring for cleaning.

According to the regulations of the *Bundesarchiv*[6] the documents over fifty years old are freely available for public use. No credentials or recommendations are necessary, but the administration reserves the right to require the identification of researchers. Documents less than fifty years old will be communicated only in exceptional cases and only with the permission of the service or department concerned.[7] Interlibrary and interarchive loans of documents (except rare or fragile ones) are made within Switzerland but not between the *Bundesarchiv* and foreign institutions.

The researcher may obtain authorization to use a typewriter if it does not disturb other visitors. The *Bundesarchiv* does not have a photographic or microfilm service for the reproduction of documents. However, it permits photostatic reproductions by an approved private photographer, who will make the reproductions under the supervision of the archives. The rates for this service are one Swiss franc (25 cents) per page or in cases of large quantities 90 Swiss centimes (22½ cents) per page.

[6] *Règlement concernant la communication et le prêt des documents des archives fédérales (du 9 mai 1944).*

[7] The minutes of the public deliberations of the two legislative houses are available regardless of date.

Other facilities available to researchers in the *Bundesarchiv* are:

1. A library containing, among many items, the collections of printed documents, debates, statutes, and reference works. There is also a card catalogue of this library.

2. Card catalogues of some of the collections since 1848 (see above under *Organization and Classification*).

3. For inventories and indexes of collections see the bibliography at the end, numbers 12, 13, 16, 23.

Those who are doing research in the *Bundesarchiv* will also find the following institutions and learned societies located in Berne:

Archives Cantonales de Berne
Archives de la Ville de Berne
Bibliothèque Nationale (Landesbibliothek)
Bibliothèque de la Ville et de l'Université de Berne
Bibliothèque Militaire Fédérale
Musée des Arts et Métiers
Musée Historique
Séminaire d'Histoire Générale et d'Histoire Suisse à l'Université de Berne
Société d'Histoire du Canton de Berne

The deliberations of the two houses of the National Assembly, when they are in session, might be of interest to visiting social scientists.

Good hotels, whether they are de luxe or moderate in price and accommodations, may be found in the center of the city, not far from the railroad station. A bus runs from this area to the *Bundesarchiv* about every ten minutes. Those who wish to find boarding houses or rooms in private homes would be advised to consult the University of Berne or Cook's tourist offices in the center of the city.

BIBLIOGRAPHY

Printed Collections of Documents

1. *Amtliche Sammlung der ältern eidgenössischen Abschiede. Die eidgenössischen Abschiede aus dem Zeitraume von 1245 bis 1798.* 8 vols. in 23. Berne, 1856–86. Collected from materials in the cantons and cities and published and distributed with the co-operation of the Bundesarchiv.

2. *Actensammlung aus der Zeit der helvetischen Republik* (1798–1803). Edited by Johannes Strickler and Alfred Rufer. 13 vols. in 14. Berne and Fribourg, 1886–1947.

3. *Amtliche Sammlung der neueren eidgenössischen Abschiede. Repertorium der Abschiede der eidgenössischen Tagsatzungen aus den Jahren 1803 bis 1813.* Edited by Jakob Kaiser. Berne, 1886. A second edition of the two following items.

4. *Repertorium der Abschiede der eidgenössischen Tagsatzungen vom Jahr 1803 bis Ende des Jahres 1813.* Berne, 1842.

5. *Urkunden zum Repertorium der Abschiede der eidgenössischen Tagsatzungen vom Jahr 1803 bis Ende des Jahres 1813.* Berne, 1843. A supplementary volume to the one listed above.

6. *Amtliche Sammlung der neueren eidgenössischen Abschiede. Repertorium der Abschiede der eidgenössischen Tagsatzungen aus den Jahren 1814 bis 1848.* Edited by Wilhelm Fetscherin under the direction of Jakob Kaiser, Federal Archivist. 2 vols. Berne, 1874–76.

7. *Offizielle Sammlung der das schweizerische Staatrecht betreffenden Aktenstücke, Bundesgesetze, Verträge, und Verordnungen, 1848.* Berne, 1850– .[8]

8. *Bundesblatt der schweizerischen Eidgenossenschaft, 1848–* .[9] A publication of the laws and decrees of the Federal Assembly, discussions and decisions of the Federal Council, proposals of federal laws and decrees, official communications of federal officials, appointments, and official acts and publications of the canton authorities.

Guides and Reference Works

9. Benziger, C. "Die Schweiz in ihren Beziehungen zu den Vereinigten Staaten von Nordamerika," *Konsular-Bulletin,* X (1931), 1 ff.

10. Ceresole, Victor. *Relevé des manuscrits des archives de Venise se rapportant à la Suisse et aux III ligues grises.* Venice, 1890.

11. Faust, Albert B. *Guide to materials for American history in Swiss and Austrian archives.* Washington, 1916.

[8]The French title is: *Recueil officiel des pièces concernant le droit public en Suisse des lois fédérales, traités, décrets, et arrêtés, 1848–1947.*

[9]The French and Italian titles are: *Feuille fédérale suisse* and *Foglio federale della Confederazione svizzera.*

12. *Generalrepertorium der Acten des helvetischen Zentralarchivs in Berne, 12 April 1798 bis März 1803* (Berne, 1876). For materials on foreign affairs see *Auswärtiges* under *Vollziehungsgewalt*, p. 17, numbers, 786–803.

13. *Generalrepertorium für das eidgenössische Archiv, 1803–1848* (only in manuscript form).

14. Haas, Leonard. "Die Schweiz und die Vereinigten Staaten von Nordamerika. Ein geschichtlicher Rückblick (1607–1917)," *Zeitschrift für schweizerische Geschichte*, XX (1940), 228–263. By an official of the Bundesarchiv and based on Bundesarchiv materials.

15. "Spanische Quellen zur Schweizergeschichte," *Schweizerische Zeitschrift für Geschichte*, I (1951), 599–608.

16. *Inventarium des eidgenössischen Archivs von 1803–1832* (a manuscript copy existing only in the *Bundesarchiv*).

17. Kaiser, Jakob. "Les archives fédérales," *Dictionnaire géographique de la Suisse*, V (1908), 337–338.

18. Kern, Léon; Henri Beuchat; Leonard Haas. *Repertorium über die Verhandlungen der Bundesversammlung der schweizerischen Eidgenossenschaft*. Vol. I (1848–74). Fribourg, 1942.

19. Kern, Léon, and Edgar Bonjour. "Summarisches Verzeichnis der Abschriften aus ausländischen Archiven, die im Bundesarchiv aufbewahrt werden," *Zeitschrift für schweizerische Geschichte*. XV (1935), 422–432.

20. Largiadèr, Anton, "Die Archive der Schweiz," *Archivar*, February 1953.

21. "Schweizerisches Archivwesen. Ein Überblick," *Festschrift Haus-, Hof- und Staatsarchiv* (Vienna, 1949), I, 23–53.

22. Plüss, A. "Mitteilungen über das Archvwesen der Schweiz," *Deutsche Geschichtsblätter*, X (1909), 163 ff.

23. *Règlement concernant la communication et le prêt des documents des archives fédérales*. Decree of the Swiss Federal Council, May 9, 1944.[10]

24. *Reglement und Plan für das eidgenössische Archiv nebst dazu gehörender Instruktion*.

25. *Repertorium über die in Zeit- und Sammelschriften der Jahre 1812–1912 enthaltene Aufsätze und Mitteilungen schweizergeschichtlichen Inhaltes*. Published by the Allgemeine geschichtsforschenden Gesellschaft der Schweiz and edited by Joseph Leopold Brandstetter and Hans Barth. 6 vols. Basel, 1892, 1906, 1943.

26. Reinhardt, H. *Schweizergeschichtliche Forschungen in spanischen Archiven und Bibliotheken*. Published by the Swiss *Bundesarchiv*. Berne, 1900.

---

[10]The German and Italian titles are: *Reglement über die Mitteilung und die Ausleihe der Akten des Bundesarchiv* and *Regolamento per la communicazione e prestito dei documenti dell'Archivio federale*.

27. Roth, Edouard. *Histoire de la représentation diplomatique de la France auprès des cantons suisses, de leurs alliés et de leurs confédéres, 1430–1704.* 10 vols. Berne. 1900–35.

28. *Inventaire sommaire des documents relatifs à l'histoire de Suisse conservés dans les archives et bibliothèques de Paris et spécialement de la correspondance échangée entre les ambassadeurs de France aux Ligues et leur gouvernement, 1444 à 1700.* 6 Parts. Berne, 1882–94. Part VI is made up entirely of two alphabetical indexes of persons and subjects.

29. Société des Nations. Institut International de Coopération Intellectuelle. *Guide international des archives. Europe.* Paris, 1934.

30. Türler, Henri. "Les archives fédérales à Berne. . . . Les archives cantonales," *Dictionnaire historique et biographique suisse,* I (1921), 385–388. This describes the classification plan of the *Bundesarchiv* and discusses the collections in the canton archives.

31. Usteri, Emile. "Berichte über Literatur, die schweizerische Archive betreffend, 1907–1927," *Archivalische Zeitschrift,* 3d Series, IV (1928), 279–316.

32. Wentzke, P., and G. Ludtke. "Die Archive," *Minerva Handbücher,* Part II, I (1932), 496.

33. Wild, Helen. *Bibliographie Schweizergeschichte, Jahrgang 1913– .* Berne, 1915–20. Zurich, 1921– .

34. Wirz, Caspar, ed., *Regesten zur Schweizergeschichte aus den päpstlischen Archiven, 1447–1503.* Collected and published by the *Bundesarchiv* in Berne. 6 numbers. Berne, 1911–18.

14 VATICAN CITY

Natalie Summers

Formerly of the National Archives, Washington, D.C.,

and

Willard Allen Fletcher

University of Colorado

HISTORY

THE earliest information concerning the Vatican archives goes back to the fourth century. At that time a part of them were deposited in the Church of San Lorenzo in Damaso, while the rest of them were located in the Turris Cartelaria iuxto Palladium, near the Roman Forum. From there they were moved to the Lateran Palace until Pope Innocent III (1198–1216) transferred them to St. Peter's. However, almost all the manuscripts prior to the reign of Innocent III are missing.[1] Pope Nicholas V (1447–55) founded in 1450 the Vatican Library (*Biblioteca Apostolica Vaticana*). The archives were kept in that library until 1611, when Pope Paul V (1605–21) established a special depository for the manuscripts, known as the *Archivio Segreto Vaticano*, independent of the library. Gradually other manuscripts were added, such as registers or copies of outgoing correspondence, copies of incoming correspondence, as well as original reports of the nuncios and legates. In time the extensive accumulation of documents necessitated the division of the materials into several collections.

Other documentary collections, significant for the study of

[1]Pp. 88–90 in no. 68 of bibliography.

Vatican diplomacy, are to be found in the libraries in Rome and in the private papers of the old and aristocratic Italian families to which some of the nuncios belonged.[2] Still other records are in the Vatican Palace. They concern ecclesiastical, juridical, ecclesiastico-political, and administrative matters.[3]

The archival collection sustained considerable losses when in 1329 it was moved to Avignon, the temporary seat of the papacy. It was returned during the years 1441, 1566, and 1783, only to be taken back to France by Napoleon I. Most of the documents were eventually sent back to Rome, some were lost, and others remained in Paris.[4]

The most important period of papal diplomacy covers approximately two centuries, the sixteenth to the eighteenth. The first nuncio was sent to Spain in the fifteenth century. In 1513 a nunciate was established near the Holy Roman Emperor and soon after a nuncio was appointed to the French court. These centuries witness the diplomatic efforts of popes anxious to fight Protestantism and Islam and to enlarge the domains of the papacy as well.[5]

It is impossible to give the exact number of volumes and bundles now deposited in the archives. There are many thousands of them, apart from the many envelopes containing documents. The bound volumes contain approximately two thousand documents each.

Since the opening of the archives in 1881 by Pope Leo XIII (1878–1903) many publications of documents have appeared. German and Austrian institutes in Rome were particularly active in this respect, while notable contributions were made by Belgian, Swiss, French, Dutch, and other scholars. In addition to the large printed collections, there exist many studies based on archival materials that form an important reference source. A good example is Ludwig von Pastor's *Geschichte der*

[2]Pp. 204–207 of number 62 in bibliography.
[3]Pp. 286–290 of number 61 in bibliography.
[4]Pp. 88–90 of number 68 in bibliography.
[5]Pp. 204–207 of number 62 in bibliography.

Päpste, covering the period from the end of the Middle Ages to 1790. His work was continued by J. Schmidlin, but unfortunately the documentation is not as thorough. The last volume ends in 1929, a period for which the archives are usually closed to the researcher.[6]

ORGANIZATION AND CLASSIFICATION

The Vatican collection may be divided into eight main groups:

1. Secret Archives
2. Archives of Avignon
3. Archives of the Apostolic Chamber
4. Archives of the Castel Sant'Angelo
5. Archives of the Dataria
6. Consistorial Archives
7. Archives of the Secretariate of State
8. Various Collections

The most important Vatican documentary collection, for the researcher in modern diplomatic history, is that of the secretariat of state (Segreteria di Stato). However, in view of the peculiar organizational structure of the entire Vatican archival collection, it is not all-inclusive, and the researcher is cautioned to refer to the other major collections of the Vatican. Moreover, when steps were taken to bring together all documents of the secretariate, much material remained in the private archives of Italian families, members of which served as secretaries of state. Some of these private collections have been deposited in the Vatican and are maintained as private and separate collections. The holdings of the archives of the secretariate of state are divided into three main groups, on a chronological basis:

A. *Fondo Vecchio*
B. *Epoca Napoleonica*
C. *Fondo Moderno*

[6]Pp. 204–7 of number 62 in bibliography.

A. *Fondo Vecchio*

This collection, terminating generally with the end of the eighteenth century, is located on the second floor of the *torre dei quattro venti*. It may be divided into four major groups: (1) *Nunziature e Legazioni;* (2) *Lettere;* (3) *Miscellanea (Varia Miscellanea);* (4) *Fondo Diverse.*

1. *Nunziature e Legazioni*

As would be expected, the reports from the nunciatures and the instructions of the Vatican secretaries of state to the nuncios abroad constitute very significant segments of the archives of the secretariate of state. The material in this group dates from the sixteenth century and terminates with the eighteenth century. The collection is of course continued, and materials are found in later *fonds*. Apart from the ordinary dispatches and coded messages, the correspondence came to include in time letters as well as enclosures. Instructions to the nuncios are preserved both in preliminary and in final drafts. It should be noted that the collection has many gaps, especially in the sixteenth century materials. Furthermore, diplomatic instructions to the nuncios were at times included in correspondence dealing primarily with nondiplomatic affairs and therefore may not always be in the archives of the secretariate of state. In the list of holdings below, an attempt is made to combine the inventory work of Katterbach, Savio, Brom, and Fink.[7] It has not been possible to ascertain in each and every case both the number of volumes and the time span:

Fondo Nunziature	*Vols. or bundles*	
Germania	818	
Francia	672	1527–1826 (and Supplement to Francia I–LV)

[7] Pp. 82–113 of number 66 in bibliography.

Fondo Nunziature   *Vols. or bundles*

Portogallo	245	1535–1851
Spagna	468	1524–1818 (and Spagna appendixes I–XXII)
Polonia	367	1567–1783
Polonia-Russia	30	
Malta	185	1572–1797
Inghilterra	34	
Genova	21	1572–1809
Venezia	420	1524–1807
Colonia	334	1575–1799
Napoli	646	1570–1824
Savoia	349	1568–1798
Svizzera	338	1532–1803
Fiandra	207	1553–1795
Firenze	271	1570–1797
Baviera	57	1786–1808
Avignone	381	1564–1789
Bologna	395	1553–1791
Ferrara	408	1597–1740
Romagna	197	1597–1740
Urbino	233	1664–1740
Corsica	11	1746–1801
Paci	71	1628–1716
Arch. Nunziature Venezia	90	

Nunziature diverse   297 *vols. or bundles*

Colonia	1605–86
Fiandra	1605–86
Firenze	1607–64
Francia	1521–1689
Germania	1591–1807
Inghilterra	1553–1686

Malta	1678–81
Napoli	1462–1686
Nimega	1676–79
Polonia	1663–1705
Portogallo	1560–1684
Savoia	1605–85
Spagna	1560–1686
Svizzera	1605–86
Venezia	1596–1686
Legazioni	1607–86
Istruzioni	Eugenius IV–1736
Lettere varie	1510–1724
Relazioni, Testi,	
Attipolitici, Affari	1546–1790

Gruppo Avvisi   159 *vols. or bundles*

a. Notices originat-
  ing within the
  jurisdiction
  of individual
  nunciatures:

Colonia	1601–97
Fiandra	1563–1746
Firenze	1651–1793
Francia	1562–1793
Malta	1667–72
Napoli	1618–1704
Polonia	1607–1770
Portogallo	1587–1672
Savoia	1616–97
Spagna	1587–1719
Svizzera	1620–96
Venezia	1605–1791
Vienna-Praga-	
Germania	1563–1709

b. Letters and
    notices from
    other places:

Ancona, Belgrado, Bologna, Dalmazia, Ferrara, Foligno, Forli, Genova, Inghilterra, Levante, Macerata, Mantova, Milano, Modena, Olanda, Parma-Piacenza, Pavia, Pesaro, Ravenna, Rimini, Roma, Spoleto, Svezia.

Memoriali e Biglietti	316
Emigrati Rivoluzione	
Francese	53
Fondo Salviati	81
Fondo Benincasa	34
Archivio Ubaldini	49

A very valuable addition to the *Nunziature e Legazioni* collection was made when the archives of the following nunciatures were brought to Rome during the pontificate of Pius XI or earlier:

	Vols.	
Bruxelles	75	
Colonia	391	
Firenze	54	
Lisbona	ca. 400	
Lucerna	448	
Madrid	307	
Monaco di Baviera	181	
Napoli	220	
Parigi	ca. 400	
Torino	220	
Varsovia	195	
Vienna	549	(and ca. 1,600 bundles)

2. *Lettere*

In addition to the correspondence found in the *Nunziature e Legazioni* collection, there exists the Lettere collection, which ranges over a wider scope, since it contains the correspondence between the curia and officials of the church universal, foreign governments, and private persons. The collection is divided into the groups listed below, but it should be noted that no rigid separation is maintained. First to be found in each group are the original communications received up to the year 1740, with material from the sixteenth and early seventeenth centuries being sparse; they are followed by communications sent, partly in copy and partly in draft. This procedure is then repeated for the period 1740 to the end of the eighteenth century. Attention is drawn to the fact that the papal correspondence found in the archives of the secretariate of state is by no means all-inclusive; many other papal offices and authorities engaged in official communications on a wealth of matters. The following are the divisions of the *Lettere* collection:

	Vols.
Lettere di cardinali	207
Lettere di vescovi e prelati	433
Lettere di principi e titolati	291
Lettere di particolari	327
Lettere di soldati	84

3. *Miscellanea (Varia Miscellanea)*

This collection in the archives of the secretariate of state is composed of items that could not easily be integrated into the other collections. Much material bearing on the history of the church from the sixteenth to the eighteenth century, such as correspondence with nunciatures, treaties, concordats, administrative documents, etc., is gathered in this collection of 1,488 volumes.

4. *Fondo Diverse*

The materials collected within this group form an integral part of the archives of the secretariate of state; they consist of the archives of individuals and families who played an important part in the affairs of the church. These papers have been deposited in the Vatican, where they are housed separately. In addition to these collections, identified below, there are other private diplomatic papers scattered through the Vatican archives. In order to locate them it is necessary to make a thorough consultation of the established indexes to various collections, such as the *Segreteria dei brevi, Brevia seu epistulae ad principes, Litterae Latinae, Segreteria dei memoriali, Fondo Confalonieri, Fondo Garampi, Fondo Mencacci, Fondo Pio, Collezione Spada, Registra Vaticana, Registra Avenionensia, Registra Lateranensia*, etc.

a. *Carte Farnesiane*:

Only 19 volumes of the extensive papers of Paul III and the Farnese family have come into the possession of the Vatican. Most of the material is located in the archives in Parma.

b. *Fondo Borghese*:

This collection, not to be confused with the *Archivio Borghese* or *Casa Borghese* in the Vatican archives, consists of the archives of the secretaries of state under Paul V (1605–21) and under his predecessor Clement VIII (1592–1605), whose political papers were taken by the Borghese family and added to its family archives. The collection came into the possession of the Vatican in 1891. It consists of four series, totaling about two thousand volumes and bundles, and constitutes a most important source for the political history of the late sixteenth and early seventeenth centuries.

c. *Fondo Barberini*:

The archives of the Barberini family that are housed in the Vatican library constitute in reality the archives of the secretariate of state under Urban VIII (1623–44). This valuable collection came into the possession of the Vatican in 1902. Of major interest are its *Carteggi diplomatici*, which contain diplomatic correspondence of the papacy.

d. *Fondo Chigi*:

The Chigi archives, housed in the Vatican library, were

acquired in 1923. They contain much valuable material of the secretariate of state during the pontificate of Alexander VII (1655–67).

B. Epoca Napoleonica

This collection, forming the link between the old and the new *fonds*, is at present in a state of reorganization, making it impossible to give a detailed summary of its contents. A great deal of the material was lost during the French Revolution and the reign of Napoleon I. As far as the diplomatic correspondence during this period is concerned, the researcher should note that part of it is still to be found in the *Fondo Vecchio* and the *Fondo Moderno*.

C. Fondo Moderno

The contents of this collection, beginning with 1816, are divided into two general groups, *Interno* and *Estero*. The *Interno* material in the Vatican archives embraces only the years 1816–33; the remainder, from 1834 to 1870, is in the Italian state archives in Rome. Of much greater significance here, the material of the *Estero* for the period 1816–70 has been in the Vatican archives for a long time. The documents for the period 1870–89 were added in 1917, those for the period 1890–1904 in 1928, and those for the period 1904–13 in 1936. The papers relating to the more recent period are still in the secretariate of state. The documents for the nineteenth century have not yet been bound, except for the years 1816–19. There are 666 bundles for the period 1814–50, 850 for the period 1851–94, and 1,005 for the *Sezione Interna* 1814–33. The *Interno* and *Estero* are divided into the following *titoli* and *rubriche*:

Interno

Titolo	I	*Affari ecclesiastici*	*Rubriche Nr.*	1–24
	II	*Amministrazione pubblica*		25–70
	III	*Materie giudiziarie*		80–99
	IV	*Finanze*		110–130
	V	*Sicurezza interna*		149–166

Estero

Titolo IX *Affari Esteri*
Rubriche:

Rubriche

269	*Prussia ministro*
270	*Paesi Bassi ministro*
271	*Hannover ministro*
272	*Toscana incaricato*
273	*Malta incaricato*
274	*Modena incaricato*
275	*Wurttemberg incaricato (anche Baden)*
276	*Lucca incaricato*
277	*Sassonia agente*
278	*Anhalt-Coethen agente (Inghilterra, Irlanda)*
279	*Affari di America*
280	*Propaganda Fide*
281	*Congregazione degli affari ecclesiastici*
282	*Ministri di Stato*
283	*Vescovi Esteri*
284	*Particolari Esteri*
285	*Consoli Pontificii in Napoli e Regno*
286	*Consoli Pontificii in Liverno e Toscana*
287	*Consoli Pontificii in Genova e suo Stato*
288	*Consoli Pontificii in Venezia*
289	*Consoli Pontificii in Trieste*
290	*Consoli Pontificii in Palermo e Messina*
291	*Consoli Pontificii in Marsiglia e Tolone*
292	*Consoli Pontificii in Corfù e Isole Ionie*
293	*Consoli Pontificii in Ispagna e Portogallo*
294	*Consoli Pontificii in Malta, Corsica, e Sardegna*
295	*Consoli Pontificii in Dalmazia*
295A	*Consoli Pontificii per gli anni 1851, 1852*
296	*Consoli Esteri Napolitano*
297	*Consoli Esteri Inglese*
298	*Consoli Esteri Diversi*
299	*Consoli Pontificii, disposizioni generali*
300	*Consoli Esteri, disposizioni generali*
301	*(Provisioni) Delagato di Constantinopoli*

Although housed separately, another collection which forms by its nature a part of the *Fondo Moderno* is the archives of the *Congregazione per gli affari ecclesiastici straordinari*. It is located in the *torre Borgia* and is not open for general consultation. Not much is known of the collection, but there is no doubt that it is of utmost significance for the political affairs of the papacy during the nineteenth and the twentieth centuries. Only for special and limited occasions is permission granted by the prefect of the archives for consultation of documents in this collection; for extensive research it is necessary to secure the permission of the Pope.

The best and most recent guide to the Vatican archives is by Fink; it appeared in 1951 and supersedes one of 1942 by the same author.[8] Another valuable guide, although somewhat outdated, is that by Brom, published in 1911.[9] Use of the Vatican archives is facilitated by the existence of a very large collection of indexes, numbering 681 volumes, prepared by Petrus Doninus de Pretis and Guiseppe Garampi for the seventeenth and eighteenth centuries. New indexes are constantly being added and they are all located in the *sala degli indici*. They are numbered consecutively, irrespective of subject, and numbers 134 and 135 are of particular importance for diplomatic history. A most valuable tool for research is the index to indexes which was prepared in 1901.[10]

ADMINISTRATION, REGULATIONS, AND FACILITIES

It would be of great advantage to anyone intending to work in the Vatican archives to familiarize himself with Fink's guide before coming to Rome. To carry on research in the manuscript records a reading knowledge of Latin is indispensable, while facility in several modern European languages is helpful. Unless the researcher is able to speak at least some Italian, he will waste much valuable time.

[8] Number 66 in bibliography.
[9] Number 63 in bibliography.
[10] Pp. 7–10 of number 63 in bibliography.

Eugene Cardinal Tisserant is the Cardinal Archivist and head of both the papal archives and the library. He was appointed to the post on September 26, 1957, and succeeded Giovanni Cardinal Mercati who died on August 22, 1957. Monsignor Angelo Mercati is the prefect of the archives. An erudite scholar, he has written a great deal about the archives and has a vast knowledge of the manuscript collection. He is very obliging and willing to help visiting scholars.

The personnel employed in the archives is small and only one of the attendants has a limited command of English. Any questions asked by the researcher will be politely answered, and he will be assisted in finding the document he wishes to have; however, the assistance will be strictly limited to that. There are no consultants as there are in many other repositories.

It is to be remembered that both the library and the archives are not public institutions and are opened to the public only as a courtesy of the Vatican authorities. The archives are open to research from the dates of the earliest documents to 1846. They are supposed to be closed for one hundred years, but so far the date has not been advanced.

To obtain permission to work in the archives it is necessary to present a letter from a university, a library, or any institution of learning. In case of emergency a letter from the embassy may be presented. The person wishing to use the archives applies to the prefect and fills out a form; a card of admission is then issued, to which a photograph of the applicant is attached. When coming the first time to apply for permission to use the archives, it is necessary to bring one's passport in order to be admitted into the Vatican City. If the applicant wishes to use the library as well as the archives, two letters of introduction to both prefects must be presented, accompanied by two photographs. In such a case two cards will be issued, and it is advisable to obtain both. The library is located across a courtyard from the archives.

There are no special rules or regulations that govern the use of the materials, once the card of admission has been issued. The person wishing to do research in the archives explains to the prefect the subject of his research, and an attendant is directed to bring the necessary index. It should be noted that this procedure is done by word of mouth and is very informal. In the library the researcher indicates his wishes and is then directed to the card catalogue and left to find the desired books. Some useful reference works are filed along the walls of the reading room and the catalogue room. If the researcher is unable to locate the volumes desired, one of the attendants will help to find them.

The reading rooms of both the archives and the library are open from 8 A.M. to 12:30 P.M. daily, except on Sundays and on Catholic holidays. Entrance is through the Sant'Anna gate. Both the archives and the library are closed for ten days at Christmas and five days at Easter. The summer holidays begin on July 15 and end on September 15. Under the present prefect, the researcher is allowed to use the archives during the summer vacation. The decision to open or close the archives during the summer holidays rests with the prefect. The library, however, is closed in any case during these summer months.

Microfilming service is offered by the library. A 35 mm. exposure costs 22 lire or about 3.5 cents at the present time. Not less than ten can be ordered. A researcher is allowed to use his own camera if he wishes. The facilities have been used extensively by different nations, and St. Louis University, St. Louis, Missouri, has microfilmed a large segment of the manuscript collection.

There is no special quarter in Rome where students live. However, the International House (*Casa Internazionale*), piazza della Rovere 83, does furnish rooms and board to men students, and is located near the Vatican. Boarding houses or rooms can be found in most parts of the city and may be located through the advertisement section of the Roman newspapers.

BIBLIOGRAPHY

Printed Collections of Documents

Austrian

Historische Kommission der Kaiserlichen Akademie der Wissenschaften in Wein:

1. Dengel, I. *Nuntius Biglia 1565–1566 (Juni). Commendone als Legat auf dem Reichstag zu Augsburg 1566.* Vienna, 1926.

2. *Nuntius Biglia 1566 (Juni)–1569 (Dezember). Commendone als Legat bei Kaiser Maximilian II. 1568 (Oktober)–1569 (Jänner).* Vienna, 1939.

3. Kramer, H. *Nuntius Biglia 1570 (Jänner)–1571 (April).* Graz, 1952.

Oesterreichisches Institut in Rom:

4. Dengel, I. "Ein Bericht des Nuntius Joseph Garampi über Böhmen im Jahre 1776," *Sitzungsberichte der kgl. böhmischen Gesellschaft der Wissenschaften. Abt. Philosophie und Geschichte,* VI (1902), 1 ff.

5. "Nuntius Joseph Garampi in Preussen, Schlesien und in Sachsen im Jahre 1776," *Quellen und Forschungen vom preussischen historischen Institut in Rom,* V (1903), 223–268.

6. *Die politische und kirchliche Tätigkeit des Monsignor J. Garampi in Deutschland (1761–1763); geheime Sendung zum geplanten Friedenskongress in Augsburg und Visitation des Reichsstiftes Salem.* Rome, 1905.

7. Steinherz, S. *Die Nuntien Hosius und Delfino 1560–1561.* Vienna, 1897.

8. *Nuntius Delfino 1562–1563.* Vienna, 1903.

9. *Nuntius Delfino 1564–1565.* Vienna, 1914.

Belgian

Institut historique belge de Rome:

10. Essen, L. van der. *Correspondance d'Ottavio Mirto Frangipani 1595–1606, tome I 1596–1598,* "Analecta Vaticano-Belgica," second series. Brussels, 1924.

11. Louant, A. *Correspondance d'Ottavio Mirto Frangipani, tome II Lettres 1597–1598 et anexes,* "Analecta Vaticano-Belgica," second series. Brussels, 1932.

12. *Correspondance d'Ottavio Mirto Frangipani (1596–1606), tome III¹ Introduction générale, lettres (1599–1606)–tome III² Lettres (1599–1606) et tables,* "Analecta Vaticano-Belgica," second series. Brussels, 1942.

13. Meerbeeck, L. van. *Correspondance des nonces Gesualdo, Morra, Sanseverino avec le secrétaire d'état pontifical 1615–1621 et annexes,* "Analecta Vaticano-Belgica," second series. Brussels, 1937.

14. Meester, B. de. *Correspondance du nonce Giovanni-Francesco Guidi di Bagno*

1621–1627, première partie 1621–1624. "Analecta Vaticano-Belgica," second series. Brussels, 1938.

15. *Correspondance du nonce Giovanni-Francesco Guidi di Bagno 1621–1627, deuxième partie 1625–1627 avec annexes et tables,* "Analecta Vaticano-Belgica," second series. Brussels, 1938.

16. Lefèvre, J. and P. *Documents relatifs à l'admission aux Pays-Bas des nonces et internonces des XVII et XVIII siècles,* "Analecta Vaticano-Belgica," second series. Brussels, 1939.

17. Lefèvre, J. *Documents relatifs à la juridiction des nonces et internonces des Pays-Bas pendant le régime espagnol (1596–1706),* "*Analecta Vaticano-Belgica,*" second series. Brussels, 1943.

18. Cauchie A., and R. Maere. *Recueil des instructions générales aux nonces de Flandre (1596–1635).* Brussels, 1904.

Dutch
Nederlandsch Historisch Instituut te Rome:

19. Brom, G. *Archivalia belangrijk voor de geschiedenis van Nederland.* 4 vols. The Hague, 1908–15.

20. Brom, G., and A. H. L. Hensen. *Romeinsche Bronnen voor den kerkelijken staatkundigen toestand der Nederlanden in de 16ᵉ eeuw.* The Hague, 1922.

21. Cornelissen, J. D. M. *Romeinsche Bronnen voor den kerkelijken toestand der Nederlanden onder de apostolische vicarissen 1592–1727. D. I: 1592–1651.* The Hague, 1932.

22. Post, R. R. *Romeinsche Bronnen voor den kerkelijken toestand der Nederlanden onder de apostolische vicarissen 1592–1727. D. II: 1651–1686.* The Hague, 1941.

French

23. Fraikin, J. *Les nonciatures de Clément VII. T.I.: Depuis la bataille de Pavie jusqu'au rappel d'Acciaccioli.* Paris, 1906.

24. Ancel, R. *Les nonciatures de Paul IV avec la dernière année de Jules III et de Marcel II. T.I: Nonciature de Sebastiano Cualtero et de César Brancatio.* Paris, 1910.

25. Richard, P. "Les origines de la nonciature de France, nonces résidents avant Léon X, 1456–1511," *Revue des questions historiques,* LXXVIII (1905).

26. "Origine et développement des nonciatures permanentes, la représentation pontificale au XVIe siècle," *Revue d'histoire ecclésiastique,* VII (1906), 53–70, 317–338.

27. Leman, A. *Recueil des instructions générales aux nonces ordinaires de France de 1624 à 1634.* Paris, 1920.

German

K. *Preussisches Historisches Institut in Rom und K. Preussische Archiv-Verwaltung:*

28. Friedensburg, W. *Nuntiaturen des Vergerio 1533–1536.* Gotha, 1892.
29. *Nuntiaturen des Morone 1536–1538.* Gotha, 1892.
30. *Legation Aleanders 1538–1539, erste Hälfte.* Gotha, 1893.
31. *Legation Aleanders 1538–1539, zweite Hälfte.* Gotha, 1893.
32. Cardauns, L. *Nuntiaturen Morones und Poggios. Legationen Farneses und Cervinis 1539–1540.* Berlin, 1909.
33. *Gesandtschaft Campeggios. Nuntiaturen Morones und Poggios 1540–1541.* Berlin, 1910.
34. *Berichte vom Regensburger und Speierer Reichstag 1541, 1542. Nuntiaturen Verallos und Poggios. Sendungen Farneses und Sfondratos 1541–1544.*
35. Friedensburg, W. *Nuntiaturen des Verallo 1545–1546.* Gotha, 1898.
36. *Nuntiaturen des Verallo 1546–1547.* Gotha, 1899.
37. *Legation des Kardinals Sfondrato 1547–1548.* Berlin, 1907.
38. *Nuntiatur des Bischofs Pietro Bertano von Fano 1548–1549.* Berlin, 1910.
39. Kupke, G. *Nuntiaturen des Pietro Bertano und Pietro Camaiani 1550–1552.* Berlin, 1901.
40. Hansen, J. *Der Kampf um Köln 1567–1584.* Berlin, 1892.
41. *Der Reichstag zu Regensburg 1576. Der Pacificationstag zu Köln 1579. Der Reichstag zu Ausgburg 1582.* Berlin, 1894.
42. Schellhass, K. *Die süddeutsche Nuntiatur des Grafen Bartholomäus von Portia. Erstes Jahr 1573–1574.* Berlin, 1896.
43. *Die süddeutsche Nuntiatur des Grafen Bartholomäus von Portia. Zweites Jahr 1574–1575.* Berlin, 1903.
44. *Die süddeutsche Nuntiatur des Grafen Bartholomäus von Portia. Schlussjahre 1575, 1576.* Berlin, 1909.
45. Kiewning, H. *Nuntiaturen des Pallotto 1628–1630, erster Band 1628.* Berlin, 1895.
46. *Nuntiaturen des Pallotto 1628–1630, zweiter Band 1629.* Berlin, 1897.
47. Meyer, A. O. *Die prager Nuntiatur des Giovanni Stefano Ferreri und die wiener Nuntiatur des Giacomo Serra 1603–1606.* Berlin, 1913.

Görres-Gesellschaft:

48. Dittrich, F. *Nuntiaturbericht Giovanni Morones vom deutschen Königshof 1539–1540.* Paderborn, 1892.
49. Ehses, St., and A. Meister. *Nuntiaturberichte aus Deutschland nebst ergänzenden Aktenstücken 1585 (1584)–1590. Erste Abteilung: Die kölner Nuntiatur. Erste Hälfte: Bonomi in Köln. Santonio in der Schweiz. Die strassburger Wirren.* Paderborn, 1895.

50. Ehses, St. *Nuntiaturberichte aus Deutschland nebst ergänzenden Aktenstücken 1585 (1584)–1590. Erste Abteilung: Die kölner Nuntiatur. Zweite Hälfte: Ottavio Mirto Frangipani in Köln 1587–1590.* Paderborn, 1899.

51. Reichenberger, R. *Nuntiaturberichte aus Deutschland nebst ergänzenden Aktenstücken 1585 (1584)–1590. Zweite Abteilung: Die Nuntiatur am Kaiserhofe. Erste Hälfte: Germanico Malaspina und Filippo Sega (Giovanni Andrea Caligari in Graz).* Paderborn, 1905.

52. Schwarz, W. E. *Die Nuntiatur-Korrespondenz Kaspar Groppers nebst verwandten Aktenstücken 1573–1576.* Paderborn, 1898.

53. Schweizer. J. *Nuntiaturberichte aus Deutschland nebst ergänzenden Aktenstücken 1585 (1584)–1590. Zweite Abteilung: Die Nuntiatur am Kaiserhofe. Zweite Hälfte: Antonio Puteo in Prag 1587–1589.* Paderborn, 1912.

54. *Nuntiaturberichte aus Deutschland nebst ergänzenden Aktenstücken 1589–1592. Zweite Abteilung: Die Nuntiatur am Kaiserhofe. Dritter Band: Die Nuntien in Prag: Alfonso Visconti 1589–1591. Camillo Caetano 1591–92.*

Swiss

55. Fry, K. *Giovanni Antonio Volpe. Seine erste Nuntiatur in der Schweiz 1560–1564,* "Frieburger Veröffentlichungen aus dem Gebiete von Kirche und Staat," I. Freiburg, 1931.

56. *Giovanni Antonio Volpe, Nuntius in der Schweiz. Dokumente. Band I: 1560–1564,* "Fontes Ambrosiani," IX. Florence, 1935.

57. *Giovanni Antonio Volpe, Nuntius in der Schweiz. Dokumente. Band II: Die zweite und dritte Nuntiatur,* "Fontes Ambrosiani," X. Stans, 1946.

58. Reinhardt, H., and F. Steffens. *Die Nantiatur von Giovanni Francesco Bonhomini 1579–1581. Einleitung.* Freiburg, 1910.

59. Steffens, F. and Reinhardt. H. *Die Nuntiatur von Giovanni Francesco Bonhomini 1579–1581. Aktenstücke zur Vorgeschichte der Nuntiatur 1570–1579. Die Nuntiaturberichte Bonhominis und seine Correspondenz mit Carlo Borromeo aus dem Jahre 1579.* Soleure, 1917.

60. *Die Nuntiatur von Giovanni Francesco Bonhomini 1579–1581. Die Nuntiaturberichte Bonhominis mit Persönlichkeiten der Schweiz aus dem Jahre 1581. Bonhominis Tätigkeit für die Schweiz während seiner Nuntiatur in Wien und Köln vom September 1581 bis zum Februar 1587.* Freiburg, 1929.

Guide and Reference Works

61. Baumgarten, Paul M. "The Vatican," *Catholic Encyclopedia*, Vol. XV, 1912.

62. Brezzi, Paolo. "La diplomazia pontificia," *Vaticano*. Edited by G. Falloni and M. Escobar. Florence, 1946.

63. Brom, Gisbert. *Guide aux archives du Vatican*. Rome, 1911. A valuable guide although somewhat outdated. The footnotes contain many references to publications from Vatican archival sources.

64. Burton, Margaret. *Famous Libraries of the World*, Vol. II of *The World's Great Libraries*. Ed. by Arundell Esdaile. London, 1937.

65. *Enciclopedia Cattolica*. Vol. XII. Article, "Archivio Vaticano," pp. 1131–34.

66. Fink, Karl A. *Das vatikanische Archiv*. Rome, 1951. The latest and most complete guide; indispensable to the researcher.

67. Glasschröder, F. X. "Archivwesen; pt. II: Vatikanisches Archiv," *Lexikon für Theologie und Kirche*. Ed. by Michael Buchberger. Vol. I, 1930.

68. Katterbach, Bruno. "Archivio e archivistica," *Enciclopedia italiana*. Vol. IV, 1929.

69. Mercati, Angelo. "La Biblioteca Apostolica e l'Archivio Segreto Vaticano," *Vaticano*. Ed. by G. Falloni and M. Escobar. Florence, 1946.

SPECIAL ARCHIVAL SOURCES

15　BAVARIA[1]

Oron James Hale
University of Virginia

ARCHIVES

BAVARIA, since 1180 when Otto von Wittelsbach acquired title to the principality, has been a duchy and later an electorate of the holy Roman Empire, an independent kingdom, a member state of the German Bund, the German Empire, and the Wiemar Republic, a National Socialist Reichsgau, and since World War II the only fully restored historic state in the German Federal Republic. Alone among the original German stem duchies, Bavaria has a tradition of independent political life that extends over a period of a thousand years. Through the centuries the original territory of the duchy, lying between the rivers Inn and Lech, was expanded to include the Rhenish Palatinate, the Franconian territories, and Swabia. Today the "Free State of Bavaria" comprises a territory approximately the size of South Carolina with a population of 9,000,000 people.

Owing to its strategic position, the size and character of its population, and the ambitions and abilities of its ruling house, Bavaria has frequently played a pivotal role in German and European politics. It was often the battleground in the struggles between the European powers. Despite the ravages of war, Bavaria's public records on foreign affairs are remarkably complete. The extraordinary development of historical studies

[1]For information on the current status of archives and libraries the author is indebted to Dr. Karl Schwend, Chief of the Bavarian State Chancellery; Dr. G. Hofmann, Director of Bavarian State Libraries; Dr. W. Winkler, Director of Bavarian State Archives; and Dr. Ludwig Maenner, Director of the *Geheimes Staatsarchiv*.

in nineteenth-century Germany had as one of its conspicuous features the preservation, organization, and publication of state and regional records. Under the patronage of the Wittelsbachs, the Royal Bavarian Academy of Sciences (1759) sponsored and supported a long and distinguished list of historical publications. With the establishment of the Historical Commission of the Academy in 1858 at the suggestion of Von Ranke, the Academy became the most important foundation in Germany in its support of historical scholarship. After the First World War, the Commission for Bavarian State History was organized by the Academy. In addition to the *Zeitschrift für bayerische Landesgeschichte*, the Commission has published important materials on Bavaria's foreign relations from French, Austrian, and Prussian archives.[2]

In its external relations during the nineteenth century, Bavaria pursued a generally consistent federal line against Prussian centralism, a *Grossdeutsch* as opposed to a *Kleindeutsch* solution of the Central European problem. The reversal of the trend in German history from centralization to federalism, which resulted from World War II, may redirect attention from the archives in Potsdam to the archives in Munich.

Until the end of the eighteenth century Electoral Bavaria maintained central document and record archives in Munich. With the union of the Wittelsbach lines of Electoral Bavaria and the Palatinate, the Munich documents archives were established in 1778 as the main archives for all Wittelsbach territories. With the further union of the Electoral house and the Pfalz-Zweibrücken line in 1799, three independent depositories were established in Munich—the Privy Country Archives (*Geheimes Landesarchiv*), the Privy State Archives (*Geheimes*

---

[2]*Gesandtschaftsberichten aus München, 1814–1848.* 15 vols. Munich, 1935– . Other notable publications are M. Ritter, ed., *et al.*, *Briefe und Akten zur Geschichte des dreissigjährigen Krieges in den Zeiten des vorwaltenden Einflusses der Wittelsbacher.* 15 vols., Munich, 1870–1948; also, A. von Druffel, ed., *et al.*, *Briefe und Akten zur Geschichte des sechszehnten Jahrhunderts mit besonderer Rücksicht auf Bayerns Fürstenhaus.* 6 vols. Munich, 1873–1913.

Staatsarchiv), and the Privy House Archives (*Geheimes Haus-archiv*). In 1929 all official record depositories were brought together to form the Main State Archives (*Hauptstaatsarchiv*) under the authority and direction of the General Director of the Bavarian State Archives.[3] As presently organized and administered there are five main divisions:

1. Bavarian Main State Archives: Division I[4]

This depository contains the records of the ministries and government agencies of the state of Bavaria and of lay and ecclesiastical territories annexed by Bavaria, excluding records pertaining to foreign relations. It is the largest collection of its kind in Germany. Address: 12 Arcisstrasse, Munich.

2. Main State Archives: Division II (formerly *Heeresarchiv*)

This division maintains the records of the Bavarian Army from 1650 to 1921 and records of the Ministry of War and its predecessor authorities to 1921. It contains about sixty-five thousand document bundles and files. Address: Leonrodstrasse 57, Munich.

3. Privy House Archives

This division administers the records of the House of Wittels-bach, including collateral lines, from 1250 to the present. The collection consists of some ten thousand bundles and files. Address: Arcisstrasse 12, Munich.

4. State Archives in the Administrative Districts. (*Staats-archive in der Regierungsbezirken*, formerly *Kreisarchive*).

5. Bavarian Privy State Archives in Munich[5] (*Geheimes Staatsarchiv*).

[3]For the early history of the Bavarian archives, the standard work is M. J. Neudegger, *Geschichte der bayerischen und pfälzischen Archive der Wittelsbacher vom 13.–19. Jahrhundert*. 3 parts. Munich, 1881–96.

[4]For a survey of the State Archives, their principal holdings, and regulations, see *Die Archive*. Minerva Handbücher. 2d Ser., Vol. I (Berlin and Leipzig, 1932), pp. 237–244. The depository designations and street addresses given in this guide no longer apply.

[5]The information presented here is drawn principally from the excellent article by Ludwig Maenner, "Die Neuordnung des Geheimen Staatsarchiv in München," *Archivalische Zeitschrift*, XLVI (1950), 104–124. A description of the archives' holdings and organization, at the turn of the century is given by G. Ritter von Böhm, "Vorstand des Geheimen Haus—und Staatsarchivs," *ibid.*, new ser., XII (1905), pp. 79 ff.

Founded in 1769 as the depository for the records of Bavaria's relations to the Reich and foreign countries, the Privy State Archives became in 1799, and remained until 1933, the archives of the Bavarian ministry of foreign affairs. It contains the extant diplomatic records of the Electoral Palatinate to 1777, of Palatinate-Zweibrücken to 1799, of ducal and electoral Bavaria to 1806, and of the kingdom and state of Bavaria since that date. The early Bavarian holdings contain some important collections not of Bavarian origin, i.e., the so-called "Protestant Correspondence, 1546–1624," presumably confiscated by the army of the Catholic League during the Thirty Years' War. Since 1799 the records appertain solely to Bavarian external relations. These comprise two main groups—the treaties and files of the ministry and the records and reports of the Bavarian legations. Most of these records were held by the ministry, or the originating missions, as current files until approximately fifty years ago when they were transferred in large blocks to the *Geheimes Staatsarchiv* (notably in 1898, 1913–14, 1921, and 1936). Over the past twenty years the *Geheimes Staatsarchiv* has effected a thorough reorganization of its holdings. As far as practicable, political and diplomatic records have been separated from other categories. The documents dealing with cultural matters, religious affairs, economic developments, and emigration have been organized, catalogued, and made accessible. One of the objects of this reorganization has been to broaden the service of the archives and to make available its holdings in fields of research outside the strictly political and diplomatic. In effecting this reorganization the administration and staff have given special attention to the mass of records dating from 1799.

As a record of Bavarian foreign relations prior to 1799, the documents consist mainly of correspondence between the German princes and their ministers, reports of missions and agents, transactions of the Imperial Reichstag, boundary disputes, princely alliances and treaties, and negotiations preliminary to war or to peace.

After the reunion of the Wittelsbach lands the creation of an enlarged kingdom during the Napoleonic period and the modernization of the state's structure during the reform ministry of Count Montgelas (1799–1817) the records of the foreign ministry not only document the external policy of an independent kingdom but also mirror the events and developments that transpired in central and western Europe from the beginning of the nineteenth century to the founding of the German Empire in 1871.

Particular importance attaches to the records and reports of the legations and missions. They are maintained under eight general classifications—princely houses and officials, foreign policy, internal administration, economy and transportation, finance, justice, cultural affairs, and armed forces. For the student of diplomatic history the second category, foreign policy and political affairs, is of primary importance. In the ministry's records the legation reports are filed by countries of origin and by years. However, it was customary in the ministry of foreign affairs to establish separate complete files for records dealing with major continuing issues. These are separately catalogued and maintained. Among them may be noted the political negotiations of the Napoleonic period, affairs of the Confederation, 1848–50, the Italian War of 1859, the Schleswig-Holstein Question, the wars of 1866 and 1870, and the Moroccan Crisis of 1904–6.

Under the new system, with the exceptions just noted, the political records have been separated from the nonpolitical and the ministry records organized chronologically according to the following plan: (1) The Reformation and Religious Wars, to 1648; (2) The Period of Absolutism, to 1799; (3) The nineteenth and twentieth centuries, to 1933. The diplomatic records of the latter period are further organized in subgroups: (a) the Napoleonic Period, 1799–1815; (b) the period 1815–66; (c) the German Empire, 1866–1918; (d) the Legation Reports, 1799–1918; (e) the German Reich, 1919–33.

Grouped as nonpolitical records for the nineteenth and twentieth centuries are those pertaining to administration of the Bavarian foreign service and the files on foreign states and their administration, economy, finance, justice, cultural relations, and armed forces. Special reference catalogues have been prepared for countries, place names, and persons.

Within the Holy Roman Empire and the German Confederation, Bavaria maintained legations at Hanover, Kassel, Wiesbaden, and the Hanse Towns, to 1866; at Darmstadt and Dresden to 1918; and at Berlin, Stuttgart, and Karlsruhe to 1934. Outside Germany permanent missions were maintained at London, Paris, Vienna, St. Petersburg, Turin-Rome, Naples, Berne, Athens, and the Vatican. Although they had no political mission after the responsibility for foreign affairs passed to the Reich government in 1871, Bavarian legations were maintained at the Vatican and the principal European capitals until 1914. The mission to the Vatican was not terminated until 1934. After 1871 the duties of the Bavarian representatives abroad were mainly cultural and representational, but they continued to report political events and developments in the countries to which they were accredited. These reports are not without value for the student of diplomatic history.

Serious losses were suffered by the archives of Bavaria during World War II. Most of the buildings housing the main divisions in Munich were so destroyed or damaged as to necessitate relocation at temporary sites. Of the actual holdings it is surprising that greater losses were not suffered. In the Main State Archives, the records of the ministry of justice were almost completely destroyed; the records of the ministry of culture likewise suffered heavy losses. The old Army Museum, which housed parts of the Army Archives, was a total loss and about 10 per cent of the records were destroyed. Regrettably the largest loss was in the military personnel records. The Royal House Archives, in the old *Residenz*, suffered considerable damage and loss to its holdings. The *Geheimes Staatsarchiv* suffered the least damage to its contents, although the building was completely destroyed. The buildings containing the archives of the administrative districts in Munich and Nürnberg were severely damaged, but owing to the protective measures taken serious loss of records occurred only to the evacuated collections at Würzburg.[6]

Approximately the same regulations that govern admission to the National Archives, Washington, D.C., apply to the Bavarian Privy State Archive and other divisions of the state archives. Foreign students should apply in advance to the General Director of the Bavarian State Archives (General-direktor der Staatlichen Archive Bayerns), 12 Arcisstrasse, Munich, or to the Director of the *Geheimes Staatsarchiv*, Leon-rodstrasse 57. Students applying for admission in person should present a letter of introduction and a request from their Consul General or Cultural Affairs Officer of the Consulate General.

LIBRARIES AND INSTITUTES

Founded in 1558, the Bavarian State Library in Munich is one of the most important in Germany. Its holdings amounted to approximately two million items in 1939, including priceless collections of incunabula, manuscripts, and papyri. While 500,000 volumes were lost by fire in World War II, its collections have been built up today to over two million volumes. Under the program of the German Research Council (*Deutschen*

---

[6]The best summary of postwar archival and library conditions in Germany is the article by Lester K. Born, "The archives and libraries of postwar Germany," *American historical review*, LVI (1950), 34–57; also, "Postwar status of chief archival institutions in Bavaria," issued by the U.S. Office of Military Government for Bavaria (1948), 37 pp. mimeo. Later assessments of damage and losses are found in *Der Archivar*, notably, *Jahrgang* 1950–51. Since the repair of buildings and relocation of archives is still in progress, scholars planning to work in German archives would do well to consult the current issues of *Der Archivar: Mitteilungsblatt für deutsches Archivwesen*, and specifically for Bavaria, the *Archivalische Zeitschrift*, published by the Bavarian State Archives. The present location and addresses of the principal German archives are given in the *Deutschland Jahrbuch 1953* (Essen, 1953), pp. 567–573.

Forschungsgemeinschaft) the Bavarian State Library is responsible for current foreign and domestic publications in the following specialized fields: General history and the historical sciences, ancient history and philology, Byzantine studies, Slavic studies (including Romanian literature), and the history and science of music. For political and diplomatic history its book and pamphlet collections are outstanding, and it possesses the largest collection of German newspapers in West Germany. The state library building on the Ludwigstrasse, constructed during the early nineteenth century, was six-sevenths destroyed or heavily damaged by bombing and fire in World War II. While the most valuable collections had been evacuated, serious losses were suffered in some of the special fields, particularly in the collections of learned society and Academy publications and historical and geographical literature, including American and Asiatic materials. Likewise, the library's excellent modern card catalog was destroyed. Except for a few important categories —maps and newspapers—the collections, as of 1954, are again available. The general reading room, with its large collection of reference works, and the music, Oriental, Slavic, and periodical divisions, have been reopened at 23 Ludwigstrasse. Plans are now completed for the further restoration and expansion of the structure, which when completed will house both the State Library and the main university library.

Prior to World War II the library of the University of Munich (Ludwig-Maximilians-Universität) contained approximately one million volumes. The university building housing the library was rendered almost totally unusable, but approximately 600,000 volumes were saved. Present holdings amount approximately to 700,000 volumes. Temporary reading rooms have been established in the various schools and departments, and book service on the general collections has been resumed in the main university building on the Ludwigstrasse, Geschwister-Scholl-Platz 1.

Although of recent origin, the Institute for Contemporary

History in Munich has a development potential which, if realized, will make it the most important center for recent history in Germany. Founded as the *Deutsches Institut für Geschichte der nationalsozialistischen Zeit*, a special research institute for the National Socialist period, the scope of its activity now embraces the period 1918–45. It is supported by appropriations from the federal government and state governments of Bavaria, Hesse, and Baden–Württemberg, and functions under the general control of an administrative board composed of representatives of the central and state governments. A council, composed of fifteen leading German historians and archivists, establishes and controls the scientific policies of the Institute, with the concurrence of the administrative board. Among the members of the policy council are such leading scholars as Bergsträsser, Kogon, Schnabel, Dehio, Hurtung, Rothfels, Ritter, Vollmer, and Winkler.

The Institute is organized in five divisions: Historical-Political, Defense and Military History, Documentation, Library, and Archives. The library of the Institute contains approximately 20,000 volumes, published mainly in the period 1933–45 and representing various aspects of German thought, culture, and politics under the National Socialist regime. Special emphasis has been placed upon the assembly of materials dealing with the early history of the National Socialist party.

The archives division maintains an information and locator file of papers and documents in private hands pertaining to the history of the National Socialist period. While the actual holdings of documentary and record material is not large, they are being steadily increased and now include such items as the papers of General Schleicher, the war diary of General Lahousen, Bavarian *Spruchkammer* records and trial proceedings of major Nazi offenders, and interrogation reports on topics such as the Fritsch crisis in 1938, the suppression of German trade unions, the 20th July in France, religious policy of the

Nazi regime, origin and early history of the NSDAP, and the German *Abwehr*. The Institute maintains a biographical record file of 2,500 names. It also possesses extensive files of Nazi newspapers and periodicals, including a file of the "Confidential Press Service of the DNB, 1938–1945."

In addition to maintaining a library and archives, the Institute has initiated a series of research projects on various aspects of German history since 1918. Some studies have been completed and published, and others are in progress. A series of documentary publications is also projected of which Hitler's *Tischgespräche im Führerhauptquartier* appeared in 1951.

One of the most important undertakings of the Institute has been the launching of the periodical, *Vierteljahresschrift für Zeitgeschichte* as a vehicle for the Institute's research and to stimulate scholarly interest in German history since 1918. The address of the institute is Reitmorstrasse 29, Munich.

16 THE LEAGUE OF NATIONS AND THE UNITED NATIONS

Robert Claus

United Nations, New York,

and

Irving P. Schiller

Formerly of the United Nations, European Regional Office, Geneva

THE United Nations, at its headquarters in New York and its European office in Geneva, has custody of a group of archival collections that should be of great interest to students of twentieth-century diplomatic history and international relations. These collections include the records of a number of organizations besides the two major ones listed in the title, and an attempt will be made here to describe each important record group briefly.[1] Except for the League of Nations records, all are now held at United Nations headquarters in New York.

LEAGUE OF NATIONS, 1919–46

One of the largest collections, and certainly a most significant one, the records of the League of Nations cover the period from

[1]It should be made clear, however, that this discussion cannot cover the many related records not in the custody of the United Nations proper. As examples one may mention the files of the League of Nations Institute of Intellectual Co-operation (held by UNESCO in Paris), of the International Court, and of the International Labour Organisation and the other "specialized agencies" associated with the United Nations (UNESCO, FAO, WHO, UPU, and others), each of which maintains its own archives.

its creation at the Paris Peace Conference in 1919 to its liquidation in 1946. Its archives were inherited then by the United Nations and are now maintained for the most part by the Geneva office, although considerable bodies of files have been transferred to the archives in New York for official use at headquarters.

In accordance with the terms of the League Covenant, three basic organs were established: the assembly, the plenary deliberative body meeting once a year; the council, the executive and security organ; and the secretariat, some six or seven hundred international civil servants, headed by a secretary-general which was responsible for providing all administrative and substantive services.[2]

To understand the records of the League (in fact, this applies to the United Nations as well) one must recognize that League policy was established by its constituent member states, each one of which was represented by a delegation speaking for the official policy of its respective government. Questions were discussed and resolutions passed by the delegates in the name of the League as an integer, while the secretariat was constantly at hand to facilitate the deliberations and carry out established policy.

The distinction occasionally becomes clouded especially in regard to the role of the higher officials of the secretariat. On that level there was a natural overlap of policy and implementation. Similarly, the registrar had a dual role to play. The registry, described below, was indeed part of the secretariat, but its responsibility was to register and maintain the correspondence, the communications, and the papers of the League in the aggregate. It is helpful, however, to bear in mind the essential difference in the roles of the international civil servants comprising the secretariat and of the delegates to the assembly,

[2]The Permanent Court of International Justice had a semi-independent status and administration, and all its records remained at The Hague and were subsequently taken over by the new International Court of Justice. Similarly the International Labour Organization (still in existence) was practically autonomous.

council, and other bodies, and it is logical, in keeping with this distinction, to divide the archives into three parts: (1) official documentation, (2) records of the secretariat sections and League commissions, (3) registry files.

1. The official documentation of the League includes the voluminous printed and mimeographed materials, which contain the procedures, debates, reports, resolutions, special technical studies, and all other propositions that relate officially to the work of the assembly, the council, and the subsidiary bodies. These records, in the course of League history, were to a great extent on public sale and were issued, of course, to the member governments, although most committee documents were circulated to committee members only. Most meetings were public, and summary or verbatim records are correspondingly available to the general public. Minutes of private meetings were incorporated in the files of the registry. Many important libraries have good collections of the published material, but the best collections are those of the two libraries of the United Nations, the one at United Nations headquarters in New York, and the other at the European office of the United Nations in Geneva (the Palais des Nations, formerly headquarters of the League). The United Nations Library in New York has recently incorporated the collection of the Woodrow Wilson Memorial Library along with its valuable catalogue.

The techniques for using the printed and mimeographed documentation with its rather involved system of symbols and sales numbers are not readily apparent, but guides and indexes have been prepared that constitute a series of keys to this labyrinth of documentation. There are four basic works:

a. *The catalogue of publications, 1920–35*, followed by six supplements, 1936–46. League of Nations, Geneva, Publications Department.

b. Carroll, Maris J. *Key to League of Nations documents placed on public sale, 1920–1929*. World Peace Foundation, Boston,

1930. There are four supplements for the years 1930–36.

c. Breycha-Vauthier, A. C. *Sources of information, a handbook on the publications of the League of Nations.* London and New York, 1939. Also published in French, Russian, German, and Czechoslovakian, 1934–37.

d. Aufricht, Hans. *Guide to the League of Nations publications, a bibliographical survey of work in the League, 1920–1947.* New York, 1951.

The value of this documentation is worth emphasizing. Those interested in international affairs professionally or avocationally will find it most rewarding to delve into these records. As Arthur Sweetser has said in the foreword to the Aufricht *Guide,* the League documents "constitute the most complete and the most compact international documentation in existence." "There in a single packet, as it were, is to be found the whole story, from smallest embryo through full flowering to final tragic ending, of mankind's first effort at permanent, organized, world-wide international co-operation to prevent war and promote well-being."

2. According to accepted definitions of source material, the documentation described above is generally of a primary nature and offers really exciting research opportunities. Much original work can be done with these documents despite their publication and wide distribution. But the next categories of records to be described have been hardly touched by students and researchers. This is particularly true of the section and commission archives. These were the records maintained in the various offices in Geneva and in the field, and they constitute a record of the day-to-day operations of secretariat and other officials. The Registry was designed to handle and file all official correspondence, and, generally speaking, the story in the Registry files is remarkably complete; inevitably, however, additional records were accumulated by practically all sections and by the special commissions. Their content, arrangement, and value vary widely, but there are useful materials inter-

mingled with much routine correspondence, and the records are described on numerous lists in sufficient detail for effective research use.

It must be explained, however, that for various reasons many records of this type are no longer available. For example, the files of the first secretary-general, Sir Eric Drummond, were deliberately destroyed in June 1940 when an invasion by German forces occupying French territory just a few miles from Geneva was feared to be imminent. Joseph Avenol, the second secretary-general, took his files with him upon resigning. Certain records held by the last League high commissioner for Danzig, 1937–39, were abandoned when that city was taken over in a sudden *putsch* by the local *Gauleiter*. Other records were destroyed because of their obvious lack of importance. Thus, when the League of Nations liaison office in Tokyo was closed in 1939, a long-time League official supervised the liquidation and, finding that most of the official correspondence was in Japanese and presuming (correctly) that correspondence in English with Geneva had been kept in the Registry, he decided "not to send it over and it has all been destroyed here in Tokyo."[3] The fate of the records of other branch offices—Rome, London, Paris, New Delhi—can be similarly reconstructed from the Registry notes dealing with the liquidation or transfer of these offices to the United Nations. Some archives were destroyed; others, especially the accounts, were dispatched to Geneva. Various governmental and nongovernmental agencies were the recipients of a third type of files, usually of general reference value.

In general, however, it is not considered worthwhile here to trace in detail the whereabouts of all these field records, since their value appears to have been relatively inconsequential. Moreover, it appears to be true that, while some source materials have disappeared for one reason or another, most of the files have been successfully retained as a result of the cautious

[3] Letter from Harada to Stencek, January 30, 1939, Registry file 18A/11022/1919.

attitude of the secretariat toward records destruction. The policy has quite consistently been to destroy nothing except materials of the most obviously ephemeral character. The following offices of the secretariat are represented in the section files:[4]

Secretary-General's Files, 1940–47 (10 feet). Correspondence arranged alphabetically by subject or correspondent. Good general coverage of League activities during World War II.

Political Section, 1919–39 (33 feet). An important collection in reasonably usable order, containing correspondence between the secretariat and delegations and other governmental agencies on all subjects of a political nature, especially those under consideration by the Council. For example, these issues are rather fully covered: Poland-Lithuania, 1920–30; Turkish minorities, 1919–21; Near East problems, 1922; Upper Silesia, 1921–22; admission of new states, especially Balkan and Baltic nations, 1920–22; Teschen Territory, 1920–23; Hungarian optants question, 1923–30; Albanian Moslems in Greece, 1924–26; Greek-Turkish frontier, 1926; exchange of Greek and Turkish populations, 1924–25; Greek-Bulgarian incidents, 1925–27; Memel, 1922–30; Japan-China, 1932, especially work of Lytton Commission; Danzig, 1920–39; and Saar, 1919–35.

Disarmament Section, 1921–37 (36 feet). Records of the Preparatory Commission for the Disarmament Conference, 1926–30; the Conference for the Control of International Trade of Arms and Munitions, 1925; the London Naval Conference, 1930; the Temporary Commission for Reduction of Armaments, 1921–24; the Permanent Advisory Committee on Military, Naval, and Air Questions; the Montreux Conference, 1936, on the regime of the Straits; the Montreux Conference, 1937, on ending the capitulation system in Egypt; and the Nyon Conference, 1937, on patrol of the Mediterranean. These files

---

[4]Section archives in many cases duplicate material contained in the Registry files; this is especially true of the Disarmament Section. Eventually a weeding process will be undertaken to get rid of duplicates.

consist mainly of reports of meetings and documents with some secretariat correspondence and memoranda.

Mandates Section, 1921–37 (50 feet). Press clippings, 1920–32; documents distributed to the Permanent Mandates Commission; miscellaneous subject files on Togoland, Palestine, Syria, Lebanon, Iraq, S.W. Africa, Kenya. Tanganyika, and problems of post-mandatory regimes.

Minorities Section, 1919–38 (13 feet). Petitions and index to petitioners; clippings, documents, and correspondence of Eric Colban, head of the section; and general files, mostly antedating 1933, dealing with such problems as Jewish and other religious minorities, and minorities in Albania, Germany, Austria, Greece, Italy, Lithuania, Romania, Turkey, and Czechoslovakia.

Health Section, 1920–38 (33 feet). Files of members of the section on their fields of interest, projects, and missions; material on nutrition, nursing, child care, and various diseases, especially malaria; reference collection of articles and publications of the United States of America relating to public health; original materials of the Intergovernmental Conference of Far Eastern Countries on Rural Hygiene, held in Bandoeng, Java, August 1937; some material of the League of Nations Epidemic Commission to China; and collections of materials used in exhibitions to illustrate the health work of the League.

Economic and Financial Section, 1920–37 (46 feet). Correspondence, memoranda, and reference material on the work of the section; files of the directors of the section: Sir Walter Layton, Sir Frank Nixon, and Sir Arthur Salter; and files of Alexander Loveday before he became the director. These materials pertain to a wide variety of economic problems especially with reference to Europe after the First World War.

Transit and Communications Section, 1920–32 (6 feet). Subject file by years dealing with all phases of work in the field. Material is included on passports; road, air, and maritime traffic; inland waterways; railroads; customs; ports; telegraph and radio communications; navigation on the Danube; franchise for a railroad between Austria and Hungary; and reform of the calendar.

Opium Section, 1929–30 (15 feet). Records of the Commission of Enquiry into Control of Opium Smoking in the Far East: minutes, files on each country visited, reference collection of laws, and accounting records.

Registration of Treaties Service, 1920–46 (125 feet). The Covenant (Article XVIII) provided that every treaty or international engagement entered into by a member of the League should be registered with the secretariat and subsequently published. Certified originals (numbers 1–4834) of the resultant published Treaty Series are on deposit; in addition, there are numerous other original signed conventions, protocols, and other international agreements concluded under the auspices of the League together with original instruments of ratification.

International Bureaux and Intellectual Co-Operation Section, 1919–48 (4 feet). General files dealing with Esperanto and with intellectual life in several countries investigated in 1923; lists of international organizations; bulletins of information; miscellaneous correspondence dealing with creation of the Institute of Intellectual Co-Operation and the Institute of Educational Cinematography; and other correspondence on educational problems.

Information Section, 1927–38 (2 feet). An odds and ends collection (of negligible usefulness) dealing with such subjects as liaison with China, double taxation, the Kellogg Pact, women and the League, and sale of League publications.

Liaison with Latin America, 1922–39 (26 feet). Correspondence with League representatives in Latin American countries and with delegations; press clippings and reference material on the Chaco affair and other Latin American disputes; and material on various phases of League activity and its effect on Latin America.

Berlin Office Files, 1928–33 (3 feet). Correspondence with headquarters in Geneva, the International Labour Organization, various German institutions and individuals, and other regional offices of the League; accounting files for liquidation; and correspondence arranged alphabetically.

Social Questions Sections. 1921–33 (24 feet). Correspondence and reference material on traffic in women and children, mostly arranged alphabetically by country or by correspondent. Of negligible usefulness; most important materials are in the Registry.

Treasury, 1920–46 (425 feet). Correspondence concerning contributions; and vouchers and accounting records.

Princeton Office, 1940–46 (25 feet). This was the successor to the Economic and Financial Section, moved to Princeton, N.J., in 1940. The files are now at United Nations headquarters. Classified general files, drafts of publications, and working papers, dealing with many aspects of international economic, financial, and fiscal problems.

In addition to the section files proper listed above, several groups of mission and commission records of considerable value are also available for study and consultation. The most important series are the following:

Governing Commission for the Saar Territory, 1920–35 (215 feet), Summary records of meetings of the commission, including typed, signed originals; complete correspondence file; and records of the commission secretariat including budgetary controls.

Plebiscite Commission for the Saar Territory, 1934–35 (9 feet). Minutes of meetings, press releases, correspondence, forms, and instructions for carrying out the plebiscite.

Supreme Plebiscite Tribunal for the Saar Territory, 1935–36 (75 feet). Registration sheets and card indexes of all voters in the territory (received from the Plebiscite Commission); and charge files, appeals, and judgments. (Complete records of important cases are in the Registry.)

Office for the Settlement of Greek Refugees, 1925–30 (7 feet).

Correspondence and working papers of this commission, which was charged with giving assistance to persons evacuated to Greece as a result of population exchange; minutes of meetings of the Refugee Settlement Commission; and material on administrative and budgetary matters and on substantive questions such as medical service and facilities for accommodating urban and agricultural population increase.

Mixed Commission on Greek-Bulgarian Reciprocal Emigration, 1920–31 (31 feet). Minutes of meetings, basic decisions of the commission, statistics, list of names and property of deportees, records of the Permanent Court of International Justice (1930) relating to legal problems of Greek-Bulgarian emigration, and basic population data of the numerous villages involved in the exchange scheme.

Mixed Commission for Exchange of Greek and Turkish Populations, 1923–34 (48 feet). Minutes of meetings, correspondence accounts, and sheets, with registration numbers, showing commission's decisions on disposition of privately-owned properties.

Nansen Office for Refugees, 1920–45 (224 feet). Correspondence of the League's High Commissioner for Refugees, Frijthof Nansen: complete set of outgoing correspondence arranged chronologically, 1922–38; systematic Registry of correspondence in two periods, 1925–29 and 1930–38; correspondence of various branch offices, especially Berlin, Athens, and Vienna; and accounting and liquidation files, 1929–45. Earliest correspondence deals primarily with Russian refugees, 1921–23. Files are in excellent condition and are generally well indexed.

Financial Reconstruction of Austria—Files of Commissioner-General, 1922–35 (54 feet). Records of the Commissioner-General, 1922–26, dealing especially with problem of inflation and loans to combat disintegration of currency system; correspondence after 1926 dealing with all phases of Austrian economy such as productive facilities, customs revenues especially from tobacco, state budget, state banks, agrarian laws, international credit position; and statistical tables, press clippings, reports, reference material, and special studies.

Financial Reconstruction of Hungary, 1923–30 (8 feet). Index files, arranged essentially by subject, covering all phases of Hungarian economic life; typical files deal with banking, budget, debts, exports, loans, statistics, tariffs, and taxation.

Mixed Commission for Upper Silesia, 1922–37 (112 feet). Case files of petitions from individuals of Polish and German extraction for redress of grievances; index register of petitions; and correspondence, press clippings, and reports dealing with discriminatory practices against minorities.

Mixed Tribunal for Upper Silesia, 1923–37 (70 feet). Case files heard by the Mixed Tribunal. These were actual disputes usually between individuals and the German or Polish governments; they involved legal problems rather than the grievances of a more personal type that were handled by the Mixed Commission. The cases were usually of a civil nature involving violation of residence, travel, and property rights. Files are basically arranged by year and by name of litigant.

Electoral Commission for the Sanjak of Alexandretta, 1937–38 (30 feet). Lists, materials on administrative procedures, and correspondence of the Commission to organize the election of the Sanjak Assembly.

Office of the High Commissioner for Refugees coming from Germany, Nov. 1933–Jan. 1936 (5 feet). Documents and correspondence of the High Commissioner for Refugees, James G. MacDonald, London. Correspondence is basically arranged by country or by name of nongovernmental organization concerned; most of the material deals with passports or substitute papers and the facilitation of emigration from Germany.

3. In spite of the length of the list of records appearing above, all that material is outside the basic single source of information about the League, that is, the Registry. It is among the Registry dossiers that one usually looks for the letters, the memoranda, the studies, and the reports of the League of Nations, 1919–46.

These files were maintained, indexed, and listed under one continuing system (with some minor modifications) from the beginning of the League. The system, based on that in use in the British foreign office, is somewhat complex, but the controls are well-nigh perfect and, with the help of the indexes and lists, the files can be used most effectively. The bulk of the material has remained in Geneva but a relatively small portion has been transferred to United Nations headquarters in New York for the use of officials there.[5]

The Registry classification system has been fully described in Egon F. Ranshoven-Wertheimer's *The international secretariat*.[6] Lists of the filing titles are available in both New York and Geneva, while the latter office has complete indexes by name and subject. The following list of the main classification for the 1933–46 period gives a good indication of the basic arrangement and scope of the files:

1. Political Section
2. Administrative Commissions
   Danzig
   Saar
3. Legal Section
   Labour
   Court of International Justice
   Treaties
   Codification of International Law
4. Minorities Section

---

[5]The decision to transfer some of the files to New York, which has been severely criticized by Frank P. Walters (*A history of the League of Nations* [2 vols. London, New York, Toronto: Oxford University Press, 1952], n. 1, Appendix) was not lightly taken, but it was found to be necessary in order that the records might be immediately available for official uses. Fears concerning the loss of papers or the breaking up of files are believed to be unfounded; storage and servicing facilities are good in both New York and Geneva, adequate controls and indexes are maintained in both depositories, and liaison between the two is excellent.

[6](Washington, Carnegie Endowment for International Peace, 1945), Appendix III, "The filing system of the secretariat," by Catherine Pastuhova.

5. Intellectual Co-operation and International Bureaux
   Section
   Intellectual Co-operation
   Youth Questions
6. Mandates Section
   Slavery
7. Disarmament Section
   Disarmament Conference
8. Health Section
   International Union
   Malaria
   Epidemiological Intelligence Service
   Sera and Biological Products
   Infant Welfare
9. Communications and Transit Section
   Inland Navigation
   Ports and Maritime Navigation
   Railways
   Electric Questions
   Road Traffic
   Ports, Telegraphs and Telephones
   Aerial Navigation
10. Economic and Financial Section
    Economic Relations
    Economic Intelligence
    Finance
11. Social Questions Section
    Traffic in Women and Children
    Child Welfare
    Information Centre for Documentation
12. Opium Section
    Permanent Central Opium Board
    Opium Supervisory Body
13. Information Section
14. Council

15. Assembly
16. Library
17. Treasury and Finances of the League
18. Internal Administration
    Buildings and Furniture
19. Legal Documents
20. Refugees
    Russian
    Armenian
50. General and Miscellaneous

INTERNATIONAL PENAL AND PENITENTIARY COMMISSION, 1893–1951

The International Penitentiary Congress in London in 1872 was the first of a series that met about every five years "to collect reliable prison statistics, to gather information and to compare experience as to the working of different prison systems and the effects of various systems of penal legislation; to compare the deterrent effects of various forms of punishment and treatment, and the methods adopted, both for the repression and prevention of crime." By 1896 formal regulations were adopted providing for equal representation of all member states on the commission and establishment of a small Executive Committee. A secretary-general was responsible for the administration of the affairs of the commission, and in 1926 his office became a Permanent Bureau. In 1929 the commission adopted the more accurate title that appears in the heading above. After a period of relative inactivity during the war years, 1939–45, the commission in 1946 offered its assistance to the United Nations and, after some years of negotiation and planning, the commission was integrated within the United Nations by a resolution of the general assembly on December 1, 1950. Its work is now carried on by the department of economic and social affairs of the United Nations secretariat.

The records of the commission consist of:

1. Accounting records, 1893–1939, including records of contributions, treasurer's reports, ledgers, and Permanent Bureau accounts (1 ft., 6 ins.).

2. Secretary-general's correspondence, 1910–26, filed chronologically with a log index (1 ft., 10 in.).

3. Registry files of the Permanent Bureau, 1925–51, classified by subject (35 feet).

UNITED NATIONS

The United Nations, established after a series of international meetings and conferences (among them the Atlantic Meeting, Teheran, Yalta, Dumbarton Oaks, and San Francisco) came into being on October 24, 1945 and held its first meeting on January 10, 1946 in London. Its basic structure had been outlined in the charter drawn up at the San Francisco Conference, while rules of procedure and arrangements for the first session had been prepared by a Preparatory Commission meeting in London at the end of 1945. The principal organs are the General Assembly, the Security Council, the Economic and Social Council, the Trusteeship Council, the International Court of Justice, and the Secretariat. Their functions are too well known to need repetition here.

Much of what has been said above about the League of Nations structure and records applies also to the United Nations. The General Assembly and the three councils, made up of representatives of member states, conduct their business in plenary sessions and by means of a large number of missions, commissions, committees, and subcommittees. The basic records of these bodies are their documents, including the published *Official Records* and the voluminous mimeographed document series, which form the first group described below.

The secretariat, headed successively by Trygve Lie and Dag Hammarskjold as secretary-general, consists principally of seven major departments, dealing respectively with political and security council affairs, economic and social affairs, technical assistance, public information, trusteeship and information from nonself-governing territories, conference services, and general services, together with an executive office and a European office in Geneva. As in the case of the sections of the League secretariat, these offices provide the document, language, communication, and other services for the general assembly and the other organs, collect and prepare technical data for them, and generally assist them in carrying on their deliberations and in implementing their decisions. Like the League also, many of the working papers and other files of these organizational units have remained apart from the Registry files and are maintained as "departmental records." Certain of the missions and commissions established by the major organs have also collected their own files, which form separately identifiable subgroups.

The United Nations Registry is responsible for registering, classifying, filing, and servicing the official correspondence of the organization as a whole; by far the major part of the most important records of the United Nations is included in the Registry files, described as the third group below.

1. The United Nations document series are extremely voluminous (about a hundred thousand pages are published yearly in English alone) and they cover the whole range of United Nations activities. A very large proportion is available to the public in printed or mimeographed form, and all are coded with symbols representing the producing organ or suborgan, identifying the type of document (summary record, working document, etc.), and placing them in chronological order. *Official Records* and many major reports are printed and widely distributed; other documents are issued in mimeographed form for extensive, "Limited," or "Restricted" distribution. Complete sets of the documents are available for consultation, subject to security and administrative regula-

tions, in the United Nations library and, in microfilm form, in the archives at New York headquarters.

The library maintains a documents reference service and prepares and publishes various special indexes as well as the two major ones indicated below. The following are the most useful guides to the document series:

a. *Check list of United Nations documents*, 1946–49, published by the United Nations in volumes dealing with individual organs of the UN; the 31-volume set is now nearly complete.

b. *United Nations document index*, published monthly by the United Nations since February 1950 (document series ST/LIB/SER.E).

c. Caballero-Marsal, F., J. K. Nielsen, and H. N. M. Winton, "United Nations documents in the United Nations Library: organization and servicing," *Journal of cataloging and classification*, VII, no. 3 (1951), 65–72.

2. The departmental records and the mission and commission files constitute a valuable source of information both on the work of the secretariat and on the various world questions with which it deals. A considerable quantity of these materials (roughly 2,600 cubic feet) has been retired to semiactive storage; the others remain in the offices which produced or received them. Because all these files are relatively recent and many of them contain confidential data received from member governments, they are made available for nonofficial use only by special authorization. For this reason, and because the quantity and character of the records are constantly changing, it is not feasible here to describe them in any detail. The researcher interested in any phase of United Nations activity may expect that pertinent material will be located both in the active files of the appropriate secretariat office and in the noncurrent files.

3. The Registry files, as in the case of the League of Nations,

contain the bulk of the official United Nations correspondence. Like the departmental files, these also must be restricted to persons specially authorized to see them. Amounting now to more than 2,000 cubic feet, they consist of three major groups: January-July 1946, August 1946–December 1947, 1948 to date. All three groups are classified by subject, the subject grouping corresponding closely to the structure of the secretariat and similarly reflecting the functional relationships of the major organs. Indexes to the more important communications are maintained in the Registry.

4. One specialized collection of United Nations records deserves mention—the sound recordings of the proceedings of the General Assembly, its main committees, and the three councils. Some thirty-five thousand double-faced 16-inch discs have been accumulated. They constitute a most significant and useful body of material for many research and informational purposes.

OTHER ARCHIVES

UNITED NATIONS INFORMATION ORGANIZATION, NEW YORK, 1941–46

This was the successor to one of the two information centers established by the Inter-Allied Committee in 1940 and 1941 to serve as clearinghouses for news and information of the allied governments. It consisted of an Information Office and a United Nations Information Board, which controlled the various technical committees on press, radio, films, etc. Its work and records were taken over by the United Nations department of public information in February 1946. The records of the parallel and co-operating London organization are not in the custody of the United Nations.

The UNIO records in the United Nations Archives consist of:

1. Reference materials produced or distributed by UNIO, dealing with the activities of the allied governments and with

the San Francisco Conference, and including press releases, periodical reviews, bibliographies, studies, reports, photographs, and sheet music, 1941–46 (56 feet).

2. Administrative records, including accounting papers and minutes of the Information Board and its committees, 1941–46 (3 feet).

UNITED NATIONS WAR CRIMES COMMISSION, 1943–48

The commission was established on October 20, 1943, by a meeting of Allied and Dominion representatives convened for the purpose at the foreign office in London. The first official meeting was held on January 11, 1944, and the commission continued its work actively until the end of March 1948.

The commission, composed of representatives of its member governments, performed valuable functions in connection with the development of principles of international law and planning for international tribunals. Its primary task, however, was to collect, investigate, and record evidence of war crimes and to report to the governments concerned those instances where the material available appeared to disclose a *prima facie* case. In carrying out this function, the commission was assisted by national offices established by each of the constituent members. Formal charges against alleged or suspected war criminals were submitted to the commission by the national offices, along with supporting data. It was the responsibility of the commission to determine whether there appeared to be sufficient evidence to warrant the listing of the persons charged as war criminals in order that they might be detained and prosecuted by the member governments. It took no part, however, in the detention of persons listed or in the prosecution of the cases, and it should be noted that only a very small proportion of the persons listed as war criminals have ever been prosecuted.

The commission carried on its work by means of a research office and three main committees, which dealt respectively with facts and evidence, enforcement, and legal questions. A Far

Eastern and Pacific Sub-Commission was also set up in Chunking in October 1944.

The following publications are useful guides to the records:

a. *History of the United Nations War Crimes Commission and the development of the laws of war*. War Crimes Commission, (London, H.M.S.O., 1948).

b. "Guide to the Records of the United Nations War Crimes Commission, 1943–1948." (United Nations Archives Reference Guide No. 19). Mimeo. (United Nations, 1951.)

c. "Index to Minutes and Documents of the United Nations War Crimes Commission, 1943–1948." (United Nations Archives Reference Guide No. 11). Mimeo. (confidential). (United Nations, 1949.)

The following are the major groups of records:

1. Minutes of meetings, 1943–48 (1 foot).

2. Documents (mimeographed), 1943–48 (1 foot).

3. Research Office publications and reference files of related materials from other sources, 1944–48 (2 feet).

4. Charge files containing formal charges, with papers submitted in evidence and other related materials, 1943–48 (45 feet). Indexed by name of suspect. (These files may be used only for official United Nations purposes.)

5. Reports and transcripts of the proceedings of national military tribunals, and of the International Military Tribunal for the Far East, 1944–48 (100 feet).

UNITED NATIONS RELIEF AND REHABILITATION ADMINISTRATION, 1943–49

UNRRA was established on November 9, 1943 when forty-four nations (later increased to forty-eight) signed an agreement, the purpose of which was to "plan, co-ordinate, administer or arrange for the administration of measures for the relief of victims of war in any area under the control of any of the United Nations through the provision of food, fuel, clothing, shelter and other basic necessities, medical and other essential services" (Article I, 2). The more important predecessor organizations were the Office of Foreign Relief and Rehabilitation Operations of the United States Department of State (OFRRO), set up on November 21, 1942, and the Inter-Allied Committee on Post-War Requirements (Leith-Ross Committee), set up in London in September 1941.

The agreement provided for a council, on which each member government was represented and which met in six sessions from November 1943 to December 1946; a central committee, consisting initially of China, U.S.S.R., U.K., and U.S.A., to make policy decisions between council sessions; a committee on supplies and various regional and special committees; and a director-general to serve as the chief executive and administrative officer. Under the latter's direction a staff numbering almost twenty-five thousand was recruited and organized in a large number of offices all over the world. Its headquarters was in Washington, D.C., and a major field office, the European Regional Office, was set up in London.

UNRRA operations came to an end in the latter part of 1946, but the demobilization of the staff and the liquidation of property and accounts continued until March 31, 1949, when the records and a few remaining functions were taken over by the United Nations.

Because of the bulk of the UNRRA files it is not possible to describe them in any detail in the limited space available here. It may be pointed out, however, that they contain vast quantities of unexploited data on all aspects of UNRRA's work, on its policies, techniques, and administrative organization and procedures, and on economic, social, and political conditions in nearly all areas of Europe and China during the critical post-war years. Nearly half the records have been destroyed, but those were primarily the routine files dealing with individual purchases and shipments. It may be said with some assurance that the UNRRA archives contain material of interest to almost any scholar working in the field of international affairs or European or Asiatic history during the decade of the 1940's.

Many UNRRA publications are easily available; the Council *Journals*, the director-general's annual reports, the periodic *Financial Reports*, and many other informative documents were printed and widely distributed. Only two items will be cited here as of special value in using the archives:

a. Woodbridge, George, and others. *UNRRA, The History of United Nations Relief and Rehabilitation Administration.* 3 vols. (New York, Columbia University Press, 1950).

b. "Index to Document Series of the United Nations Relief and Rehabilitation Administration, 1943–1949." (United Nations Archives Reference Guide number 18). Mimeo. (United Nations, 1951.)

Some fifty unpublished stacklists, descriptive lists, and other guides to parts of the UNRRA files have been prepared in the United Nations Archives and are available for consultation there.

The records fall broadly into the following major groups:

1. Documents and other publications, 1943–49 (25 feet). Printed or mimeographed; classified, listed, and indexed in the "Index" cited as (b) above.

2. Headquarters records, divided as follows:
Executive Office, 1943–49 (380 feet). Includes papers of the director-general, the general counsel, the public information division (with a fine collection of photographs), the historian, and others.
Bureau of Administration, 1943–49 (1200 feet). Includes personnel files and the classified central registry files covering all phases of UNRRA work.
Bureau of Supply, 1943–48 (470 feet). Contains detailed records of the operating divisions dealing with agricultural

rehabilitation, food, clothing, textiles, and footwear, and with procurement and shipping generally.

Bureau of Areas, 1944–45 (60 feet). The files of a short-lived bureau set up to co-ordinate field work.

Bureau of Services, 1943–48 (100 feet). Material pertaining to repatriation and welfare work, displaced persons programs, and relations with associated voluntary agencies.

Controller, 1943–49 (260 feet). The accounting, budget, and statistical records, containing much useful data on the source and distribution of funds.

3. European Regional Office (London), 1944–49 (340 feet). These consist mainly of a large and valuable classified subject file dealing with all aspects of operations in Europe, together with some accounting files.

4. Mission files, 1944–48 (1500 feet). Papers of the offices in countries listed below. Some of them were engaged in distributing supplies, maintaining welfare services, or operating displaced persons camps; others were purchasing missions; and still others were merely shipping offices.

Albania	Ethiopia	Italy	Trieste
Austria	Finland	Korea	Turkey
Belgium	France	Luxemburg	Ukraine
Byelorussia	Germany	Norway	Yugoslavia
China	Greece	Philippines	Balkans
Czechoslovakia	Hawaii	Poland	Middle East
Denmark	Hungary	Sweden	Southwest Pacific
Dodecanese	India	Switzerland	Latin America

SAN FRANCISCO CONFERENCE, 1945

The United Nations Conference on International Organization met at San Francisco on April 25, 1945, for the purpose of agreeing upon a structure and terms of reference for the United

Nations organization that had long been envisaged. Basing their work on a draft prepared by the 1944 meetings at Dumbarton Oaks, the representatives of the 50 participating governments signed the United Nations Charter on June 26, 1945 and at the same time set up a Preparatory Commission to arrange the first United Nations General Assembly.

The conference acted through four general committees—on conference direction, credentials, procedure, and draft coordination—and four commissions to plan the charter sections, dealing respectively with general provisions, the general assembly, the security council, and judicial organization. Each commission was divided into two or more technical committees. A secretariat, headed by Alger Hiss of the United States, provided conference services.[7]

1. Mimeographed and printed documents (27 feet) constitute the principal conference records. They contain the resolutions, committee reports, minutes, and draft texts that led to the final charter. They are classified by committee symbols and are most valuable sources for interpretation of the intent of the founders with regard to the charter provisions. The following are the most useful guides to the documents:

a. *Documents of the United Nations Conference on International Organization, San Francisco, 1945*, 22 vols. (London and New York), United Nations Information Organizations and United Nations, 1946–56. (A photo-offset published series; contains a subject index.)

b. "Guide to the records of the United Nations Conference on International Organization, San Francisco, 1945" (United Nations Archives Reference Guide number 10). Mimeo. (United Nations, 1949.)

c. Bruce, William J. "The San Francisco UNCIO documents," *The American archivist*, January, 1946, 6–16.

[7]Most secretariat files, together with the signed copy of the charter, remain in the custody of the United States department of state, which also has the records of the Dumbarton Oaks Conference.

d. Goodrich, Leland M., and Edvard Hambro. *Charter of the United Nations, commentary and documents.* 2nd and revised ed. (Boston, World Peace Foundation, 1949).

2. Unpublished verbatim minutes of committee meetings (6 feet).

3. Conference correspondence and general files (13 feet).

4. Commission and committee working papers (9 feet).

5. Credentials, charter texts, and related materials, presentation and publicity files, photographs, and sound recordings (26 feet).

UNITED NATIONS PREPARATORY COMMISSION, 1945–46

Established at the San Francisco Conference in June 1945, the commission met only briefly at that time and convened its executive committee in London on August 16 for the purpose of preparing for the first United Nations general assembly and formulating recommendations concerning transfer of League of Nations assets, organization of the secretariat, and other matters. The executive committee report was completed and submitted to meetings of the full commission beginning on November 24. The final report of the commission was adopted and the meetings adjourned on December 23, 1945, but the organization continued in existence legally until superseded by the United Nations secretariat when the secretary-general took office on February 2, 1946.

Both the executive committee and the Preparatory Commission carried on their work by means of a series of committees, each entrusted with the task of discussing and formulating recommendations concerning one aspect of the work of the United Nations. A secretariat, headed by Gladwyn Jebb, assisted the committees in their work.

There are four principal groups of records:

1. Official documents, August-December 1945 (4 feet). Classified by committee and described in:

a. "Index to the documents of the United Nations Preparatory Commission, 1945–1946." (United Nations Archives Reference Guide number 1). (United Nations, 1947.)

b. "Index to the documents of the executive committee of the United Nations Preparatory Commission, 1945." (United Nations Archives Reference Guide number 2). (United Nations, 1948.)

c. Dougall, Richardson. "The archives and documents of the Preparatory Commission of the United Nations," *The American archivist*, January, 1947, pp. 25–34.

2. Verbatim records of meetings of the commission, its technical committees and the executive committee, June 1945–February 1946 (3 feet).

3. Working papers of the technical committees, 1945–46 (1 foot).

4. Correspondence files, classified by subject, with card indexes, 1945–46 (6 feet).

NOTES CONCERNING THE DEPOSITORIES

Most of the records described above are located in the Secretariat Building at United Nations headquarters, 42nd Street and 1st Avenue, New York. They are in the custody of the Archives Section in the library and of Record Retirement in the Registry, both located on the 19th floor, where reading rooms and the assistance of reference staff are available to qualified scholars and researchers on Monday through Friday from 9:30 A.M. to 6:00 P.M. Microfilm readers and listening booths for sound recordings may be used, and arrangements can be made to obtain copies of photographs, sound recordings, or other materials (on microfilm or photostat) at cost.

The regulations governing access to the archives vary widely; some of the restricted materials have been indicated above. It is suggested that inquiry concerning availability of any particular body of records be addressed by mail to the Chief, Archives

Section, who can also provide fuller descriptions of the archives as well as assistance in using the facilities of the United Nations library at headquarters and the archives in Geneva.

The bulk of the League of Nations archives are located in the secretariat wing of the Palais des Nations, Geneva, Switzerland, where they are in the custody of the registrar. Close liaison is maintained with the headquarters Archives Section, and scholars would find it advisable first to consult the nearer repository, whatever records they may wish to use.

17 PUBLIC OPINION AND FOREIGN AFFAIRS

I. THE PRESS

Joseph J. Mathews

Emory University

HISTORIANS are not in complete agreement regarding the value of the newspaper as a source for the study of foreign affairs. As documentary evidence, newspapers have demonstrable limitations. At best they may give information that is incorrect, or misleading because it is incomplete, or biased by virtue of having been designed to support a viewpoint. They may contain no reference whatever to diplomatic developments of great moment. The nature of the newspaper makes some of these limitations inevitable regardless of the freedom, integrity, or the ability of the journalists who write for them, a fact that is too well recognized to require amplification. No reputable historian accepts an uncorroborated press account of a diplomatic development without first bringing into play the critical skills of his profession. But, as James Ford Rhodes, one of the earliest American scholars to make extensive use of newspapers, observed: "He (the historian) does not make his materials. He has to take them as they are."[1] The real question for the student of the history of foreign affairs, especially for the period since the early nineteenth century, should be *how* to use newspapers, not *whether* to use them. Properly used, newspapers can be of great value for many aspects of international relations. For problems dealing with public opinion and foreign affairs, the

[1] James Ford Rhodes, "Newspapers as historical sources," *Atlantic monthly,* CIII (May, 1909), 651.

348

daily press organ is an indispensable source. Certainly no source of comparable value is generally available.

Possibly the most difficult of all problems that the student faces in using newspapers is the extent to which they may be utilized to measure public opinion. The difficulty here is a compound one: not only is the character of the public mind elusive, and in any absolute sense unmeasurable, but also the newspaper is a peculiarly treacherous instrument to employ for the purpose. The fact cannot be ignored that the newspaper was not designed primarily as a mirror of the public mind. Only rarely, even among the most circulation-minded of journals, is there a conscious and consistent effort to cater exclusively to the tastes of the public. Even in these instances, as J. A. Spender has pointed out, the journalists "who are in this peculiar way detached from individual judgment inevitably take the line that their commercial interests favour." And he added: "What the public of a particular newspaper wants is by no means always what the majority of the country wants."[2] Lucy Maynard Salmon has gone even further to assert that "the very nature of the press prevents it from representing public opinion, even in the imperfect way in which it may be said to be represented by its regularly chosen delegates in a legislative body." Miss Salmon also points out that "each paper may have its own constituency, but as a rule ignores, and perhaps to a certain extent must ignore, public opinion outside of that constituency."[3] When all the vagaries in the historical evolution of the newspaper press are taken into account, and all of the controls and pressures, whether governmental or private, group or individual, that have influenced the contents of its pages are recalled, the pitfalls that face the student who attempts to use the press in order to determine popular opinion may seem too numerous and too serious to warrant the attempt. Yet, the sum total of difficulties does not add up to an impossible problem.

[2] J. A. Spender, *The public life*. 2 vols. (London, 1925), II, 109.
[3] Lucy Maynard Salmon, *The newspaper and the historian* (New York, 1923), p. 439.

The first of the two basic difficulties mentioned, that which stems from the nebulous character of public opinion itself, is in part a real one and in part an artificial creation. The problem becomes unnecessarily, perhaps hopelessly, complex when a concept of public opinion is used that embraces both static and dynamic opinion, views and emotions that do not find means of direct public expression as well as those that do, "not only the deliberative judgments of the rational elements within the collectivity, but the evanescent common will."[4] The student who seeks to appraise public opinion in its fullest sense will— almost needless to say—find his newspaper materials inadequate.

One solution is to replace the concept of public opinion with a more restricted one such as publicity and to keep one's investigations within the limits of the term.[5] The substitution has the merits of seeming to clarify, and of steering the scholar away from certain recognized dangers, but it can also be misleading. Publicity implies almost exclusively the process of persuasion and is related intimately to the acts of informing, advertising, and propagandizing. The press serves as a medium of publicity, of course, but save under conditions of relatively rigid control it also reflects in some measure the opinion that has been persuaded. The commonplace expression that "the press sometimes follows, sometimes leads public opinion" is a valid generalization even if it is irritating in its lack of precise meaning. No one who has followed an issue for a considerable period in the pages of a varied selection of newspapers is likely to deny that there is frequently a marked change in the trend of newspaper attitudes in response to what is at least assumed to be the opinion of the public. The foreign secretary who attempts to publicize a particular viewpoint in the press is often launching a "trial balloon" in order to obtain reactions. Publicity and

[4]Hans Bauer, "Public opinion," *Encyclopaedia of the social sciences*. 15 vols. (New York, 1930–35).

[5]Oron James Hale, *Publicity and diplomacy, with special reference to England and Germany, 1890–1914* (New York, 1940), pp. vii–viii.

opinion are not in reality as neatly separable as the student might wish.

If that segment or phase of general opinion that finds public expression is sufficiently strong to influence the course of diplomatic developments, then it must be recognized as a significant force whether or not it satisfies the broadest definition of public opinion. If, for example, government officials assume on occasions that such public expressions are in fact public opinion and are influenced in their decisions by what they take to be expressions of the general will, then these public expressions have pre-empted for the occasion the role of *vox populi* as a whole. The diplomatic documents published by the European powers for the period from 1870 to 1914 contain numerous examples that illustrate how the statesmen of the period used the newspapers not only in attempts to influence opinion but also to determine public reactions. The primary objective of the newspaper clipping activities of an embassy or consulate was that of ascertaining trends in public opinion in order to keep the home government informed. This is not to say, however, that cabinets, kings, and foreign secretaries were invariably guided by what they found in the press—possibly all statesmen have been guilty at one time or another of calling up an imaginary dictate of the general will to support their position—or that the press was at any time the sole instrument used for gauging public feeling. The degree to which a statesman relied on the press of a country as a guide to its opinion varied widely with time and circumstances. Public officials often placed greater faith in the papers of some foreign states than in their own. In the latter case, they possessed a more intimate knowledge of the influences that shaped the newspapers and had other ways of gauging opinion. Also, the extent to which an official felt impelled to heed the public voice was a variable. The diversity of the problem adds to its complexity and makes a detailed and precise knowledge of the influences that shape the contents of the press a necessity.

Bismarck is said to have declared that true history cannot be written from official documents because the historian does not always know what was in the minds of the authors of the documents. In commenting on this statement, G. P. Gooch adds, "but it is equally true that history cannot be written without them."[6] Both points have an applicability to the problem of using newspapers in the writing of diplomatic history, at least for certain periods. One period that can be used to demonstrate the value of newspapers in the study of foreign affairs is the era just before World War I. Here we have ready availability to more extensive publications of official documents by a number of powers than for any other period of similar length and importance. We have also notable special studies, such as those of E. Malcolm Carroll and Oron J. Hale,[7] which examine in detail the relationships of the press of certain countries to the diplomacy of the time. While these two scholars approach the problem from somewhat different points of view, their findings prove beyond question that a study of the press, particularly the relationships between government officials and the press, broadens and clarifies our knowledge of diplomacy. Even such advocates of secret diplomacy as Bismarck and Salisbury have to be viewed in a different light when we see their relations to the press. In fact, these studies enable us to maintain with confidence that for this period a full knowledge of diplomatic history cannot be obtained without study of the press.

For the historian to know what was in the mind of the journalist is at least as formidable an assignment as to know what was in the mind of the diplomat, but it is no less necessary to understanding. The authors of the official history of the London *Times* place great stress on the necessity of "knowledge

[6]G. P. Gooch, "European diplomacy before the war in the light of the archives," *International affairs*, XVIII (January–February, 1939), 78.
[7]E. Malcolm Carroll, *French public opinion and foreign affairs, 1870–1914* (New York, 1931); *Germany and the great powers, 1866–1914* (New York, 1938); Hale, *Publicity and diplomacy.*

of the intentions behind the policy of newspapers." This they consider a "vital requirement." Paraphrasing a statement by Hans Münster, they assert: "Newspapers can only be used as an historical source when one has in each case examined and weighed the various influences on the production of the paper." And "these influences," they declare, "cannot be scientifically weighed without reference to the correspondence between the proprietorial, managing and executive department of the newspaper with its agents at home and abroad."[8]

The position of the authors of the *Times's* history is vindicated by the work they have produced. This monumental four-volume study,[9] which was some twenty years in preparation, and which made use not only of the voluminous records fortunately preserved at Printing House Square but also of a great variety of additional materials, including those that were pertinent in numerous European foreign offices, points up as no other kind of study could have done how intricate and significant was the role of a great newspaper in European diplomatic developments. The sober and painstaking scholarship of the work is recognizedly unusual in the field of newspaper history. More than that, the implications of the study place in a most unfavorable light the numerous historians of diplomacy who occasionally leave their official documents for a side excursion into the press, which they quote with at least the inference that public opinion of some sort is represented. Too often the historian who applies the most rigid rules in evaluating his other sources, or even in evaluating the press for purposes other than as a mirror of public opinion, selects his newspaper at random and justifies his references with nothing more than a suggestive adjective—the influential *Post*, the usually well-informed *Temps*, or the liberal *Tageblatt*.

Scholarly study of the press is still in its infancy, and until

[8] *The history of the Times.* Vol. III, *The twentieth century test, 1884–1912* (New York, 1947), p. 809.
[9] *The history of the Times.* 4 vols. (London, 1935–52).

greater progress has been made the historian of diplomacy will of necessity be retarded in his use of it. Unfortunately, there are few cases where private newspaper records have been preserved to the extent they have for the London *Times*. Unhappily, too, the directions taken by some of the studies related to the problem have not been calculated to ease the task of the historian. Some, though fortunately by no means all, of the work sponsored by the German *Zeitungwissenschaft* in the 1930's was useless pedantry. Some of the recent American studies by the public opinion "experts" who count columns, parse newspaper sentences, and list adjectives and adverbs according to propaganda types, muddy the water more often than they make it clear. To attempt to establish any general canons to be applied to the use of newspapers at varying times, under differing governmental restrictions, and in a number of countries, is an impossibility. The historian must take into account not only the controls and influences on the press at a specific time and place but also how much information on foreign affairs was available to the press. Harold Temperley has concluded that the trend in Great Britain from the early nineteenth century to World War I was consistently in the direction of greater secrecy in the handling of diplomatic matters.[10] Yet, it was Salisbury who declared in 1901 that "the diplomacy of nations is now conducted as much in the letters of special correspondents as in the dispatches of the Foreign Office."[11]

Even a single issue of a newspaper presents more than one problem. The newspaper is not one document but a series of them. A news item differs from an editorial or leader; the news may be private or official in origin; it may be impossible to determine its origin; the news may deal with one of the many aspects of international relations that seldom comes within the province of the official documents but which in the long view

---

[10]Harold Temperley, "British secret diplomacy from Canning to Grey," *Cambridge historical journal*, VI (No. 1, 1938), 1–32.

[11]Quoted in Sir Sidney Lee, *King Edward VII*. 2 vols. (New York, 1929), II, 279.

may affect public opinion and the relations between two countries more than a treaty. Like public opinion itself, the press possesses infinite variety and complexity. Sound knowledge of public opinion as reflected in the press depends necessarily upon sound knowledge of the press no less than of public opinion. In recent decades new mediums for the dissemination of news have appeared—the radio, cinema, and television—which promise to make the problem of the historian increasingly difficult. It may be that the historian in "1984" will view the "newspaper era" as a comparatively uncomplicated one.

The systematic collection and preservation of newspapers for scholarly use is of relatively recent origin. In 1866 when Eugène Hatin published his famous *Bibliographie de la presse périodique*, the *Bibliothèque Impériale (Bibliothèque Nationale)* was only beginning to catalogue its newspapers and periodicals, which had been collected haphazardly. The first cataloguing effort was of dubious value in that the attempt was made to divide newspapers into the same categories used for printed books. In the numerous additional depositories in Paris where newspapers were kept, only two or three were accessible to the student in such a way that he could make good use of them.[12] At about the same time (1869), the British Museum began to receive directly copies of all British newspapers and periodicals when the abolition of the last of the taxes on newspapers in that year made it no longer necessary for newspaper proprietors to deposit copies at Somerset House. Fortunately, the Museum had previously obtained newspapers from Somerset House when they were no longer needed for official purposes. Since the 1860's the work of collecting and preserving newspapers, and of making them readily available to students, has made steady progress the world over. There are numerous depositories where working conditions and the presence of reference tools

---

[12]Eugène Hatin, *Bibliographie historique et critique de la presse périodique française* (Paris, 1866), pp. vii–xi.

make the work of research in newspaper files compare favorably with research in other source materials. New reproduction techniques, moreover, have proved extremely valuable in making newspaper files available in libraries other than the few great depositories. Only rarely is a "complete run" of an important newspaper available in a single depository, but microfilm fills in the gaps and makes possible wide and relatively inexpensive distribution. One of the more striking examples of the usefulness of microfilm in making newspapers more generally available is that of a recent project sponsored by the University of California Library at Berkeley. The excellent South American newspaper collection in the British Museum, one of the best in the world, has been microfilmed by the California institution and is now available in the western hemisphere. The project also included the filming of western North American and Canadian papers in the British Museum collection.[13] The great majority of newspaper depositories now supplement their newspaper holdings with microfilm.

Among the large European newspaper archives, none is superior in the number and extent of its holdings to the British Museum. With the exception of London newspapers prior to 1801, which are still housed in the British Museum, Bloomsbury, most of the national newspaper collection is in the British Museum Newspaper Library at Colindale, some twenty minutes from the center of London by the Underground. Since they fall in the earlier period, the famous Burney and Thomason collections of newspapers, tracts, etc., are to be found at Bloomsbury in the main Museum building. Also located at Bloomsbury are the files of the *London, Edinburgh, Belfast* and *Dublin Gazettes*, along with additional files of the *Times* since 1809.[14]

[13]This information, along with statistical and general data pertaining to their collections, was kindly furnished the writer by members of the staff of the British Museum Newspaper Library, Colindale.

[14]By legal definition a newspaper in England is a periodical containing advertising and news that appears at least each twenty-six days. Hence monthlies are ruled out. Certain periodicals, however, have been deposited at Bloomsbury or Colindale for varied reasons and their locations cannot always be predicted.

But the bulk of the Museum's newspaper collection is, of course, located at Colindale where there are an estimated four hundred to four hundred and fifty thousand volumes of bound papers occupying roughly fifteen to fifteen and a half miles of shelving. These holdings are increased annually by some five thousand English volumes that come to the Library by virtue of the Copyright Act (1911 and previous acts), and by roughly fifteen hundred foreign and colonial accessions obtained by purchase. There are separate catalogues for British and foreign journals, but in each case the listings are according to the place of publications. Unfortunately, shortage of space recently has led officials to restrict service on non-British papers to those issued during the past two years. There is hope that a new wing to the building, which has been projected, will again make all the resources of the library available. Although the working period is brief (10 to 4 on week days), at least from the American viewpoint, working conditions are excellent at Colindale and the service is rapid measured by the standards of any library. The student who is interested in English newspapers of the earlier period may need to consult the Bodleian Library at Oxford or other depositories as well as the holdings of the British Museum, but this need is unlikely to arise for the student interested in the nineteenth and twentieth centuries. In addition to its British papers, the Colindale Library is uniquely rich in journals from virtually every part of the globe. For the nineteenth century the German and Austrian holdings are somewhat better than the French, and the French somewhat better than the Italian or other European collections.

Scholars have been heartened to learn that the direct bomb hit during World War II on one of the buildings at Colindale did not do as much damage as was at first feared. The work of assessing the damage is still in progress at the time this statement is being written, but Museum officials estimate the loss at roughly five thousand volumes. The losses sustained were entirely in the English provincial and Irish papers. Scottish papers and a few important papers such as the *Manchester Guardian* and *Irish Times* were fortunately not damaged. For the present, Irish papers for the period 1865–1930 are unobtainable, and provincial papers from their beginning to 1932 are available to students on a limited basis only.

Facilities for research in newspaper files are rarely as concentrated in continental centers as they are in the British Museum in London. The student, unless his needs are restricted to, say, military or special types of periodicals, or the journals of a single country for a short period, is apt to find it necessary to pursue his studies in several depositories. The great number and the specialized character of many of the continental depositories, together with restrictions imposed by the present writer's lack of firsthand knowledge of more than a few archives, make it impossible to offer here anything better than selected examples and suggestions. Ordinarily, of course, the student whose interests are in the newspapers of a particular country will find it advantageous, perhaps even necessary, to work in that country. There is, for example, a more complete collection of nineteenth-century Dutch papers in the *Koninklijke Bibliotheek* in The Hague than can be found outside the Netherlands, although there are several excellent university and public newspaper collections elsewhere in the country. The *Koninklijke Bibliotheek* also has files of a number of early Dutch journals, along with reasonably comprehensive twentieth-century holdings, although the Dutch Royal Library does not receive copies of all papers by virtue of a copyright law as does the British Museum.

The numerous special and even general newspaper collections in Paris present the student with a sometimes tedious but by no means insoluble problem. The logical starting point is the *Bibliothèque Nationale* where the holdings are the most extensive and where there are available catalogues, bibliographies, guides, and counsel to enlighten the student. In the catalogue of the *Bibliothèque Nationale*, French newspapers and periodicals are listed by centuries. For a particular period such as the French Revolution, there is available the comprehensive work of Gérard Walter in the fifth volume of the *Catalogue de l'histoire de la Révolution française*,[15] which supersedes earlier bibliographies by Hatin and Tourneux. The location in Paris depositories of non-French periodicals can be readily ascertained by consulting a recently completed list of foreign periodicals which presents them alphabetically, geographically, and according to subject.[16] The overflow from the *Bibliothèque Nationale*, consisting mostly of provincial periodicals and those infrequently used, is sent to a *dépôt* at Versailles where the student must go to use them. Among the more important depositories in Paris that contain newspaper collections of varying size and importance are the *Bibliothèque historique de la Ville de Paris*, the *Bibliothèque de l'Arsenal*, the *Bibliothèque du Sénat*, the *Bibliothèque de la Chambre des Députés*, and the *Archives Nationales*.

Taken as a whole, the task that confronts the student who works with newspapers is a formidable one, but the problem of locating and gaining access to newspaper files is becoming progressively easier. It is hoped that this fact will encourage more students to accept the challenge that these materials present.

2. THE PROBLEM OF PUBLIC OPINION UNDER DICTATORSHIPS

Lynn M. Case
University of Pennsylvania

In the first half of this chapter one has seen the difficulty of determining both static and dynamic public opinion from any

[15]Bibliothèque Nationale, Département des Imprimés, *Catalogue de l'histoire de la Révolution française*, par André Martin et Gérard Walter. 5 vols. (Paris, 1936–43).

[16]Bibliothèque Nationale, Département des Imprimés, *État sommaire des périodiques étrangers. Reçus dans les bibliothèques et les centres de documentation de Paris en 1948* (Paris, 1950).

source. In resorting to the press as a source on public opinion one has naturally to limit himself to dynamic opinion or, as Oron J. Hale has called it, to "publicity." Again, as we have seen above, the difficulty with the dynamic press publicity is one of distinguishing between expressions of editorial opinion and editorial attempts to create or influence public opinion by official inspiration, private propaganda, or trial-balloon soundings. Thus the problem of determining even the dynamic opinion is filled with complications and hazards that beset the historian of foreign affairs at every turn.

There are periods and places in the nineteenth and twentieth centuries, however, when it is well-nigh impossible to ascertain any sort of approximation of even dynamic public opinion because of dictatorial regimes and their ruthless suppression of public expression of opinion, whether at the parliamentary tribune, on the electioneering rostrum, or in the press. Examples of such regimes are often found right at the periods when foreign affairs are most significant and when a knowledge of even dynamic opinion would be of considerable value. We are reminded of such regimes as the Orleans Monarchy in France after the passage of the September Laws of 1835, the authoritarian Second Empire in France between 1851 and 1868, the Bismarck era in Prussia and Germany between 1862 and 1890, the Czarist and Communist regimes in Russia before and after 1917, the Fascist regime in Italy from 1922 to 1943, the Nazi regime in Germany from 1933 to 1945, and the French Vichy regime between 1940 and 1944. Indeed, it seems to be one of the great paradoxes of our age that at a time when the material means of publicity have been multiplied and extended by telegraph, telephone, railroad, motor highways, aviation, power presses, moving pictures, radio, and television, there have been more successful mass efforts to stifle opinion by censorship and distort thought by propaganda than in any previous eras. The twentieth century has been famous for its widely developed educational systems and high degree of literacy and at the same time most infamous for its iron curtains and brain-washing.

Such well-known conditions are the despair of the historian when he realizes that an adequate account of diplomatic history requires a knowledge of public opinion and that insuperable obstacles have been put in the way of ever obtaining such a knowledge. And yet there is one bright hope in all this darkness: the fact that most of these dictatorships were dependent in one way or another on an acquiescing public opinion. Not only were there great ministries of propaganda established to propagandize the ideologies of the regimes but considerable secret effort was made to ascertain accurately both static and dynamic opinion (alas, most of it was static) by such means as reports of administrative officials, totalitarian party workers, and the secret police. If the historian could once obtain access to these reports after the downfall of these dictatorships and if the successor regimes would be far-sighted enough to save these reports for the use of unprejudiced scholars, then some tentative approach at least could be made to the problem of public opinion and foreign affairs even in periods of dictatorship. The present writer had the opportunity to be in Italy soon after the downfall of the Fascist regime, and he saw such material in governmental offices and party headquarters. Whether this has been preserved for subsequent historical use remains to be seen.

In the nineteenth century there was one such dictatorial regime, the French Second Empire (1851–70), which made systematic and comprehensive surveys of opinion on foreign and domestic affairs through administrative and police channels, and the successor regime, the Third Republic, managed to preserve a considerable amount of the material in the French *Archives Nationales*. Therefore the Second Empire will be used in this chapter as an example of this unique approach to the conquering of the seemingly insurmountable barriers blocking the determination of public opinion in dictatorships.

However much Napoleon III was a dictator in the French Second Empire, both he and his party leaders were ever conscious of public opinion. If for no other reason, this attitude could be explained by his affirmation of the principle of popular sovereignty, which he invoked by secret plebiscite votes. Furthermore, he adhered in principle to the device of universal manhood suffrage, however much it was thwarted in practice. Hence Napoleon III could not ignore public opinion.

Likewise the emperor had a broad interpretation of what public opinion was. He seemed to consider static opinion to be more important than the dynamic. A little unsigned note in his handwriting was found in the Tuileries Palace after his downfall, which asked and answered the much debated question of what public opinion was:

But, who are the people? Are they by chance the five or six thousand people in Paris who meet together at the clubs or at the *Redoute* and who think they are speaking in the name of all France? Are they the drawing-rooms, the shops? Are they the [newspapers?]? Are they the young people, drunk with enthusiasm? Are they the old people longing for the past? Are they the army? Are they the legislative body?

No, the people are the whole mass of the nation, those who exercise the universal suffrage. They are the masters of us all; and those little groups [*coteries*] who call themselves the people commit a blasphemy.[17]

This was not just an idle meditation on his part. All during his reign we see his concern for public opinion,[18] and no better single incident could be cited than that reported in 1866 by Baron Beyens, the Belgian minister in Paris:

The emperor . . . has been able to determine better each day on how the country is opposed to war and irritated at Prussia and Italy. Although this sentiment has been affirmed in more ways than one, although the police reports from all over the empire confirm it,

[17]Robert Holt, ed., *Papiers sauvés des Tuileries* (Paris, 1871), p. 25.
[18]See Lynn M. Case, *French opinion on the United States and Mexico, 1860–1867. Extracts from the reports of the procureurs-généraux* (New York, 1936) and by the same author *French opinion on war and diplomacy during the Second Empire* (Philadelphia, 1954).

they wanted to consult again the opinion of the common people [*classes populaires*]. Prefects were ordered to Paris, secret soundings were made by the mayors in various parts of their territories, and everywhere the answer was an ardent desire for peace. His Majesty did not conceal the impression produced on him by this result.[19]

And in this instance Napoleon III obeyed public opinion by staying out of the Austro-Prussian War, even though that decision in the long run turned out to be a misfortune for France. A few years later he confided to the Spanish ambassador:

It cost us a great deal to recognize the state of affairs which the battle of Sadowa created in Germany. We tolerated it, although not without regret. French public opinion was at that time very emphatic in favor of peace, and I was resolved to respect that tendency [*ce courant*].[20]

If the French press of the Second Empire, severely censored and subjected to governmental pressures, is not a fit source for the study of public opinion, to what collections of reports may we turn as a substitute? Fortunately in the case of this regime, the administrative reports are rich and varied. The two most important ones are the reports of the procureurs general and those of the prefects, both found in the French *Archives Nationales* in Paris, which will be discussed separately below.

One of the channels to which the emperor-dictator turned for confidential information about opinion was his procureurs general, or in a sense district attorneys, who were in charge of prosecution duties in the twenty-eight court-of-appeal districts in France. As early as 1849, when he was still President of the Second Republic, he had his minister of justice request such reports on a monthly basis. In 1852 they were made quarterly reports; in 1853, semiannual; and finally in 1859 they became

[19]Beyens to C. Rogier, Paris, June 10, 1866, Service des Archives. Belgian Foreign Ministry Archives, Brussels, MSS, Correspondence politique, series Légation française (hereafter cited as AEB, CP), XXIII, number 83.

[20]J. Conrad Kern, *Souvenirs politiques* (Paris, 1887), p. 205.

quarterly again for the remainder of the empire. The instructions of the minister of justice in 1859 to his procureurs general are particularly good in revealing the seriousness and thoroughness with which they went about the task of polling opinion:

It will not suffice [wrote the minister of justice] for you to observe and report to me in a general way the state of public opinion; it is indispensable that I find in your communications evidence of a personal study and a clear and exact evaluation of everything characterizing the period in question and of anything revealing the tendencies and needs of the people. . . . I attach a great deal of importance to these periodic communications.

I also think it to be of great importance that you give me the results of your observations on the principal economic questions with which the government and the country are concerned. Consequently I should welcome with great interest whatever you may have to report on the condition of industries in your district, the causes of their prosperity or decline [and] the condition of the workers employed.[21]

It was as a result of such instructions as these that the procureurs general undertook four times a year a regular Gallup poll of the people of all classes in their districts. Their subordinates all the way down the hierarchy engaged in these periodic surveys: advocates general, imperial procureurs, assistants (*substituts*) in each department, and the justices of the peace in each canton. As the instructions went down, so the reports came back up the ladder of administration, until finally the procureur general incorporated the full story in an official report to Paris. There were even efforts to make careful rechecks on some of the surveys, as is revealed by the following report from Besançon:

The heads of the courts' legal staffs [*parquets*] of Vesoul, Gray, and Lure tried hard to verify with the greatest care by their own personal investigations the information transmitted to them by the

[21]Circular of the minister of justice to the procureurs general, Paris, March 11, 1859, Archives Nationales, Paris, MSS, Rapports des Procureurs-généraux, series BB³⁰, carton 367 [hereafter cited as procureur reports].

unanimous reports of the justices of the peace. They interviewed officials, industrialists, landowners, farmers, and plain workmen, and they all did not meet one single person who showed the least sympathy for a war [a war which they knew was favored by the government].[22]

The people in the ministry of justice took the reports as seriously as did the procureurs and their subordinates. Their pages are filled with red-penciled underlinings; their margins are cluttered with lines, checks, and comments. Particularly in the period between 1866 and 1869, when various crises arose, the passages dealing with foreign affairs were copiously underlined. Many digests, accompanied by illustrative extracts, were prepared for higher officials, presumably for the emperor. One entire carton (368) is set aside for digests and extracts for the period between 1853 and 1863. During the Austro-Sardinian War in 1859 weekly reports were demanded of the procureurs general.[23]

Very few of the quarterly procureur reports had less than ten pages; some individual reports were ninety pages long; the average length was about twenty-five pages. They fill about sixty-six bulky cartons, numbered from BB[30] 367 to BB[30]451; those from 370 to 389 are the main separate files from each district. In these cartons of the separate districts the reports are bound into about six books of manuscripts (a total of about 115 books). Each report is usually divided into three sections: political (i.e. opinion), economic, and moral. The political is subdivided into opinion on domestic and foreign questions, and these in turn by marginal headings are subdivided into current topics. Taken all together, the procureur reports form a vast and detailed Domesday Book of all France, not just Paris, for the twenty years before 1870.

The numbers and contents of the cartons of series BB[30] are indicated as follows:

[22]Procureur report, Besançon, April 9, 1859.
[23]Circular of May 12, 1859, procureur special reports, carton 369.

370	(Agen, Aix)
371	(Angers [mostly for 1864] and Amiens)
372	(Bastia [Corsica])
373	(Besançon)
374	(Bordeaux, Bourges)
375	(Caen, Chambéry)
376	(Colmar)
377	(Dijon, Douai)
378	(Grenoble, Limoges)
379	(Lyons)
380	(Metz, Montpellier)
381	(Nancy)
382	(Nîmes, Orleans)
383	(Paris)
384	(Paris, Pau)
385	(Poitiers)
386	(Rennes, Riom)
387	(Rouen)
388	(Toulouse)
367	Instructions to procureurs general
368	Summaries of reports
369	Weekly reports during the Austro-Sardinian War
389	Regular reports from October 1868 to October 1869. These were not put in the separate district files.
395–423	Political affairs.
425	Inventory of Series BB30.
427–443	Elections of 1863
450–451	Agitation on the Roman question.[24]

[24]Other discussions of the procureur reports may be found in Lynn M. Case, *War and diplomacy*, pp. 6–10; Case, *U.S. and Mexico*, pp. xiii–xx; Case, "New sources for the study of French opinion during the Second Empire," *Southwestern social science quarterly*, XVIII (1937), 161–170; Jean Maurain, *Histoire ecclésiastique du Second Empire* (Paris, 1930), p. 23; *Cambridge modern history*, XI (New York, 1909), 927; Charles Seignobos, *Bulletin de la société de l'histoire moderne*, Year VI, No. 49, June 1907.

But, however systematic and complete were these procureur reports of opinion, the emperor was not satisfied with having just one channel of information. From the beginning of his presidency and all through the period of the empire he required similar periodic reports from his prefects in the eighty-eight departments of France.[25] They vary from being quarterly, tri-monthly, bimonthly, to monthly. After 1865 they continued to be monthly reports. The prefect likewise used his administrative hierarchy for the surveys: the subprefects of the arrondissements and the mayors of the communes. Some of the subprefect reports are fairly detailed, and many of them have been forwarded on to Paris. But the reports of these subordinates are not too helpful on foreign affairs because these officials were much more absorbed with questions of domestic politics and political agitation and unrest. The reports of the prefects themselves are just as disappointing because they were usually drawn up on four-page printed forms where the prefect merely filled in a few remarks under each heading. A great deal of attention was paid to the local press and its degrees of conformity, which is interesting for a history of the press but just to the same extent valueless for a survey of opinion. For one third of the period of the Second Empire (1859–65) the prefect reports have been lost or destroyed. After the lifting of the press censorship in 1868, the prefects seem to have been asked only to write special reports on opinion when required.[26] Furthermore, there are no digests, extracts, or economic reports.[27]

One of the special reports requested of the prefects after 1868

[25]Archives Nationales, Paris, MSS, series F¹ᶜ III, Ministère de l'Intérieur, Administration générale, Esprit public et élections. Série départementale. Comptes-rendus administratifs (hereafter cited as prefect reports).

[26]Prefect report, Isère 7, April 6, 1868.

[27]On the collection of the prefect reports (F¹ᶜ III) see Case, U.S. and Mexico, pp. xi–xiii; Case, War and diplomacy, pp. 10–13; Maurain, Histoire ecclésiastique, pp. xi–xii; E. Malcolm Carroll, French public opinion and foreign affairs, 1870–1914 (New York, 1931), p. 7; Carroll, "French public opinion on the war with Prussia in 1870," American historical review, XXXI, 681.

was that of July 1870, asking urgently for a description of the public reaction to the Spanish throne incident and to Gramont's declaration in the legislative body. Within a week these reports were telegraphed in to Paris, but they are not found in the *Archives Nationales*. They were probably destroyed by the fires attending the Communard Revolt in 1871, but fortunately most of the significant passages were published in the *Journal Officiel* of October 2, 1870.

These prefect reports, making up series F¹ᶜ III of the *Archives Nationales*, consist of about one carton for each department, with the documents unbound but tied together with a cloth band.

However less adequate the prefect reports were in comparison to those of the procureurs general, they were still examined and noted by the cabinet ministers in Paris. In 1866 Goltz, the Prussian ambassador, wrote that La Valette, the minister of interior, was becoming more favorable to the pope "partly as a result of the prefect reports on the attitude of the country." A year later another member of the Prussian embassy staff, Solms, wrote home that he received this information directly from La Valette: "In his capacity as minister of interior he received from all sides and from all departments the most exhaustive reports on the feeling of the French people, and he could assure me that in France the people wished for nothing more heartily than peace."[28]

In addition to these two main collections of administrative reports on opinion mention should be made of the police reports and the reports of the Paris prefect of police, although few of these reports seem any longer to be in existence. We have already seen that Beyens spoke of "police reports from all over the country" in 1866 (cited above). Ten years earlier he wrote: "It was especially by the secret and confidential reports of the

[28]Goltz to Bismarck, Paris, Oct. 26, 1866; Solms to Bismarck, Paris, Aug. 30, 1867; in *Auswärtige Politik Preussens*, edited by the Historische Reichskommission under the direction of Erich Brandenburg, Otto Hoetzsch, and Hermann Oncken (10 v. Oldenburg, 1933–39), VIII, 117; IX, 198.

prefect of police that the emperor has been informed in recent times."[29] This is confirmed by a conversation Senior had with a Commandant Blanchard, an official in the ministry of interior who kept in correspondence with local police officials. Blanchard told Senior: "Their reports are interesting and amusing; they are intended to reflect public opinion on every subject. At first they used to alarm me, but one gets callous to repeated denunciations of hostilities and plots. I was employed on them today (March 6, 1858) from seven in the morning to five in the evening."[30] It was evidently some such provincial reports as these which the Paris prefect of police combined with his own findings to report to the emperor. Evidently, too, these were as frank and objective as were the procureur reports. Unfortunately, few of the reports of the prefect of police for this period seem extant. None was located by the staff of the *Archives Nationales*. The *Archives Départementales de la Seine* and the *Archives de la Préfecture de Police* in Paris both fear that these collections may have been destroyed in the Commune fires of 1871. Nevertheless, this last collection is mentioned here with the faint hope that some enterprising scholar, thus forewarned, may yet uncover them in some unexpected place.

The *Archives Nationales*, which is the place of deposit for the procureur and prefect reports, is located in Paris on the corner of the Rue des Archives and Rue des Francs-Bourgeois. It is open from Monday to Friday from 9:30 to 12:00 and 1:00 to 5:00 and on Saturdays from 1:00 to 5:30. It is closed in the summer from July 1 to July 15. To gain permission to consult its documentary collections, a researcher needs to have a letter from his embassy or legation. The *Archives Nationales* also furnish a microfilming and photostatic service. As to the more important extracts on opinion on foreign affairs in the procureur reports, the present writer possesses microfilm copies with an

[29]Beyens to Vilain XIIII, Paris, Nov. 6, 1856, AEB, CP, Légation française, XVIII, number 60.

[30]Nassau Senior, *Conversations with Thiers and Guizot and other distinguished persons during the Second Empire, 1852–1860* (London, 1878), II, 167.

accompanying identification calendar at the University of Pennsylvania.

This matter of sources on opinion during the dictatorial Second Empire in France furnishes an example of what may be found later in many other countries that suffered from dictatorial rule. The preservation and future availability of this material may depend upon a multitude of factors: upon the absence of a blind destructive hatred by hostile successor regimes, upon the adoption by governments of more enlightened policies concerning scholarly interests in an age when humanity seems to be sinking back socially and intellectually into semi-barbarism, and upon the desperate hope that, by some miracle of human endeavor, atom bombs will not be dropped on the world's metropolitan centers, where so many of the official archive collections are housed.

18 UNESCO[1]

Richard H. Heindel

Wagner College

DIPLOMACY has never been totally oblivious to educational, scientific, and cultural matters, so often the actions of individuals or nongovernmental organizations. But it is apparent that during recent decades intercultural relations, "people speaking to people," have become a more mature interest of the diplomatic, governmental world, nationally, bilaterally, and multilaterally. Appraisals of the significance of these cultural factors offer an inviting field to scholars of many disciplines. However, some time may elapse before this kind of research is integrated satisfactorily into the exposition of international relations.

The analysis of international-intercultural relations will of necessity take the researcher into many scattered files. But it may be useful, as a brief case study, to refer to the United Nations Educational, Scientific and Cultural Organization (UNESCO), whose constitution was framed in London, November 16, 1945 and which is now composed of eighty member states. UNESCO has deliberated, operated, and stimulated correspondence on a very wide range of problems. Its principal organisms are its legislative body, the general conference which has changed from annual to biennial sessions, an executive board, the secretariat, headed by a director general, and the various national commissions in member states. Though subject to frequent reorganization, the secretariat at UNESCO House is presently divided into six program departments—education, natural sciences, social sciences, cultural activities,

[1]The author has drawn heavily upon data prepared by J. Opocensky, Head of the Archives Division of UNESCO, and wishes to acknowledge this assistance.

mass communications (including public information) and technical assistance. Services now include: documents and publications and exchange of persons. External relations, now called bureau of relations with member states, has been shifted to the office of the director-general; statistics to the department of social sciences. The rehabilitation division was first replaced by voluntary international assistance and since 1955 by public liaison division, attached to the mass communication department.

Administrative units exist for management, budget, control, personnel, conference planning, and general services. UNESCO has relationships through contracts, subventions, conferences, seminars, and correspondence with many international non-governmental organizations. The protocol relating to the entry into force of an agreement bringing UNESCO into official relationships with the United Nations was signed February 3, 1947.

On January 4, 1922 the League of Nations set up an International Commission of Intellectual Cooperation to serve as a consultative organ. On January 16, 1926 an International Institute of Intellectual Cooperation was created with headquarters in Paris for the purpose of insuring the continuity of the work of the commission. They existed until 1946 when they were liquidated with the other institutions of the League of Nations. The Archives of UNESCO now include the following papers of this League organization:

1. Correspondence of the I.I.I.C. 1926–46;
2. Roneographed documents of the I.I.I.C., 1926–46;
3. Roneographed documents of the International Commission of Intellectual Cooperation, its committees and sub-committees, 1925–38.

Unfortunately some documents were lost during the war.

The UNESCO Archives also inherited the archives of the Conference of Allied Ministers of Education, which was convened during the war in London by the British ministry of education to plan for cultural reconstruction in war devastated countries. The conference was a direct precursor of UNESCO. The papers of CAME devoted to cultural reconstruction are divided into the following categories:

1. The plenary meetings of the conference;

2. The conference's executive bureau, with its finance and establishment committee and its commissions: books and periodicals commission, history committee, science commission with its technical committee, audio-visual aids commission with its school-broadcasting committee, commission for the protection and restitution of cultural material, basic scholastic equipment commission with its committee on the needs of a unit, commission on special educational problems in liberated countries, and commission on Belgian memorandum on denazification of Eupen and Malmédy.

The CAME papers concerned with the establishment of UNESCO are as follows:

1. Documents of the two open meetings with the United States delegation;

2. Documents of the drafting committee on the constitution of UNESCO;

3. Papers of the working committee for the preparation of the international conference for the establishment of UNESCO.

The summary records of meetings and other important papers are bound.

The UNESCO Archives were not organized until 1948. Hence attention had to be given to the preservation and classification of the documents and correspondence of UNESCO in its first two years of existence. Since January 1, 1949 the Archives collect, register, and index all the documents and publications produced by UNESCO, establish the indexes of the records of the general conference, and co-operate with the UNDI (United Nations Documents Index). Some 269 agreements concluded by UNESCO with member states, the United Nations and specialized agencies, and intergovernmental organizations have been registered. The Archives also serve as an information center for UNESCO documents and publications and as a liaison between UNESCO and the International Council on Archives. The responsibility for correspondence is divided between Archives and Registry. The two divisions have been united recently into one administrative unit within the bureau of conference planning and general services. The Archives keep the dead files of correspondence.

With the exception of a few restricted documents, the Archives in the Annex of UNESCO House, third floor, are open to research workers every day from 10 A.M. to 6 P.M. without special permission. UNESCO House is located at 19 Avenue Kléber, Paris 16, and the Annex is on Rue la Perousse. In the new headquarters, 109 Avenue de Suffren (Place Fontenoy), Paris 7, the Archives will be located on the first floor near the registry, the library, and other documentation services. A microfilm service will be set up upon the completion of permanent headquarters in Paris. Microfilming is permitted.

"A periodical subject list of publications and documents of UNESCO" (classified alphabetically by subject) is easily available in the United States at depository libraries. A cumulative index of UNESCO documents is in preparation. UNESCO publications, such as the records of the general conference, the annual report of the director general, the reports of member states, and UNESCO periodicals are available from UNESCO'S agency, the Columbia University Press, 2960 Broadway, New York City, 27, and UNESCO Publications Center, 152 W. 42nd Street, New York City, 36.

The Archives do not have a complete file of documents and publications covering the related work of the member states and national commissions.[2]

---

[2]It is interesting to note the total number of documents per session of the General Conference in one language: (2nd) 482; (3rd) 499; (4th) 346; (5th) 515. Charles S. Ascher, *Program making in UNESCO, 1946–51* [Chicago, Public Administration Service, 1951], p. 77. Subsequent figures are: 6th session, 1951: 437; 7th session, 1952: 491; 8th session, 1954: 632 in each language.

Depository libraries[3] receive the more important mimeographed documents of UNESCO, as well as its publications. These include reports of meetings of the executive board, resumés of activities, study papers, etc. However, they do not receive documents which UNESCO classifies as "working series"—documents and minutes of committees of experts, working papers, and the like. While these are not restricted in the sense of being classified material, they are effectively restricted by limitations on the number of copies produced. Documents of the executive board and some of the "working series" papers are available in the reference files of the U.S. National Commission for UNESCO and at the UNESCO Liaison Office at UN Headquarters.

In the early years a lack of coordination between departments of UNESCO in establishing a coherent documentation system resulted in a confusing variety of symbols and frequent changes or variations within series. Since 1950, symbols were standardized as follows:

ED   —Education
EXP   —Exchange of Persons
CUA   —Cultural Activities
MC   —Mass Communications
NS   —Natural Sciences
SS   —Social Sciences
TA   —Technical Assistance

The advantages of such standardization are obvious. The disadvantages of too general a classification are in some cases

[3]UNESCO depository libraries in the United States are: Library of Congress, Washington, D.C.; Columbus Memorial Library, Pan American Union, Wash., D.C.; New York Public Library, New York, N.Y.; University of North Carolina; Library, Chapel Hill, N.C.; Harvard University Library, Cambridge, Mass., University of Chicago Library, Chicago, Illinois; Cleveland Public Library, Cleveland, Ohio; Louisiana State University Library, Baton Rouge, La.; St. Louis Public Library, St. Louis, Missouri; University of Texas Library, Austin, Texas; University of California Library, Berkeley, California; University of California Library, Los Angeles, California.

offset by a subsidiary classification, such as ED/SEN for Seminars. However, no such system has been established for the CUA papers, which include in one consecutively numbered series, without differentiation of any kind, such loosely related material as papers on libraries, museums, copyright, historical monuments, philosophical studies, music, and the theater.

The letter C/ . . . preceded by the number of the session has always been the symbol of the general conference: 1C/ . . . 2C/ . . . etc. Since its sixth session, the executive board documents have been indicated by EX/ . . . preceded by the number of the session.

Index